AMERICAN MIRROR

AMERICA IN THE WORLD

Sven Beckert and Jeremi Suri, Series Editors

For a full list of titles in the series, go to https://press.princeton.edu/catalogs/series/title/america-in-the-world.html

American Mirror

THE UNITED STATES AND BRAZIL
IN THE AGE OF EMANCIPATION

ROBERTO SABA

PRINCETON UNIVERSITY PRESS

PRINCETON & OXFORD

Published by Princeton University Press
41 William Street, Princeton, New Jersey 08540
99 Banbury Road, Oxford OX2 6JX

press.princeton.edu

All Rights Reserved

First paperback printing, 2024
Paper ISBN 978-0-691-20269-3
Cloth ISBN 978-0-691-19074-7
ISBN (e-book) 978-0-691-20535-9
LCCN: 2020049839

British Library Cataloging-in-Publication Data is available

Editorial: Eric Crahan, Priya Nelson and Thalia Leaf
Production Editorial: Jenny Wolkowicki
Jacket/Cover design: Layla Mac Rory
Production: Danielle Amatucci
Publicity: Alyssa Sanford and Charlotte Coyne
Copyeditor: Joseph Dahm

Jacket/Cover credit: Porto de Santos, Brazil, ca. 1880. Marc Ferrez / Gilberto Ferrez Collection / Instituto Moreira Salles

This book has been composed in Arno Pro

For my parents
Paulo and Dirce

Whatever may be their use in civilized societies, mirrors are essential to all violent and heroic action.

—VIRGINIA WOOLF, 1929

CONTENTS

NOTES ON ORTHOGRAPHY AND CURRENCY

CHANGES IN THE rules of nineteenth-century written Portuguese make for multiple spellings of the same word. In the interest of clarity and homogeneity, I have adopted the most recent orthography for personal names, places, and institutions.

The Brazilian currency in the monarchical period was the mil-réis. One mil-réis could be divided into one thousand réis. One thousand mil-réis was called one conto de réis.

AMERICAN MIRROR

Introduction

The bourgeoisie . . . has been the first to show what man's activity can bring
about. It has accomplished wonders far surpassing Egyptian pyramids, Roman
aqueducts, and Gothic cathedrals; it has conducted expeditions that put in the
shade all former exoduses of nations and crusades.

—KARL MARX AND FRIEDRICH ENGELS, 1848

SLAVE LABOR WAS central to the making of the modern world. It gave Europeans the means to occupy and develop the Americas. The trade in slaves
helped merchants accumulate capital that was reinvested in agriculture, industry, and infrastructure. Slave plantations produced the sugar, cotton, and coffee
that propelled the industrial revolution in the North Atlantic countries. As the
nineteenth century progressed, slaveholders acquired new lands and more
slaves. They deployed the powers of the state to build sprawling inland empires
and protect their property. The power of the lash ensured that enslaved people
would keep working until their deaths.

The United States and Brazil, the two major independent slave societies in
the Western world, were the main beneficiaries of the expansion of slavery. By
the 1850s, at the apex of the system, the former enslaved approximately four
million people, the latter nearly two million. Slavery fueled the economies of
both countries, producing valuable agricultural commodities for the global
market. Slaveholders wielded great political power in both states, occupying
key positions in their central as well as local governments. Whereas societies
like Haiti and Jamaica experienced economic decline after emancipation,
American and Brazilian elites grew richer and more powerful by exploiting
enslaved Africans and their descendants.

Its efficiency and profitability notwithstanding, slavery eventually collapsed in these two countries. The United States, shaken by a bloody separatist war and the mass flight of enslaved people from Southern plantations, led the way in the mid-1860s. Brazil, agitated by a mass abolitionist movement that included free and enslaved people, followed suit in the late 1880s. But neither of these two societies was caught off guard. On the contrary, as slavery unraveled in the western hemisphere, Americans and Brazilians came together to stimulate and direct this transformation. This book traces how a cosmopolitan group of antislavery reformers connected these two emancipation processes to boost capitalist development in both countries. It argues that modern capitalism emerged not from the remaking of slavery in the nineteenth century but from its unmaking. Between the 1850s and the 1880s, American and Brazilian antislavery reformers succeeded in creating economic systems that surpassed anything that slave societies had ever created.

––––––

The crisis of slavery in the Western world was intertwined with the expansion of industrial capitalism. Previously restricted to a few regions of the North Atlantic, such as the textile-producing centers of Lancashire and New England, industrial capitalism began to expand by the middle of the nineteenth century. Railroads reached into the interior of continents, and steamships crossed oceans, transporting countless human beings and commodities. Nation-states at once regulated their economies, protecting certain industries and building infrastructure, and tore down barriers to the movement of capital, labor, and goods. Pressured by labor shortages or workers' demands, trying to catch up with domestic or international competitors, or simply enthusiastic about the newest inventions, entrepreneurs applied science and technology to production. As time went by, steel, fertilizers, the assembly line, streetcars, petroleum, telegraphy, harvesters, futures markets, electricity, and many other innovations revolutionized the global economy.

Of course, the rise of industrial capitalism was not a story of unmitigated prosperity. Periodic busts—the most dramatic being the long depression beginning in 1873—were constitutive parts of this capitalist boom. In the long run, however, crises led to more innovation and greater growth. For developing countries disadvantaged by Great Britain's free-trade policies, periods of recession offered a valuable opportunity to refashion national economies and create new international networks. Economic nationalism and new forms of cosmopolitanism sprang up at the expense of British interests in the second half of the nineteenth century.

Perhaps more important, a highly unstable economic system made an almost inexhaustible workforce available to the owners of capital. Having their livelihoods constantly disrupted by boom and bust cycles, massive contingents of working people entered the ranks of the proletariat. Although uneven and protracted, proletarianization was a global phenomenon that accelerated as the nineteenth century progressed. New technologies, integrating markets, changing legislation, expanding credit mechanisms, demographic pressures, recurrent wars, and environmental degradation combined with periodic economic collapses to dissolve traditional communities. As the historian E. P. Thompson puts it, "The experience of immiseration came upon them in a hundred different forms."[1] And so immiserated human beings had no choice but to search wherever they could go for someone who would pay for the labor power contained in their arms and legs.

A group of American and Brazilian reformers sought to make their societies compatible with and integrated into the brave new world opening before their eyes. These men were bourgeois modernizers, determined to swiftly develop productive forces within their countries and simultaneously speed up the flow of commodities, capital, ideas, and human beings across international borders. They were immersed in what the historian Eric Hobsbawm describes as "the drama of Progress, that key word of the age: massive, enlightened, sure of itself, self-satisfied but above all inevitable."[2]

Living in the richest and most expansive slave societies in the Western world, these modernizers singled out slavery as the main impediment to the full development of their countries. Unimpressed by the slaveholders' achievements, they argued that slave labor was backward and irrational. Fearlessly, they insisted that the downfall of slavery and the triumph of free labor in the form of the wage system would lead to the emergence of unparalleled agroindustrial empires. These changes, they believed, would promote investment, attract immigrants, and encourage innovation. The new order would redistribute labor and capital in more rational ways. For these reformers, antislavery was not a romantic quest to free an oppressed race; it was rather a modernizing project that would build strong nation-states and prosperous capitalist economies.

The modernizers pointed to several problems that made slavery into a burden in the age of industrial capitalism. They often compared slave societies with free societies. The United States was a case in point: Brazilian as well as American antislavery reformers used the census, travel narratives, and even the writings of Southern proslavery ideologues to demonstrate that, in the antebellum period, the free North was superior to the slave South in manufacturing output, population growth rates, transportation and urban infrastructure, literacy levels, educational facilities, number of registered patents, and more. Even in agriculture, the enterprise that Southerners were most proud of, the North displayed advantages. Antislavery reformers pointed out that the free states were well ahead in the number of farms, improved acreage, average value per acre, value of farming implements and machinery, productivity per acre, productivity per worker, and total agricultural output.[3]

To claim, like many proslavery ideologues did, that slavery was indispensable to produce the commodities that made the world go round seemed ludicrous to these modernizers. They understood capitalism as a system whose main feature is constant change and adaptation. They argued that alternative fibers could replace cotton, alternative stimulants could replace coffee, and alternative sweeteners could replace cane sugar. More important, they believed that wage earners could replace slaves in plantation agriculture, producing even more cotton, coffee, and sugar than slave labor produced. Their goal was not to uproot plantation agriculture in Brazil or the United States but to make it more dynamic and efficient, while better integrating agricultural commodities into national and global networks of trade, production, and consumption.

As for the apparently declining postemancipation Caribbean, the antislavery reformers were confident that vast, diverse, and autonomous countries such as Brazil and the United States would not suffer the fate of colonial islands. In fact, these modernizers contended that it was slavery that made plantation areas play the role of colonial societies, sacrificing their own development to supply manufacturers—especially the British—with cheap agricultural commodities. Antislavery reformers lamented that slaveholders were attached to the power of human muscle, unable to take full advantage of the mechanical advancements of the age. They understood that although planters could (and sometimes did) adopt industrial technology on their plantations, they had little incentive to save the labor of enslaved people, who received no wages and held no formal rights. Worse, slave societies were unable to invent and produce the technologies they needed, having to constantly import machines and implements from free-labor societies. In short, the modernizers saw slavery as a counterproductive embarrassment.

American and Brazilian antislavery reformers felt that the institution of slavery held their enterprises and their societies back in an age of progress. They argued that slavery had to be eliminated so that industrial capitalism could flourish in plantation areas. Surveying the problem of slavery in the British West Indies, the historian Thomas Holt writes that "while historians might conclude retrospectively that slavery was logically compatible with capitalism, the men who fashioned the emancipation law completely rejected that notion."[4] The same was true for the men who forged the process of emancipation in the United States and Brazil.

American Mirror traces how, as the problem of slavery shook their countries, American and Brazilian antislavery reformers acted concertedly to turn upheaval into opportunity. This transnational modernizing collaboration crossed four decades, beginning in the 1850s, when the United States was about to erupt into a destructive conflict over the extension of slavery, and triumphing in the late 1880s, when Brazil completed its gradual emancipation process. In addition to famous antislavery activists, like John Greenleaf Whittier and André Pinto Rebouças, this reform movement included broader social forces that opposed slavery, bringing together businessmen, diplomats, engineers, journalists, lawyers, merchants, missionaries, planters, poets, politicians, scientists, students, and teachers.

However diverse their backgrounds, the main characters in this book shared important attributes. They belonged to ascending national bourgeoisies, having much of their training, businesses, and political activities connected to growing urban centers such as New York, Rio de Janeiro, Chicago, and São Paulo. They nonetheless maintained ties to the rural world, seeking to export to plantation areas the expertise and technology developed in the cities. In the United States, they usually supported the Republican Party. In Brazil, most were dissidents within the Liberal Party, and some were members of the Republican Party. Most of these antislavery reformers were entrepreneurs of some sort: they devised infrastructural projects, produced agricultural commodities, engaged in foreign commerce, managed factories, published periodicals, and established private schools. They were also brokers, connecting people with shared interests and similar ideas across the hemisphere. This book traces their trajectory and influence. It shows how, by building networks between the United States and Brazil in the age of emancipation, they triumphed where proslavery advocates failed.

———

A new wave of scholarship posits that by the middle decades of the nineteenth century American slaveholders had risen as modern capitalists and powerful policy makers. Southern proslavery advocates apparently found no match for their influence at home and abroad. Slaveholders' success in covering the Mississippi Valley with cotton plantations and influencing the American government, some historians claim, served as a model for planter elites elsewhere.[5] When scholars look at the second largest slave society in the Western world, they argue that the success of American slaveholders reassured Brazilian planters that unfree labor would indefinitely expand. Powerful Brazilians thus embraced the strategies and worldviews of the slave South.[6] Proslavery forces emerge from this scholarship as hemispheric hegemons.

American Mirror challenges the argument that proslavery advocates offered viable projects of national development or international cooperation. The analysis of US-Brazilian relations demonstrates that, among several other frustrations, powerful Southerners utterly failed to attract the most obvious partner to the proslavery cause. The argument that slave labor was the basis of modern civilization, and that without it the United States and Brazil could not produce their main staples, did little to allure Brazilian planters, who had been experimenting with free labor since at least the 1840s. Moreover, Brazilians understood that the cotton-producing American South had little to offer them in terms of products, technology, and expertise. Further souring this relationship, Southern proslavery expansionists treated Brazil as an inferior society available for manipulation and conquest in the decades leading to the American Civil War and during the conflict. Not surprisingly, Brazilian elites kept their distance from the slave South.

Antislavery Northerners, on the other hand, succeeded in befriending slave-holding Brazil. Frustrated by the reactionary stands of Southern cotton planters before and after the secession crisis, Northerners found in the Brazilian slave society a new chance to vindicate their vision of gradual emancipation. Thus, the same people who attacked and ultimately crushed slavery in North America took a constructive approach to the process of slave emancipation in Brazil. Recognizing an opportunity to form profitable alliances, reform-minded Brazilians—a group that included wealthy slaveholders—did not hesitate to welcome Northern influence. It was clear to anyone willing to see it then that the free North was at the forefront of innovation. The Brazilian elite understood that whereas Southern slaveholders were desperately fighting for a lost cause, Northern antislavery reformers were shaping the future in their own image.

In addition to addressing the failure of proslavery projects, this book engages with the growing historiography on the abolitionist struggle in the western hemisphere. Questions pertaining to the broadening of the public sphere, the strengthening of republicanism, the emergence of social movements, and the advancement of civil and political rights occupy the most recent works on antislavery in Brazil and the United States. Scholars propose that the campaign against slavery in these countries was a constitutive part of a Western phenomenon inaugurated by the political revolutions of the late eighteenth century and advanced by nineteenth-century popular struggles. They further argue that the fight against slavery anticipated trends that would give rise to the discourse on human rights.[7]

Although a valuable contribution to the study of political change, this scholarship overlooks the importance of antislavery movements to the making of capitalism. *American Mirror* contends that the struggle against slavery in the United States and Brazil was a constitutive part of "the drama of Progress." The need to expand markets, build infrastructure, integrate the countryside with the city, spread technical education, and set up industrial enterprises animated the antislavery reformers. The most consequential legacy of antislavery in the western hemisphere was an economic order based on the exploitation of wage earners. Whereas democratic participation and human rights remained distant aspirations for millions of impoverished people in their countries, American and Brazilian antislavery reformers succeeded in expanding capitalist production and trade.

This book also contributes to discussions of American foreign relations in the period extending from the Civil War to the Spanish-American War. For decades, the so-called Wisconsin School set the tone of the debate, arguing that overproduction in the post–Civil War era inexorably led Americans to aggressive commercial expansion and imperialist intervention abroad.[8] In response, a new wave of works proposes that the road to imperial expansion was not predetermined. Scholars now argue that uncertainty and improvisation marked American actions in the global arena during the second half of the nineteenth century. Americans demonstrated a pungent anxiety about their marginal role in a globalizing order and found themselves playing by the rules of stronger powers, especially Great Britain. Unable to defeat the Old World empires, scholars conclude, the United States increasingly became more similar to them. As time wore on, Americans embraced an Anglo-Saxon identity that distanced themselves from Latin America.[9]

The current approach to foreign relations tends to obscure Americans' role in refashioning capitalism in Latin America and Latin Americans' creative appropriation of American capital and expertise. This book incorporates a Latin American perspective into the making of American foreign relations. And it does so by examining how class interests aligned across national borders. It shows that the demands and interests of the Brazilian planters helped shape the ascent of the United States to global power in the late nineteenth century. By advancing the modernizing projects of the Brazilian elite, American antislavery reformers were able to forcefully challenge European empires and strengthen capitalist enterprises at both ends of the hemisphere.

―――――

Situated at the intersection of studies on proslavery politics, abolitionism, and foreign relations, *American Mirror* proposes that antislavery reformers engaged in a transnational process of class formation, which tied seemingly disparate groups such as manufacturers in the American North and planters in the Brazilian southeast. In addition to expanding markets for their products abroad, these groups collaborated in the search for new ways to control and exploit the working masses. The great transformation that these modernizers brought about in the late nineteenth-century world was the widening of the divide between a cosmopolitan coalition of owners of capital and a growing class of impoverished workers.

By investigating how the American North engaged with the Brazilian slave society, this book shows that antislavery laid the groundwork for a long-term and highly profitable partnership between capitalists from the most powerful countries of the western hemisphere. However influential Americans became among Brazilian elites, the United States established neither a formal nor an informal colonial relationship with Brazil during the nineteenth century. And precisely because they did not have the upper hand in their relationship with Brazil, Americans learned invaluable lessons in capitalist expansion. Together, American and Brazilian antislavery reformers elaborated newly efficient forms of labor exploitation in Brazil's coffee regions, making Brazilian coffee planters all the more powerful. In the process, American manufacturers acquired an avid consumer for their products, and American merchants secured a reliable supplier of cheap coffee.

American influence also helped Brazil in its long effort to counter British imperialism and limit its reliance on British capital. Shrewdly, antislavery Northerners presented themselves as a benign alternative to British abolitionists, who had long been flexing their imperial muscle against Brazil's interests.[10] Instead of patrolling the Brazilian seacoast with warships and imposing invasive treaties on Brazil, as Great Britain had done for decades, the American North offered technology and expertise that would ease Brazilian planters' reliance on slave labor. Working alongside Brazilian reformers, Northerners were able to portray the United States as a modernizing force and challenge the overbearing influence of the British Empire in the western hemisphere.

———

Free labor in the form of the wage system was not the natural or inevitable replacement for slave labor. The working poor in the nineteenth century tried to push freedom well beyond the point that elites wanted it to go, seeking to acquire land, tools, or anything that would give them a high degree of independence. This tendency contradicted projects to build expansive trade networks, large-scale commercial agriculture, and advanced industrial enterprises. Thus, in reaction to the workers' struggle for self-sufficiency, other forms of unfree labor, like peonage and convict labor, were tested in communities of ex-slaves in the Americas and expanded in Africa, Asia, and Eastern Europe throughout the nineteenth century.[11]

Yet despite persisting pockets of unfree labor that endure today, wage labor eventually became the fulcrum of capitalism, spreading from the cities to the countryside, from the center to the periphery, conquering all branches of the global economy. For half a century after the historian Eric Williams published his seminal *Capitalism and Slavery* (1944), some remarkable studies sought to explain why the battle against slavery gave rise to a mode of production based on wage labor. Either by engendering new forms of labor discipline, imposing urban interests on rural societies, encouraging inland and overseas migrations of formally free workers, or liberating capital and commodity flows, the dismantling of slavery resulted in a labor system that forces the majority of humanity to sell their labor power to a minority who owns plantations, mines, factories, or other productive facilities. Far from representing the ultimate salvation of the working class, the wage system serves well the interests of powerful capitalists.[12]

Because of their agricultural might, long dependence on slave labor, and aspirations to develop and integrate vast territories, the United States and Brazil became prime testing grounds for the deployment of formally free workers—white and black, native-born and immigrant—to advance capitalist enterprises. As antislavery reformers from these two countries came together, the question became how to make the slaves' cause into the capitalists' cause. Hence, their transnational antislavery struggle went hand in hand with projects to concentrate capital, develop infrastructure, privatize natural resources, strengthen corporations, foster domestic and international commerce, regulate labor migration, and defeat working-class movements. In the end, antislavery reformers contributed to making the free poor and freedpeople into wage earners and building capitalist enterprises that slave societies could not have dreamed of creating.

Drawing on the scholarly tradition initiated by Eric Williams, this book examines how the transition from slave to free labor advanced capitalist relations of production in the United States and Brazil. Antislavery reformers did not envision free labor as self-reliance and small proprietorship. These modernizers took advantage of the crises of emancipation in the largest slave societies of the Western world to advance an economic system based on the concentration of capital in the hands of very few and the destitution of the working masses. With a few exceptions (who usually saw the problem too late), the antislavery reformers who appear in *American Mirror* were not concerned about the well-being of slaves, proletarians, or any member of the working class. The central argument of this book is that these bourgeois modernizers, in their struggle against slavery, were in fact making, normalizing, and entrenching free labor in the form of the wage system.

———

Born in the coffee-growing region of São Paulo to a planter family, José Custódio Alves de Lima studied at Syracuse University in New York during the 1870s. In 1878, he wrote that "the American Union is a mirror in which the Brazilian must look if he wants to contribute his part to the material development of the country."[13] The mirror metaphor comes in handy when exploring relations between the United States and Brazil in the second half of the nineteenth century. For Northerners, Brazil became a mirror of what the American South could have been if only cotton planters had accepted the supremacy of free labor and had embraced gradual emancipation. For Brazilians, the American North and its extension to the American West became a mirror of what Brazil could become if coffee planters made the right choices, phasing out slavery while modernizing and diversifying the economy.

The mirrors in this story also offer a reflection on transnational history. Auspiciously, the transnational approach has already entered the academic mainstream. This trend has revitalized the discipline, and excellent studies have been published during the last two decades. Yet, with few exceptions, transnational historians, while emphasizing exchange and mobility, give little thought to broader processes simultaneously shaping the lives of different societies around the globe. In other words, transnational studies are very effective at describing the circulation of people, commodities, ideas, and technologies, but rarely discuss structural changes such as the emergence of the modern state or the consolidation of the capitalist mode of production.

Seeking to understand structural changes as well as mobility and exchange, this book draws on works that have applied the principles of political economy to transnational analyses. According to Richard Franklin Bensel, political economy "is a combination of *economy* and *state policy*," forming "a dynamic organizing structure within society that shapes the potential replication of social groups and activities, and thus determines the developmental trajectory of the nation."[14] The most successful works of transnational history show that, under capitalism, the *economy* engenders a global market, recruits highly mobile workers and experts, and creates industrial centers along with suppliers of raw materials. They further demonstrate that, in the modern world, *state policy* continuously responds to the policies of other states and the pressures of international movements and institutions. As a result, the *transnational political economy* emerges as a dynamic organizing structure within a connecting world that shapes the potential replication of—national and international—social groups and activities, and thus entangles the developmental trajectories of different nations.[15]

———

This book is divided into two parts. Part I moves from the height of proslavery expansionism in the United States, in the 1840s, to the beginning of gradual emancipation in Brazil, in the early 1870s. Chapter 1 discusses how proslavery Southerners' foreign policy alienated the Brazilian elite and ruined any possibility of a proslavery alliance emerging. Antislavery Northerners, on the other hand, succeeded in bringing Brazilian society closer to the Union by portraying Brazilian slaveholders as progressive planters willing to phase out slavery and modernize their economy. Chapter 2 shows how shared anti-British sentiments created an alliance between Brazilian Liberals and American Republicans during the American Civil War. Whereas American diplomats took the Brazilian side in the geopolitical imbroglios of the time, American entrepreneurs invested in transportation infrastructure in Brazil and the two countries established steamship communication. Chapter 3 focuses on the influence of Massachusetts intellectuals on Brazil in the late 1860s. Relying on friendly antislavery figures from the American North and attentive to what had happened to the American South, the Brazilian political elite embraced a project of conservative modernization.

Part II extends from the beginning of Reconstruction in the United States, in the late 1860s, to the remaking of labor on the Brazilian coffee plantations after the Golden Law, in the late 1880s. Chapter 4 examines three groups of Americans who settled in the Oeste Paulista, the fastest growing coffee-producing region of Brazil, after the American Civil War. They were ex-Confederates who took up mixed commercial farming, manufacturers from the American North who established industrial enterprises, and Protestant missionaries who built private schools for the planters' children. All of them contributed to the modernizing projects of the local elite. Chapter 5 reconstructs the trajectories of Brazilian men who visited, studied in, or worked in the United States during the 1870s. Enjoying the hospitality of Northern capitalists, Brazilian observers celebrated the consolidation of wage labor and bought into Liberal Republican projects to favor big capital in North America. Chapter 6 addresses the seemingly contradictory connections between an expanding market for slave-grown Brazilian coffee in the United States and the American contribution to slave emancipation in Brazil. Whereas the coffee trade became a most lucrative enterprise for American businessmen and the temperance movement used coffee to discipline the working class in American cities, Brazilian planters used money from the coffee trade to improve their plantations and complete the transition to wage labor.

———

Neither in the United States, where slave emancipation happened suddenly and violently, nor in Brazil, where all the major industries relied on slave labor until emancipation came, did the demise of slavery create a profound crisis. On the contrary, thanks to the work of antislavery reformers, the postemancipation history of these two countries was one of immediate and continuous economic advancement. From the outbreak of the secession crisis in the United States to the signing of the Golden Law in Brazil, American and Brazilian antislavery reformers worked side by side to create economic systems based on industrial technology, scientific expertise, and wage labor. They did not wait for slavery to crumble, but intentionally replaced it with a more dynamic and efficient mode of production. The accomplishments of this transnational group of modernizers confirmed what Karl Marx and Friedrich Engels had already seen in 1848, when they wrote that "the bourgeoisie cannot exist without constantly revolutionizing the instruments of production, and thereby the relations of production, and with them the whole relations of society."[16]

PART I

A New World Unchained

A Hand-Mirror

Hold it up sternly—see this it sends back, (who is it? is it you?)
Outside fair costume—within, ashes and filth,
No more a flashing eye—no more a sonorous voice or springy step,
Now some slave's eye, voice, hands, step,
A drunkard's breath, unwholesome eater's face, venerealee's flesh,
Lungs rotting away piecemeal, stomach sour and cankerous,
Joints rheumatic, bowels clogged with abomination,
Blood circulating dark and poisonous streams,
Words babble, hearing and touch callous,
No brain, no heart left—no magnetism of sex;
Such, from one look in this looking-glass ere you go hence,
Such a result so soon—and from such a beginning!

—WALT WHITMAN, 1855

1

Distant Slave Empires

IN MAY 1844, Secretary of State John C. Calhoun sent detailed instructions to the newly appointed US minister to Brazil, Henry A. Wise. If the British Empire ever managed to destroy the slave system of either Brazil or the United States, Calhoun speculated, "it would destroy the peace and prosperity of both and transfer the production of tobacco, rice, cotton, sugar and coffee from the United States and Brazil to [the British] possessions beyond the Cape of Good Hope." Hence, Calhoun commanded, "you will avail yourself of the occasion to impress on the Brazilian government the conviction, that it is our policy to cultivate the most friendly relations with all the countries on this continent, and with none more than with Brazil."[1] Despite Calhoun's wishes, neither Wise nor any other Southerner would be able to build a proslavery coalition with Brazil, the second largest slave society in the Western world in the nineteenth century.

The problem of slavery polarized the United States during the 1840s and 1850s. The Mexican War reopened questions about the balance between free and slave states that the Missouri Compromise had kept at bay. A new compromise was forged in 1850, but it failed to stem the conflict. As the 1850s progressed, slaveholders' imperial voracity intensified: they now wanted to take Kansas, increase their influence in western territories, and promote filibustering expeditions in the Caribbean and Central America.[2] The Republican Party emerged as a response to aggressive proslavery expansionism. Confronted by fire-eaters, Republicans put their foot down: slavery was not to expand beyond the South.[3] The United States was on the brink of civil war.

The institution of slavery also shook Brazil by the middle decades of the nineteenth century. Pressured by the British Empire, the Brazilian government had made the importation of African slaves illegal in 1831. But the law was disregarded, and with the cooperation of influential Brazilian politicians, the traffic only increased thereafter. The British government renewed its pressure and, in 1845, unilaterally gave the Royal Navy the right to intercept and search any Brazilian vessel suspected of carrying slaves.[4] In addition to the instability that slavery generated, Brazil got involved in border skirmishes that became a full-blown war against Argentinians and Uruguayans between 1851 and 1852. Although Brazil did not increase its territory, it flexed its imperial muscle with little reservation in South America.[5]

The geopolitical agitation of the era bred friction between the United States and Brazil. The involvement of American merchants and sailors in the illegal transatlantic slave trade to Brazil in the 1840s provoked a negative reaction from Henry A. Wise, who became embroiled in heated disputes with Brazilian authorities and threatened to attack Rio de Janeiro. As relations between the two countries were still shaken by the early 1850s, the expansionist projects of American proslavery ideologues aggravated Brazilians once again. The Brazilian elite now feared Matthew Fontaine Maury, a Tennessee slaveholder and superintendent of the American Naval Observatory, who nurtured plans to explore and settle the Amazon Valley, repeating the process of Anglo-American conquest successful in Mexican Texas. An empire of its own, Brazil forcefully opposed Southern impositions.

As the secession crisis escalated in the United States, however, Southern fire-eaters tried to make Brazil a client of the emerging Confederacy. But a missionary and writer from Indiana named James Cooley Fletcher, acting as an agent of Northern entrepreneurs and abolitionists, formulated a competing approach. He not only established strong ties with the Brazilian elite but also elaborated a compelling narrative about their progressive character, which he then used to criticize proslavery Southerners. All the while, Fletcher fostered commercial exchanges with Brazil by exhibiting the industrial prowess of the American North to Brazilian audiences.

Rejecting an older approach that regarded slave societies as precapitalist,[6] scholars now emphasize the great power that slaveholders acquired in the nineteenth century. Historians of American slavery posit that Southern cotton planters were audacious capitalists who elaborated successful expansionist projects reaching well beyond North America.[7] In turn, historians of Brazilian slavery assume that Southerners' success helped stabilize the institution in Brazil, where the local elite embraced proslavery ideology.[8] The study of US-Brazilian relations in the 1840s and 1850s, however, reveals that, no matter how boastful Southern slaveholders had become, they could not establish an effective foreign policy in defense of slavery or promote it as a viable system for the future of capitalism. The South failed to convince Brazil, a country that held some two million slaves, to embark on a proslavery crusade. The Northern approach, on the other hand, seemed quite appealing to Brazilians willing to modernize their economy and slowly reform their institutions. By the end of the 1850s, American antislavery reformers had planted the seeds of a transnational cooperation that would isolate the slave South and set the stage for a transition to free labor in Brazil.

Filthy Business

Henry A. Wise, a slaveholder and politician from Virginia, had been elected six consecutive times to the House of Representatives, serving from 1833 to 1844 and gaining notoriety as a staunch proslavery advocate. All in all, he seemed like the perfect candidate to foster closer relations between American and Brazilian slaveholders.[9] Yet as soon as Wise arrived in Rio de Janeiro, he made clear that a binational proslavery alliance would not be as easy to build as John C. Calhoun's instructions had implied.

By the 1840s, the British Empire had coerced the major players in the transatlantic slave trade—Spain, Portugal, and Brazil—to permit the Royal Navy to police their ships. The United States was the only exception. Hence, the American flag was widely used to cover up the illegal slave trade to Brazil.[10] As Wise put it in one of his first reports to Calhoun, "Our flag alone gives the requisite protection against the right of visit, search and seizure; . . . in fact, without the aid of our citizens and our flag it [the slave trade to Brazil] could not be carried on with success at all."[11]

Americans living in Brazilian coastal cities could make easy profits by obtaining sea letters from US consulates and fitting out vessels for slavers. As slave prices soared due to British policing, traffickers organized several shipments of goods such as arms, gunpowder, iron, rum, tobacco, and cloth to Africa. American ships were fast, American seamen had expertise, and American merchants had access to these goods. More important, American traffickers had few reasons for concern. Despite the existence of harsh anti–slave trade legislation in the United States, the Department of State and the Navy usually acted leniently toward slavers as long as they did not land in American ports.[12]

Unlike some of his compatriots, Wise had many reasons to abhor the African slave trade. As a white Virginian, he identified the influx of Africans to the Americas with the threat of slave rebellion. Since the time of Thomas Jefferson, "Africanization" reminded Virginians of the Haitian Revolution.[13] Moreover, memories of Nat Turner's Rebellion were still fresh.[14] Yet more important, born in 1806, Wise came to adulthood at a time when his native state had established itself as an exporter of slaves to the cotton regions of the United States. Like his fellow Virginians, he feared that a new increase in the African slave trade would encourage Mississippi Valley planters to overthrow the 1807 act banning the importation of slaves into the United States, thus disrupting Virginia's lucrative domestic business.[15]

An enemy of abolitionism, Wise also believed that American involvement in the African slave trade could open a door to a British assault on American slaveholders. "In immediate connection with this subject of the slave trade," Wise advised Calhoun in January 1845, "is that of interference by Great Britain with the domestic slavery of the United States." A consternated Wise told his superior that the same British abolitionists who were attacking the African slave trade to Brazil were seeking information about slavery in the United States.

> They not only inquire about population, about the importation of slaves against our own laws in our own jurisdiction, about the laws for the protection of slaves, about the civil capacities and disabilities of slaves by law, about their relative increase or decrease, about the melioration of laws in respect to them, about their general relative condition, but they pry into the treatment of the slaves by their private owners, into their food and raiment, into the disposition of masters to manumit them, and into the existing extent and influence of private societies or parties favorable to the abolition of slavery among us.

If American merchants and seamen continued to participate in the African slave trade to Brazil, Wise reckoned, the British would persist in their "impudent and dangerous intrusion," threatening "the very sanctity of our private lives and of our private rights."[16]

Vexed by the ease with which traffickers acted in Brazil, Wise decided to demonstrate force. In late 1844, he received intelligence that an American brig called *Porpoise*, whose crew was composed of American and Brazilian seamen, had been chartered by Manoel Pinto da Fonseca, a powerful Portuguese slaver and resident of Rio de Janeiro. Fonseca placed one of his agents, a Brazilian named Paulo Rodrigues, in command of the *Porpoise* and sent it to the coast of Africa, where, according to Wise, it supplied Fonseca's slave factories "with cachaça, (agua ardente, or the white rum of this country,) with muskets and fazendas, (or dry goods and groceries,) and with provisions, sailing from port to port, the captain and crew seeing the slaves bought at various times and places, and shipped on board of other vessels, and lending her boats and ship's crew from time to time to assist in shipping slaves." When the *Porpoise* was completing its trip back to Brazil in January 1845, Wise commanded the USS *Raritan* to capture it within the harbor of Rio de Janeiro.[17]

Outraged by the assault on Brazilian sovereignty, the Brazilian minister of justice promptly asked Wise to order the release of the *Porpoise*. What followed demonstrated how much esteem Wise had for the country that Calhoun viewed as an important ally. "I decided in my own mind to go on board of the *Raritan*," Wise reported, "and proposed that, if the minister of justice would send an officer to take Paulo [Rodrigues] and the other [Brazilian] passengers into custody for trial under the laws of Brazil, I would interpose for their release." The vessel and the American citizens, Wise determined, would remain detained by the captain of the *Raritan* until the Brazilian government agreed to extradite them.[18]

The Brazilian minister, appalled by Wise's insolence, ordered gunboats of the Brazilian Navy to surround the *Raritan*. Wise complained that this demonstration of force was done "in a very rude and insulting manner" and insisted that he was going to extradite the detained American citizens with or without the permission of Brazilian authorities. Yet the captain of the *Raritan* did not concur with such a confrontational proposition. The *Porpoise* and its crew were handed to the Brazilian Navy, but not without more haranguing from Wise. "Allowing Fonseca to walk aboard with impunity," he ranted, "releasing Paulo [Rodrigues] and his companions, . . . and, finally, sheltering all the criminals on their return under the protection of [Brazil's] sovereign jurisdiction" was an insult that "could not be submitted to by the United States, as far as their flag and citizens were concerned."[19]

While the *Porpoise* affair was still making the headlines, Brazil decided not to renew the 1817 right-of-search treaty with Great Britain. Signed by Portugal before Brazilian independence, the treaty allowed British ships to police vessels heading to Brazil. In response to Brazilian refusal, the Earl of Aberdeen, the British secretary of state, pulled off a diplomatic coup in 1845. Going back to a treaty that the Brazilian government had signed in 1826, he found that the first article classified the slave trade as piracy. Soon, Brazil learned about the Aberdeen Act, which unilaterally affirmed that British warships could search any Brazilian vessel suspected of carrying slaves. After all, Aberdeen argued, even according to Brazilian treaties, the slave trade constituted piracy. Further twisting Brazil's arm, he determined that going forward the traffickers would be judged not by Anglo-Brazilian mixed commissions (created in 1817) but by the Great Britain High Court of Admiralty. Brazilians protested in vain.[20]

The proslavery Wise did not side with the angry Brazilians against the abolitionist Aberdeen. Instead, just when Brazil was facing one of the most serious threats against its sovereign rights on the seas, he decided to wage a new attack on Brazilian sovereignty, this time targeting law enforcement in the Brazilian capital. On October 31, 1846, the Rio de Janeiro police arrested three drunken American sailors of the USS *Saratoga* for fighting with knives in front of the Hotel Pharoux, situated near the wharf. Their superior, Lieutenant Alonso B. Davis, charged the Brazilian officers with a sword and threatened to enter the guard room of the imperial palace, where his men had been detained. When Davis was arrested, Wise exploded with rage, demanding the immediate release of the four Americans. Brazilian authorities soon released Davis, and the sailors were quickly tried and acquitted. Nonetheless, Wise continued complaining, requesting the punishment of the responsible police officers and an official apology from the Brazilian government.

Bento da Silva Lisboa, the Brazilian minister of foreign affairs, was scandalized. He remarked that during the negotiations of the Davis affair, Wise "questioned Brazil's sovereign rights on its beaches (*in litore*); disparaged the public forces for neither wearing shiny uniforms nor having light-colored faces; qualified as treason and cowardice the capture of Lieutenant Davis; and saw in it an insult to the [American] flag."[21] Not satisfied, Wise threatened to bombard Brazil's capital city. In a letter to *O Mercantil*, an outraged observer recalled that "Mr. Wise has directed to our Minister of Foreign Affairs the most unjust and ridiculous complaints . . . and some say that he even threatened to *raze Rio de Janeiro with all his frigates*!! !! !!"[22] Adding insult to injury, at the height of the imbroglio Wise ordered an American battleship stationed in the harbor of Rio de Janeiro not to salute the baptism ceremony of Princess Isabel and Dom Pedro's birthday celebration.

As the Davis affair unfolded, Wise did not waste the opportunity to express his contempt for Brazil. When justifying his position to Secretary of State James Buchanan, who had replaced Calhoun in March 1845, Wise asserted that "this people are yet uncivilized and ought to be taught a lesson." The imprisonment of Davis and the three sailors, Wise explained, was just one of many cases of Brazilian brutality against Americans occurring since he had arrived in Rio de Janeiro. He claimed that Brazilian authorities had humiliated several American citizens, including his own son. A certain Mr. Southworth, Wise recounted with indignation, had been "imprisoned and fined severely, without judge or jury, because one of his employés struck a drunken negro who was abusing him in the most insufferable manner." The offense against an officer of the US

Navy had been the last straw for Wise: "You must, in a word, *make* this people respect us. They are ignorant, insolent, and touched by a false sense of dignity; but they are selfish enough to know what concerns them, and will not lightly trifle with a Power which can injure them as deeply as the U. States can, if compelled to resent their insults and outrages."[23]

Wise's contempt grew out of his view of Brazil as a society at the mercy of vile slavers. In the middle of his exchange with Buchanan about the Davis affair, Wise railed once again against the traffic. Yet this time Brazilian politicians, and not merchants and seamen, were the target of his fury. "It is not to be disguised nor palliated," he argued, "that this Court as well as this whole country is deeply inculpated in that trade." According to Wise, in Brazil the slavers were either the men in power or those who financed and controlled the men in power. "Thus, the Govt itself is in fact a slave trading Govt against its own laws and treaties." Ignoring Calhoun's initial instructions, Wise delighted in having become "very obnoxious . . . to this country, whose most wealthy and influential citizens are all hindered and obstructed by me in their slave-trade profits."[24]

In one of his tirades, Wise saw fit to attack Great Britain for being much closer to the Brazilian slave trade than Americans had ever been. Writing to Charles James Hamilton, the British minister to Rio de Janeiro, Wise claimed that every diplomat and politician knew that British merchants supplied the Brazilian traffickers with goods specifically designed to acquire slaves in Africa. "A vast proportion of the dry goods, and the powder and muskets, and a great variety of articles under the general names of 'fazendas estrangeiras' [foreign goods] or 'mercadorias e varios generos' [merchandise and assorted articles]," he contended, "are of English manufacture, and many made expressly as 'panos da costa' [cloths of the coast]."[25] Clearly then, as Wise saw it, British "manufacturers and merchants cannot but know that these goods are made of a peculiar pattern from the fact of their being required for the Slave Trade, and that they are ordered and intended for that traffic."[26]

The British had no right to attack American slaveholders, Wise told Hamilton, because they were accomplices of the Brazilians in a horrific crime. "Indeed," he concluded, "I am more than ever confirmed in the conviction that the largest interests in the world, next to those of Brazilian subjects, now favoring the Slave Trade, are those of a certain class of British manufacturers, merchants, and capitalists."[27] Wise's anti-British feelings did not lead him to side with Brazilian slaveholders. All he had in mind when he attacked Great Britain was his native region's own interests. He could not have cared less about the future of slavery in Brazil.

Before long, the Brazilian political elite understood that, when it came to impinging on Brazilian sovereignty, Americans were no different from the British. During the Davis affair, the Brazilian minister of foreign affairs suspended relations with Wise and requested that the US Department of State recall him. Buchanan nonetheless kept Wise in Rio de Janeiro. Anti-American voices rose in Brazil then, and influential newspapers demanded Wise's deportation.[28] One member of the Brazilian Parliament exclaimed in April 1847 that "we will be the first blamed if we do not forcefully express ourselves, protesting before the country and demanding the employment of all energy and vigor in this negotiation, because justice is on our side."[29]

Confronted by Brazilian politicians and the Rio de Janeiro press, Wise positioned himself as a victim of the slave trade interests. "The Ministers and Councilors of State and Senators and Delegates in the Legislative Chambers," he told Buchanan in April 1847, "are, undoubtedly, engaged in this bold as well as horrid traffic, and its principal capitalists are the owners of the newspaper press in this city which prevented more than any other cause a course of conciliation on the part of the Imp[erial] Govt respecting the imprisonment of Lt Davis and the three seamen."[30]

Mindful of the hemispheric context in which Wise was acting, Antonio Pereira Rebouças, the son of a freed slave and a Portuguese tailor who had fought for independence in the 1820s and become a prominent jurist and politician, told Parliament that Brazilians should keep their eyes wide open. "For a question of little importance," Rebouças charged in May 1847, the United States had "revived in the Americas, the land of Liberty, the principles of the ancient barbaric and semi-barbaric nations, invading territories of the Mexican Republic with the intention to conquer them by force and at gunpoint, making an effort to introduce discord among the peoples of that country by the most atrocious means." Rebouças feared that Brazil would have the same fate as Mexico if the American envoys continued to conduct diplomacy through the "ostentation of the intemperance of American soldiers; deducing from this intemperance a right over our country, as if they were disembarking at an abandoned beach; and, after flaunting as a right this act of intemperance, they insult the Brazilian nationality for the accident of the epidermis!"[31]

Wise had affronted the Brazilian police because of their skin color, questioned Brazilian sovereignty in Brazilian territory, and threatened to attack Rio de Janeiro. All the while his superiors in Washington had supported him. Brazilian elites were not willing to bear such humiliation anymore. "The Rubicon was crossed," *O Mercantil* raged against the United States, "the mask of hypocrisy fell off, and the much-vaunted protection of American interests, it is now clearly made evident, is nothing more than a pretext to boast superiority in relation to other states of the continent."[32]

Echoing Rebouças, other politicians demanded a forceful response from their government. Deputy Gabriel José Rodrigues dos Santos cried in Parliament that two recent diplomatic episodes had deeply wounded the Brazilian sense of national honor. First, the British, considering Brazil a vanquished country, had subjected Brazilian seamen to "the judgment of non-Brazilian tribunals." Yet, he lamented, the Brazilian government had lowered its head cowardly. Second, in the quarrel with Wise, Brazilian officials had demonstrated "the same tepidity, the same weakness, the same indecision. . . . After having got all he wanted through our humiliation, he intended to express, make it very clear, very manifest to the eyes of all, his triumph against our national dignity and the vilification that he had thrown over the Brazilian government." Brazil could not remain silent before the likes of Aberdeen and Wise, the outraged Rodrigues dos Santos concluded.[33] Similarly, Deputy Urbano Sabino Pessoa de Melo advised that "Brazil cannot continue with the system that to this day has directed our foreign relations. Our exaggerated acquiescence, our trepidation, a terrified panic that we manifest in all our affairs, have brought us the most serious difficulties."[34]

In August 1847, after challenging Brazilian sovereignty on more than one occasion, disparaging Brazilian politicians as lackeys of the slave traders, affronting Brazilian police forces because of their skin color, remaining silent about the Aberdeen Act, and threatening to bombard Rio de Janeiro, Wise returned to the United States by his own request. Ignoring Brazilian formal complaints, the US Department of State did not apologize for his actions. Back in Virginia, Wise would resume his proslavery advocacy, becoming a delegate to the state Constitutional Convention of 1850 and state governor in 1855. In 1859, he would sign the death sentence of the abolitionist John Brown.[35]

Having a slave population of approximately two million and being the only other independent slave society in the western hemisphere, Brazil might have seemed like the natural ally of Southern proslavery advocates.[36] Yet Southern slaveholders like Wise refused to establish a coalition with Brazil. In the 1840s, powerful Southerners, concerned about their own regional interests and regarding the Brazilians as an inferior people, demonstrated that they cared little about Brazil's destiny and would do what they could to impose their will on Brazil. Accordingly, Brazilian elites recognized American proslavery foreign policy as a threat akin to British antislavery imperialism. Wise departed as an enemy, rather than a friend, of Brazilian slaveholding interests. The image of Southern hostility that he left behind would not be easily erased.

Making matters worse for the Brazilian elite, at the time Wise left British cruisers were moving to single-handedly enforce the Aberdeen Act.[37] Yet what seemed like a double defeat for Brazil was transformed into victory. The Conservative Party, returning to power in September 1848, now sought to find a way to end the slave trade. The Liberals and Dom Pedro II favored abolition, and a large section of the public opinion understood that Brazil should free itself from the traffickers' corrupting influence. As major slavers were becoming identified with foreign capital—including American capital—Brazilian politicians argued that the end of the traffic would contribute to preserving national sovereignty. As the historian Leslie Bethell explains, "In the course of a tumultuous debate [in Parliament] more than one deputy expressed marked hostility towards the slave trade, which all were agreed was controlled by foreigners and therefore 'not properly speaking a Brazilian interest' and which, moreover, was directly responsible for recent British outrages against Brazilian sovereignty."[38] On September 4, 1850, an anti–slave trade law was ratified.

Thereafter, the Brazilian Navy reinforced its patrols of the coast; the central government made sure that provincial presidents, local judges, and police chiefs swiftly enforced the law; and special maritime courts, dispensing with the necessity of trial by jury, deported well-known foreign slavers. Slave ships continued trying to land their cargoes in Brazil for years, but the traffic was reduced to a trickle. Then an opportunity appeared to demonstrate that Brazilian society had once and for all repudiated the African slave trade. Auspiciously for the Brazilian authorities, it involved the apprehension of a schooner flying the American flag.[39]

In January 1856, the Brazilian Navy captured the *Mary E. Smith* off the Brazilian coast transporting nearly four hundred enslaved Africans. Chartered by Portuguese and American firms, the *Mary E. Smith* had sailed directly from Boston to Central Africa and from there to Brazilian waters. When the vessel was taken to the port of São Mateus, in the province of Espírito Santo, dozens of Africans started to die of cholera. The local population was horrified and loudly called for the punishment of the traffickers. The occasion was propitious for Brazilian authorities to affirm national sovereignty. "This apprehension, lacking nothing to be complete," Minister of Foreign Affairs José Maria da Silva Paranhos stated, "evidently demonstrates the restless solicitude of the imperial government and its agents. The repulse that the smugglers found in the population of the province is one more proof that the extinction of the slave trade is today the Brazilians' general desire."[40]

Based on the Law of 1850, Brazilian authorities charged the ten members of the *Mary E. Smith* crew—five of whom were American citizens—with slave trafficking. They were sent to Brazilian prisons for two or three years and had to pay the expenses of sending the enslaved survivors back to Africa. In spite of the complaints from American diplomats, who claimed that the seamen had been tricked by the ship's captain, only one of the prisoners was pardoned— and not before spending two years in jail—for old age.[41]

Brazil now posed as an international crusader against the slave trade in the face of the United States. As Paranhos reported in 1857, the Brazilian government "has worked to obtain information through its agents in the countries where, we suspect, the speculators act, especially the United States, Portugal, Spain and its possessions."[42] Reversing Wise's accusations, Brazilian authorities transferred the stigma of the slave trade back to the Americans. But Wise's compatriots would not leave Brazil alone. As the African slave trade was coming to a halt, Southerners would try to take their own slaves to the Brazilian Amazon.

Texas in Amazonia

During the 1840s, the superintendent of the American Naval Observatory, Matthew Fontaine Maury, a Tennessee slaveholder from a prestigious Virginia family, conducted a project to map ocean currents and winds. One of his most lauded discoveries was that the currents of the Gulf of Mexico formed a highway connecting the estuaries of the Mississippi and the Amazon. "Here, upon this central sea," Maury posited, nature "has, with a lavish hand, grouped and arranged in juxtaposition, all those physical circumstances which make nations truly great. Here she has laid the foundations for a commerce, the most magnificent the world ever saw. Here she has brought within the distance of a few days, the mouths of her two greatest rivers."[43] It was the calling of his people, Maury preached, to take advantage of such a marvelous system of lands and waterways.

Unlike the Mississippi Valley of the mid-nineteenth century, dense forests still covered the Amazon Valley, and the local inhabitants were mostly indigenous people who engaged in hunting, fishing, and subsistence agriculture. Afraid of losing this sparsely populated area, the Brazilian government prohibited foreign vessels from traveling and trading on its northern rivers while tightly controlling immigration to the region.[44] Determined to enter the

Amazon Basin, by early 1850 Maury petitioned the US Congress and Department of State, which, in turn, pressured Brazilian diplomats. After some hesitation, the Brazilian government granted permission for a scientific expedition. Maury put two naval officers from Virginia in charge of the exploratory parties: Lieutenant William Lewis Herndon—who happened to be his brother-in-law—was assigned to navigate from Peru into Brazil; Lieutenant Lardner Gibbon would go from Brazil into Bolivia.[45]

Despite all guarantees by the American government that the intentions of the expedition were purely scientific, Maury's instructions to Herndon evinced his real designs. "Shall it [the Amazon Valley] be peopled with an imbecile and an indolent people," he inquired in a letter dated April 1850, "or by a go ahead race that has energy and enterprise equal to subdue the forest and to develope [sic] and bring forth the vast rescource [sic] that lie hidden there? The latter by all means." A man of the seas, Maury looked well beyond the North American interior as the future of Southern slavery. The Amazon Valley "is to be the safety valve for our Southern States," he advised. "When they become overpopulated with slaves . . . they will send these slaves to the Amazon. Just as the Miss[issippi] Valley has been the escape valve for the slaves of the Northern now free States so will the Amazon valley be to that of the Miss[issippi]."[46]

Maury envisioned a process of conquest similar to what had taken place in Mexican Texas: "American influences will give the ascendency there and the [Amazon] valley in a few years will become [sic] to be regarded for all commercial purposes as a sort of an American Colony." He made clear to his brother-in-law that "your going is to be the first link in that chain which is to end in the establishment of the Amazonian Republic." Maury believed that if the United States forced Brazil to sign a river navigation treaty, "it can no more prevent American citizens from the free as well as from the Slave States from going there with their goods and chattels to settle and to revolutionize and republicanize and Anglo Saxonize that valley than it can prevent the magazine from exploding after the firebrand has been thrown into it."[47]

Herndon's and Gibbon's reports, sent to Maury between 1851 and 1852, depicted the Amazon Valley as a vast wilderness inhabited by a half-civilized population. The racial composition of the Amazonian people was of particular interest to the explorers. Herndon found that the whites were very few and could be considered white only "in contradistinction to the Indian."[48] The Virginians were all the more surprised to learn that these "half-breeds" were in charge of securing the western borders of Brazil. In Mato Grosso, on the Brazil-Bolivia border, Gibbon scorned the Brazilian soldiers' efforts to impress: "While they respectfully saluted Uncle Sam's uniform, we noticed, for the first time, how very awkwardly the negro handles the musket."[49]

Herndon came to the only conclusion that would have pleased his superior: the Amazon Valley was in need of "an industrious and active population, who know what the comforts of life are, and who have artificial wants to draw out the great resources of the country." As he crossed sumptuous forests and rivers, Herndon dreamed of what his people would accomplish in the South American interior: "Let us suppose introduced into such a country the railroad and the steamboat, the plough, the axe, and the hoe; let us suppose the land divided into large estates, and cultivated by slave labor, so as to produce all that they are capable of producing." Subjected to American colonial rule, the Amazon would certainly surpass "the grandeur of ancient Babylon and modern London."[50]

Unfortunately for Maury and his disciples, Brazilian authorities were not willing to cooperate. While negotiating permissions for the expedition, the Brazilian minister to Washington, Sérgio Teixeira de Macedo, wrote a detailed report to Minister of Foreign Affairs Paulino José Soares de Souza, the future Viscount of Uruguay. Teixeira de Macedo analyzed the recent territorial expansion of the United States, pointing out that "this country presents a system of conquest and usurpation unknown in past times and in the Old World, a system that is incarnated in the population, constitutes part of their opinions, of their prejudices, that is practiced independently of the Government." The United States, Teixeira de Macedo added, did not conquer territories by using a standing army, as the French and British empires did. In a strange sort of democratic expansionism, American farmers and planters would simply settle whatever lands they desired, be they owned by European, indigenous, or Latin American people. War usually followed, and the Americans, already settled in, triumphed. The ease with which thousands of families from the eastern United States had occupied former Mexican lands was enough, for Teixeira de Macedo, to demonstrate that they could go anywhere, including the Amazon. Forwarding American newspapers to Soares de Souza, Teixeira de Macedo drew attention to "the contempt with which the Anglo-Saxon-American looks at other peoples, and especially at us, and how he convinces himself that he is the civilizer par excellence of the Americas."[51]

Teixeira de Macedo also warned Soares de Souza that Brazilians should not fool themselves and expect that the sectional conflict raging in the United States would weaken Maury's expansionist drive. "The southern faction," he wrote, "is the most invested, most interested in these invasions. In the present state of union with the North, which does not find immediate gain in such conquests, the plans of the South often find themselves thwarted by the federal government." If the separation between slave and free states materialized, though, "whatever the confederation of the South judges convenient, it will quickly execute, without having to deal with the bridles that now are presented by the commercial interests of the North."[52] Teixeira de Macedo knew well where Maury was coming from. American slaveholders' imperialism terrified the slave empire of South America.

In response to Herndon's and Gibbon's expedition, the Brazilian government sent its own agents to negotiate treaties with Brazil's Amazonian neighbors. By restricting navigation on the Amazon Basin, Brazil had long prevented vessels coming from the Atlantic Ocean from reaching the interior of New Granada, Ecuador, Peru, and Bolivia. Because the Andes made access from the Pacific coast to the Amazon very difficult, these four republics had been dissatisfied with Brazil's policy.[53] In 1851, Brazil proposed a treaty to Peru that would grant free intercourse on rivers common to both countries for Brazilian and Peruvian ships only. In 1852 it was Venezuela's turn, and in 1853 New Granada and Ecuador. Moreover, on August 30, 1852, the Brazilian government conceded to the Baron of Mauá, an influential Brazilian entrepreneur, a thirty-year exclusive privilege, along with large financial incentives, to navigate the Amazon Basin. The contract also prescribed that the navigation company would help establish sixty government colonies on the banks of the Amazon and its tributaries.[54]

Such developments infuriated Maury. In a series of articles for the Washington *Union* and the *National Intelligencer* published under the suggestive pseudonym of Inca, he initiated a public campaign against Brazilian control of the Amazon Basin. These anti-Brazilian texts were soon translated and published in Lima, Rio de Janeiro, and La Paz, immediately gaining Maury notoriety in South America.[55] He portrayed a paradise in the Amazon comprising lands suitable for large-scale agriculture and mining. Yet, he protested, Brazil had decided to shut the doors of the region to the Anglo-Saxon civilizer. "So fearful has she been that the steamboat on those waters would reveal to the world the exceeding great riches of this province," Maury charged, "that we have here re-enacted under our own eyes a worse than Japanese policy; for it excludes from settlement and cultivation, from commerce and civilization, the finest country in the world." He ranted that Brazilian pressure on the Amazonian republics was an attempt "to hood-wink them, to retard their progress, to seal up tighter than ever their great arteries of commerce, and thus perpetuate the stagnation and death that have for 300 years reigned in the great Amazonian

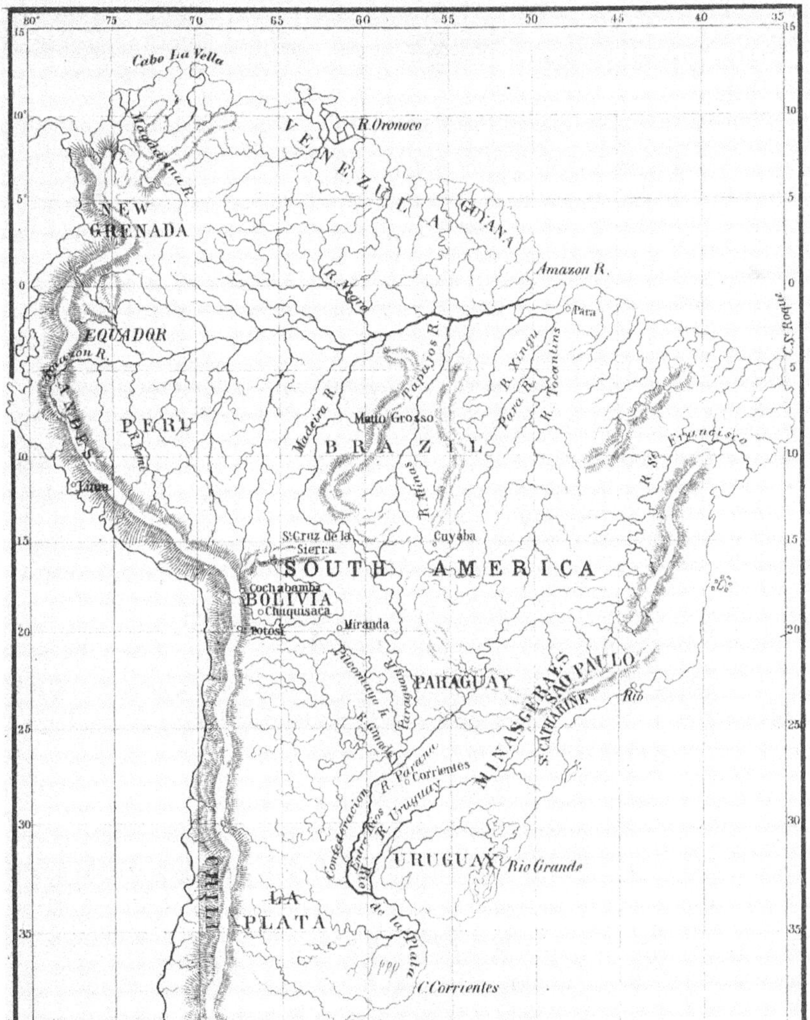

FIGURE 1.1 Seeking to confront Brazil, Maury included a map in the collected
edition of his articles that erased national borders and showed an open Amazon Basin.
Matthew Fontaine Maury, *The Amazon, and the Atlantic Slopes of South America:
A Series of Letters Published in the National Intelligencer and Union Newspapers,
under the Signature of "Inca"* (Washington: F. Taylor, 1853).
Courtesy of the American Antiquarian Society, Worcester.

water-shed." The concession to Mauá was "one of the most odious monopolies that ever were inflicted upon free trade, or that now retard the progress of any country."[56]

Maury's campaign against Brazil gained some high-level endorsements in the United States. Writing for the *Southern Quarterly Review* in October 1853, the South Carolina senator and proslavery leader James Henry Hammond remarked that "by the united action of wind and stream," the Amazon Valley was closer to Charleston than to Rio de Janeiro. Like Maury, Hammond claimed that "Providence appears to direct—by the natural laws alluded to—into the waters of the United States, the future valuable and varied productions of an Empire. Energetic man must appropriate the blessing." Hammond thought that the Brazilian notion of national interest was quite absurd: "Like the man who boasts to the world of a splendid (unimproved) estate—lying waste, and giving comparatively no return to the owner—Don Pedro will laud his possessions too; but neither improve them himself—for he is really incompetent—nor permit another to do so." But Hammond knew well what the Brazilian monarch worried about: "He fears our ambitious desire to annex his Empire!"[57]

Hammond clarified that the United States had other priorities for conquest: the rest of Mexico, Cuba, the West Indies, and Central America. Nevertheless, "reasoning from the increasing power and grandeur of America . . . and from the long tested propensities of her dominant race for the acquisition of *land*, and for the *order* and *good government* of the world, it may be said . . . that Brazil, empire as it is under a monarchical sovereign, must inevitably partake of the glorious destiny of the United States!" Hammond objected to Maury's idea that the American South needed a safety valve for its excess slave population as he thought that there was plenty of room for slavery to expand in North America for another thousand years. Still, he enthusiastically joined Maury in rallying "our southern planters, with their slaves, in large numbers, in the course of time, to emigrate to the fertile valley of the Amazon."[58]

According to Francisco Inácio de Carvalho Moreira—the successor of Teixeira de Macedo as Brazilian minister to Washington—Maury's campaign had done more than kindle Hammond's imperial imagination. By August 1853, he feared that American filibusters were preparing to occupy the Amazon.[59] Despite being reassured by the US Department of State that those were only rumors and that the US Navy had been watching for any unauthorized expedition, Carvalho Moreira insisted that several sources had provided him with precise intelligence "that reckless [American] ship-owners had intended to dispatch steamers to force their entrance to that river in search of ports in Peru and Bolivia, on the pretext that the governments of these two republics have declared their ports free to foreign commerce." The Brazilian diplomat had heard that these plans of aggression were so advanced that a lieutenant of the US Navy was ready to take command of the invading troops, having received permission from the federal government. Even if the American government denied protection to the filibusters, Carvalho Moreira feared, "they were disposed to continue their sinister projects either way, taking on their own the risks of so temerarious an enterprise."[60]

If, on the one hand, Carvalho Moreira's fears of an armed invasion of the Amazon did not materialize, on the other, the US Department of State continued to advance Maury's agenda. American diplomats approached the Amazonian republics about establishing their own treaties of commerce and navigation. Brazilian diplomacy suffered serious setbacks then as Brazil's northern neighbors opened their interior rivers to American ships by the mid-1850s. Nationalist elites of northern South America, aware of Brazil's aggressive policies toward the republics of the Plata and concerned about their own borders, saw Brazilian imperialism as the great menace in the region. The influence of the United States in the Amazon Basin, they reckoned, could be a shield against Brazilian impositions.[61]

While American agents helped raise anti-Brazilian feelings in northern South America, a new US minister arrived in Rio de Janeiro. A native of North Carolina, William Trousdale had served as a brigadier general during the Mexican War and later became governor of Tennessee. On October 28, 1853, Trousdale proposed to Antonio Paulino Limpo de Abreu, who had replaced Soares de Souza as minister of foreign affairs, a treaty of amity, commerce, and navigation. "I was told," an angry Trousdale reported back, "that if they treated with us, the Government of Great Britain . . . would not only ask for one also, but would insist on it, without revoking the bill introduced by Lord Aberdeen in 1845, containing a clause giving the British the right to search vessels under Brazilian colors on the sea." Therefore, Trousdale concluded, "a treaty with the United States had always been delayed or prevented."[62] By juxtaposing the Amazon question to that of the slave trade, Brazilian authorities had found a (not so) subtle way of saying that they were not willing to risk, again, getting involved with powers that could injure Brazilian sovereignty.

Trousdale nevertheless persisted, managing to meet with Dom Pedro II. But the monarch was not of much help either, telling him that "it had become of late the settled policy of Brazil to decline entering into Treaty Stipulations with Foreign Powers, in order to avoid entanglements and interpretations which would be adverse to the interests of the Empire."[63] When José Maria da Silva Paranhos replaced Limpo de Abreu in the Ministry of Foreign Affairs, Trousdale renewed his efforts, now arguing that "Brazil is an American nation; she is in friendship with the United States; they are both the most powerful and wealthy nations on this Continent; both are slave-holding powers; the trade between them is advantageous, particularly to Brazil."[64] Trousdale repeated the same argument to a member of the Council of State, emphasizing that Brazil's "social institutions, particularly slavery, which must be preserved, pointed to the necessity of a closer alliance with the American Union."[65]

After years of friction, Trousdale now proposed that slavery should be the basis of an alliance between Brazil and the United States. Yet, to his chagrin, the Brazilians would have none of it. After all, as Trousdale himself recognized, "the idea had been frequently held out in the Brazilian papers and elsewhere that the object of the Americans in endeavoring to secure the opening of the Amazon was to gain a foothold, with a view of ulterior annexation to the United States."[66] In this point Trousdale was right: Maury's writings had become frightening specters for Brazil. Furthermore, the memory of Wise still haunted the Brazilian public, who wished to keep a safe distance from the slave South. In other words, wary Brazilians knew that Trousdale's proslavery rhetoric of friendship did not match Southerners' actions in foreign affairs.

In 1854, the Brazilian Army colonel João Batista de Castro Morais Antas, who had participated in several expeditions to the Amazon, published a series of articles assailing Maury and his inaccurate geography. Morais Antas denounced Maury's arrogant belief that Americans could "impose happiness by force onto Peru, Bolivia, and Brazil." He feared the repercussions of such ideas in a country "where the illusions propelled without reply by the press may one day tend to disturb the modest prosperity of other peoples." It was time, Morais Antas urged, "to draw the attention of the civilized world to this system of conquest by absorption, which starts to characterize some spirits in the United States." Even if the Amazon remained undeveloped, he asserted, "in no case it could be derived from this that the United States or any other nation has the right to create embarrassments and, much less, occupy that region, cultivate it, and colonize it."[67]

Another critic of Maury, Pedro de Angelis—a Brazilian resident in Montevideo—published a long pamphlet in French, the lingua franca of nineteenth-century diplomacy, to demonstrate that Brazil alone had the right to control the Amazon Basin. "Supported by the *droit de gens*, by the customs of nations, by the Treaty of San Ildefonso," Angelis argued, "Brazil can reserve the exclusive right of navigation on its interior rivers and exclude any foreign power, even the Spanish-American republics." Brazil nonetheless had extended its generous arm to its neighbors, spontaneously providing them access to the Atlantic. Very different from benevolent Brazil, Angelis continued, was the United States. "Vis-à-vis Texas," he accused, "the Americans have been rehearsing a system that seems to have triumphed among them now." The more territories Americans conquered, the hungrier they got, and a system created by bloodthirsty filibusters had now become the official foreign policy of the United States: "No longer timid aspirations, desires contained by respect for treaties, a tacit protection given to bands of adventurers; it is now in the Senate, taking the form of a motion presenting the theories of invasion for public applause." Quoting from speeches for the annexation of Cuba by Democratic senators, Angelis portrayed a nation of thugs dedicated to sending its filibusters all over the hemisphere.[68]

The last word in the quarrel with Maury came from the former minister of foreign affairs Soares de Souza. In regard to the question of interior navigation, he told the Council of State in April 1854, "Brazil is in the same position that it was recently in regard to the traffic. If we openly and completely oppose ourselves to the navigation of the Amazon, we will have all against us, and no one for us. We will be, in spite of ourselves, dragged, and whoever is dragged cannot dominate and direct the movement which drags him so that he can take advantage of it." Once again, the problem of the African slave trade reared its ugly head. If they wished to preserve national sovereignty, Soares de Souza argued, Brazilians could neither oppose the spirit of the age nor wait for some foreign power to force them into it. "If the Amazon is penetrated without us, and without any serious resistance," he insisted, "we will be deceived, and lose any moral force that we might have."[69]

Soares de Souza asked for renewed negotiations with the Amazonian republics and the reinforcement of Brazilian navigation and colonization projects—whatever it took to avoid American encroachment. Seeking to convince the Council of State about the urgency of the question, he narrated the histories of American conquest of Texas, California, New Mexico, and Oregon. Cuba and Sonora were next; and then, the Amazon. "American migration to the Amazon would be an immense threat," Soares de Souza remarked. "It would extinguish our race, our language, our religion, our laws. Our industry would never emerge, and if any existed, it would be suffocated." Anglo-Americans would not mingle with other people, he believed. Aided by their government and American companies, these invaders would "either get rid of all competition from our settlers or subjugate them."[70]

Soares de Souza asserted that the Brazilian government could not repeat the mistake of the Mexicans, who let Texas be colonized by Anglo-American slaveholders. Neither could Brazil passively watch its neighbors yield to the invaders. If Peru and Bolivia were willing to open navigation and distribute lands to American settlers, Brazil should not hesitate to take measures "to counterbalance this population, by peopling our frontier." Soares de Souza asked Brazilian diplomacy to be even more aggressive in protecting the Amazon: "This way we will give the law, otherwise we will receive it."[71]

Maury overestimated his powers and underestimated the resolve of other peoples to protect their own interests, following a pattern that had become all too common among proslavery Southerners. Disregarding such evidence, part of the scholarship emphasizes proslavery expansionists' own version of their hemispheric projects, portraying them as successful empire builders who exerted their power all over the Americas.[72] In reality, proslavery expansionists like Maury achieved very little after the Mexican War. By the 1850s, Southern expansionism had become a series of pipe dreams based on an unrealistic interpretation of foreign affairs. Filibustering expeditions were resounding failures. And the project to take over the Amazon never became anything more than a bluff. On the other side of Southern imperialism stood another slave empire that would not yield to Southerners' machinations. Brazil would open the Amazon River to foreign ships only in 1867, after the free North had crushed the slave South in the American Civil War.

Again, proslavery Southerners had treated Brazil with contempt. And, again, Brazilians had responded in kind. Through Morais Antas, Angelis, and especially Soares de Souza, the Brazilian response to Maury had become a forceful affirmation of Brazilian imperialism in northern South America. Incapable of breaking the Brazilians' resolve and engulfed in the secession crisis at home, fire-eaters would now try to make Brazil a client of the emerging Confederacy. They did not expect, however, that antislavery Northerners would formulate a more effective approach to Brazil.

The Mission

As Maury's campaign raged, a missionary from Indiana arrived in Brazil. James Cooley Fletcher was the son of a powerful lawyer, banker, and railroader from Indianapolis, who was also a Free Soiler and eventually became a member of the Republican Party. Fletcher studied at Brown University and the Princeton Theological Seminary, became a Presbyterian minister, and spent part of his youth in Paris and Geneva. In 1851, at the age of twenty-seven, he went to Brazil to work as chaplain for the American Seaman's Friend Society. His first impressions of the country were quite positive. "This people," he wrote to his father, "(among whom there is free press, tolerant laws, a language easy to acquire, and more [religious] indifference than bigotry) it appears to me, that here in a growing kingdom, a flourishing empire, there is as much if not more reason to hope for fruit than in India or China."[73] Although Fletcher's primary intention was to preach to American seamen and spread the Protestant faith among Brazilians, his eyes were wide open for business opportunities. From the perspective of American merchants and manufacturers, he soon understood, Brazil could be a much better customer than the Far East.

In 1852, Fletcher's meager missionary earnings led him to apply for the position of secretary of the US legation in Rio de Janeiro. In contrast to most American missionaries and diplomats who preceded him, he eagerly sought to become close to the Brazilian elite. An opportunity to cultivate good relations came when Dom Pedro II accepted an invitation for a tour of the USS *City of Pittsburg* and Fletcher was designated to accompany the monarch. Exultant, he described this "splendid experience" in a letter to his family. "The etiquette of the Court is very great, very precise," he began, "but on that day the Emperor—a fine looking young man, more than 6 feet [tall] and of great dignity—conversed with me like 'any brether,' while ministers, generals, and commodores were most respectful and distant in their approach to His Imperial Majesty." Dom Pedro II had "many fine steamers and vessels in his navy," Fletcher continued, "but he was perfectly surprised at the richness and luxury and magnificence of the *City of Pittsburg*." The monarch walked around the American steamer, examined the machinery, and studied its blueprints for a long time. But Dom Pedro II was not the only Brazilian to demonstrate interest in American-made technology. In the same letter, Fletcher described a visit to a coffee plantation and told his brother—a railroad engineer and inventor—that "you ought to come here and apply science to the machinery of coffee plantations. They need you here."[74]

Some months later, Fletcher returned to the subject of the Brazilian need for American technology: "They are building a railr[oad] here over the mountain. I told the engineer about the locomotive which climbs the hill at Madison." Referring to the cogwheel system, which permitted locomotives to climb a steep hill in Indiana, Fletcher urged his family to help his Brazilian friends. "Will you so soon as you receive this," he addressed his brothers, "ask Morris or someone who knows to answer the following questions—What is the descent to the mile of the Madison hill—Who invented the Engine—Has he any to sell—and Where can they be manufactured—for doubtless they are patented. I should not wonder if three or four of that kind should be ordered by this Govt."[75]

After a brief return to the United States in 1854, Fletcher decided to put his connections with American manufacturers and influential Brazilians to work. Back in Rio de Janeiro in 1855, he organized an exhibition of American goods at the Imperial Museum. His professed desires were "to see men of science and learning in Brazil linked with the kindred spirits of our vigorous land; to behold good school-books in the hands of Brazilian children; and to see our manufactures taking their stand in this country, which is so great a consumer."[76]

Entering the exhibition, the visitors could see the American and the Brazilian flags together, hanging over the portraits of George Washington, Dom Pedro I, and Dom Pedro II. Several publications, small manufactured articles, and agricultural tools—all made in the United States—were displayed to demonstrate the development of American industry. To Fletcher's great satisfaction, Dom Pedro II was the first to visit, "made many inquiries, and manifested a most intimate knowledge with the progress of our country."[77] Flattered, Fletcher decided to reciprocate Dom Pedro's kindness by going in person to the imperial palace and presenting the royal family with books, engravings, and maps from the exhibition. Before returning to the United States, he wrote to the monarch promising that "when I return to my home in Philadelphia I shall, if agreeable to Your Majesty, forward, so far as I am able, whatever there is new in the department of science in the United States."[78]

After Dom Pedro II, hundreds of visitors crowded the museum to see the objects from the United States. "Astonishment and admiration were constantly upon the lips of the Brazilians," Fletcher celebrated.[79] Rio de Janeiro newspapers took notice of Fletcher's effort, reporting that he had brought from his country "a magnificent collection of maps, photographic specimens, and diverse manufactures."[80] The *Correio Mercantil* remarked that, through Fletcher's exhibition, the Brazilian people could see "the industrial progress of the United States, because it gathers works of all qualities, from the plow of the humble mechanic from Newark to the deluxe editions of the foremost publishers and engravers of the Union."[81]

José Martiniano de Alencar, a famous writer in Brazil at the time, saw in Fletcher's exhibition the material possibility of amicable relations between the United States and Brazil. He was fascinated by the "industrial products of the United States," the samples of photography, chromolithography, geographical charts, and "a bust of [Daniel] Webster that Mr. Fletcher says was made by machinery." After listening to Fletcher speak on the need to make Brazil known in the United States, Alencar declared with excitement that "if Mr. Fletcher succeeds in this idea, for which he seems to work with much enthusiasm, he will be providing a great service to the Americas. From these new relations a great idea of an American policy may be born, which will in the future direct the destiny of the New World, and put an end to European intervention."[82]

Fletcher, for his part, was convinced that the Brazilians' positive response proved that "a proper exhibition of American arts and manufactures, arranged by business-men and those who have means to carry it out, would redound a thousandfold to the benefit of American commerce."[83] Through Fletcher, Northern manufacturers found avid consumers in Brazil. As the years went by, other Northern agents carried his work forward, and Brazilian demand for American products, especially agricultural and transportation technologies, expanded rapidly.

Back again in the United States, Fletcher started speaking about Brazil to American audiences. In January 1857, a *Correio Mercantil* correspondent reported that Fletcher had lectured at the New York Historical Society. After exhibiting books, newspapers, and engravings from Brazil, he presented "a magnificent portrait of our monarch, which was received with thundering applause once Mr. Fletcher declared that such was the portrait of a prince of great virtues as a man, and of superior merit as head of a country where true Liberty is enjoyed." The correspondent also noted that, thanks to Fletcher, articles about the commerce of Brazil appeared in popular American publications such as the New York *Merchant's Magazine*. "I have finally heard good things being said about our country," the delighted writer concluded, "and without adulation or lies."[84]

Fletcher used his lectures to promote what would become one of the most popular books about a South American country in the nineteenth-century United States. Although including passages from the travel journal of Daniel Parish Kidder, a Methodist missionary who lived in Brazil during the 1830s, the book *Brazil and the Brazilians: Portrayed in Historical and Descriptive Sketches*, first published in 1857, resulted mostly from Fletcher's efforts.[85] The work opened with a reprimand to American readers for their ignorance in relation to the largest country of South America. Brazil was much more than a territory of mighty rivers, virgin forests, and wild animals. According to Fletcher, Brazilians were "the most progressive people south of the Equator."[86]

In *Brazil and the Brazilians*, Fletcher was particularly invested in contrasting the national paths taken by Brazil and Mexico. Although both countries were similar in territorial extension, population size, and resources, he maintained, Mexican instability had impaired its development while Brazil had been steadily progressing. Not surprisingly, Brazilian "commerce doubles every ten years; she possesses cities lighted by gas, long lines of steamships, and the beginnings of railways that are spreading from the sea-coast into the fertile interior; in her borders education and general intelligence are constantly advancing."[87]

Yet more remarkable, for Fletcher, was the contrast between the slave society of Brazil and that of his own country: "The subject of slavery in Brazil is one of great interest and hopefulness. The Brazilian Constitution recognises, neither directly nor indirectly, color as a basis of civil rights; hence, once free, the black man or the mulatto, if he possess energy and talent, can rise to a social position from which his race in North America is debarred." Although acknowledging that slaves in Brazil faced serious problems such as high suicide rates, cruel punishments, and brutal exploitation, Fletcher insisted that "in Brazil every thing is in favor of freedom."[88] By emphasizing what he perceived as the benevolence of the Brazilian slave society, Fletcher set up an attack on the proslavery American South.[89]

In addition to lauding Brazilian laws and customs concerning race relations, Fletcher was optimistic about the attitudes of those who should have been most interested in the perpetuation of slavery in Brazil: the coffee planters. For him, the Vergueiros, a prominent family from the province of São Paulo, represented all the best impulses of the Brazilian planter class. Fletcher was delighted to visit their model plantation of Ibicaba, situated in the township of Limeira. The peculiarity of Ibicaba, he explained, "consists in the fact that free labor is employed in carrying on its vast operations; and those whom Senator Vergueiro and his sons have brought to displace the Africans are men of the working-classes from Germany and Switzerland." Fletcher regarded the Vergueiros as visionaries for employing European immigrants as sharecroppers on their plantation: "We shall see . . . that they have adopted that plan which has not only been productive of great and profitable results to themselves, but that they have helped to elevate and greatly benefit the condition of those who were in narrow circumstances at home. The Vergueiros have solved the question, so often asked, 'What is the true mode for colonization in Brazil?'"[90]

The planter, Nicolau Pereira de Campos Vergueiro, was a Liberal senator, many times a minister, and once regent of the empire. His sons, all of whom had been educated in Europe, were plantation managers and agricultural modernizers. Fletcher was jubilant to learn the Vergueiros' views of their own

FIGURE 1.2 "Colonia Vergueiro." Daniel Parish Kidder and James Cooley Fletcher, *Brazil and the Brazilians: Portrayed in Historical and Descriptive Sketches* (Philadelphia: Childs & Peterson, 1857), 411. Courtesy of the American Antiquarian Society, Worcester.

enterprise: "I demanded of Sr. Luiz Vergueiro if it were mere philanthropy which prompted their efforts to introduce free labor: he replied, most promptly and decidedly, 'We find the labor of a man who has a will of his own, and interests at stake, vastly more profitable than slave-labor.'" Brazilian planters, Fletcher believed, had accepted the superiority of free labor and had already devised a feasible sharecropping system to replace slavery. After visiting another plantation belonging to the Vergueiros, Fletcher noted that "hitherto blacks have been employed upon this large estate; but it is the intention of the proprietor to introduce, as soon as possible, free white laborers." From this and other observations, Fletcher concluded with pleasure (and quite a bit of haste) that "slavery is doomed in Brazil."[91]

In his book, Fletcher reproduced images that reinforced the idea of order and well-being on Brazilian plantations. The engravings represented the benign free labor system that Fletcher claimed he had found at Ibicaba. His textual narrative was no less idealized: "I visited the cottages of the colonists, about one mile from the manor. As I passed along, I was constantly saluted by cheerful Swiss and German workmen, some of whom were surrounded by noisy and joyous fair-headed children, who capered about with as much life and glee as if at the foot of the Hartz or in the valleys of the Oberland."[92]

As it turned out, the always watchful Fletcher chose not to discuss the growing discontent of the Ibicaba sharecroppers, which led to an uprising in late 1856. The historian Emília Viotti da Costa explains that the sharecropping system was an attempt "to reconcile the interests of the planters, accustomed to slave labor, with those of the colonists, who were eager to acquire property, improve their living conditions, and rise in the social scale. The result did not please either group."[93] Poorly treated by the supervisors, feeling cheated by the planters and the merchants, restricted in their mobility and ability to communicate with the outside world, paying abusive interest rates on the money advanced for transportation, and unable to accumulate enough money to acquire their own lands, the sharecroppers rebelled. When the incident became known in Europe, Swiss and German authorities prohibited peasants from migrating to Brazil. The Vergueiros and other planter families of São Paulo nonetheless persisted in their experiments with free labor by slowly improving the sharecropping system and combining it with the wage system.[94]

A committed antislavery reformer, Fletcher did not want to know about setbacks. Neither did he mention that, by the 1850s, Ibicaba employed over two hundred slaves and that the Vergueiros kept buying more captives while experimenting with sharecropping. In fact, Fletcher twisted the truth to demonstrate that Brazilian prospects in relation to the transition from slave to free labor were extremely bright. "The system inaugurated by Sr. Vergueiro and Sons," he insisted, would "prove a great blessing to Brazil and to the poorer classes of Europe." Fletcher imagined that the sharecropping system would be expanded to all plantations of Brazil and the immigrants' children would grow up healthy, well educated, and attached to the soil; "and, if nothing untoward occurs, Brazil, in half a century, will have a host of small proprietors infusing a new lifeblood into the body politic."[95]

Fletcher's omission of the coffee planters' brutal methods and cold calculation would become the norm among American antislavery reformers who engaged with Brazil. As long as they were willing to improve their economy and experiment with free labor, Northerners thought that Brazilian slaveholders should take their time, phasing out slavery in a way that would preserve political order and economic inequality in Brazil. From the very beginning, it was clear that the free North favored an emancipation process in Brazil that would maintain—perhaps even increase—the power of the planter class. Together, these two groups worked to turn slaves and immigrants into free—but also destitute—workers who would sell their labor power cheaply to the owners of capital.

In the presence of men such as the Vergueiros, Fletcher condemned the attitudes that some of his (Southern) compatriots had been adopting in relation to Brazil. To his embarrassment, Fletcher was residing in Rio de Janeiro when the Brazilian press published Maury's writings. "I well remember the commotion his communications on the Amazon caused at the capital," he lamented, "in connection with a report that a 'filibustiering' [sic] expedition was fitting out at New York to force the opening of the great river." Fletcher never hesitated to defend Brazilian sovereignty. "As the case stands," he echoed Angelis and Morais Antas, "Brazil certainly has the right, and the sole right, to control the rivers within her own borders, no matter if they do rise in other states."[96] Fletcher was further disheartened by the appointment of William Trousdale as US minister to Brazil. Accusing the diplomat of having ruined all possibilities of an amicable treaty between the two countries, Fletcher told his father that Trousdale had become "the laughing stock of the Court, the diplomatic corps and his own countrymen. He is a man who asks advice of nobody and takes none from whoever that attempts to give it."[97]

But Fletcher did not think that American citizens should completely remove themselves from the waters of Brazil. A new approach to the question was necessary, and in contrast to Maury's proslavery expansionism, Fletcher favored the posture of an Ohio entrepreneur he had met in Rio de Janeiro. Born in North Carolina, Thomas Rainey had moved to Cincinnati during the 1830s, joined the Whig Party, become an educator and the editor of the *Ohio Teacher*, and taken great interest in steamship navigation. In 1854, he headed to Brazil. After getting in touch with Brazilian politicians and businessmen, Rainey proposed the creation of a steamship line connecting New York to Belém, in the northern province of Pará, to be integrated there with Brazilian lines into the Amazon and to the southern provinces. Unlike Maury, however, Rainey was not seeking to colonize the Amazon with Anglo-American planters and their slaves. For him, the markets of Brazil were more attractive than its jungles.[98]

Back in the United States, Rainey started a public campaign to gather support for his project. In 1856, he petitioned Congress for a contract for carrying mail and goods between the United States and Brazil. In 1857, Rainey gave a lecture at the New York Historical Society on the Brazilian trade. He pointed out that American merchants complained that the federal government gave them no means for conducting trade with Brazil. "They complain," Rainey specified, "not so much that Great Britain has the monopoly of this trade, . . . not so much that she has even four lines of steamers and weekly communication, . . . but that the citizens of the United States are not permitted to enter into a fair competition for this trade."[99] In 1858, Rainey published a long pamphlet titled *Ocean Steam Navigation and the Ocean Post* and distributed five hundred copies to American legislators. It explained that "our immense trade with Brazil and other portions of South-America, which if properly fostered would increase with magic rapidity, . . . is compelled to use the necessarily selfishly arranged, and circuitous, and non-connecting lines of Great Britain."[100]

In the same spirit of Fletcher, Rainey emphasized that Brazil was a progressive country, enumerated Brazil's abundant agricultural products, and remarked that its navigation networks were being extended and its railroads pushed to the interior. Rainey further noted that "Brazil, having now most heartily abandoned the slave-trade in fact and principle, finds that the labor of white colonists, so far from being unable to supply the demands of the country, is really largely increasing its production, and adding more rapidly to the permanent wealth." Fletcher applauded Rainey's effort and reproduced his 1857 lecture as an appendix to *Brazil and the Brazilians*.[101]

Fletcher's efforts to bring men like Rainey closer to Brazil were met with praise in the American North. Popular publications such as the Boston *Littell's Living Age* were enthusiastic to learn that "by an intelligent, vigorous, and persistent policy of internal and foreign government, [Brazil] may, one day, rival in wealth, in power, and in moral and intellectual splendor, the great empires of past or present times."[102] The idea that Brazil had great potential was not new; what was really groundbreaking in Fletcher's approach was the idea that a policy of collaboration—instead of subjugation—would be the best one to secure American interests in Brazil. The Philadelphia *Saturday Evening Post* regretted that "Brazil, alarmed and incensed by the construction put upon some American newspaper articles regarding the opening of the Amazon river, . . . has shrunk from us, and now discourages any commercial connection." The editor hoped that, through Fletcher's initiative, the two countries would finally establish friendly relations.[103]

In a very positive review of Fletcher's work, the Washington *National Era* highlighted that Brazilians deserved to be respected, especially because "everything is in favor of freedom in Brazil."[104] Antislavery publications were particularly interested in the future of that country. "Slavery is essentially and unchangeably evil," the New York *Methodist Quarterly Review* remarked. "Yet there are facts which greatly mitigate the curse, and render Brazilian slavery less hopeless than the *domestic* institutions of this 'Land of the free and home of the brave!'" Exalting Fletcher's Brazilian friends, the reviewer joyfully asserted that, in Brazil, "free labor is everywhere coming into contact with slave labor, and the result is obvious."[105]

As expected, the reception of *Brazil and the Brazilians* in the slave South was very different from what took place in the free North. Southern reviewers wasted no time in claiming that Fletcher was mistaken. J. D. B. De Bow, an influential proslavery ideologue based in New Orleans, alerted his readers that "it is to be observed that we are dealing with an antislavery authority." De Bow stressed the political elements of Fletcher's work: "Had Brazil been part of our South, we should have had 'painted devils' enough portrayed in its slave fields." A Yankee, Fletcher could never be "a proper judge of what is fitting or not fitting to the institution of African slavery." Fletcher erred, De Bow rebuked, when claiming that the institution was doomed in Brazil. "Based upon the experience of the rest of the world, and upon its necessity in that country," slavery would not only persist but expand there. The political stability and economic development of Brazil resulted, in reality, from the existence of a strong slave regime. All things considered, De Bow proclaimed that the United States and Brazil stood "together, though nearly alone in the world, in maintaining African slavery, and deriving from it that strength and consideration which experience has shown must result from it in all agricultural countries."[106]

An even angrier reaction emerged when Fletcher lectured about Brazil in Memphis, Tennessee. One of the audience members was scandalized by Fletcher's contention that "abolition would be entirely in accordance with his wishes, and would redound to the glory and prosperity of Brazil, and the entire American continent." The spectator aggressively challenged Fletcher: "By what sort of labor is the great valley of the Amazon to be cultivated, if slavery be abolished in Brazil?—What is to become of the surplus slave population in the South, in the ages to come, if not profitably transferred to that immense valley?" Following Maury's logic, the critic argued that "Fletcher is evidently behind the age. While all the outside world is modifying its views in regard to the 'peculiar institution' of the South, he comes into the midst of the South itself, and boldly makes war upon the very foundation-principle of that institution!"[107]

The problem of Brazilian slavery became such a momentous quarrel in the United States that, in April 1857, the proslavery *Charleston Mercury* urged

President James Buchanan to appoint "men of ability and capacity" to represent Southern interests in Brazil. The newspaper stressed that Brazil, along with the United States, was the only independent country "which recognizes and sanctions negro slavery"; and this institution would form "an identity of interest which should bind the two nations in the closest alliance, and which entitles the United States, in virtue of its superior power, to a sort of protectorate over the weaker neighbor."[108] It did not take long for the Buchanan administration to go along with the project of making Brazil into a client of Southern proslavery interests. Richard Kidder Meade became US minister to Brazil in December 1857. A former congressman for Virginia, Meade was, in the words of the *New York Tribune*, "a well-known politician of the extremist Calhoun school."[109]

Fletcher's work about Brazil had fallen on fertile soil as anti- and pro-slavery positions hardened along sectional lines in the United States. Each side manipulated facts about Brazil's slave society to advance its own agenda. Each side formulated a specific approach to Brazil. Each side sent its own envoy to negotiate with the Brazilians. Whereas Fletcher successfully helped antislavery Northerners establish a vibrant network connecting the two countries, proslavery Southerners continued to demonstrate their incapacity to build an alliance with slaveholding Brazil. It became clear then that Brazilian society had little interest in what the slave South had to offer. Northern antislavery reformers—and not Southern planters—lured elite Brazilians who were trying to bring their country up to date with the innovations of the time.

An Easy Choice

As soon as Meade arrived in Rio de Janeiro and had the opportunity to address Dom Pedro II, he mentioned the need for strengthening the bonds between Brazil and the slave South. After a short note about giving "additional life and energy to an already growing and prosperous commerce," Meade reminded the Brazilian monarch that "an institution common to both countries, fixed and deeply rooted in their soil (with many hostile prejudices to encounter from without), does now establish an affinity between them, and will insure for mutual defense, a unity of action and feeling that will prove invincible in the future."[110]

Meade's address to Dom Pedro II caused consternation among the enemies of slavery in the United States. The Republican senator Henry Wilson of Massachusetts demanded that the president communicate to the Senate the instructions given to Meade.[111] The *National Era* supported Wilson's request, arguing that the American people had the right to know whether Buchanan had authorized Meade "to propose to Brazil an alliance offensive and defensive, on the ground of the existence of Slavery in one half of this country and in the whole of that country, for the purpose of rendering it irrevocable."[112]

Meade's proposition also created some anxiety in Brazil. Commenting on his address, the *Diário do Rio de Janeiro*, whose editor in chief was José Martiniano de Alencar, alluded to the recent past: "We cannot imagine that, being the ones extending their hand to this alliance of two continents, the United States are aiming at a selfish interest and hoping to deceive our government so that they can, under the shadow of this policy, practice offensive acts against the sovereignty of other peoples." Having Henry A. Wise and Matthew Fontaine Maury fresh in their memories, Brazilians dreaded Meade. Now that "the fast means of communication connect the world through commercial relations," Alencar's newspaper hoped, "the time of conquest is far away."[113]

Other Rio de Janeiro newspapers responded to Meade's address. They all reinforced the idea that Brazil favored commercial relations over a proslavery alliance. The *Correio Mercantil* suggested that Brazil and the United States could be brought closer "through fruitful lines of steam navigation."[114] Nothing was said about the protection of slavery. The *Correio da Tarde* expressed similar feelings, emphasizing that commerce was the greatest incentive for two countries willing to become allies, "and since steam considerably shortened distances," all peoples should connect.[115] Again, not one word about the protection of slavery. The *Jornal do Commercio* emphasized "the influence that the Empire [of Brazil] produces on the balance of trade of America."[116] Once again, the protection of slavery was absent.

Southerners' proslavery ideology and policies did not shield Brazilian slaveholders' interests or foster a sense of safety among the Brazilian elite, as some scholars contend.[117] The economic growth of the slave South and its aggressive expansionism never guaranteed a stable existence for the Brazilian planter class. On the contrary, at the height of their power, proslavery Southerners became a major threat to Brazilian sovereignty. Their actions bred great instability in the international system, making an already embattled country like Brazil all the more distressed. Not surprisingly, Brazilians like Alencar—himself a Conservative connected to slaveholding interests in the province of Rio de Janeiro—wanted to steer clear of the slave South.

The Brazilian refusal to embark on a proslavery crusade with Southern fire-eaters did not go unnoticed in the United States. "The Brazilian Government is very far from regarding Slavery as 'fixed,' or even as 'deeply rooted' in the soil," the *New York Daily Tribune* noted. In fact, Brazilians regarded slavery "as

an antiquated colonial institution . . . not suited to its more advanced condition." Meade had, therefore, "totally deceived himself in expecting to find in
Brazil any 'unity of action and feeling' in resisting outward pressure—or hostile
prejudice, as he calls it—against the institution of Slavery."[118] More emphatically, William Lloyd Garrison's *Liberator* reproached Meade for embarrassing
all Americans in front of the Brazilian people: "The very first time he makes his
appearance at court, . . . with an impertinence never equaled, he brings up the
subject of Slavery, and thinks thus to advance himself in the esteem of the powers that be." Meade had made a fool of himself as "the true state of the slavery
question is set forth in the following extracts from the new work entitled, '*Brazil
and the Brazilians*,' from which it will be seen that there are causes at work to
produce a termination of bondage in the empire." After attacking Meade, the
Liberator quoted extensive sections of Fletcher's work discussing the lack of
legal racial barriers and the free labor experiments in Brazil.[119]

Southern fire-eaters nonetheless insisted that Brazil would ultimately be on
their side. On June 25, 1858, the *Charleston Mercury* published Meade's address
to Dom Pedro II. In the very next section, it transcribed a letter from a Southern merchant living in Rio de Janeiro who dismissed Fletcher's view on Brazilian slavery: "You have read (especially in 'Brazil and the Brazilians,' by
Fletcher) about the prospect of the future emancipation of the slaves here.
There is just such a prospect as exists in Louisiana." Echoing De Bow, the correspondent concluded that "the quiet and order in Brazil is due to the presence
of that 'institution.'"[120]

In December 1860, informed of Abraham Lincoln's election, Meade made
a final attempt to reach out to the slaveholding interests of Brazil. Writing to
the secessionist leader Howell Cobb of Georgia, a political ally and personal
friend, Meade explained his efforts.

> I say truly when I tell the Brazilians, which I often do, that the *Institution* [of
> slavery] is the great conservative principle of their Government, and that
> emancipation would result in its overthrow, to be succeeded by the same
> unsettled state of things, which distinguishes the Spanish American Gov-
> ernments; that it was as essential to the growth of coffee as of cotton, and
> without it neither Brazil nor the South United States would be fit for a white
> man to live in.

The persistent Meade even tried to approach Dom Pedro II again. "I had a
short conversation with the Emperor on this subject, but when I said that
slavery was the normal and proper condition of the African," a discouraged

Meade recalled, "he dissented. I was much tempted to tell him that his throne rested upon the conservatism of the coffee planter, as our constitution and freedom did on the slave owners." Meade learned that Brazilians were indeed interested in the future of the Union, but not because of slavery per se. "The effect of our commotions is not yet much felt here," he remarked, "but is greatly dreaded. We consume more than one half of all the coffee that is made here, and a diminished demand in the United States would seriously affect their commerce."[121] Try as he might, Meade failed to make Brazilians forget about trade with the North and rally behind the rising Confederacy.[122]

As the fire-eaters were failing to attract Brazil to the cause of Southern secession, a group of people on the Northern side of the conflict continued to foster good relations with Brazil. Now famous for his *Brazil and the Brazilians*, Fletcher went on a tour lecturing at places such as the New York Historical Society and the Smithsonian Institute.[123] "On the subject of Slavery," the *New York Times* paraphrased one of Fletcher's lectures in November 1860, "the Brazilians have no questions, no fusion and no confusion. The putting down of the African Slave Trade in 1850, has virtually done away with Slavery in that country, and a few years hence it will have ended altogether."[124]

Northern interest in Brazil grew as the Civil War unfolded, and Fletcher's book had five editions before 1865. In February 1863, a few weeks after Lincoln signed the Emancipation Proclamation, the author spoke to the Boston Mercantile Library Association about Brazil. Fletcher told the audience that he "had yet to see the first man in Brazil who held to the doctrine of Divine right of Slavery. They all, without exception, admitted it to be an evil, and acknowledged it to be their duty to do all in their power to mitigate and eventually to exterminate the curse." Fletcher's exposition certainly made many Northerners involved in a protracted civil war wish that the Southern section of their country were more like Brazil. "Under the action of influences now at work in Brazil," he optimistically predicted, "it was generally believed that slavery would come to a final and peaceful end within twenty years."[125]

Meanwhile, Fletcher's portrayal of Brazil flattered Brazilian observers. Unlike the British, who used their warships to impose antislavery treaties on Brazil, Fletcher and his Northern supporters seemed willing to accept Brazil's own pace toward emancipation, no matter how slow. Once news of his Boston lecture arrived in Rio de Janeiro, the *Correio Mercantil* praised "the considerable services rendered to our country by one of the enthusiasts of our wealth and a sincere friend of our progress, Mr. Fletcher," who was then going to Europe, where he planned to continue lecturing on Brazil. Brazilians had much to gain by the promotion of Fletcher's views on their progressive character before European audiences.[126]

Fletcher's idealized narrative about the Brazilian slave society appeared at a time of heightened geopolitical tension. His Northern audience appropriated his ideas about "the most progressive people south of the Equator" in response to the hardening of proslavery attitudes in the slave South. Antislavery Northerners used *Brazil and the Brazilians* to demonstrate that Southern slaveholders were rebelling against the spirit of the age.[127] Not surprisingly, proslavery commentators rejected Fletcher's account, formulating their own approach to Brazil. But they were unsuccessful. Based on previous experiences with Southerners, Brazilians had many reasons to believe that they had much to lose by supporting the cause of Southern secession. The industrial products and patient antislavery of Fletcher and his Northern allies, on the other hand, pleased the Brazilian elite.

Fletcher did not act alone to reconcile Brazil and the Union at the onset of the American Civil War. He was a broker, a link between two very different societies interested in complementing—rather than fighting—each other. The missionary from Indiana along with his Boston and New York audiences had something quite appealing to offer Brazil. For Brazilians in the 1850s, commercial ties with a booming industrial society appealed much more than fighting for the eternal preservation and aggressive expansion of slavery. Moreover, Northerners were willing to take a very patient approach to the problem of slavery in Brazil, slowly treading the path toward free labor. Fletcher made it clear from the very beginning that this path would favor Brazilian planters, helping them profitably employ free workers. At all events, it was not much of a contest: Brazilians hesitated little to choose Fletcher over Meade, Trousdale, Maury, and Wise.

2

The Enemy of My Enemy

ON SEPTEMBER 28, 1865, a *New York Times* correspondent in Rio de Janeiro reported that "there is, in some respects, much competition here between the English and American interests in certain fields of enterprise. Perhaps I shall more truthfully state the case by saying much disposition is shown on the part of the lion to drive the eagle from this entire empire."[1] The writer might as well have said that the eagle fought back and did all it could to scare the lion away from Brazil. Brazilian observers were quite happy to watch this clash play out. At a time of acute geopolitical tension, the foreign policy of Great Britain, the mightiest empire of the nineteenth century, was responsible for consolidating a partnership between Brazil and the American Union.

During the American Civil War, supporters of the Union grew hostile to Great Britain. To begin with, British authorities nurtured plans to mediate peace negotiations that could consolidate Confederate independence. Adding insult to injury, elite Britons often stated that the Northerners were rough plebeians trying to oppress Southern aristocrats.[2] The Union also complained that the British sold warships to the Confederacy and offered their colonial ports for Confederate raiders to refit. Moreover, Northerners resented the way that British authorities dealt with a naval affair at the end of 1861, forcing the Union to release the two Confederate agents who had been removed from an intercepted British ship, the RMS *Trent*.[3] Further vexing the Union, other European empires, with the tacit approval of the British, were taking advantage of the crisis in the United States to exert their power in Latin America. By late 1861, Napoleon III ordered an incursion into Mexico and, by 1864, established a puppet Habsburg monarch there. Also in 1861, Spain attacked the Dominican Republic in an attempt to revive its colonial domination of Hispaniola and, in 1864, occupied the guano-rich Chincha Islands in the Pacific, which belonged to Peru.[4]

Within this turbulent context, a British intervention in South America seemed imminent, and Brazil appeared as the greatest prize for British imperialists. It was clear to all then that Great Britain was using the problem of slavery to intimidate Brazilian authorities. Following the Aberdeen Act of 1845, Brazil had terminated the African slave trade by the early 1850s. Still, British diplomats and politicians continued to bully. During the 1860s, they pressured Brazilian authorities about the so-called *emancipados*: Africans found aboard slave ships, liberated by a mixed Anglo-Brazilian naval court, and taken by Brazilian authorities for a fourteen-year period of apprenticeship and subsequent liberation. Most of the emancipados, however, were subjected to slave-like conditions in Brazil. By January 1863, tensions between the two countries escalated as British warships blockaded the port of Rio de Janeiro. As a result, Brazil and Great Britain severed diplomatic relations.[5]

Diplomatic troubles between Brazil and the Union also erupted during the American Civil War. The Army general and Republican editor James Watson Webb started his tenure as US minister to Brazil on the wrong foot, trying—and failing—to send liberated slaves from the American South to the Brazilian Amazon. Before long, Brazilian official neutrality in regard to Southern secession and the activities of Confederate raiders off the Brazilian seacoast enraged Webb. Yet distrust was put aside as anti-British sentiments ended up bringing Rio de Janeiro and Washington to conciliation. When Webb confronted a British diplomat who had been pestering Brazil about the emancipados, Brazilian public opinion hailed him as the bearer of the best practices of the Monroe Doctrine.

Contributing to the process of conciliation, as the conflict unfolded in the United States, Brazilian politicians began to invite Northern engineers and entrepreneurs to conduct infrastructural works in and around Rio de Janeiro. American investment in railroads, ferries, and streetcars presented a serious challenge to the dominance of British capital in Brazil. Concurrently, Northerners increased their coffee imports from Brazil as Union soldiers were gulping as much caffeine as they could to keep fighting the secessionists. Consolidating the partnership between the two countries, as the American Civil War was coming to an end, the Brazilian Liberal Party and the American Republican Party came together to subsidize the first direct steamship line connecting Brazil to the United States.

The American Civil War transformed the international status of the United States, as it gave Northerners an opportunity to simultaneously confront Southern secession and European imperialism. Scholars of foreign relations, countering the narrative of inexorable expansion formulated by the Wisconsin School,[6] now propose that the United States took a cautious approach to international matters in the Civil War era. They stress that, confronted by a much stronger empire, Americans found themselves treading on eggshells, now seeking to avoid conflict, now trying to collaborate with Great Britain.[7] But a very different story unfolded in the largest country of South America. As the geopolitical environment went from bad to worse, Northern diplomats and entrepreneurs presented the Union as a benign modernizing force in the hemisphere and actively challenged Great Britain. The relationship with Brazil took center stage for the Union then. By taking the side of the Brazilians in their imbroglio with the British and strengthening economic bonds with Brazil, antislavery Northerners recast the United States as a nation capable of exporting progress even in times of grave disruption. The fact that Brazil still preserved slavery made the American Republicans all the more interested in engaging with it. For their part, Brazilian Liberals had no qualms about associating with the Union. Instead of submitting to proslavery Southerners or British abolitionists, new leaders rose in Brazil as they joined American antislavery reformers in charting a path forward.

The Waters of Brazil

The son of an American Revolutionary hero from Connecticut, James Watson Webb spent his youth in the Army fighting frontier wars and eventually rose to the rank of general. By the late 1820s, he became a newspaper editor and established the *New York Courier and Enquirer*. Webb soon gained notoriety for spreading fears of racial amalgamation. In 1834, his writings contributed to inciting the bloody antiabolitionist riots in New York City. A Jacksonian Democrat during the 1830s, Webb moved to the Whig Party in the 1840s and eventually became a Republican. A close ally of William Henry Seward's, Webb became an ardent advocate of the new party and a harsh critic of Southern fire-eaters. When the Civil War erupted, Webb was convinced that President Abraham Lincoln would appoint him major general of the Union Army; instead, Webb had to content himself with an appointment as US minister to Brazil.[8]

Unhappy with his new position, Webb decided to use it to increase his fame and wealth, single-handedly devising a plan to colonize slaves freed during the American Civil War in Brazil. His project, presented to Secretary of State Seward in May 1862, called for the creation of a joint stock company to direct the enterprise. The American government would loan the company an amount to match the stockholders' investment. This money would be used to send freedpeople to the Brazilian Amazon, where they would become apprentices bound to the colonization company for three years. The Brazilian government would donate to the company one hundred acres of land for every colonist introduced and for every child born to the colonists. At the end of the apprenticeship period, the ex-slaves would be given a small farm, a hut, agricultural implements, and some money. From then on, they would become Brazilian citizens and completely cut formal ties with the company. No more than one-fifth of the acquired lands would be distributed to the black colonists. The remainder would be used or sold by Webb for profit.[9]

Drawing on the language of benevolent colonization promoted by the American Colonization Society since the early nineteenth century, Webb claimed to be an instrument of Divine Providence. "The finger of God, in my mind," he wrote to Seward, "points to the northern provinces of Brazil as the future home of the manumitted negro of the United States." All would benefit from his scheme, Webb believed. By welcoming millions of freedpeople from North America, Brazil would be acquiring "precisely the species of laborers and citizens best calculated to develop her resources and make her one of the great powers of the earth." By moving to the Brazilian Amazon, the American-born freedman would find a home where "the woolly-headed and thick-lipped descendant of Africa has his place side by side with his 'White brother.'" Last but not least, the United States would be "blessed by his *absence*, and the riddance of a curse which has well-nigh destroyed her."[10]

To guarantee the success of the enterprise, Webb explained, the Brazilian government would "cause such additional legislation as may be necessary, to insure a faithful discharge of their duties as 'apprentices.'"[11] In other words, Brazil would have to modify its laws in order to guarantee the orderly conduct of the company's indentured laborers. Not surprisingly, Webb's colonization scheme was stillborn. Seward's response was a much-needed lesson in diplomatic courtesy: a proposition to colonize Brazilian lands could never be devised "without having first some overture from the head of that empire." And he doubted that Dom Pedro II would be willing to welcome ex-slaves from North America as colonists. "We have no right to assume," Seward continued, "that the Emperor of Brazil would prefer an expelled caste from this country to other possible supplies of population for the improvement of the laboring classes of the empire."[12]

As Seward had predicted, Webb received a negative response from the Brazilian minister of foreign affairs, Miguel Calmon du Pin e Almeida, the

Marquis of Abrantes. "Nothing of that sort may possibly be tried in our country," he put it bluntly, "as we have a positive law that expressly interdicts the admittance of any freed negroes within our limits."[13] In case Webb had any difficulty understanding what was being said, Abrantes transcribed the Law of November 7, 1831. He was not only rejecting Webb's colonization scheme but also making clear that Brazil would not submit to the demands of American speculators. After all, not long ago, Matthew Fontaine Maury had tried to establish a foothold in the Brazilian Amazon, alarming Brazilian authorities about American encroachment. Without support for his colonization scheme, Webb would have to find other ways to make the best of his time in Brazil.

Following this first fiasco, Webb decided to focus all his energy on a pressing diplomatic issue emerging on the Brazilian seacoast. In September 1861, the Confederate ship *Sumter*, commanded by the famous sea captain from Alabama Raphael Semmes, had spent one week coaling at the port of São Luís, on the northern coast of Brazil. Responsible for capturing, plundering, and burning eighteen Northern commercial vessels, the CSS *Sumter* terrorized Union diplomats and naval commanders during the first months of war.[14]

Although Webb was quick to protest the incident in São Luís, Brazilian authorities, following the lead of Great Britain and France, declared their neutrality in regard to the American Civil War. "In the same position in which the so-called Confederate states find themselves today," the Brazilian minister of foreign affairs argued in a letter to Webb dated December 1861, "once were the United States, and after them Brazil and all the republics that had been colonized by Spain; in Europe, Greece and Belgium, and not long ago Hungary, Italy, and other countries."[15] Furious, Webb retorted that Semmes was a raider working for a desperate group of rebels whose goal was to "restore the infamous slave traffic with the Coast of Africa and establish a southern confederation based on the institution of slavery."[16] Webb knew well what the African slave trade meant to Brazilians concerned about protecting their sovereignty.

During the time he spent in Brazil, Semmes never hid the true meaning of Southern separatism. The historian Don H. Doyle notes that, when addressing European audiences, Confederate agents had to "tone down the hysterical rhetoric about abolitionism, play up the South's alienation over tariff policy, and place the South's desire for free trade with Europe front and center."[17] In slaveholding Brazil, on the other hand, Semmes had no qualms about expressing the proslavery foundations of the Confederacy. While in São Luís, he told the provincial president that "this war was in fact a war as much in behalf of

Brazil as of ourselves, and that if we were beaten in the contest, Brazil would be the next one to be assailed by Yankee propagandists."[18]

Yet despite Brazil's potential as a proslavery ally, Semmes could not overcome Southerners' prejudices against Brazilian society and ended up following in Matthew Fontaine Maury's and Henry A. Wise's footsteps. In Semmes's eyes, an insurmountable gap separated his people from his Brazilian hosts. He underscored that, in Brazil, the free black was "the equal of the white man, and as there seems to be no repugnance, on the part of the white race—so called— to mix with the black race, and with the Indian, amalgamation will go on in that country, until a mongrel set of curs will cover the whole land." Not invited to a grand ball in São Luís for the celebration of Brazil's Independence Day, Semmes considered that there was no reason for lamenting such exclusion. "The only feeling excited in us, by this official slight," he wrote in his memoir, "was one of contempt for the silliness of the proceeding—a contempt heightened by the reflection that we were a race of Anglo-Saxons, proud of our lineage, and proud of our strength, frowned upon by a set of half-breeds."[19]

Consistent with his sense of racial superiority, Semmes saw Brazil as a weak power that could be subjugated and manipulated. When, in April 1863, Semmes returned to Brazilian waters—this time commanding the faster and stronger CSS *Alabama*, which the Confederacy had purchased from Great Britain—he found out that Brazilian authorities had limited the stay of both belligerent parties in Brazilian ports. After a productive raiding journey around the archipelago of Fernando de Noronha, Semmes left for Salvador, the capital city of Bahia. There, he received an order from the provincial president to depart within twenty-four hours. That was a great opportunity, Semmes reckoned, to put Brazilians in their place: "I really wanted nothing—though I afterward took in a few boat-loads of coal, merely to show the president that I was disposed to be civil—and this consideration, along with the fact that I had the heaviest guns in the harbor, induced me to be rather careless, I am afraid, in the choice of phraseology, as I penned my dispatch."[20] After insulting Brazilian authorities in writing, Semmes refused to leave, remaining one more week in Salvador.

The Confederacy never sought to establish an alliance with slaveholding Brazil. From the height of his rank as the most powerful Confederate naval commander, Semmes perpetuated Wise's and Maury's hostile attitudes toward Brazil. His bravado alienated Brazilian diplomats and politicians, who, for a short while, had been willing to recognize the Confederate cause as one of self-determination. Brazilian observers understood that Semmes was just one of the many filibusters who had been plaguing Latin America for more than a decade. The interactions between Semmes and Brazilian authorities clearly indicate that, even when it desperately needed allies, the slave South failed to establish an effective foreign policy to defend its interests.[21]

Whereas the proslavery Semmes ruined any possibility of a Confederate-Brazilian alliance, the antislavery Webb almost created a war between the Union and Brazil. As two more Confederate raiding vessels, the CSS *Georgia* and the CSS *Florida*, started using ports in Bahia and Pernambuco to refit and sell their plunder, Webb emphatically protested, ranting that "the scenes which history informs us were rife in the 17th century, in the islands of the West Indies, are now being enacted in the 19th century, in the ports of Brazil." Captured American sailors and passengers, Webb continued, "have been compelled, in the ports of a friendly nation, to witness their clothing and jewelry, and even family relics, sold on the wharves and in the streets of Bahia and Pernambuco by their piratical captors, at a tenth of their value."[22] Following Webb's depiction of Brazilian ports as a safe haven for pirates, on October 14, 1864, the USS *Wachusett* entered the harbor of Salvador without the authorization of the Brazilian Navy and seized the CSS *Florida*. Under very suspicious circumstances, the seized Confederate vessel sank on its way to a Union port.

To the surprise of outside observers, however, the Brazilian minister of foreign affairs reported to his government that, immediately after the seizing of the *Florida*, Webb had come to him "not only to express to the imperial government all his regret for the deplorable event, but also to reassure us that the government of the Union, disapproving the proceeding of the commander of the *Wachusett*, would not hesitate to offer His Majesty the Emperor [Dom Pedro II] a proper reparation." Along with Webb's apology came a note from Seward containing a list of guarantees: first, the commander of the *Wachusett* would be suspended and court-martialed; second, the US consul in Salvador would be discharged; third, the Brazilian flag would receive the appropriate honors; fourth, the crew of the *Florida* would be freed; and, finally, were it not for an accidental shock with a warship that had sunk the *Florida* near Virginia, it would have been returned to the Brazilian port.[23]

Semmes was appalled. Reflecting on the incident, he raged that the *Wachusett* had "violated the neutrality of the port [of Salvador], by seizing her [the *Florida*], and carrying her off; and the Yankee nation, rather than make the amends which all the world decided it was bound to make, by delivering back the captured ship to Brazil, ordered her to be sunk by *accident* in Hampton Roads!"[24] What the Confederate raider did not know was that, at the moment that the *Florida* affair threatened to unsettle diplomatic relations between the Union and Brazil, the actions of a pesky British diplomat had brought both countries closer than ever before.

The Lion and the Eagle

In 1862, Webb and William Dougal Christie, the British minister to Brazil, got into what seemed to be a petty quarrel. In a letter to Seward, Webb gave his version of the incident. Christie had invited Webb, who lived in Petrópolis (the mountain summer retreat of the Brazilian elite), to spend a week at his house in Rio de Janeiro. Webb responded that he had to consult his wife. "What do you or I care," Christie rudely retorted, "for our wives objecting in such a case, intended to show the good feelings which exist between our countries." Although uneasy, Webb ended up accepting the invitation. But, during his stay, Christie became even more discourteous, sparing no opportunity to mistreat him in front of other diplomats. It did not take long for Webb to speak up and leave Christie's residence. Moreover, he wrote directly to Lord John Russell, the British foreign secretary, accusing Christie of intemperance. Infuriated, Christie cut ties with the US legation.[25]

As personal as such a quarrel seemed to be, Webb's justification to Seward proved that there was much more involved in the matter than a clash between two ill-mannered personalities. "If there had been no Rebellion at home," Webb explained, "no Trent affair, and no bad blood existing between England and the United States, there would not have occurred any quarrel between their representatives in this far distant quarter of the world."[26] Even Seward, who had a well-established reputation as an Anglophobe and never completely dismissed a war against the British, thought Webb had gone too far in his pro-Union bravado and reproached him. Webb did not apologize, however. He insisted that were it not for the American Civil War "there would have been no reverses before Richmond, no General McClellan to sneer at and abuse, and no Northern Army to be characterized as inferior in courage to the rebels, and wanting in the chivalry, which pertains to the gentle blood of the Cavaliers! And this from a base-born, vulgar, Scotchman."[27]

Webb's timing could not have been better. By early 1863, he had gained all the attention he had been seeking. The *New York Times* and other American newspapers published the story along with his letters to Christie and Russell.[28] Webb happily left aside his colonization scheme and the Confederate pirates to concentrate on the dispute. He bragged not only that he had defended the honor of his country against a vile pro-Confederate Briton but also that he had improved the image of the Union in Brazil. Writing to Seward, he claimed that it was a "well-known and openly conceded fact, here, in Brazil, that the Court, from the Emperor down, . . . justify my conduct, as not only expedient and necessary, but under the circumstances, absolutely unavoidable."[29]

There was, indeed, a great deal of truth in Webb's conceit. Before his altercation with Webb, Christie had managed to make many enemies in Brazil. Since his arrival in 1859, Christie had been pressing Brazilian authorities about the emancipados. In 1861, he wrote to the Brazilian minister of foreign affairs that he had been instructed to request "a list of the free blacks who were handed over by the [Anglo-Brazilian] Mixed Commission to the care of the Brazilian authorities, specifying what has become of them, whether dead, emancipated, or still in service."[30] Aware that Brazilian authorities, in spite of Brazil's treaties, had overlooked the reenslavement of Africans rescued from slave ships by the Royal Navy, Christie kept insisting on his request.[31]

Already persona non grata, Christie found two more excuses to attack Brazil. First, he accused Brazilian authorities of negligence in a case of plunder and alleged assassination of the crew of the *Prince of Wales,* a British merchant ship that wrecked off the coast of Rio Grande do Sul in June 1861. Ignoring all Brazilian efforts to solve the case, Christie made undiplomatic maneuvers, sending two British warships to the region and ordering a captain of the Royal Navy to intervene in the investigation. While the *Prince of Wales* case remained unresolved, in June 1862 three drunken British officers of the HMS *Forte* were beaten and imprisoned by Rio de Janeiro policemen. Although the three men were quickly released with no charges, Christie was outraged. Once again he made exaggerated demands, asking for official apologies from the Brazilian government, the punishment of the policemen, and the dismissal of the Rio de Janeiro police chief. All the while, Russell supported Christie's attitudes.[32]

As Brazilian authorities refused to meet Christie's demands, on December 31, 1862, he ordered British warships to blockade Rio de Janeiro, seizing all Brazilian vessels trying to leave or enter the harbor. A commotion ensued and an angry mob surrounded the British legation. On January 3, 1863, Brazilian authorities agreed to pay, under protest, for the plunder of the *Prince of Wales* and proposed to submit the *Forte* affair to arbitration by a third party. It took three more days for Christie to command the Royal Navy to release the seized Brazilian ships.[33]

Nevertheless, it was a pyrrhic victory for the British diplomat. In June 1863, Leopold I, King of the Belgians, who had been selected as arbiter in the *Forte* case, decided in favor of Brazil. Now Brazilian authorities accused Great Britain of breaking basic diplomatic rules by sending warships to Rio Grande do Sul and seizing ships in the Rio de Janeiro harbor in peacetime. When the British government refused to offer formal apologies and pay for damages, Brazil severed diplomatic relations with Great Britain.[34]

The Christie affair made Webb's colonization scheme and the seizing of the CSS *Florida* seem like minor mishaps. Brazilian newspapers hailed Webb as "a model diplomat," who, in his quarrel with Christie, "behaved as a true gentleman."[35] It did not take long for Brazilian observers to go beyond the immediate feud and imagine Webb as the bearer of broader hemispheric interests. "We recently learned that General Webb, the United States Minister," the *Diário de Pernambuco* reported, "in his relations with our government, has given proof of his great benevolence, giving up on all the petty questions that emerge between nations, with the objective to manifest to our government that Brazil has to connect itself to the United States in order to advance an American policy, thus putting an end to European pretensions of invasion and domination."[36]

In June 1863, Webb himself promoted these ideas by having one of his letters to the American steamship entrepreneur Thomas Rainey published in Brazilian newspapers. "The relations between the two governments are the most cordial," Webb started his friendly note, "and I hope that they will be as longlasting as the friends of constitutional systems and the promoters of an American policy, who demand that the Americas be governed by Americans, may desire." After blaming the British for fitting out the *Alabama* for Confederate pirates—and thus being the source of their crimes off the Brazilian coast— Webb concluded with a reference to the Christie affair: "These few egoistic men who think that the retaliations made by England against the commerce of Brazil were just, and approve the insult made against the sovereignty of the Empire, they certainly do not like to see the cordial relations that now exist between the two great nations of the American continent."[37]

Contributing to Webb's campaign, James Monroe, the US consul in Rio de Janeiro, wrote to Secretary of the Treasury Salmon P. Chase that, after succeeding his clumsy proslavery predecessor Richard Kidder Meade as minister to Brazil, Webb had "raised the American name from disgrace and reproach to respect and honor." Now, Monroe continued, "every American who walks the street in this city feels that he is treated by every Brazilian he meets, with more respect, on account of the spirited and patriotic course of his Ministry."[38] Even Americans living far away from Rio de Janeiro made sure that they sided with Webb. J. B. Bond, a merchant resident in Pará, told Webb that "I do not at all doubt you being a favorite with the Braz[ilian] Govt. You were so even before your row with Christie, and community of dislike has now no doubt increased the former Govt preference for you."[39]

Not coincidentally, when the USS *Wachusett* seized the CSS *Florida* in the harbor of Salvador, Brazilians and Americans were prepared to promptly reestablish friendly relations. In November 1864, the *Jornal do Commercio* noted that Webb's attitudes "make us hopeful that Lincoln will not treat Brazil with the brutality that Lord Russell did at the time of the retaliations against us." The violation that the commander of the *Wachusett* had perpetrated against Brazilian sovereignty would "sooner or later be redressed by a satisfactory explanation, which will be given as if this incident had taken place on the waters of the most powerful maritime nation in the world." The *Jornal do Commercio* concluded that Webb's "way of addressing our government is in blatant contrast with that offered us by Mr. Christie, of *inglorious* memory."[40]

In January 1866, an auspicious coincidence took place off the coast of Santa Catarina, in southern Brazil. The USS *Wachusett* now found itself without fuel and in distress. Brazilian authorities not only supplied the needed coal but also declined to accept payment for it. William Van Vleck Lidgerwood, a New Jersey businessman who served as chargé d'affaires at the US legation while Webb was on leave, expressed his gratitude to the Brazilian minister of foreign affairs, declaring that the American people would take "this additional courteous act of the Brazilian Government as renewed evidence of the feelings of friendship and good understanding which should exist between the leading powers of America." A new hemispheric policy, Lidgerwood believed, was emerging: "We shall hereafter be not only close friends but practically we shall become firm and fast allies."[41] Writing to Seward in April 1866, Lidgerwood reported that "the Brazilian people generally believe that the *Florida* Affair is settled, and in an entirely satisfactory manner to this Government, voluntarily so upon the part of the United States, and therefore the frequent comparison made by the Brazilians of the justice of the United States Government, as shown in the *Florida* Affair, and the injustice of the British Government evidenced in the Christie Affair."[42]

To be sure, Lidgerwood could have been exaggerating when he told Seward that Americans were now regarded by the Brazilian people "as just as we are known to be powerful, and hence the frequently expressed desire for an alliance, offensive and defensive between the United States and Brazil, by Brazilian citizens, which is never desired with any other nation."[43] Webb was certainly going through one of his delusions of heroism when he communicated to

Seward that the Christie affair, "which has so widely separated this [the Brazilian] government and people from England, and drawn them so much closer than ever before to the United States, was the consequence of his private quarrel with me, resulting in his complete overthrow and disgrace."[44] Exaggerations and delusions aside, at a time when so many tensions erupted all over the Atlantic, Webb's feud with Christie certainly contributed to improving relations between the Union and Brazil.

For Brazilian and American observers, the Christie affair became one more example of European imperial opportunism. Old World powers were taking advantage of the Civil War in North America and the weaknesses of Latin American states to intervene in the western hemisphere. The French had invaded Mexico, the Spanish had attacked the Dominican Republic and Peru, and now the British threatened war with Brazil. All the while, British agents seemed very interested in supporting the Confederate bid for independence against the American Union. Not surprisingly, Americans residing in Brazil took a hostile stand against the British. All things considered, Webb's failed project to colonize the Amazon with ex-slaves and the quickly resolved *Florida* affair had been minor bumps on the road to rapprochement.

Recent studies of American foreign relations in the Civil War era portray the United States as a hesitant player in the geopolitical game of the western hemisphere, taking a conciliatory approach to the British Empire and often failing to make inroads into Latin America.[45] This was certainly not the case of American relations with Brazil. The Christie affair gave Northerners a precious opportunity to present themselves as a benign alternative to British imperialists, and Webb grasped it. And his attitudes were not isolated. As Webb was confronting Christie, Northern entrepreneurs were acting to solidify the image of the Union as a modernizing influence in slaveholding Brazil.

Dom Pedro Segundo Railroad

In the mid-1850s, Brazilian politicians devised plans for the expansion of their country's transportation infrastructure, starting from Rio de Janeiro and its surrounding areas. The British played an important role in this process. According to the historian William R. Summerhill, "In the southern hemisphere Brazil was the single largest Latin American recipient of British capital through the 1880s."[46] By the late 1850s, however, Brazilian authorities began to rely on American capital to ease their dependence on British investors. A country that continued to develop its infrastructure while facing a secession crisis, members of the Brazilian Liberal Party reckoned, certainly could challenge the British and help Brazil move forward.

In 1855, private investors and the Brazilian government formed a joint stock company to build the Dom Pedro Segundo Railroad, connecting the port of Rio de Janeiro to the coffee-producing region of the Paraíba Valley. The company acquired a loan amounting to 1.5 million pounds sterling from Great Britain. Along with the loan came the British contractor Edward Price and the British chief engineer Christopher B. Lane. They took charge of building the first section of the railroad, connecting the harbor to the foot of the Serra do Mar, the mountain range extending into the interior. Soon, the chairman Cristiano Benedito Ottoni—a member of a well-known Liberal clan from Minas Gerais—demonstrated his dissatisfaction with the services of the British railroaders. In addition to delays and waste, according to Ottoni, "it became clear that Lane was working with his countryman Price to deceive us. It seems that their plan was to take control of the railroad, one as engineer, the other as manager, eliminating the [Brazilian] Board."[47]

When the Brazilian government announced the plan for the second section of the railroad, Ottoni established certain conditions in order to curb foreign contractors. First, the board would take charge of determining routes, deadlines, and budgets; second, the contractors would be fined for any delays; and third, the company would "contract preferably American engineers, experts in building great lines through sharp slopes such as the Alleghenies."[48] Ottoni then hired Charles F. M. Garnett of Virginia as chief engineer and Andrew Ellison of Massachusetts as Garnett's assistant. Both men had worked together on the Virginia and Tennessee Railroad. Under Ottoni's supervision they projected the section of the Dom Pedro Segundo Railroad that would climb the Serra do Mar. During construction, Ellison replaced Garnett as chief engineer.

Price, still working on the first section, was upset with the arrangement. He wrote to the Brazilian government that "the work that Mr. Ottoni wants to execute will cost two million pounds sterling; . . . it is possible to cross the sierra spending one and a half million; I am ready to undertake this work if you fire the American engineers, with whom I cannot get along."[49] Yet, to Price's chagrin, Ottoni not only kept the American engineers' project but also hired an American contractor to build the second section. By following through with his decision to hand railroad construction to American engineers, Ottoni took a decisive step to reshape material improvements in nineteenth-century Brazil. This move had the support of an ascending group of Liberals who were seeking to tighten the bonds of friendship with the Northern United States.

In January 1858, William Milnor Roberts arrived in Brazil carrying some impressive letters of introduction. "I have known Mr. Roberts professionally," the chief engineer of the Pacific Railroad wrote, "during twenty nine years during the whole of which time he has been actively employed upon the public works of Pennsylvania, Ohio, and Missouri. During this time he has been chief engineer of several important canals, slack water navigation, and railroads, whose successful completion bears testimony to his ability and skill."[50] Born in 1810 into a Philadelphia Quaker family, Roberts started working at the Union and Lehigh Canal at age fifteen. He quickly rose to chief engineer of major railroad and canal projects in the Northeast and the Midwest. During the 1850s, he became the contractor for the St. Louis and Iron Mountain Railroad and the Keokuk, Des Moines and Minnesota Railroad.[51] The second section of the Dom Pedro Segundo Railroad, which would climb twenty-five steep kilometers, was a challenging enterprise, and Roberts seemed like the right man for the job.

When he arrived in Brazil, Roberts joined other Northern entrepreneurs to form Roberts, Harvey & Co. Being the most experienced partner, he assumed the presidency of the firm and became the main supervisor of the works.[52] In a letter to American newspapers, the contractors measured their task up to that of the British: "You are aware that the first section of this important national work was commenced by an English party, Mr. Edward Price. His contract covered only the first thirty-eight miles—all light work, over a flat country." The second section, they boasted, "or *Mountain* division, is totally different from the first. It runs along the sides of the mountains, and encounters very heavy work—deep cutting through rock, heavy embankments and walls, and twelve tunnels in as many miles."[53] It became clear very soon that the enterprise was more than a private matter for Americans residing in Brazil. "The Brazilian Government has always shown a very great willingness to encourage American enterprise," the *New York Times* reported in June 1860, "although it still holds to the old idea of European superiority. This railway will, however, prove that science in the New World is not less advanced than in the Old."[54] Failure in climbing the Serra do Mar, one of Roberts's subcontractors wrote to the *New York Herald*, would represent a bitter defeat for the United States: "It will be a thing to lament should the American company fail to finish the entire second section. The English would gloat over it."[55]

The success of Roberts, Harvey & Co. would not only provide American entrepreneurs the opportunity to prove themselves superior to the British but also dissipate Brazilian fears of the United States. Having Wise, Maury, and Semmes in mind, the *New York Times* correspondent reminded the American public that not long ago, in Brazil, "the fear of American enterprise, of American trade, of American shipping, as opening wedges to American filibusterism, pervaded all ranks, and effectually excluded our citizens, as well as our diplomatic representatives, from the confidence of the Government." Now, thanks to entrepreneurs like Roberts, things were changing: "The completion of the contract for the extension of the Dom Pedro II Railroad gives a new hold to your countrymen upon the internal improvement system of Brazil. In fact the prejudice against the Yankees is rapidly vanishing."[56] The building of the second section would help entrepreneurial Northerners to distance themselves from the aggressive foreign policy of proslavery advocates.

General optimism notwithstanding, the extreme incline, hard rocks, heavy rains, and tropical vegetation of the Serra do Mar made the construction a herculean effort. Even with all his experience, Roberts considered that "the work on the Dom Pedro Segundo Railroad was much heavier than any I had ever met with on any improvement in the United States."[57] At the end of the day, however, the difficulties heightened Roberts's sense of accomplishment. In a long report written sometime in 1864 and addressed to the author of *Brazil and the Brazilians*, James Cooley Fletcher, Roberts remarked that "future contractors in Brazil may take advantage of the knowledge derived from the great experience of the builders of the Mountain Section of the Dom Pedro 2° Railroad; and why not future engineers too; and future Railroad Companies?"[58]

In addition to expertise for future enterprises, Roberts created some good business opportunities for his countrymen. Following his advice, Ottoni ordered "several locomotives from the United States, which are now being manufactured at the extensive works of Baldwin & Co. of Philadelphia, which have had much experience in constructing and adapting locomotives to heavy grades and hard curves."[59] Like American contractors working in Brazil, Baldwin had to innovate to meet Brazilian needs. Writing in 1897, a historian of the company recalled that "steel tires were first used in the [Baldwin] works in 1862, on some engines for the Dom Pedro II Railway of South America.... No tires of this material were then made in this country [the United States]."[60]

During the 1870s and 1880s, Baldwin continued to produce locomotives adapted to its Brazilian customers' demands. And other American companies followed suit. In 1876, the *Railroad Gazette* reported on a new railroad project in Brazil.

Estrada de Ferro de Sao Paulo e Rio de Janeiro.—This road is of 39 ⅔ in. gauge, is built by an American contractor. It will run from Sao Paulo, northwest, connecting with the Dom Pedro II Railroad, and will be completed within a few months. The rolling stock, bridges, etc., are American, as follows: Baldwin locomotives, Jackson & Sharp Company's cars, Sellers' machinery, Keystone (it is believed) bridges. When this road is completed passengers can go from Rio de Janeiro to Sao Paulo and Santos by rail, thus avoiding the sea voyage of 20 to 30 hours.[61]

By the mid-1880s, according to the *Railway World*, "the largest and most powerful locomotives" ever built in the United States were the Decapods: "12-wheeled locomotives, built at Baldwin works, one of which was for the Dom Pedro II Railroad of Brazil."[62] In 1887, the American geologist John Casper Branner observed that Brazilian customers were so satisfied that "almost all the locomotives used to-day upon the railways of Brazil . . . go from the shops of the Baldwin Locomotive Works in Philadelphia." Baldwin's business with Brazil had increased to such an extent that the company kept one of its engineers residing in Rio de Janeiro for the purpose of setting up and maintaining the engines. "The American locomotives have therefore grown so in favor," Branner concluded, "that the English manufacturers have been forced, in order to retain any share of their trade in Brazil, to construct their locomotives upon the plan of the Baldwin engines."[63] Eventually, the Baldwin locomotives became so ubiquitous that "Balduína" became synonymous with locomotive in Brazil.[64]

When he set out to work on the Dom Pedro Segundo Railroad, however, Roberts believed that he was doing much more than creating a market for American technologies. He acted as an antislavery reformer, taking a critical stand in regard to the order that unfree labor engendered in Brazil. Observing the plantations close to the Serra do Mar, he lamented that the Brazilian economy still remained in a primitive condition. No farming community existed in Brazil, he claimed. "What land is cultivated in the country (only about 150th part) is chiefly in the hands of large holders—chiefly coffee and sugar planters. Each planter is an *institution* by himself." The planter and his dependents—"wife, children, and slaves, among whom he is the Patriarch"— seemed to have little to do with outsiders so far as their agricultural practices and interests were concerned. Roberts also noticed that very few agricultural associations and regional fairs existed in Brazil. "Each Patriarch digs in, from year to year," he continued, "usually increasing in wealth and consequence;

but still not conducing by any joint action with others to the general improvement of agriculture or the general settlement of the country."[65]

Ultimately, Roberts hoped, Brazilian agriculture would be the great beneficiary of his work. He thought of slavery, first and foremost, as an economic problem, which had until the Civil War made the American South a backwater and still made Brazilian agriculture fall short of its full potential. Slavery bred backwardness, he argued, because it prevented knowledge and wealth from spreading to all classes. The railroad would open the plantations to the outside world and open the minds of the backward planters, he believed, leading Brazil to a gradual process of emancipation.[66] Through entrepreneurs like Roberts, Northern antislavery became synonymous with economic development.

However much he condemned the permanence of slavery in Brazil, Roberts did not see the Brazilians as an ignorant people. On the contrary, like his friend Fletcher, he was pleased to see that they were willing to move forward. Besides the good climate, well-organized government, and healthy population existing in Brazil, he wrote in 1862, "the Brazilian mind is quick in apprehending and appropriating; in contriving and arranging; and the spirit of enterprise having taken root, it is fair to infer that it will soon grow to be a tree which shall bring good fruit abundantly." The railroad, Roberts added, would help the Brazilians develop the countryside: "The vast interior of Brazil is yet a wilderness; so, fifty years ago, was nearly all the country west of the Ohio River in the United States." After explaining how the railroad had opened up the American Midwest to be settled by free immigrant farmers, Roberts imagined that Brazil could follow the same path. "The construction of the railroads through the interior," he maintained, "is almost the only means of originating and sustaining such a stream of foreign population."[67]

Roberts espoused the Northern belief that the expansion of transportation infrastructure and the universalization of free labor formed the only sustainable model of development for vast national territories.[68] "All of Brazil can never be held by planters merely," he asserted. Confident in his vision of the future, he added that "there must come a day when there will be a population of *Farmers*; men who will own a comparatively small extent of land; who, with their sons and their daughters and their free man servants and maid servants, will earn their bread by the sweat of their brow; and who will constitute the Yeomanry of Brazil." Roberts felt that he had done his part by climbing the mountains with the railroad and hoped that Brazilian elites would do theirs: "It is in the power of the statesmen at the head of affairs acting in harmony

FIGURE 2.1 "Dom Pedro II Railroad. Upper Portal to Tunnel n. 2 on 2nd Section." Carlos Linde, *Brasil: Estrada de Ferro de D. Pedro II* (Rio de Janeiro: Typ. do Imperial Instituto Artistico, ca. 1867). Courtesy of the Fundação Biblioteca Nacional, Rio de Janeiro.

with the Emperor to retard or to advance the settlement of the interior by the external and internal policy they may pursue."[69]

A rising group of Brazilian politicians welcomed Roberts's modernizing vision. In June 1862, members of the Brazilian Liberal Party gathered for the inauguration of a tunnel along the second section. Martinho Álvares da Silva

Campos, a political ally and business partner of the Ottoni family, proposed a toast "to the United States, to the entrepreneurial genius of the Americans, to the services they offer around the world to the cause of progress and civilization." The older Ottoni brother, Teófilo, raised his glass "to American labor, of which we have just seen beautiful examples. May they conclude soon this gigantic enterprise and conclude it with glory for all the national and foreign entrepreneurs."[70]

For decades, Roberts's work stood out as an extraordinary feat in Brazil. By 1880, the board of the Dom Pedro Segundo Railroad praised him for "the wonderful design of the Serra do Mar," observing that it constituted "a great pride to our country: indeed, the mountain covered with virgin forest, the steep slopes, the extremely deep transversal valleys, the difficult progress, and the height difference of 427 meters . . . were major difficulties that tested the entrepreneurial genius of industrial innovators."[71] As late as 1887, one of Roberts's compatriots who lived in Rio de Janeiro noted in a travel guide that "a journey over the *serra* section of the D. Pedro II railway will give the traveler a chance to see the best specimen of railway engineering in Brazil, and one of the best in the world."[72]

In 1865, Roberts left Brazil for the United States to engage in ambitious enterprises such as the Atlantic and Great Western Railroad, the improvement of the Ohio River, and the Northern Pacific Railroad. By successfully climbing the Serra do Mar, he had left a door wide open for other American entrepreneurs willing to work in Brazil. Furthermore, he had opened an opportunity for antislavery reform to enter Brazil via material improvement. During the remainder of the 1860s into the 1870s and 1880s, other skilled Northerners would emulate Roberts's example. They would confidently challenge British capital and work on advancing the cause of free labor in Brazil. Hailed as a great modernizer by the Brazilian elite and American residents in Brazil, Roberts would return to the country in the 1880s to redesign seaports and enhance river navigation.[73]

Companhia Ferry

A few months after Roberts left, a *New York Times* correspondent noted that the completion of the second section of the Dom Pedro Segundo Railroad represented the opening of a new era for American enterprise in Brazil.

> The first and level portion of the road is of English build, with English cars and English locomotives. The second and mountain section is of American

construction, of American material, and has heavy American engines, with eight drivers, built by M. W. Baldwin & Co., of Philadelphia. This portion of the road runs through a wild mountain region of Brazilian forest to the valley of the Parahyba, where is opened up, perhaps, the finest and largest coffee growing district of the whole empire, if not the world. . . . The Don Pedro Secundus [sic] Railway stands a witness and a monument to superior American engineering ability.

The competition between British and American entrepreneurs extended beyond railroads. "The ferry running across the bay to Praia Grande and Saint Domingo," the correspondent continued, "is of American origin and under American control. The very boats now running here have ploughed a thousand times the waters of New York bay, between South Ferry and Staten Island." Unhappy with this additional sign of the growing American influence in Brazil, "an English company was about reviving a line in opposition to this, . . . but failed in the attempt."[74]

The Companhia Ferry was a creation of Thomas Rainey, James Cooley Fletcher's and James Watson Webb's ally who had tried to establish a steamship line between New York and Pará. In 1858, Rainey obtained a twenty-year concession to run ferryboats across the Guanabara Bay, connecting the center of Rio de Janeiro to the growing suburbs of Praia Grande and São Domingos, in the township of Niterói. In September 1860, Rainey was in New York City for the launch of the ferryboat *Primeira*, built by the Novelty Iron Works.[75]

After watching the ferry glide across the East River, the Brazilian minister to the United States declared that he regarded the event "as a beginning to drawing still closer the bonds of friendship and commerce" between the two countries. He was "glad that the United States had at last entered the list in competition with other countries in this important branch of business and industry." Rainey and other New York businessmen warmly applauded such words. They understood well what the Brazilian diplomat meant by "competition with other countries." As the *New York Times* put it, "The British have built all of the steamers hitherto for the Brazilian government, companies and individuals, and consider themselves to have the rights exclusive and almost patent to this business for the future. Dr. Rainey has by this large contract broken their prestige and opened a place for the beautiful works of our own country."[76]

Back in Rio de Janeiro in 1861, Rainey wrote to New York newspapers that "my works create a great enthusiasm here, and the ferry depot in the city will be altogether the handsomest structure in Brazil."[77] On June 29, 1862, a large

FIGURE 2.2 Companhia Ferry Pier, Pharoux Street, Rio de Janeiro, ca. 1865.
Courtesy of the Fundação Biblioteca Nacional, Rio de Janeiro.

crowd, which included the royal couple, gathered to watch the inauguration of the line of ferries. Not everything went as planned, however. Because of the intense traffic in the Guanabara Bay, the *Primeira* hit a barge and two sailboats, forcing the boatmen to throw themselves overboard. As the commander of the ferryboat tried to avert other collisions, the *Primeira* ended up stranded on a nearby shoal.[78] These incidents prefigured some other troubles to come.

A few months after inauguration, local newspapers were denouncing the filthiness, delays, explosions, and crashes (some of which were fatal) to which Rainey's ferries subjected the inhabitants of Rio de Janeiro and Niterói. Some of the writers urged that Rainey should be criminally charged for the accidents and that the Brazilian government should intervene in the company. *A Vida Fluminense*, published in Niterói, organized a relentless campaign against Rainey in 1868, attacking him for indulging in "mortifying the miserable users of his barges, keeping them filthy, with broken or crooked seats, poorly lit and having the boilers in a *yankeely* frightening state of safety."[79] After several trips were canceled without prior notice, *A Vida Fluminense* editorialized that "*El Mariscal Rainey* continues to treat us as a conquered people!"[80]

Rainey was shrewd enough to blame British interests for the campaign against his company. In February 1868, he published a story in the *Jornal do Commercio* about a passenger who had accused him out loud in the ferry of being "always drunk, from the morning to the night." The offender was a well-known British resident of Niterói. A few days after the incident, Rainey approached his critic on the street and spoke out in defense of his honor: "You have abused and slandered me very much during the last two or three years, I am tired of this and want to make it clear to you that, if you do not stop these abuses, I will take a whip and will apply it to your back."[81]

Rainey claimed that the Britisher was a rude customer who often used the entrance reserved for barefoot passengers (i.e., slaves) and had once encouraged some scoundrels to break the windows of the ferry house. And there was more: "He is the one who two or three years ago suggested to my brother that we should steal from the Brazilians by all means possible, because they are, he claimed, all miserable thieves who live off the foreigners." The British customer went so far as stating that Brazilian authorities were corrupt and "the Emperor was an idiot, only capable of attending mass and producing state chicanery." Worse, "during and after the Christie affair," he had proposed "to catch a dozen Brazilians and send them to London so that Lord Palmerston could throw them into a cage and exhibit them as monkeys."[82] Real or imagined, Rainey's foe was the kind of pesky Briton whom Brazilians—and Americans living in Brazil—loved to hate. The reference to the Christie affair, the treatment of Brazilians as thieves and monkeys, and the disrespect for Brazilian authority made this character a perfect representative of the haughty Englishmen whose supremacy the American entrepreneurs and diplomats had been challenging in Rio de Janeiro.

Rainey knew very well what side to take in Brazil of the 1860s, doing everything he could think of to convince Brazilian public opinion that he was a faithful servant of the country. He often went to the imperial palace to pay homage to Dom Pedro II, made his ferries salute the Count of Eu (the French prince married to the Brazilian princess) when he returned from his post as general commander of the Brazilian forces in Paraguay, gave money to various charities, sponsored artistic events, organized regattas, guided Brazilian visitors through American gunboats stationed in the Rio de Janeiro harbor, offered free fare to students of the Normal School of Rio de Janeiro, and—true to his antislavery origins—even organized a maritime tour to raise funds for the Niterói Abolitionist Society.[83] In January 1869, an amused Brazilian passerby witnessed Rainey ripping out a poster of a humoristic publication titled *Carambolas* that had been glued to the wall of his ferry house: "It was hilarious to see Mr. Rainey in his *Yankee* rage resembling a Don Quixote who throws himself, raising his fists, against a serene windmill. . . . He furiously cried, vociferating [in ungrammatical Portuguese]: '*Goddam*! Me not want *Carambolas* in this pier; this book be *republican*, against government, *goddam*!'"[84]

Despite Rainey's investment in public relations, in 1868 the Brazilian government granted to Carlos Fleiuss, the son of a rich German merchant family, the right to establish a line of ferries to compete with the Companhia Ferry. The simple announcement of Fleiuss's enterprise, according to *A Vida Fluminense*, forced Rainey to improve his services. One could now see how he "grabs a mop, washes the barges, piers, stations, and even the faces of his employees, sweeps and dusts everything, glazes the windows that for long have been naked, rebuilds one of his small barges, fixes the old pier of S. Domingos, tears his lips in an angelical smile, and promises to all champagne at all times and a ready reduction of fare prices. A toast to competition!"[85]

The improvements made the Companhia Ferry thrive. In 1874, Rainey sold his valuable stocks and left Rio de Janeiro a wealthy man.[86] Established in the Long Island City neighborhood of Ravenswood, he started working on a bridge connecting Manhattan to Queens.[87] Although not as polished as Roberts, Rainey had successfully played the role of the American entrepreneur who could bring all sorts of improvements to Brazil. By establishing the Companhia Ferry in the early 1860s and advancing urban transportation in Rio de Janeiro for over a decade thereafter, Rainey strengthened the modernizing mission that the American North had been devising as it crushed the rebellion of slaveholders at home and confronted the British Empire abroad.

Botanical Garden Rail Road Co.

Like Rainey's ferries, American streetcars would connect the capital city of Brazil to its growing suburbs. In 1858, the Brazilian government offered a concession for the establishment of a line of mule-drawn streetcars connecting the central part of Rio de Janeiro to the neighborhoods of Botafogo and Laranjeiras. The Brazilian entrepreneurs who acquired the concession, however, failed to establish the service, and put it up for sale a few years later. The former manager of the Bleecker Street Horsecar Company of New York, Charles B.

Greenough, heard of the opportunity and consulted with James Cooley Fletcher about the prospects of investing in Brazil. As expected, Fletcher provided much valuable information. After acquiring a loan from the New York railroader Erastus Corning, Greenough traveled to Rio de Janeiro and bought the concession. Because Brazilian investors did not want to gamble on streetcars, Greenough raised some more capital in the United States and formed the Botanical Garden Rail Road Co. in 1867.[88]

On October 9, 1868, Greenough's streetcars started operating. During the inaugural ceremony, a Brazilian politician proposed a toast "to the free and fruitful labor that radiates from the United States to all the peoples of the universe." Someone else raised his glass "to the American people, who occupies the first place at the vanguard of civilization." Yet another Brazilian enthusiast of the United States spoke of "the fraternity of American peoples, condition of greatness for the present and for the future." Present at the ceremony, Dom Pedro II was impressed with the elegant streetcar imported from New York, which glided smoothly over the one mile of tracks that Greenough had managed to lay by then.[89]

A few days after inauguration, the humor magazine *Semana Illustrada* reminded its readers that the new streetcars had not yet been baptized. "It is a matter of giving a popular name to the new cars of Botafogo. Some think they should be called *yankees*, others say *bonds*. Which one will catch on?"[90] Bonds—or *bondes*—it would be. The origin of this name was not clear even to contemporaries. An American diplomat learned during the 1880s that "the money for the undertaking was raised by the sale of the company's bonds, and from that fact the streetcars in Rio are universally called 'bondes.'"[91] A British visitor heard at roughly the same time that "the name arose from the simultaneous issue of the bonds of a national loan and the tickets of this company, which later were used as currency for small payments."[92] Whether people knew how they got their name or not, Greenough's bondes were a success. "If the [Brazilian] treasury bonds have limits," the *Semana Illustrada* observed in 1869, "those of the Americans do not."[93] By 1870, the Botanical Garden Rail Road Co. had about eight miles of tracks and a dozen cars, which transported three million passengers a year. By 1875, it had over thirteen miles of tracks and more than seventy cars, which transported about six million passengers annually.[94]

One week after the Botanical Garden Rail Road Co. initiated service, "An Old Englishman" wrote to the *Jornal do Commercio* that riding the streetcar "has been the most interesting event that has ever taken place in my life." The tumultuous crowd waiting at the stop reminded the chronicler of the French

Revolution. Once on board, he felt as if in a sardine can. Soon after the streetcar started moving, it derailed. Once fixed, it continued. A few feet ahead, it derailed again. And again. And again. A fellow passenger asked the Englishman: "Will we regress?" The answer was pure sarcasm: "No sir, don't you know that these cars only move toward progress? How do you expect them to regress!?" All the while, the passengers complained about the hard wooden benches, the derailing, and the slow pace, leading the scornful British observer to remark that Greenough's "company will be as beneficial as that of Mr. Rainey."[95]

British envy aside, the experience of riding the streetcars—of waiting and sharing a ride with anonymous people, of getting to places much faster than on the old carriages and omnibuses, of adapting to impersonal rules—gave rise to the sentiment that Rio de Janeiro was finally becoming a modern metropolis. As a character who represented the common people of the city on the pages of the *Semana Illustrada* observed, "Young men, old men, men, women, children, blacks, whites, filthy, clean, necktied, un-necktied; ultimately, every odd-looking animal that walks around on two legs has had the pleasure to enter, for 200 réis or a piece of yellow paper, the terrestrial ships that the Americans call some strange names but the boys, my little friends, call simply *bonds*."[96] Greenough's bondes were now integral part of daily life in Rio de Janeiro.[97]

While his streetcars filled with people of all classes, Greenough himself became the embodiment of how Yankee efficiency (and greed) could overpower British aristocrats. Famous for his grouchiness and tight management, Greenough was precious material for the *Semana Illustrada*: "The man acts like a sergeant in his stables at Machado Square. He gesticulates, screeches, my goodness! He looks like a madman, or a prophet of times long gone." For all his hard work, the *Semana Illustrada* continued, Greenough deserved "the gratitude of those who wait under the sun and the rain, are then pressed in to be pampered with kicks, scrubs, unrequired rubs, and sometimes even theft by highly skilled acrobats. Viva Mr. Green O, cream of the crop of altruism, jewel of the philanthropists, perfection of abnegation!"[98] While humorists had fun with the mixed feelings that Greenough's success raised in Rio de Janeiro, the Botanical Garden Rail Road Co. continued to grow. More people moved to the suburbs, and Greenough got richer.[99]

In 1877, another humor magazine, the *Revista Illustrada*, told Greenough's story, this time through cartoons. The illustrated narrative began with a Brazilian businessman acquiring a concession for streetcars in the late 1850s but deciding to put it away. Greenough then arrived and bought the concession.

Há mais de 20 annos, tinha-se concedido privilegio para bonde a um respeitavel brazileiro, o qual re-
ceiando que lhe desse a tropa, tratou de o passar ao Sr barão
de Mauá ... hoje visconde.

Sua Ex.ª preoccupado com os seus
negocios bancarios, e tendo já levado
essipiga com a Mazambomba, julgou
prudente guardal'o de quarentena.

Um bello dia, apresentou-se ao
Sr de Mauá, um Norte-Americano, o
Sr Greenough, que lhe propoz a compra
do privilegio mediante 80 contos.

Feita a transa
tratou logo de formar
Côrte, e passar acções
com enthusiasmo.

Effectivamente, com a renda do transito,
entre a cidade e o largo do Machado, construiu-se
toda a linha até o Jardim Botanico, tendo os pou-
cos accionistas apenas feito uma entrada de 22 ½ %

Debalde as antigas diligencias procurarão
lutar; em pouco tempo ficarão esmagadas
pela poderosa adversaria.

A empreza Botanical Garden continuou cada
vez mais prospera, operando uma revolução entre os
nossos costumes, centuplicando o movimento de passa-
geiros, enchendo as ruas de familias que viviam ente-
rradas em suas casas e beneficiando assim o Comm...

Apezar do Governo ter exigido onus taes que bas-
tava unicamente os que 'eram applicados á Camara Municipal e a Instrucção publica para rebentar
qualquer Companhia

Cada provincia teve bonds.
Houveram propostas até para bonds
na cidade de Meia pataca e Madre
de Deus do Angú

Estabeleceu-se grande jogo de acções. Os m...
desfizeram-se dellas deixando-as nas mãos dos ...
ficaram, como no jogo do burro, bastante en...

FIGURE 2.3 "Questão de Bonds," *Revista Illustrada*, November 24, 1877. Courtesy of the
Fundação Biblioteca Nacional, Rio de Janeiro.

uninda então meia duzia de amigos, que não receiavam
ar o seu dinheiro, deu logo commeço aos trabalhos
via ferrea. Os nossos capitalistas riam-se e diziam:
ha de ser o nosso dinheiro que se ha de enterrar alli!

A actividade e energia do Americano, obtiveram
um esplendido triumpho. Os bonds commeçaram a
funccionar e o publico ficou embatucado diante tão
bello resultado.

Queremos acções! Queremos
acções, gritaram então os capitalistas.! Agora é tarde e alem
disso não preciso mais de dinheiro

terrenos se venderam e arremataram,
iram e milhares de casa se edificaram
mente a renda Municipal e do Thesouro

Considerado o negocio de
bonds como o nec plus ultra
das californias, milhares de
propostas subiram para os
altos poderes do Estado,

Onde, durante alguns
annos, criaram soffri-
vel quantidade de bolor.

Ao Cons.º Costa Pereira coube
a importante e espinhosa missão
de distribuir os bondificos privi-
legios.

As acções na praça forão logo
pedidas, disputadas e arrancadas
dando immediatamente 50 e 100
mil reis de premio,

BANCO DO BRAZIL

u-se a comprehender que só havia no Brazil
Janeiro e um Botafogo; e os bonds desceção
na estima de seus admiradores e o enthusi-
ou de uma vez!

Foi uma febre fatal, uma febre bondicidia!
Quantos accionistas não terão dito a olhar para certos trilhos:
—Ahi jarem os nossos cobres!

E mestre Greenough tira
todos os ditos para o banco
alguns contos de reis que re-
presentam mais de 200 % de
lucro!

FIGURE 2.3 (continued)

Brazilian investors refused to acquire the company's stocks and laughed at his works. "We are not burying our money here," they said. Nevertheless, Greenough's energy triumphed and all were glad with the new service. Brazilian investors now wanted stocks, but it was too late. Greenough's tracks and dividends expanded in tandem, and the old means of transportation went out of business. The Botanical Garden Rail Road Co. became ever more prosperous, bringing a true revolution to Rio de Janeiro, expanding the circulation of people, filling the streets with families, and benefiting commerce. Property along the tracks increased in value, new buildings were erected, and the city profited greatly. Seeing streetcars as the best of all businesses, everyone came up with a project for a new line. The government distributed new concessions, and Brazil was taken by a streetcar-stock-speculation fever. All provinces, no matter how small their cities, created their own streetcar lines. But the government imposed heavy burdens, breaking most new companies. The game continued for a while, and some ended up with useless stocks in their hands. In the end, all realized that there was only one Botanical Garden Rail Road Co. in Brazil. The fatal streetcar fever drove many bankrupt. But not Greenough, the *Revista Illustrada* concluded its cartoon narrative, who continued to cash in his splendid profits.[100]

In 1874, an American engineer who visited Brazil as an agent of the Jackson & Sharp Co. Delaware Car Works noted that, starting off with little capital, Greenough had become very successful. "The profits realized from this section were so great that in a few months the company extended its track as far as the Botanical Garden, which doubled its length, and passed en route the beautiful suburbs of Botafogo. The last annual dividend was 18%, which equals more than the entire first cost of the road." The line had "proved a literal gold-mine to its projectors" and done great good to American enterprise in Brazil: "What is more, its success led to the most unbounded confidence in any enterprise that had its origin in America."[101]

Similarly, an American naturalist who explored Brazil in the mid-1870s observed that, when Greenough first arrived in Rio de Janeiro, "people who could not afford a carriage of their own, must ride in dirty, crowded omnibuses, or go on foot, as the most of them did." After Greenough created his company, things changed. "The Yankee idea was received with favor and opposition, in about equal measure," the observer continued. "However, it was carried out, and now the Botafogo line is probably the finest of its kind in the world; the stock three or four hundred per cent above par." By demonstrating the excellence and profitability of American enterprise, Greenough had rendered valuable services to his own countrymen as well as to the Brazilians. "The road was economically built, and it is carried on with true Yankee acumen," the naturalist concluded.[102]

Arriving in 1879 to serve as US minister to Brazil, Henry Washington Hilliard could not stress enough the importance of the Botanical Garden Rail Road Co. for Rio de Janeiro. Of the means of transportation that connected the suburbs to the city center, Hilliard noted, "the Botanical Garden Railroad is by far the finest and the most important. Through the central part of the city, beginning at the Ouvidor, its finest street, it extends through the aristocratic quarter, Botafogo, to the magnificent Botanical Gardens, and to the suburb beyond them."[103]

Indeed, the streetcars had become so important for the people of the capital city that when, on January 1, 1880, the government enforced a tax of twenty réis per ticket, a violent uprising took place. The rioters attacked cars, tracks, horses, and drivers. The Army intervened. The cabinet of ministers fell. On January 4, the tax was indefinitely suspended and the revolt abated, leaving at least three dead.[104] One day earlier, while the people of Rio de Janeiro were still shedding blood for their right to ride the streetcars that Greenough had brought to their city, he died in France, where he had gone to treat his health. But his bondes lived on. By the late 1880s, an American journalist living in Rio de Janeiro testified to the enduring importance of Greenough's work: "The Botanical Garden line serves to connect the city with the suburban districts of the Cattete, Larangeiras, Botafogo, Copacabana, Lagoa and Gavea. Much of this part of the city is comparatively modern and the streets and residences are more pleasing to the eye."[105]

Greenough's streetcars, Rainey's ferries, and Roberts's railroad represented major accomplishments for American capital, generating immense profits and consolidating the influence of the United States in the largest country of South America. None of these American entrepreneurs had a free hand, however. They always worked under the close supervision of Brazilian authorities, customers, and journalists. As they strove to attend to Brazilian interests, the agents of the free North learned invaluable lessons in how to build transnational business networks. Before long, American enterprise would reach beyond Rio de Janeiro and transform all sorts of economic activities in Brazil.

Seeking to deconstruct the older scholarly narrative of relentless American capitalist expansion, historians now characterize American entrepreneurs as hesitant novices, incapable of challenging the predominant influence of British capital in undeveloped countries in the nineteenth century.[106] A more nuanced characterization emerges from the study of the Americans who were investing and working in Rio de Janeiro between the 1860s and the 1870s. True, Americans came from a position of disadvantage in relation to the British and had much to learn as they engaged with Brazilian society. Yet precisely because they were willing to work in concert with the Brazilian elite, Americans succeeded in confronting British capital.

Thanks to these entrepreneurs and the alliances they established with members of the Brazilian elite, Northern capital presented itself in Brazil as a progressive alternative to both Southern proslavery expansionism and British imperialist abolitionism. Their accomplishments shed light on how the United States emerged as a world power in the wake of a bloody domestic conflict. From the perspective of the only remaining independent slave society in the Western world, the American North seemed capable of exporting progress even as it faced a major crisis at home.

The Hermit and His Friends

In 1858, when Roberts, Harvey & Co. signed the contract to build the second section of the Dom Pedro Segundo Railroad, an American citizen living in Brazil penned an enthusiastic letter to the *Philadelphia Bulletin*.

> All the Americans in Rio de Janeiro regard the making of the present contract as a strong movement toward American interests in Brazil; believing that it will be the means of introducing many enterprising Americans in various walks of life, as well as many American inventions and manufactures; besides strengthening the bonds of friendship which ought forever to exist between the two greatest Governments of the western hemisphere. . . . American mechanics, laborers and contractors will now, therefore, receive a double welcome in Brazil; from Brazilians, as well as from their own countrymen.

The writer maintained that all that was needed now was "a *steamship* communication between the two countries to induce a large social as well as commercial intercourse, and this cannot long be delayed." Both countries would gain from such direct connection: "The United States, being the *largest* coffee customer of Brazil, has to pay annually a heavy balance in *specie*," while Brazil "spends this same specie in England in purchasing such articles as can, and *will be*, hereafter and ere long, furnished at lower prices in the United States." In other words, the new steamship line would favor Americans and Brazilians at the expense of British middlemen.[107]

The need for a direct connection became all the more evident as the demand for coffee rapidly expanded in the United States during the Civil War. Since early in the nineteenth century, Brazil had been supplying between one-half and two-thirds of all coffee consumed in the United States each year. Americans had been drinking coffee produced by Brazilian slaves not only at home and work, but also at war. President Andrew Jackson had made coffee part of the military ration in 1832. At the outbreak of the Civil War, American soldiers could not imagine fighting without the stimulant. "The coffee ration was most heartily appreciated by the soldier. When tired and foot-sore, he would drop out of the marching column, build his little camp-fire, cook his mess of coffee," a former Massachusetts artilleryman recalled. "It was coffee at meals and between meals, and men going on guard or coming off guard drank it at all hours of the night."[108] By 1864, the Union government was buying forty million pounds of coffee to keep up morale in the Northern Army. Brazil took advantage of the situation, and coffee prices jumped from fourteen cents per pound in 1861 to forty-two cents per pound in 1865.[109]

While Union soldiers drank overpriced coffee, Confederates could hardly get any of it due to the Union naval blockade. Southern merchants thus tried to make whatever they had in hand taste like coffee: nuts, sweet potato, rye, chicory, okra seed, melon seed, and even bark. As usual, advocates of secession tried to sugarcoat the desperate situation of the rebellion. "We have been favored, by a friend, with a sample of Cotton Seed Coffee," the *Charleston Courier* reported in January 1862. "The aroma is very like that of coffee, and its flavor is similar to that of coffee."[110] But soldiers could not be fooled and did all they could to get the real thing, even if it meant trading with the enemy. A British officer who visited the Confederacy in 1863 observed that "the loss of coffee afflicts the Confederates even more than the loss of spirits."[111]

While soldiers in North America craved caffeine, the coffee trade received vital help from a young Brazilian politician with a passion for all things Yankee. The son of a declining oligarchical family from Alagoas (an impoverished province in northern Brazil), Aureliano Candido Tavares Bastos had entered the Pernambuco Law School at the age of fifteen, in 1854. The next year, he moved to the São Paulo Law School, where he joined a group of radical intellectuals and became an avid reader of Alexis de Tocqueville's *De la démocratie en Amérique*. In 1858, Tavares Bastos joined the Liberal Party and was appointed to an administrative post in the Brazilian Navy. In 1861, at the age of twenty-two, he was elected to the Chamber of Deputies. Before long, he became the most prominent of all Brazilian antislavery reformers.[112]

Soon after his election, Tavares Bastos made an impression in Parliament by delivering a speech condemning the obsolete structure of the Brazilian Armed Forces. And he did so in the presence of the ministers of the Navy and War. Tavares Bastos immediately lost his post in the Navy but gained fame and new opportunities to express himself about issues that, he thought, held Brazil back in an age of progress. He then started publishing a series of letters in the *Correio Mercantil* under the pseudonym of O Solitário (The Hermit). From education to the military, from public employment to the judicial system, from foreign trade to slave labor, Tavares Bastos assailed the status quo with relentless energy. In 1862, he compiled these letters in the form of a book titled *Cartas do Solitário*, which he expanded and republished in 1863.[113]

Attentive to the global transformations of the nineteenth century, Tavares Bastos sought to refashion the Brazilian liberal tradition.[114] A strong state, he contended, would intervene in society to optimize its potentials. The central state should use its resources to expand infrastructure instead of imposing restrictions to trade and association or feeding a swarm of unproductive bureaucrats. Tavares Bastos wanted the government to "facilitate interior communications in the country; bring the population centers closer to each other; connect the extreme points of the Empire; build railroad lines; promulgate freedom of navigation; make innumerable steamers cross our coast and our navigable rivers; in one word, develop the material elements of the country." Inspired by the likes of Abraham Lincoln, Otto von Bismarck, and Napoleon III, Tavares Bastos merged the language of nation with the language of capital. He believed that the proper way to build a polity integrated by the spirit of comradeship and mutual interests would be to develop a robust economy based on free enterprise. "Such is the true path toward our greatness; such is also, as it has always been, the true direction of the human spirit," he proclaimed.[115]

Tavares Bastos's nationalism rejected any form of chauvinism or isolationism. He was a cosmopolitan liberal who understood that countries should cooperate and learn from each other.[116] In *Cartas do Solitário*, more so than in any other work by a Brazilian author at the time, the United States appeared as an example to be emulated. "The North-American Union," he believed, "is the rendezvous of the civilized world." Among German, Irish, French, and English immigrants, all living "in the shade of liberty" in the United States, one could easily spot the "audacious Yankee, generous, fervent with activity, breathing the personal dignity of the Apollo Belvedere, indefatigable and strong, in his agitated life of assemblies, meetings, clubs, press, in his vigorous life, which is the only one worth living." For Tavares Bastos, the United States was, above all, a model of capitalist development: "It is from this country that will come to us the practical experience that will improve our agriculture, our economic condition, which has striking similarities to that of the Union." He urged his fellow countrymen "not to be afraid of the civilizing, democratic, evangelical, humanitarian, and fraternal spirit of the North Americans."[117]

In a letter addressed to the American merchant resident in Rio de Janeiro George N. Davis, Tavares Bastos lauded American entrepreneurs who were investing in Brazil during the 1860s. "We meet with Americans in all parts of Brazil," he celebrated. "In Rio de Janeiro Americans have rendered commerce the labor-saving machines of their agriculture, which is analogous to ours. In the province of Rio de Janeiro our great man of enterprise, Mr. C[ristiano Benedito] Ottoni, hands down to Americans his vast undertakings." Tavares Bastos praised the "indomitable perseverance and extraordinary energy" of William Milnor Roberts and other American railroaders. "They have filled up valleys," he rejoiced, "perforated through the Serra do Mar with tunnels, and at this moment locomotives made in their northern home take possession of the heights over [our] Thermopylae."[118] He also admired Thomas Rainey: "Steam is today the great means of transportation. See the marvelous Bay of Rio de Janeiro, which should be crisscrossed by elegant *steam-boats* in every direction, like the beautiful vessels of the Companhia Ferry."[119] Tavares Bastos sought to invite more Northern entrepreneurs to his country. "Brazil needs new *blood*," he continued his letter to Davis, "it needs the *Yankee* spirit, this intrepidity, this energy, this masculine spirit of invention and progress."[120]

For Tavares Bastos, the Union was a force for progress that could help Brazilian society enter the modern world. Thus, he used his position to advance American enterprise in Brazil. In December 1865, for example, he arranged a meeting between Rainey and the minister of agriculture, commerce, and public works to discuss the future of the Companhia Ferry.[121] He also held twenty-five hundred shares in the Dom Pedro Segundo Railroad Company and supported Ottoni's moves.[122] Tavares Bastos constantly corresponded with the engineer Andrew Ellison, inquiring about different steps of the construction of the second section and discussing costs, labor, materials, and technical matters.[123]

Tavares Bastos's admiration for the free North was intertwined with his contempt for the slave South. The battle between the Union and the

Confederacy, he believed, was a crucial episode in the nineteenth-century battle between progress and backwardness. Lynching and human hunting were just some of the evils becoming ever more common in the slave South, he noted. "In comparison to the cruelty of the slave breeders of Delaware, Maryland, Kentucky, Missouri, etc., and the extravagant barbarities of the inhabitants of the southern United States during the present war, most of our slave masters deserve some praise." Brazilian masters should not conclude, however, that they were free from the deleterious influence of slavery. Tavares Bastos sarcastically pointed out that, in Brazil, "slavery flaunts daily edifying scenes: suicides, cruelties, assassinations."[124]

Not only cruel, slavery was a heavy economic burden on Brazil. "It is undeniable," Tavares Bastos asserted, "that the institution of slavery was and is the central cause of our moral and material misery." He saw the slave as "a bad property . . . whose indiscriminate purchase explains the ruin of many rich planters." The slave, he feared, would soon become "the primary cause of a constant crisis" in Brazil.[125] To be sure, Tavares Bastos was not the first Brazilian to identify slave labor with backwardness.[126] Yet he was among the first and most influential Brazilian politicians to use the sectional divide in the United States to clarify what progress and backwardness meant. Tavares Bastos had no doubt that free labor was on the side of progress, and slavery on the side of backwardness.

As the American Civil War raged, in July 1862 Tavares Bastos asked the Brazilian Parliament to subsidize a monthly line of steamers connecting Rio de Janeiro to New York with two hundred contos de réis (approximately 110,000 dollars) annually. While some more cautious Brazilian politicians doubted that it was a good time to tighten the bonds with a country going through a convulsive domestic conflict, Tavares Bastos thought otherwise. He confidently told his peers that "after the present struggle—a glorious battle, because it opposes freedom to servitude, progress to barbarism—it is the destiny of the great republic of Washington to become the major power of the world."[127] Tavares Bastos reckoned that Brazil would profit much from a faster way to export coffee to the United States. Yet he envisioned other, loftier benefits stemming from his proposed subsidy. The antislavery North would help advance free labor in Brazil.

Though the subvention he asked for failed to pass by six votes in the Chamber of Deputies, Tavares Bastos succeeded in attracting valuable American attention to his project. In January 1863, James Watson Webb informed the young Brazilian politician that he had found someone willing to help Brazil and the United States connect through steam navigation: "I enclose here a very valuable and important letter from the great man of our country, whose word in such circumstances is *law*, Commodore Vanderbilt. You certainly know him by reputation, and I believe him when he says that I am the only living man who could induce him into such an enterprise."[128] Having been trying to profit from his tenure in Brazil since he had arrived, Webb planned to use his personal connections to take charge of the steamship line.

According to Webb, his friend Cornelius Vanderbilt—a shipping magnate and the richest man in the United States at the time—had calculated that the line of steamers would need a subsidy of fifty thousand dollars per round trip, amounting to six hundred thousand dollars annually, well beyond the amount that Tavares Bastos had asked the Brazilian government for. But, from Webb's point of view, even one million dollars would be a small price for Brazil to pay in order to encourage trade with the United States. Americans were the most avid consumers of Brazil's most valuable commodity: coffee. And there was more—the increased influx of American manufactured products to Brazil "would reduce the *profits* on British goods at least fifteen millions, and fan that amount to the people of Brazil."[129]

Tavares Bastos wrote to Davis in March 1863 that he felt honored to know that "Mr. General Webb has devoted some of his precious attention to this very important subject." In spite of the initial setback in having the subvention approved by the Brazilian Parliament, Tavares Bastos was hopeful. Seeking to reassure Davis, he echoed Webb: "Now who is the most directly interested in the closer relations of which I have spoken? Without a doubt Brazil, and above all the planters and dealers in coffee." American capital would also benefit: "The English, who almost monopolize our market in cotton and woolen fabrics, send to Brazil articles of a high price and inferior quality, hitherto without competition. If American manufacturers obtain information of this market and study near at hand the wants and tastes of nine million people, I have no doubt that in a short time they will be strong competitors of the English." Inciting Americans to challenge the British, Tavares Bastos did not forget to mention the Christie affair. "The recent arbitrary conduct of England," he told Davis, "excites in the whole of Brazil a great distrust in all European Governments, and by this means some of the most obstinate minds have been opened to the idea of an intimate alliance with the United States. The moment is propitious."[130]

The United States would furnish Brazil with processed food, furniture, agricultural implements, and other goods. More important, Tavares Bastos highlighted that "the Dom Pedro Segundo Railway Company have formed so good an opinion of your foundries and machine shops that they now prefer American locomotives and American cars." Beyond material needs, the United States would supply Brazil with precious expertise. Tavares Bastos was confident that the steamship line would attract to Brazil "civil engineers, men of enterprise, intelligent laborers, men habituated to new inventions, and they themselves inventors. . . . Let us have a line of steamers between the United States and Brazil, and then we shall see the development of our country by an advantageous influx of Americans."[131] As the Civil War was tearing American society apart, Tavares Bastos trusted that communications with the antislavery side of the conflict would be a boon to his country.

Despite his appreciation for Webb and their shared views, Tavares Bastos soon found another American partner to promote his project. "I read in the New York *Journal of Commerce* of September 16 a letter from our good and respectable friend Rev. Mr. Fletcher on this subject," he informed Davis.[132] James Cooley Fletcher and Tavares Bastos had met a few weeks after the Chamber of Deputies had rejected the subvention to the line of steamers. "In 1862 I went to Brazil," Fletcher recounted, "and had long conferences with Hon. Tavares Bastos, the youngest of Brazilian statesmen." Unlike Webb, Fletcher had no plans to take charge of the enterprise. Moreover, he agreed to lobby for a subsidy from the American government equal to the one that Tavares Bastos was asking from the Brazilian government. With a joint subsidy of around two hundred thousand dollars annually, they calculated, the concession for the steamship line would find many bidders.[133]

Perhaps because of Webb's popularity since the Christie affair, Tavares Bastos decided not to sever relations with him and agreed to present his proposition to the Brazilian Parliament in April 1864. After mentioning how an increase in coffee exports to the United States and a reduction in price of American manufactured goods would challenge British interests, Tavares Bastos told his peers that the new line of steamers would contribute to the enlightenment of Brazil. "The Brazilian agriculturalist," he envisaged, "instead of unproductively consuming the luxuries of Paris," would have a means to go straight to the United States "to examine the innumerable improvements of the industry that constitutes his profession, from the most curious mechanisms to the steam-powered plow." Brazilian travelers would be able to contemplate "the most amazing scenes of human progress, the marvels of a truly prodigious industry." Tavares Bastos emphasized that, in the United States, "our young men will get used to indefatigable labor, to fervent activity, fertilized by a solid education, practical, indispensable, fundamental, professional, the only one capable of saving our youth."[134] Although Tavares Bastos's ideas were enthusiastically applauded, the Chamber of Deputies balked; the subvention that Webb sought was too costly for Brazilian coffers. Nevertheless, Tavares Bastos's arguments had made a good impression, and he could now move forward alongside Fletcher.

While Webb's project floundered in Brazil, Fletcher was succeeding in securing a subvention in the United States. In August 1863, the Boston Board of Trade met for Fletcher's lecture on the commerce of Brazil. He started by declaring that he "wished, as some of the most liberal and important propositions had been made in the Brazilian Parliament, that an expression of hearty sympathy might go out from this community, to encourage those who were endeavoring to link the United States and Brazil by lines of steamships and by closer ties of amity." After showing through statistics that the United States was losing a crucial commercial battle against Great Britain by not establishing a direct connection with Brazil, Fletcher read translated passages of *Cartas do Solitário*. Impressed, the Boston Board of Trade resolved, first, "that in view of the growing commerce between the United States and Brazil, we deem it for the highest interest of both countries to have direct steam communication"; second, "that we appreciate the endeavors of Hon. A. C. Tavares Bastos and coadjutors"; and third, "that we recognize in these propositions, and in the large vote in their favor, . . . a spirit of liberality and enlarged views that demand perseverance on the part of their projectors in Brazil, with cordial cooperation of the United States."[135]

Good news soon arrived in Brazil. "I enclose a paragraph cut from a Boston paper," Davis wrote to Tavares Bastos in February 1864, "by which you will see that our friends have organized a Steam Ship Company and have obtained an Act of Incorporation from the State of Massachusetts." If the Brazilian government would join the Union government to subsidize the steamship company, Davis enthused, "we shall soon have steam communication with the United States."[136]

On April 15, 1864, influenced by Fletcher and the Boston Board of Trade, the Republican congressman John B. Alley of Massachusetts introduced a bill authorizing the US postmaster general to work with the Brazilian government in jointly subsidizing direct steamship service between the two countries. Explaining the steamship line project to his peers, Alley stressed that "the leaders of the [Brazilian] Liberal Party have been its earliest advocates. That party has lately come into power, and it is thought by well-informed persons now in Brazil, and in official relations with our Government, that the Brazilian

Government is now prepared to act in full cooperation with our own." As an example of the good feelings existing among Brazilian Liberals for the American Union, Alley read in the House of Representatives the letter that Tavares Bastos had sent to Davis in March 1863.[137]

In support of Alley, the Republican congressman John V. L. Pruyn of New York noted that "the relations existing between Brazil and Great Britain . . . are not as cordial as they have been." He rallied his peers to approve the subvention to the steamship line: "I sincerely trust that this bill will receive unanimous assent of the House, and that we will show to Brazil, which is so well disposed toward us, by prompt and unanimous action, that the American people fully appreciate their good feeling toward us and are anxious for the closer relations which we trust will soon grow between the two countries."[138]

Alley concurred that the establishment of the steamship line would be a first step in securing American influence in Brazil. Invoking the Monroe Doctrine, he told the House of Representatives that "the South American nations are all anxious to establish more intimate political and commercial relations with this country. They dread the encroaching and grasping policy of the Governments of the Old World, and they are looking to the Government of the United States as a barrier and shield to the aggressions and usurpations of European policy."[139] Alley, Pruyn, and the rest of the Republican Party understood that slaveholding Brazil offered a unique opportunity for antislavery Northerners to assert their modernizing mission in opposition to British imperialism.[140]

Writing to Tavares Bastos directly in April 1864, Fletcher congratulated him and enclosed a copy of Alley's speech. According to Fletcher, Alley had "studied the statistics of Cartas [do Solitário] and those I have provided." He was happy to tell his Brazilian friend that "in our Congress and throughout the United States, Tavares Bastos is well-known."[141] In May 1864, Lincoln signed the Alley bill into law. The Republican administration would subsidize the line of steamers connecting Brazil to the United States with up to 150,000 dollars per year.[142]

Immediately after the Alley bill was ratified, Fletcher traveled to Brazil to lobby for a measure to complete the deal. On arriving, he wrote to Tavares Bastos that "I have come to B[razil] with the most philanthropic intentions, to give light in regard to the steamship line and the law passed by the U.S. Congress and sanctioned by the President." Fletcher admitted he was glad that Webb's project had failed: "It was too much and besides the Deputies here and the people in the U.S. saw a *speculation* in this."[143] Tavares Bastos also felt relieved not to be bound by Webb's exaggerated requests and replied that "as soon as the law of the American Congress (Alley bill) became known here, more than 40 deputies signed the project, which you have seen, authorizing the [Brazilian] imperial government to concede the subvention of two hundred contos de réis to whichever company receives from the government in Washington the subsidy voted by Congress."[144]

After meeting with Fletcher, by late August 1864 Martinho Álvares da Silva Campos, the political associate of the Ottoni brothers, brought into the Brazilian Parliament a project to complement the Alley bill.[145] Silva Campos's speech at the Chamber of Deputies echoed Alley's arguments at the House of Representatives.

> The United States is the only one of the great nations in the world against whom we have no real complaints (*cheers*), and from whom we have never received an offense. (*Cheers*). . . . And it is the only one of the great nations in the world from whom we have received constant and never contradicted proofs of benevolence, and from whom we can find support, without which we might not live (*cheers*), given the impudent tone and the haughtiness with which we have been treated in the English Parliament by the British Prime Minister. (*Long applauses*).

Taking into consideration the "interventionist and aggressive spirit" of European powers and their recent attacks on the Dominican Republic, Mexico, and Peru, Silva Campos concluded that Brazilians should "adopt an American policy, a policy that, creating harmony between us and the American nations, will give us strength to obtain the kind of justice that has been denied to us."[146]

The imminent victory of the free North in the American Civil War became a strong argument in favor of the subvention in the Brazilian Parliament. Antonio Francisco de Paula Souza, a rich coffee planter and Liberal leader from São Paulo, marveled at the resilience of the Union. "To prove the greatness of that nation," he remarked, "it is enough to observe that today, after three years of a fierce struggle never before seen, a battle of titans, giants, mythological gods, . . . [the American] people has not ceased to provide examples of development in all kinds of human activity." Interrupting Paula Souza, another deputy argued that the Americans were suffering from the vices of their own institutions. "Vices that we share," he retorted. "What is the cause of the South in this war? It is a cause that also exists among us. The American people is destined to provide us plenty of examples on how, one day, we may solve our great social problem."[147]

Like Tavares Bastos, Paula Souza was an antislavery reformer who trusted that closer relations with the United States would bring valuable lessons to

Brazil. Having a direct means of transportation to the United States, young Brazilians would be able to attend agricultural schools "with excellent teachers, the first in the universe," and would have access to "ready-made [agricultural] models and machines." Beyond intellectual and material gains, in North America Brazilian youths would have "a school of morality, of elevation and personal dignity."[148]

In early 1865, a group of New York entrepreneurs—who had asked for a total subvention of 240,000 dollars to complete twelve round trips per year—obtained the concession from the American government, henceforth establishing the United States and Brazilian Steamship Company. In March of that year, an agent of the new company went to Brazil to work with Fletcher. Together, they "prepared a pamphlet, more fully explaining the law of the United States, and bringing the statistics of our own [American] commerce to bear upon the subject, to prove the necessity of immediate action on the part of Brazil."[149] Writing from New York City, the president of the steamship company courted Tavares Bastos: "Considering Your Excellency one of our best friends and defenders, we trust in your most valuable support and great influence."[150]

In May 1865, the members of the Rio de Janeiro Chamber of Commerce wrote a petition to the Brazilian Parliament suggesting that the benefits of subsidizing a line of steamers would go well beyond immediate pecuniary gains. The merchants expressed their fascination with "the magnificent spectacle that is presented by that laborious, bold, energetic, and rich democracy, in which abound all the resources of modern life." Such a spectacle, they believed, "must produce great and beneficial impressions upon those who behold it." Like Tavares Bastos and Paula Souza, the petitioners envisaged that, in a short time, Brazilian youths would go "to the United States to study the useful arts and sciences of daily use and application; to learn agriculture, the trades, and the arts through practice—how to construct canals and rail-roads, and how to optimize their time by employing it constantly in useful pursuits." On their return to Brazil, these young men would "bring with them some of that spirit of enterprise, of that energy of character, of that love of labor, which so preeminently distinguish the American democracy."[151]

The 149 merchants who signed the petition chose Tavares Bastos to present it to the Chamber of Deputies. And Tavares Bastos did so in a dramatic fashion, taking advantage of an unexpected circumstance. He told his peers that he was touched to present the petition "at this moment, when news of a tragic event arrives to disturb the minds of all friends of Liberty and Peace, when an irreparable disgrace darkens nineteenth-century civilization!" Referring to the assassination of Lincoln and the attempt on the life of Seward, Tavares Bastos sought to create an emotional link between Brazil and the Union. "The noble act of the Chamber of Commerce clearly demonstrates," he concluded, "the deep sympathy that the people of Rio de Janeiro nurture for the great country of real Liberty, known as North America, for the cause represented by the honorable President Lincoln and his illustrious Secretary [of State]!" Teófilo Ottoni presented the same petition to the Senate one week later.[152]

Contributing to Tavares Bastos's effort, in June 1865 William Van Vleck Lidgerwood, the New Jersey entrepreneur who also served as chargé d'affaires, spoke in favor of the subvention to the steamship line at a meeting of the Sociedade Auxiliadora da Indústria Nacional (Auxiliary Society of National Industry; SAIN), the most important scientific association in Brazil at the time.[153] He argued that it would permit the Brazilian planter to "meet the demand for coffee in the United States through a continuous supply of this product, avoiding the price fluctuation that currently feeds speculation and injures him. All these problems will cease to exist thanks to the steamship line, because the planter will constantly receive information about the real value of his coffee in New York."[154] The sum that Brazil would contribute to subsidize the steamship company would thus quickly be repaid. After a short deliberation, the members of the SAIN approved Lidgerwood's speech and forwarded it to the Brazilian Parliament.

When the discussion reached the Senate, the Liberal senator João Lustosa da Cunha Paranaguá of Piauí explained that his party favored an American policy that would save Brazil from episodes such as the Christie affair. He rejoiced that the steamship line would bring his country "closer to those who give us prompt and loyal reparations for the insults made by their subjects, unlike those who attack us through their ministers and admirals, those who withhold our property and who try by all means to demonstrate their malice."[155] In addition to fostering economic and intellectual development, a direct connection with the American North would shield Brazil against British impositions. Little did it matter that Webb, the hero of the day when Christie confronted Brazil, had been left out of the steamship deal. Now the bonds between the two countries were strong enough not to depend on one diplomat. The subvention passed in the Senate and Dom Pedro II signed it into law on June 28, 1865.

This was a major achievement for the most progressive wing of the Liberal Party, the group led by Tavares Bastos. The steamship line would not only carry Brazilian coffee to the United States but also inspire profound social and political change in Brazil. By associating with the American Republican Party and Northern entrepreneurs, antislavery Liberals had become the driving force of momentous changes in Brazil by the middle of the nineteenth century. They inserted their country into the emerging capitalist world order and remade the central government into a force for economic development. They were Brazil's great modernizers. Undaunted, they welcomed the crisis of slavery in the western hemisphere and charted a path forward for their country. In concert with their American allies, they would shape free labor to serve the interests of the Brazilian planter class.[156]

In 1866, Cornelius K. Garrison acquired the United States and Brazilian Steamship Company. A New York entrepreneur, he had operated steamships on the Mississippi River and the Caribbean Sea, worked with Vanderbilt transporting prospectors to California during the Gold Rush, and served as mayor of San Francisco between 1853 and 1855. Garrison now sought to profit from trade with the largest country of South America. Counting on the joint subsidy offered by the Brazilian and the American governments, he maintained three steamships in service connecting New York to Rio de Janeiro for a decade.[157]

Northerners saw the steamship line as a symbol of their growing influence in the world economy. Celebrating the ongoing construction of the transcontinental railroad, which would connect the eastern railroad network to the Pacific coast, in 1867 *Harper's Weekly* compared its potential benefits to those of the United States and Brazilian Steamship Company: "A letter [from New York City] will reach Hong Kong by way of San Francisco much quicker than when it went by way of Liverpool, just as our enterprise had shortened the time of our communication with Brazil."[158] Such transportation networks, *Harper's Weekly* predicted, would transform New York City into "the commercial centre of the world."

The establishment of the monthly line of steamers resulted from a partnership between antislavery reformers from both ends of the hemisphere. Tavares Bastos and his allies had established a strong bond with Lincoln's Party, the group of men who had just crushed an aristocracy of slaveholders. Brazilian Liberals now made plans to buy new technologies from the United States and send Brazilian youths to study at American universities. Furthermore, the steamship line represented a new wide door for American entrepreneurs willing to repeat, or expand, what Roberts, Rainey, and Greenough had been achieving in Brazil. More important, the steamship line represented a joint victory over British imperialism. It was a message from Brazil that it was not to be bullied anymore and a message from the American Union that a new hemispheric policy had emerged.

3

A Hemispheric Battle

IN JULY 1867, upon learning that Brazil had opened the Amazon River to foreign vessels, the poet John Greenleaf Whittier published a tribute to the Brazilian people in the *Atlantic Monthly*.

Freedom in Brazil

With clearer light, Cross of the South, shine forth
In blue Brazilian skies;
And thou, O river, cleaving half the earth
From sunset to sunrise,
From the great mountains to the Atlantic waves
Thy joy's long anthem pour.
Yet a few years (God make them less!) and slaves
Shall shame thy pride no more,
No fettered feet thy shaded margins press;
But all men shall walk free
Where thou, the high-priest of the wilderness,
Hast wedded sea to sea.[1]

A Massachusetts abolitionist, Whittier had been a founding member of the American Anti-Slavery Society in the 1830s, achieved national fame for his *Poems Written during the Progress of the Abolition Question in the United States* (1837) and *Voices of Freedom* (1846), joined the Free Soil Party and later the Republican Party, and supported the Union with fervor during the American Civil War. When Whittier wrote about Brazil, he had joined the effort of the Radical Republicans, seeking to secure freedom in the postwar United States and extend it abroad. He hoped that the Brazilians, after opening their river, would liberate their slaves. In Brazil of the 1860s, however, Whittier's ideal of freedom would become synonymous with capitalist modernization.

The immediate aftermath of the American Civil War seemed to be undoing much of what men like Whittier had fought for. Unreconstructed white Southerners carried on the conflict after Robert E. Lee's surrender through guerrilla warfare and terrorist acts.[2] Contradicting the principles of the Thirteenth Amendment, Southern state legislatures enacted the Black Codes, which restricted the civil rights of freedpeople, punishing vagrancy and reducing many to peonage. Meanwhile, President Andrew Johnson adopted conciliatory measures toward former Confederates. Radical Republicans fought back, weakening Johnson and passing the Fourteenth and Fifteenth Amendments, which were intended to guarantee the civil and political rights of ex-slaves. They also placed the Southern states under military rule and extended the powers of the Freedmen's Bureau.[3]

While the American soil was still soaked with the blood spilled during the Civil War, Brazil became involved in a brutal foreign conflict. The war for the control of the Plata Basin against the Paraguayans, whom Brazilian elites regarded as barbarians, proved to be much longer and bloodier than expected, lasting from 1865 to 1870. The war crisis brought about an avalanche of indictments against the social system prevalent in Brazil.[4] Compounding the political turmoil, in 1868 Dom Pedro II replaced a coalition of moderate reformers from both parties with the Conservatives. The Liberals protested by presenting a long list of desired reforms, the most important of which was gradual slave emancipation. In the meantime, an abolitionist movement emerged with radical propositions. Excluded from the central positions of power, these activists began to assail the status quo through the press and new associations.[5]

Louis Agassiz, a close friend of Whittier's, visited Brazil between 1865 and 1866. Accompanied by James Cooley Fletcher, Agassiz served as director of a Harvard scientific exploration of the Amazon Valley. In addition to his scientific duties, Agassiz engaged with Brazilian reformers such as Aureliano Candido Tavares Bastos and expressed his antislavery opinions. As a gesture of sympathy toward the famous naturalist and his Northern friends, the Brazilian political elite set aside old fears, opening the Amazon River and promising to deal as soon as possible with the problem of slavery.

The influence of Massachusetts intellectuals, the victory of the Union, and Abraham Lincoln's martyrdom seemed to be pushing Brazil to antislavery reform already in the mid-1860s. But now Brazil had its own war to wage, and the Brazilian government vacillated when it came to acting against slavery. Agassiz,

Fletcher, and Whittier nonetheless remained faithful to Brazil, going so far as defending Dom Pedro's merciless war against Paraguay before American critics and claiming that Brazilians were on the right track to slave emancipation. Then, exasperated by official procrastination, the Brazilian abolitionist movement redoubled its pressure on the political elite. Hoping to contain further agitation and seeing an opportunity to set Brazil on the path of capitalist development, the Conservative government enacted the Law of the Free Womb on September 28, 1871.

The transnational approach has revitalized the study of the American Civil War. Historians underscore the political consequences of Northern victory for other countries, suggesting that the United States became a beacon of freedom and equality in a troubled world. The survival of the American republic, they argue, inspired processes of democratization across the globe.[6] In Brazil, however, the victory of the Union led to something quite different. As the free North defeated the slave South, American antislavery reformers shut their eyes to Brazil's imperialist policies and undemocratic institutions. Although radical abolitionists nurtured egalitarian visions for Brazil, moderate groups were able to take control and enact a gradual emancipation project that would ensure the continuation of the Brazilian planters' rule. Seeking to avoid the social upheaval that had taken place in the United States, political and intellectual elites from the two countries favored selective change in Brazil. They consciously set in motion a process of conservative modernization.

The King of Naturalists

Louis Agassiz's interest in Brazil dated back to the late 1820s, when, as a student at the University of Munich, he had assisted his mentor, Carl Friedrich Philipp von Martius, in classifying and describing a collection of fish from Brazilian rivers.[7] During the 1840s, when Agassiz moved to the United States and became a professor of zoology at Harvard, he concentrated on studying North America. By the 1860s, however, Agassiz became convinced that the study of the tropical environment, varied species, and geological formation of the Amazon Valley would help him debunk Charles Darwin's *On the Origin of Species*, first published in 1859. Agassiz believed that a supernatural intelligence had created life once, wiped it out through glaciation, and created it again after the Ice Age. Thus, he could not accept Darwin's revolutionary idea that chance was the cause of order or, in other words, that life on Earth was the product of random events.[8]

Besides Martius and Darwin, another person attracted Agassiz to Brazil. James Cooley Fletcher was living in Newburyport (thirty-five miles northeast of Cambridge) during the 1860s. Having several friends in common in Massachusetts, such as John Greenleaf Whittier, Agassiz heard about Fletcher's travels to Brazil and, in 1862, commissioned him to conduct a field trip to the Amazon Valley to collect little-known specimens of freshwater fauna.[9] On that occasion, Fletcher had a long meeting with Dom Pedro II, who showed great interest in American works of science and literature. "He spoke of Agassiz, of Mr. Ticknor, author of Spanish Literature, and of Mr. Everett, as gentlemen well-known to him, and of his works which H[is] I[mperial] M[ajesty] had just received, asking after Mr. Bancroft, Mr. Longfellow, and John G. Whittier."[10]

On July 12, 1862, Dom Pedro II registered in his diary that "Fletcher has met with me and brought several works from the United States, and letters from notable men among which is one from Agassiz, which he promptly gave me."[11] In his letter, the Swiss-born Agassiz, accustomed to aristocrats from Europe and the United States alike, paid tribute to the Brazilian monarch: "The civilized world admires Your Majesty, not only as the paternal and generous sovereign of a people full of love and devotion, but also as an instructed man, protector of the arts and sciences, and friend of everything that tends to elevate the human species." As a token of friendship, Agassiz sent through Fletcher his most recent book on the natural history of North America to Dom Pedro II.[12]

Agassiz also asked if Dom Pedro II would be willing to "establish direct relations between the savants of Brazil and those of the United States, and particularly with the Museum of Cambridge," whose director was Agassiz himself.[13] Dom Pedro II did not hesitate to accept the offer, guaranteeing that he would personally take detailed notes on some curious specimens of Brazilian fish and "send to you some objects of natural history that, according to what Mr. Fletcher told me about the nature of your study, will perhaps interest you."[14] Always communicating in French, the naturalist and the monarch became scientific collaborators and personal friends, exchanging letters about sick relatives and birthday parties as well as plants and animals.

Back in the United States in 1863, Fletcher lectured on Brazil at the Boston Mercantile Library Association, "giving an interesting and vivid description of that 'King of Waters,' interspersed with numerous anecdotes of his personal experience while navigating its bosom." Fletcher added that the king—or emperor—of Brazil was as majestic as the Amazon River: "The speaker closed by paying a high tribute to the rare qualities of head and heart which distinguish the present Emperor of Brazil and render him the greatest and best monarch now living."[15]

Fletcher's lectures and the material he had collected for Agassiz generated enthusiasm about Brazil in Massachusetts elite circles. In early 1865, when Agassiz decided to organize his expedition, the Boston banker Nathaniel Thayer told him to "select your assistants, organize your expedition, proceed to your work, and send the bills to me."[16] Writing to Dom Pedro II a few days after the announcement of the Thayer Expedition, Fletcher emphasized Americans' support for the scientific enterprise: "Your Majesty can hardly appreciate the great interest that is felt here [in the United States] by men of science in this contemplated visit of Professor Agassiz."[17]

Agassiz arrived in Rio de Janeiro on April 22, 1865, where he stayed for several weeks before going to the Amazon. Along with the naturalist came his wife Elizabeth Cabot Cary Agassiz (the daughter of a Boston Brahmin family), several Harvard students (including William James, Stephen van Rensselaer Thayer, and Charles Frederick Hartt), the painter Jacques Burkhardt, and James Cooley Fletcher.[18] It was a very propitious moment for a scientific expedition. The United States and Brazilian Steamship Company had just started operating its monthly line between Rio de Janeiro and New York. Meanwhile, the Companhia de Navegação e Comércio do Amazonas (Amazon Navigation and Commerce Company) had been expanding its fleet, the volume of cargo and number of passengers transported, and the waystations integrated into the river transportation system. For most Brazilians, Matthew Fontaine Maury's expansionist projects and fears of American occupation of the Amazon Valley were already forgotten.

By the early 1860s, some Brazilian political leaders had become convinced that the time for a thorough development of the Amazon Valley had arrived. They had been arguing that the opening of the river to foreign vessels would be the first step in that direction. As the minister of agriculture, commerce, and public works put it in his 1863 report, "The opening of the Amazon River to the commerce of all nations that are in peace with Brazil is certainly one of the things that the imperial government desires the most to see, and it is something that I hope will bring happy results."[19] In 1864, the discussion had reached Parliament, and Aureliano Candido Tavares Bastos had become the leader of those supporting the opening.[20]

Under such circumstances, the Brazilian political elite welcomed Agassiz as a celebrity. Always having Fletcher by his side, he visited his friend Dom Pedro II and made more than one stop at Parliament, always receiving tributes.

They also visited the most important scientific institutes of Rio de Janeiro and, escorted by William Milnor Roberts, inspected the works of the Dom Pedro Segundo Railroad.[21] Invited by the monarch, Agassiz delivered free public lectures at the Colégio Dom Pedro II. Rio de Janeiro newspapers transcribed Agassiz's lectures in full, filling their pages with theories about glaciation and freshwater fish.[22] After attending two lectures, the editor of the *Semana Illustrada* declared that he was "anxiously waiting for the third lecture, the fourth, the fifth, the thousandth; because to listen to this notable naturalist is to harvest from each one of his expositions the seasonal fruits from the Tree of Knowledge." A full-page portrait of "The Sage Agassiz" accompanied this article.[23]

Before the Thayer Expedition left Rio de Janeiro for the Amazon, the Imperial Institute of Fine Arts organized a banquet for fifty guests to pay Agassiz homage. The first toast to Agassiz and his crew was proposed by Antonio Francisco de Paula Souza, the Liberal leader from São Paulo and Tavares Bastos's ally who was then serving as minister of agriculture, commerce, and public works. Several other toasts by Brazilian politicians and intellectuals followed. Fletcher was not forgotten. Deputy Pedro Luiz Pereira de Souza, "in a brief and warm improvisation, mentioned the new era being opened to Brazil with the inauguration of the steamship line to the United States, which will strengthen the bonds that must connect two great brothers, and proposed a toast to the promoter of this line, Mr. Fletcher." Then, Fletcher raised his glass and started speaking of the friendship between North and South America. Agassiz, taking center stage, interrupted his friend, saying that "there is only one America now." The Brazilians rejoiced.[24]

Brazilian authorities provided Agassiz with everything he needed to accomplish his scientific goals in the Amazon Valley. "The kindness of the Emperor of Brazil, who is a man of no common culture," the *Boston Daily Advertiser* reported, "had followed him [Agassiz] wherever he had gone and had facilitated in the most generous and effective manner all the scientific purposes and plans which Mr. Thayer's magnificence had enabled Professor Agassiz to arrange and undertake a year ago." Dom Pedro II placed a government steamer at the service of the Harvard naturalists and furnished them with letters of introduction.[25]

Minister Paula Souza also took interest in the Thayer Expedition. Among other things, he requested that Agassiz collect Amazon specimens for the Imperial Museum in Rio de Janeiro.[26] "Allow me to say," Agassiz responded, "that I not only accept your request with pleasure but also believe that your collaboration will be very useful to our enterprise."[27] Paula Souza appointed João

Martins da Silva Coutinho, a major in the Brazilian Army Corps of Engineers who had distinguished himself for his works on the Amazon during the 1850s, as guide to the Thayer Expedition.[28] Agassiz was delighted to have Coutinho by his side, writing from the province of Pará to inform Paula Souza that "the profound knowledge that Coutinho possesses about everything that relates to the Amazon has been the main source of all the ease that I am finding to conduct my work with promptness and in a vast scale."[29]

Coutinho made sure that everything needed for Agassiz's research—such as fuel, tools, and containers—would be readily available in the Amazon Valley.[30] Coutinho admired Agassiz's manners as well as his work, informing Paula Souza that "he does not refrain from saying that before coming to Brazil he had a narrow view of our things, but now he realizes that only in France and the United States has he encountered the same dedication to the sciences from the government as he has found here." Coutinho was delighted when Agassiz compared Brazil to the United States, pointing to the "the tranquility that we [Brazilians] enjoy, the liberty that we possess, even in times of war." Agassiz's opinions, Coutinho believed, would not only improve the image of Brazil in the United States but also foster closer relations between the two countries.[31]

Another figure who impressed Agassiz was Tavares Bastos, who met with the Thayer Expedition in Manaus, capital city of the province of Amazonas. "To our great pleasure," Elizabeth and Louis Agassiz wrote in their travel journal, a river steamer "brings Mr. Tavares Bastos, deputy from Alagoas, whose uniform kindness to us personally ever since our arrival in Brazil, as well as his interest in the success of the expedition, make it a great pleasure to meet him again."[32] In March 1866, the *Atlantic Monthly* published a letter from Elizabeth Agassiz describing Tavares Bastos. "Although not yet thirty years of age," she started, "he is already distinguished in the politics of his country; and, from the moment he entered upon public life to the present time, the legislation in regard to the Amazons [sic], its relation to the future progress and development of the Brazilian empire, has been the object of his deepest interest." A leader of those who advocated for progressive reforms in Brazil, Tavares Bastos had "already urged upon his countrymen the importance, even from selfish motives, of sharing their great treasure with the world."[33]

In his 1863 *Cartas do Solitário*, Tavares Bastos had posited that opening the Amazon was essential to the economic development of northern Brazil. "Let us decidedly open the great river," he demanded, "so we conquer the sympathy, which we now lack, of the civilized world." An open-door policy, Tavares Bastos envisioned, "would promote labor, increase transactions, spread abundance, people the wilderness, and multiply transportation. It is the natural order of things, and this is the harmony of interests." Tavares Bastos admitted that, in the 1850s, Maury and his proslavery followers had made plans to annex the Amazon; but he guaranteed that the aggressive Southern expansionists were now a defeated minority in the United States. To prove his point, Tavares Bastos reminded his readers that, "in the final chapter of the work *Brazil and the Brazilians*, Mr. Fletcher condemned these [Maury's] exaggerations, but simultaneously insisted on the great advantages to foreign commerce that the opening of the Amazon would bring." Fletcher's writings were definitive proof for Tavares Bastos and other Brazilians that it was "an error to believe that every American is a filibuster, and that the political motto of the nation of Washington, Franklin, and Jefferson is invasion and conquest. Nothing could be more inaccurate." Inspired by Fletcher and the supporters of the Union, Tavares Bastos insisted that "the enlightened part of that country and, above all, the Republican Party profess the impartial principles of Monroe."[34]

Now, in addition to Fletcher and the Republican Party, Tavares Bastos had the naturalist Louis Agassiz on his side. In a series of articles for the *Diário do Rio de Janeiro* (later published as a book titled *O Valle do Amazonas*), he resumed the work begun in *Cartas do Solitário*. Tavares Bastos argued that the Amazon was not a river, but "a fresh-water ocean: this is what Mr. Agassiz told me about the Negro River, when, in front of the Solimões [River]"—both of which are tributaries of the Amazon River—"looking left and right, one loses the horizon on the vast aquatic plain. . . . It is, thus, the same as any inland sea of the globe, a system of communication that must be put in service of the peoples of the world, because the seas belong to all."[35] Tavares Bastos, the young Brazilian modernizer, dreamed of Americans bringing economic development to the Amazon Valley.

Agassiz left no doubt that he was invested in making his trip to Brazil something more than a scientific quarrel with Darwin. After months exploring the Amazon Valley, he returned to Rio de Janeiro, where he lectured before over four hundred prominent figures, including the royal family, on the resources of that region. "It was his opinion," the *New York Herald* reported, that the Amazon Valley "would one day become the mart of the world, supporting in comfort twenty millions of inhabitants."[36] Agassiz publicly joined forces with Tavares Bastos: the treasures of the Amazon Valley should be open to all friends of Brazil.

The famous naturalist also offered a helping hand to Tavares Bastos's most urgent cause. Along with books and equipment, Agassiz carried to Brazil a letter from Whittier to be delivered to Dom Pedro II. "I have long, in common with all our literary and scientific men," the poet wrote to the monarch, "cherished a high respect for the humane and enlightened ruler of a great empire." After the praise, Whittier did not "lose this opportunity to thank thee from my heart for the friendly attitude of the Brazilian government toward my suffering country in the hour of her great trial. Our terrible struggle seems drawing to a close and everything indicates that, with the withdrawal of the evil and disturbing element of slavery, we are to be henceforth a truly united people."[37] By mentioning the problem of slavery, Whittier was, at once, condemning the proslavery rebellion against the Union and trying to push Brazil toward reform.

Following Whittier's lead, Agassiz was not afraid to touch on the problem of slave emancipation in front of Dom Pedro II.[38] Violating the etiquette that he knew so well, Agassiz engaged in a frank conversation about slavery with the royal couple during a dinner at the palace. Elizabeth Agassiz reproduced the dialogue in a letter to a friend. Dom Pedro II asked about Agassiz's impressions of Brazil. "Everything delights me with one exception," he answered, "and perhaps that exception is one which it would be indiscreet to speak of here." "No, no," Dom Pedro II said, "be perfectly frank. I like to have your observations, favorable or unfavorable." Agassiz then expressed his antislavery feelings: "I must say it shocks me to see numbers of negroes who are crippled in their limbs in consequence of the numerous burdens they carry on their heads. It is a hideous consequence of slavery here." Dom Pedro II responded earnestly that "slavery is a terrible curse upon any nation, but it must and it will disappear from among us." His wife Teresa Cristina "took up the strain and said she considered it the saddest feature in their social system." To Agassiz's joy, the royal couple seemed to have "no hesitation in expressing their horror and detestation of it and their hope that it would be rooted out."[39]

Mr. and Mrs. Agassiz were no radical abolitionists. In fact, it did not take much to convince the couple of naturalists that the prospects of emancipation were bright in Brazil. After a few inquiries with Brazilian political leaders, they happily remarked that "the subject of emancipation is no such political bugbear here as it has been with us. It is very liberally and calmly discussed by all classes; the general feeling is against the institution, and it seems to be taken for granted that it will disappear before many years are over." Unlike the antebellum United States, Brazil seemed to have no law or custom that restrained the march of emancipation. "These are the things which make one hopeful about slavery in Brazil," Louis and Elizabeth Agassiz concluded, "emancipation is considered there a subject to be discussed, legislated upon, adopted ultimately, and it seems no uncommon act to present a slave with his liberty."[40]

The couple of naturalists, who often stayed in plantation houses while exploring the country, became quite sympathetic to Brazilian slaveholders. In *A Journey in Brazil* (1868), they described the Santa Anna plantation, located in the province of Minas Gerais: "Its owner carries the same large and comprehensive spirit, the same energy and force of will, into all his undertakings, and has introduced extensive reforms on his plantations." Mr. and Mrs. Agassiz arrived at Santa Anna during the coffee harvest. "The spectacle was a pretty one," they exulted. Buying into Brazilian slaveholders' ideology of benevolent management and strategies of gradual and individualized emancipation, the naturalists were satisfied to see the slaves receive rewards for extra work. "A task is allotted to each—much to a full-grown man, so much to a woman with young children, so much to a child—each one is paid for whatever he may do over and above it. The requisition is a very moderate one, so that the industrious have an opportunity of making a little money independently." The American visitors rejoiced to learn that those who saved enough would be able to buy their own freedom.[41]

It may be true, as some historians point out, that many Northerners held on to the belief that the cause of the Union could advance democracy and equality abroad.[42] Nevertheless, when it came to the last independent slave power in the Americas, a country that enslaved nearly two million human beings, influential agents of the Union were more interested in fostering international trade and securing the power of the planter class. Hoping that the Brazilian path to slave emancipation would be smoother than the American path, distinguished members of Massachusetts elites were glad to compromise with the interests of Brazilian slaveholders and accept their own pace of reform.

Sensing what was going on with the Thayer Expedition, the Philadelphia *Daily Age* noted in November 1865 that "Brazil is yet a new, undeveloped country. It may, therefore, be reasonably doubted if any previous event of its history has so affected its agricultural and mineral development, not to say its civilization and Christianization, as the scientific explorations now making under the supervision and direction of Professor Agassiz."[43] Its exaggerated tone aside, the paper was right that Agassiz's visit had a profound impact on Brazil. The famous naturalist left for the United States in July 1866. A few months later, the Brazilian Parliament issued a decree establishing that, from September 7, 1867, onward, the navigation of the Amazon River would be open to all friendly nations.[44]

FIGURE 3.1 "Fazenda de Santa Anna in Minas Geraes." Louis Agassiz and
Elizabeth Agassiz, *A Journey in Brazil* (Boston: Ticknor and Fields, 1868).
Courtesy of the Biodiversity Heritage Library.

It would take a little longer before the Brazilian political elite moved against
slavery. Nonetheless, Tavares Bastos was exultant. Writing to his friend Quintino Antonio Ferreira de Souza Bocaiuva, who was in New York City in December 1866, he could not contain himself: "The Amazon is open. Give me a
hug for this! . . . What a battle! But we won." The enthusiastic Tavares Bastos
asked Bocaiuva to "send without delay to my old friend Fletcher and to Professor Agassiz (Boston) two copies of my book [*O Valle do Amazonas*]. Don't
take too long. It is an honor that I owe them."[45] To Tavares Bastos, it was clear
that Fletcher's and Agassiz's interest in the Amazon had convinced powerful
men in Brazil that Americans and Brazilians could work together in making
the mighty river a center of civilization. And he was confident that this was
just the first of many reforms to come.

As soon as Agassiz arrived in the United States, he started lecturing on the
Amazon and his elite Brazilian friends. The *New York Herald* revealed how
enthusiastic the audiences were about the opening of the river. "This is a most
important concession in view of the vast and productive territory which thus
thrown open to the commerce and enterprise of this country," the newspaper

noted. "We have the authority of Professor Agassiz," it emphasized, "who has just returned from a tour of scientific investigation in Brazil," and guaranteed that "the valley of the Amazon is an immense extended plain" capable of supporting a population of over one hundred million.[46]

Powerful Americans celebrated that they had overcome one major hurdle in their relationship with Brazil: the "King of Waters" was open. In his annual message of 1867, President Andrew Johnson remarked that "Brazil, with enlightened sagacity and comprehensive statesmanship, has opened the great channels of the Amazon and its tributaries to universal commerce."[47] This measure came to complement the steamship line, American investment in Brazil's infrastructure, and the shared antipathy toward British imperialists and proslavery Southerners.

As the conflict in North America reached a resolution, the Union and Brazil strengthened a friendship that had begun to germinate in the 1850s. In this context, the opening of the Amazon River—and the new opportunities for commerce and development it entailed—represented a notable accomplishment for modernizing forces led by men like Tavares Bastos, Fletcher, Paula Souza, and Agassiz. Capitalizing on this additional achievement, they now looked forward to definitively setting Brazil on the path to capitalist development.[48]

War Measures

The rosy picture that the Massachusetts intellectuals painted of Brazil obscured the bitter disagreement that Brazilian observers were having when discussing the meaning of the antislavery measures of the Union. Perhaps more so than any other people at the time, Brazilians fully understood that the Emancipation Proclamation had taken the American Civil War to a point of no return. Besides leading some two hundred thousand black men to join the Union Army, this war measure reassured enslaved women, children, and elders that their struggle for freedom would be recognized by the federal government. According to the historian Stephanie McCurry, "The Emancipation Proclamation profoundly upped the ante for the C.S.A. in their battle for the hearts and minds of their own slaves. . . . Jefferson Davis was thus not far off the mark in charging that by the Emancipation Proclamation ('the most execrable measure recorded in the history of guilty man') 'President Lincoln has sought to turn the South into a San Domingo.'"[49] Brazilian journalists quickly comprehended that the interpretation of this war measure and its consequences had the potential to advance or obstruct antislavery reform in Brazil.

In response to the conflict in North America and the rise of antislavery leaders like Tavares Bastos, a proslavery reaction began to form in Brazil of the 1860s. Brazilian proslavery advocates, however, were never as organized or aggressive as their American counterparts. As the sociologist Angela Alonso puts it, "Unlike the explicit American proslavery ideology, Brazilian proslavery ideology operated through a technique of invisibility."[50] Elite Brazilians had long portrayed slavery as a given part of life, which had been inherited from colonial times, and thus could not be blamed on the present generation. When confronted, instead of portraying slavery as a positive good, proslavery spokesmen in Brazil adopted the rhetoric of "necessary evil": slavery was so deeply rooted in Brazilian soil, they argued, that it would create more damage than benefits to try to remove it.

The American Civil War provided an opportunity for proslavery Brazilians to demonstrate how pernicious the attempt to mess with slavery could be. Traditionally allied with the Conservative Party and the coffee planters of the Paraíba Valley, the *Jornal do Commercio* gave voice to the reactionaries, claiming that the Emancipation Proclamation was "not a legal measure of pacific abolition, but an arbitrary act of vengeful and cruel Servile War! . . . Its only goal is to excite a slave rebellion." No matter how much Lincoln talked about his Christian piety, for the *Jornal do Commercio*, "God will never approve an act that, under the pretext of emancipation, seeks to reduce the South to the horrific condition of Saint Domingue."[51]

Responding to the proslavery reactionaries, the *Diário do Rio de Janeiro* began to portray the Emancipation Proclamation as a heroic act. Edited by Tavares Bastos's associates, traditionally allied with the Liberal Party, sometimes tending to republicanism, and often supporting social reform, the *Diário* lauded Lincoln in January 1863 as he admitted "slavery as the cause of the War" and proclaimed that "through the abolition of slavery the Union will be restored."[52] By freeing millions of human beings, "Mr. Lincoln has marked his name in one of the greatest acts of justice in history," the editor asserted in February. "Come what may, as lamentable as it is to see violence in service of justice, this is a great act; the idea for so long incubated has hatched; from now on slavery is dead!" The only act that all should be lamenting was Jefferson Davis's "savage proclamation announcing a sanguinary retaliation against the acts of the federal government: death to all officers who command armed slaves; death to all slaves enlisted in the federal troops; death without pity, without mercy, outside of the battlefield, even to those who surrender." The *Diário* concluded with a provocation: "What will the partisans of the South say about this terrible decree?"[53]

For the *Jornal do Commercio*, there was nothing barbaric in the Confederate response to the Emancipation Proclamation. Southern slaveholders needed "preventive measures of repression . . . to avoid the insurrection that it encourages."[54] The proslavery reactionaries responded to their reformist interlocutors that Lincoln's measures were truly barbaric, only contributing to more bitterness on the side of the rebels and a longer and bloodier conflict. Had Lincoln preserved slavery, "it would still be possible to find understanding and harmony between the South and the North." Yet, the *Jornal do Commercio* alleged on January 3, 1863, the Emancipation Proclamation had "shattered the last bond, . . . and the war will now take an even more horrific character."[55]

Brazilian reactionaries were not alone in condemning Lincoln's war measures. Similar responses were emerging in Europe at the time. In October 1862, as the news of the preliminary emancipation proclamation reached Great Britain, the London *Times* accused Lincoln of doing "his best to excite servile war in the States which he cannot occupy with his arms." The influential British newspaper, which claimed to defend the cause of humanity, pointed its finger at the American president: "He will appeal to the black blood of the African; he will whisper of the pleasures of spoil and of the gratification of yet fiercer instincts. . . . Mr. Lincoln avows, therefore, that he proposes to excite the Negroes of the Southern plantations to murder the families of their masters while these are engaged in the war. The conception of such a crime is horrible."[56]

Such sensationalist pronouncements only demonstrated that the likes of the *Jornal do Commercio* and the *Times* were desperately embracing a lost cause. For most foreign observers, the Emancipation Proclamation represented a moral victory for the Union. Socialists in Germany, Republicans in France, and Garibaldians in Italy praised Lincoln for his courageous stand against slavery.[57] Labor activists organized mass meetings in working-class districts of Lancashire to celebrate American emancipation, and none other than Karl Marx, who lived in London then, trumpeted that "the New World has never achieved a greater triumph than by this demonstration that, given its political and social organization, ordinary people of good will can accomplish feats which only heroes could accomplish in the old world!"[58]

As the Emancipation Proclamation took effect and Western public opinion swung in favor of the Union, the *Jornal do Commercio* realized that the conflict had reached its crucial moment. "It is not a battle of governmental principles that can be harmonized with concessions from the parties," the newspaper started. "It is a social war, which admits no conciliation of ideas, because its raison d'être is as implacable as the *be not be* of Shakespeare. Slavery or not slavery."[59] In January 1865, the *Diário do Rio de Janeiro* proclaimed that "it does not matter anymore, especially to the Brazilian thinker, to know if the American Constitution permits the meridional states to secede from the motherland." What was really at stake at the time was that "the fratricidal battle, while its bloody combats multiply, threatens the whole of humanity in its morality, in its dignity, in its essential progress, because the prize that both sides dispute is called—*slavery*."[60] A few months later, slavery crumbled and the Confederacy was crushed.

While Brazilian reformers were celebrating the victory of the Union, however, some dramatic news arrived from the United States. Elizabeth and Louis Agassiz wrote in their journal that, on May 21, 1865, "as we drove up to the Hotel Inglez after dark that evening, hoping to get a glimpse of an American paper, . . . we were greeted by the announcement of the assassination of Lincoln and Seward, both believed at this time to be dead."[61] More news arrived in the following days: Secretary of State William Henry Seward had survived, but President Abraham Lincoln had died.

Now all major Brazilian newspapers, including old critics, paid tribute to Lincoln. The reactionary *Jornal do Commercio* described John Wilkes Booth's act as the "most terrible of all modern crimes" and lamented "the assassination of President Lincoln at the precise moment the world expected so much from him, and when his plans for the restoration of peace began to ripen in the plenitude of his capacity and moderation."[62] The *Diário do Rio de Janeiro* reflected on the sadness of the American people and praised their effort to honor the deceased president during his funeral: "Pomp never seen before, an enormous and plaintive multitude waited for the remains of the heroic man, the martyr of the causes of progress and humanity. It was a triumphal march among the tears and longing of a free people. The most beautiful of all spectacles and the most fecund of all lessons."[63]

Brazilian public opinion quickly transformed Lincoln into a martyr. In July 1865, a pamphlet came out containing a description of the funeral, a Portuguese translation of Reverend Phineas D. Gurley's eulogy, and a biographical sketch of the late president.[64] The Brazilian poet Felix Ferreira published *A Morte de Lincoln: Canto Elegiaco*, and the leader of the Presbyterian mission in Brazil delivered his own public eulogy in Rio de Janeiro.[65] Ads for "photographic portraits of President Lincoln" appeared in Brazilian papers, and the assassination became a favorite topic for Brazilian illustrated publications.[66]

Another eloquent tribute to Lincoln came from the Grande Oriente do Brazil, the most important masonic lodge in the country. In June 1865, the

FIGURE 3.2 *Bazar Volante*, December 10, 1865. Courtesy of the Fundação Biblioteca Nacional, Rio de Janeiro.

freemasons addressed the American people through James Watson Webb, the US minister to Brazil, lamenting the death of "the most energetic, if not the foremost, representative of the cause of progress," "a benefactor of humanity." Declaring themselves cosmopolitan apostles of freedom, the Brazilian freemasons stated that "the blood of Abraham Lincoln was the supreme baptism for the Christian idea in the modern era, an idea that he embodied with sublime perseverance and indomitable courage."[67]

Commemorating the author of the Emancipation Proclamation was especially meaningful to the Brazilian people because their country was entering its own violent conflict and would soon have to deal with the problem of waging war while holding onto slavery. Intervening in Uruguay's internal quarrels in 1864, the Brazilian Navy had singlehandedly shut down the Port of Paysandú on the Uruguay River. The Paraguayans deeply resented the measure as they lived in a landlocked country and depended on the rivers of the Plata Basin to reach the ocean. Thus, the Paraguayan dictator Francisco Solano López sought to unify discontented factions all over the region in an effort against Brazilian imperialism. Yet afraid of López's intensions to acquire a maritime outlet for his country, the Uruguayan and Argentine governments formed a coalition with Brazil. One of the most devastating wars of the nineteenth century ensued.[68]

Worried about the lack of manpower as the war dragged on, in November 1866 Dom Pedro II consulted the Council of State about the possibility of emulating Lincoln, recruiting slaves to fight. The Liberal leader from São Paulo José Antonio Pimenta Bueno, the Marquis of São Vicente, responded affirmatively, arguing that Sparta, Athens, and Rome often used slave soldiers in their legions and "the United States has recently offered a new example of this practice."[69] José Tomás Nabuco de Araújo, a Liberal from Pernambuco, agreed with São Vicente, reminding Dom Pedro II that "in the United States President Lincoln, through his proclamations of September 22, 1862 and January 1, 1863, ordered the slaves having the necessary aptitude to be enrolled in the Army and the Navy. Thousands were enlisted and served well." To support his position, Nabuco de Araújo quoted parts of the 1863 report by the American Freedmen's Inquiry Commission on the service of fugitive slaves in the American Civil War. Among other things, he read the opinion that "the Negro has a strong sense of the obligation of law and of the stringency of any duty legally imposed upon him. The law in the shape of military rule takes for him the place of his master, with this difference, that he submits to it heartily and cheerfully without any sense of degradation."[70]

Not all councilors agreed, however. Francisco de Sales Torres Homem, a former Liberal who had moved to the Conservative Party, argued that "what has been done in the United States during the last civil war cannot serve as a model for Brazil." Torres Homem's opinion entailed not a criticism of Lincoln or the Emancipation Proclamation but the acknowledgment that, by using slaves as soldiers, the Union Army had "employed its natural allies, who combated in favor of their own cause, and therefore were the most interested in the triumph of the Union." In the context of a war to crush a slave power, he continued, "there was no risk in the measure provided that slave emancipation would be general and those who did not take part in military service would have the same benefit." But Brazil was itself a slave power, and notwithstanding the promise of individual emancipation, slaves would not fight for a country that kept their families in chains. Brazil was between a rock and a hard place, according to Torres Homem: it could either proclaim general emancipation and displease the most powerful men in the country or leave things as they were and reject the support of hundreds of thousands of able-bodied men who were enslaved. Torres Homem chose the second option, and so did most of his peers and the monarch.[71]

Slave men served in the Brazilian Army during the Paraguayan War. But upholding property in slaves, the Brazilian government paid masters for slave recruits and accepted slaves as substitutes for slaveholders' relatives or protégés who had been drafted. On returning from Paraguay, the slaves who survived the sanguinary war were liberated. Though not as numerous as in the Union Army, slaves represented a significant source of recruits in the Brazilian effort against López. More than six thousand slaves, nearly 5 percent of the total Brazilian soldiers, fought. Slave recruitment was particularly important during the years of 1867 and 1868, when popular enthusiasm for the war was waning.[72] Yet at the end of the day, Torres Homem's assessment proved to be correct: since Brazilian politicians were not willing to let go of the institution of slavery once and for all, unlike the slaves who fought for the Union in the American Civil War, few of the Brazilian slaves went to Paraguay willingly.[73]

The American Civil War did not engender a new era of equality in Brazil. In fact, by the mid-1860s, Brazilian elites became all the more aggressive in their imperialism. Moreover, they refused to adopt a war measure similar to the Emancipation Proclamation and held on to slavery while waging war.[74] For the Brazilian government, the war against López was nothing more than a war against a people deemed inferior who dared to try to control the Plata Basin. Nevertheless, in their genocidal campaign against Paraguay, the Brazilians would receive enthusiastic support from Massachusetts antislavery reformers.

The Slave Empire

Initially, the American press favored Dom Pedro II over Francisco Solano López. Brazil's enemies, according to a *New York Times* article from March 1865, were no different from some of the populations who were being attacked by the forces of the Union in the American West.[75] "More than half of Paraguayan blood is native American," the newspaper remarked, "and the language of the sons of the forest is spoken in the streets of their metropolis. . . . The president, the Grand Sachem, is the father of all. . . . He holds the country and uses it much as we might suppose a Southern overseer would manage who never expected to meet the owner of his agent."[76] Some American commentators believed that by defeating an indigenous population and their cruel master, Brazil's civilizing mission in the Plata would create opportunities for foreign merchants in the interior of South America. "Now is the time for the European Powers and American also," the New York Herald correspondent in Rio de Janeiro urged in June 1865, "to unite with Brazil in opening the Paraguay River to [the Brazilian province of] Mato Grosso, where an important custom house should be established, and push Lopez and his policy aside to reach it."[77]

Discussions about recruiting slaves for the Brazilian war effort made American observers optimistic. Newspaper correspondents hastily emphasized that progressive slaveholders were willing to let go of their property. "Many planters and others," the New York Herald correspondent noted early on, "have presented slaves to the government to serve as soldiers. They have certificates of freedom given them which grant all the rights of citizens, and they will be entitled to bounty lands the same as white volunteers."[78] Reporting on the debates in the Council of State, the same writer spread rumors that the Brazilian government was planning to expropriate thirty thousand slaves for the war effort. "This measure, if carried out," he speculated in November 1867, "will be borne with full resignation by the majority of Brazilians, who in reality are not great lovers of the institution of slavery. Of late they have been realizing the disadvantages under which the empire has been laboring for the last fifty years, owing to the institution."[79] Similarly, the New York Times maintained that "Brazil, pressured from within and without to abolish slavery, is prepared to furnish men to fill up the gradually depleted army of invasion."[80]

Not all American observers, however, bought into the antislavery and civilizing narratives of the Brazilian war effort. From the outset of the conflict, some had been expressing their concerns about Brazilian expansionism in the Plata. "The war arises out of the long-determined and selfish desire of Brazil to extend her boundaries to the Rio de la Plata, on the south, and the Uruguay on the west," the Boston Daily Advertiser contended in August 1865. "Such an acquisition of territory would give Brazil control of la Plata, and the fertile lands which that large stream and her tributaries drain, a tract of 70,000 square miles in extent."[81]

As it became clear that the war would not change the plight of most Brazilian slaves, anti-Brazilian sentiment surged in the American press. In June 1868, the *Boston Daily Advertiser* proclaimed that it was the duty of all civilized nations, and especially of the United States, to stop the destruction of Paraguay by the "unwholesome empire of Brazil, ruled more villainously than any other country on the face of the earth, by a wretched oligarchy of Portuguese slaveholders."[82] In February 1869, the *New York Herald* correspondent explained that "the existence of slavery as a Brazilian institution makes them [the Paraguayans] fear the imperial views, and they are therefore fully prepared to believe what their leaders are careful to impress upon them, that the Brazilians design reducing them to slavery."[83] Such a statement was easily manipulated, and in December 1869 an editorial piece in the same newspaper speculated that Brazilian victory would mean "the extension over the eastern portion of the [South American] Continent of an empire based on human slavery and liberal exclusion." Brazil would not only absorb Paraguay, Uruguay, and Argentina to expand chattel slavery to the Plata but also close the waterways of the region, "for Brazil has always opposed the opening of those rivers."[84] Suddenly, the country that had been hailed by Agassiz and Whittier became an aggressive slave empire jealous of its rivers.

An incident involving American diplomats contributed to damaging the Brazilian cause even further in the United States. In early 1866, the Brazilian Navy barred the US minister to Paraguay, Charles Ames Washburn, from reaching Asunción. After almost one year, during which Washburn remained stranded in Argentine territory, the US chargé d'affaires William Van Vleck Lidgerwood successfully pleaded with Brazilian authorities to let the American diplomat quietly pass the river blockade. Further complicating the situation, in 1867 Brazilian authorities vehemently rejected offers of mediation that James Watson Webb had presented in the name of the American government. In the United States, some called for a demonstration of force. "Brazil declines the friendly intervention of our government in bringing about a peace between the Emperor and his neighbors," an outraged observer wrote to the *New York Times*. "That is an insult, and must be avenged."[85]

Things got out of hand when, in 1868, López accused Washburn of conspiring against the Paraguayan government and put him in jail. Then, Webb gave orders to the commander of the USS *Wasp* to go up the Paraná River, reach Asunción, and rescue Washburn. But the Brazilian Navy enforced the blockade once again. Furious, Webb threatened to break diplomatic relations with Brazil. The Brazilian government then decided to take Washburn out of

Asunción on a steamer of the Brazilian Navy and hand him over to the commander of the *Wasp*. Webb, not satisfied with this arrangement, behaved in a
way reminiscent of his British foe William Dougal Christie, bringing back to
life claims of four American merchants against Brazilian naval authorities dating back to the 1850s. When Brazil refused to pay, Webb went beyond threats
and broke diplomatic relations between the two countries for thirteen days in
May 1869. Brazil finally paid and diplomatic relations were reestablished.[86]

While Webb raged against Brazil, General Martin Thomas McMahon, who
had served as aide-de-camp to General George B. McClellan during the American Civil War, became US minister to Paraguay, replacing Washburn. To everyone's surprise, McMahon developed a friendship with López. Back in the
United States at the end of 1869, he depicted the Paraguayan dictator as a benevolent and beloved leader. When questioned about the causes of the war,
McMahon responded that "Brazil would have a hostility against any republic
situated on the borders of her slave-holding empire."[87] For McMahon, López's
Paraguay represented a free republic fighting Brazilian proslavery expansionism. "At the beginning of the contest," he told an audience at the New York
Cooper Institute in February 1870, "Paraguay contained a million happy
people—today two-thirds of the population have perished and the remainder
are wandering on the mountains and learning to look forward to death as a
welcome deliverance from Brazil. The rule of Brazil brought misery and wrong,
and death was less terrible than starvation and lifelong persecution."[88]

In the face of American diplomats' and journalists' open hostility to the
Brazilian war effort, Dom Pedro's Massachusetts friends did not fail him.
Fletcher wrote to the monarch in July 1866 that he had no doubt "that the
cause of Brazil—the cause of justice and civilization—will triumph."[89] In Oc-
tober 1866, Agassiz reassured Dom Pedro II that the Brazilian war against
López would "advance the cause of humanity and progress, freeing the Para-
guayans from the frightful despotism under which they groan."[90] In July 1868,
Whittier requested that Fletcher inform "the Emperor that the intelligent
people of the U.S. understand that the struggle now going on is waged by
Brazil and her allies in the cause of civilization and progress."[91]

From his home in Newburyport, Fletcher engaged in a public campaign to
defend the cause of Brazil, writing articles for popular American publications.[92]
Already in September 1865, an anonymous article for *Harper's Weekly* argued
that "it is folly to claim the sympathy of civilization for the stern and solitary
despotism of Paraguay; and it is unpardonable to represent the contest as a
struggle between monarchy and republicanism." Unlike Paraguay, Brazil was

a constitutional monarchy based on a representative political system. "Paraguay is actually and in spirit," the article concluded, "the least republican State upon the continent, while Brazil and the Argentine Republic, open to all the world, are constantly advancing in liberal civilization."[93] In October 1865, *Harper's Weekly* reminded its readers that Dom Pedro II "is an admirer of American writers" and had welcomed Agassiz as "a kind friend and warm supporter." More important, "the great purpose of his life seems to be to elevate the Brazilians to the position of a free people. During his reign Brazil has taken gigantic strides in material progress." Paraguay, on the other hand, "is without doubt one of the most despotically governed countries in the world."[94]

In the sixth edition of *Brazil and the Brazilians* (1868), Fletcher lamented that, in regard to the Paraguayan War, "there has been as much ignorance in both the United States and England as there was in Europe concerning the late Rebellion in North America."[95] Fletcher constantly drew parallels between the Paraguayan War and the American Civil War. A central point of these comparisons was an alleged manipulation of facts by unscrupulous journalists. "As in our [American] civil war we were constantly misrepresented by Englishmen," Fletcher wrote to Dom Pedro II in July 1866, "so we have a *few*, a *very* few, who sympathize with Paraguay, but I have been on the alert from the beginning of hostilities to set the public right through the means of some of our journals."[96]

By late 1866, two news reports arrived in the United States that contributed to the pro-Brazilian campaign. The *New York Times* informed the American public that the Amazon River would be open and that "two hundred slaves belonging to the Brazilian Government have been set free by the Emperor. . . . They desired to go to the war, and were enlisted and sent South [to Paraguay] as volunteers."[97] Agassiz wrote an optimistic letter to his friend Dom Pedro II.

> The United States is passionate about slave emancipation and I am sure that from now on many voices will rise in the secret of the hearts of Republicans asking for the Heavens to bless Your Majesty for the initiative taken in the regeneration of a suffering race. Furthermore, the opening of the Amazon will stimulate pecuniary interests and give a new impetus to this adventurous spirit that makes Americans the pioneers of modern civilization.[98]

From early on, *Harper's Weekly* had been emphasizing the antislavery tendencies of Dom Pedro II, no matter how vague they were. "The Emperor's ideas of the abolition of slavery are well known," an October 1865 article claimed.[99] In December 1865, the magazine further speculated that "Brazil has been quietly doing away with slavery by the mild process of her laws since 1850, but the complete downfall of the 'institution' in our land has led the South American Empire to consider the best means to be more speedily rid of that which weighs like an incubus upon any country."[100]

While Dom Pedro II had freed his family's slaves and the rivers of his empire, the American advocates of Brazil now argued, López had done exactly the opposite. Brazil's allies often compared the Paraguayan dictator to the enemies of the Union in recent conflicts. "The people of Paraguay are the slaves of Lopez," *Harper's Weekly* remarked in May 1868, "who is the only great trader in the country, and who might be left to himself, like any other barbarian, if he did not molest innocent people."[101] Furthermore, López had tried to close the Plata "as the rebels once did the Mississippi River to Northern steamers." Thus, "the people of Brazil and the Argentine and Uruguayan republics determined, as did the people of the North, that the rivers should be opened. This was the cause of the war."[102] In *A Journey in Brazil*, Louis and Elizabeth Agassiz reinforced the idea that Brazil deserved "the sympathy of the civilized world, for it strikes at a tyrannical organization, half clerical, half military, which, calling itself a republic, disgraces the name it assumes."[103]

By the war's end, Fletcher's and Agassiz's opinion had won the debate. H. Hargrave, writing in June 1870 for the popular *Lippincott's Monthly Magazine*, criticized Americans who expressed "their fears that the overthrow of Lopez will necessarily end in the absorption of that country by Brazil, and thus be instrumental in the extension of African slavery and anti-republican principles." The anti-Brazilian writers were completely mistaken, Hargrave continued. Paraguay had been a slave power under López. Brazil, on the other hand, had entered the path to civilization: "On August 22, 1866, the emperor, Dom Pedro II, voluntarily and spontaneously declared his intention of commencing the work of abolishing slavery at the close of the war; and it is hardly probable that so enlightened and liberal a monarch would, of his own free will, make such a declaration without intending to put it in force." The provisional government of Paraguay, set up at Asunción by the invading forces, had already issued "a decree which reflects the greatest honor on its members, and which for ever abolishes slavery in that country." Hargrave came to a rhetorical conclusion that Fletcher and Agassiz certainly approved: "Can any reflecting mind bring itself to believe that such a decree would have been issued if the intention of Brazil had been the extension of slavery? Nay more, is it not in itself an evidence of the sincerity of the emperor, Dom Pedro II, in his desire to abolish it in his own dominions?"[104]

After his forces assassinated López, Dom Pedro II finalized an atrocious war that killed over two-thirds of the Paraguayan adult male population—in addition to causing the deaths of uncountable women and children—and imposed a puppet regime on what was left of the country.[105] True, Dom Pedro II had freed his family's slaves and the invading forces had terminated slavery in Paraguay; but he would never become the antislavery hero that his Massachusetts admirers expected. Still, overlooking his wrongdoings, the pro-Brazilian campaign in the United States did not let Dom Pedro II down. Contemplating the commercial bounty of the South American interior, antislavery Northerners upheld Brazilian imperialism in the Plata region.

The Radicals

Well before Dom Pedro II considered doing anything about the institution of slavery, other political leaders had been fighting human bondage in Brazil. Born in the western province of Goiás in 1811, José Inácio Silveira da Mota built his political career among the Liberals of São Paulo. In the early 1850s, Silveira da Mota was elected to the Chamber of Deputies and, in 1857, presented a bill to ban slavery in Brazilian cities. This time, Silveira da Mota drew only laughs and scorn from his peers. A few years later, however, he did not seem so quixotic. During the early 1860s, Silveira da Mota's antislavery agenda reemerged through propositions to ban public slave auctions and prohibit foreigners, religious orders, and the state from owning slaves in Brazil. As early as May 1861, he was arguing in the Senate that "had the states of the South of the American Confederation adopted a system to ameliorate the legal condition of the slaves, perhaps, gentlemen, we would not see today a threat to the American Union, perhaps we would not see today two flags in the United States."[106]

Fighting alongside Silveira da Mota was the senator from Bahia Francisco Gê Acayaba de Montezuma, the Viscount of Jequitinhonha. A radical Liberal who had participated in the process of Brazilian independence and never let go of his romantic views, Jequitinhonha confronted slavery earlier than most Brazilian politicians. In 1831, when it became clear that the Brazilian ban on the African slave trade was not going to be enforced, he denounced the vicious traffic and asked his fellow legislators for stern measures. During the early 1860s, Jequitinhonha presented bills for freeing slaves who had performed military service and the children of enslaved women who had been donated or ceded by their owners.[107]

Since the Brazilian Parliament would not even consider their bills, the opponents of slavery found other means to attract attention to their cause. The outcome of the American Civil War offered them valuable opportunities. In 1865, Jequitinhonha published a pamphlet celebrating the defeat of the slaveholders' rebellion in North America: "To punish the defenders of such an iniquitous institution, Providence made a body of freed slaves the first to enter Richmond, the capital of the Southern Confederacy."[108] When Lincoln was assassinated and the Brazilian Senate resolved to send condolences to the American Senate, Jequitinhonha did not miss the chance to say that Brazil should glorify the deceased president "as a benefactor of humanity, as someone who recognized the justice of a great cause and struggled for it." To honor his death, Jequitinhonha continued, "it is our duty to demonstrate that, if a cancer that weakens us still exists, it does so because circumstances of high politics force Brazil to postpone justice." When some of his peers accused Jequitinhonha of imprudence, he became even louder, clarifying that by "great cancer" he really meant "the institution of slavery."[109]

In the 1866 edition of his best-selling book *Brazil and the Brazilians*, Fletcher praised Silveira da Mota and Jequitinhonha for their efforts against slavery, remarking that "after the collapse of the so-called 'Confederate States'" they had "brought this subject most prominently before the Brazilian people." Fletcher then added a third member to the parliamentary battle for emancipation in Brazil: "A. C. Tavares Bastos, in the Chamber of Deputies, has been a persevering advocate of emancipation."[110] Tavares Bastos had joined Silveira da Mota's and Jequitinhonha's struggle immediately after he was elected. He boldly proposed in the Chamber of Deputies measures for the immediate emancipation of newborn slaves, the proscription for state institutions and religious orders to own slaves, the banning of public slave auctions, and the end to breakups of slave families through sale. In his *Cartas do Solitário*, Tavares Bastos warned his countrymen that antislavery was sweeping the world and would not take long to arrive in Brazil: "I believe that the liberal movement, which, from 1834 in the English colonies to this day, has gradually freed the slaves, will not stop, will not disappear now in the second half of this century." Recently, the Dutch Empire had taken steps to free over thirty thousand slaves in Guiana, he observed, and now "the United States rehearses, in the midst of an honorable struggle, plans to solve once and for all the question of slavery." Tavares Bastos anticipated that the "time will also come to Brazil when this problem will enter the order of the day."[111]

Always ready to act, Fletcher did not let his radical Brazilian friends down. In March 1865, several American newspapers, including William Lloyd Garrison's *Liberator*, published an article signed by Fletcher. "I have just received," he explained, "a letter from Hon. Tavares Bastos, a leading member of the Brazilian Chamber of Deputies, requesting that I should send him immediately all the works pertaining to slavery that I can collect." During his most recent stay in Brazil, Fletcher had received the same request from several other Brazilian politicians. "Certain Brazilian statesmen," he continued, "have looked upon our struggle with intense interest; for while their own slavery will, by their own laws on the subject, doubtless become extinct in twenty years, yet there are a great many leading minds who desire to take measures for the extinction of bondage for the 2,000,000 slaves (there were, in 1850, 3,000,000 slaves) before a half decade shall have gone." Fletcher further pointed out that Agassiz had been assured that "in Brazil they were looking forward to emancipation," and Senator Silveira da Mota had "brought in resolutions to check the accursed thing last session." Although the Brazilians were "united in their detestation of slavery," the discussions in Parliament would not be simple. "Therefore," Fletcher concluded, "come these pressing requests for books, pamphlets, speeches, etc., etc., on this subject. I appeal to members of [the US] Congress, editors of newspapers, publishers, ministers, and private citizens, to all interested in the weal of their fellow-man, to aid in this matter."[112]

The request yielded immediate results. In May 1865, the New York *American Missionary* reported that "last March Rev. J. C. Fletcher, Boston, at the request of a leading member of the Brazilian Chamber of Deputies, made an appeal for books, pamphlets, speeches, &c, on the subject of slavery, to be forwarded to Rio de Janeiro, for circulation. We have reason to believe that the appeal was promptly and liberally responded to." Following Fletcher's lead, other Northern missionaries were engaging in the battle for emancipation in Brazil. "Bishop Potter, of Pa.," the report continued, "just before leaving for Rio de Janeiro last month, made application to this office for printed documents on the subject of slavery, that he might put them into the hands of proper persons, as he understood that the subject of the abolition of slavery in Brazil is to come up in May in the National Assembly for consideration."[113]

Moreover, Fletcher's appeal brought the attention of the British and Foreign Anti-Slavery Society (BFASS) to Tavares Bastos's work. "As I found your name referred to in a letter which appeared in the American papers by Reverend Mr. Fletcher, in connection with the question of emancipation," the secretary of the BFASS wrote to Tavares Bastos in May 1865, "I take the liberty of forwarding to you a copy of a letter which I addressed to a correspondent of ours in Rio, on the ___ February 1865." The BFASS asked for information about the slave trade, the conditions of freed Africans, the number of slaves, and the progress of the antislavery cause in Brazil.[114] Tavares Bastos's response left no doubt that, in general, Brazilians were willing to move toward emancipation. He underscored that Brazilian society was "more advanced than the society of the vain knights of the golden circle, the planters of the South of the [American] Union. . . . A well-designed reform, based on practical experience, will never cause a terrible crisis in Brazil like the one that has just taken place in the North American Union."[115]

Wary of the commotion that Tavares Bastos and his allies were creating, Dom Pedro II asked one of the councilors to analyze possible means for gradual emancipation in Brazil. In January 1866, the Marquis of São Vicente presented five antislavery propositions to the monarch: the first one would free the newborn; the second would create provincial committees responsible for regulating slaves' self-purchase; the third would compel slaveholders to register their slaves in a government database; the fourth would free the slaves of the state; and the fifth would free the slaves of religious orders.[116] However, as the war against López became ever more complicated, Dom Pedro II pushed aside antislavery reform to focus on slaughtering the Paraguayan population. São Vicente's propositions were shelved, and not until the war was over did they reappear.

Tavares Bastos continued to act in spite of Dom Pedro's procrastination. In June 1866, he presented to Parliament two antislavery bills: one would free the slaves of religious and civil associations; the other would free the slaves of the state.[117] Neither bill passed. Too worried about López, the Progressive League—a coalition of moderate reformers from both Brazilian parties that was in power then—adopted Dom Pedro's posture. The radical Liberals were outraged: the government not only conducted a most inept war against Paraguay but also seemed incapable of acting on pressing social reforms. Adding insult to injury, instead of turning to more progressive members of the Liberal Party to solve the crisis, in 1868 Dom Pedro II ousted the Progressive League and gave power to the Conservatives.[118]

For Brazilian abolitionists, it was time to fight from outside political institutions. An organized abolitionist movement began to emerge in Brazil then.[119] And now the activists could use images from North America as weapons in their struggle. The poet Antonio Frederico de Castro Alves became nationally famous for his 1869 "Slave Ship," one of the greatest antislavery poems ever written. Before writing his magnum opus, though, Castro Alves dedicated some of his ink to the American Civil War. In 1865, he published "The Century."

> Fight. There is a sublime law
> That says: "In the shadow of crime
> Revenge shall march."
> Don't you listen to a cry from the North,
> Which reaches the feet of infinity,
> Which will awaken Franklin?[120]

Castro Alves's view of the American Civil War as a death struggle between freedom and slavery reappeared in his 1868 "Verses of the Hermit," likely a tribute to Tavares Bastos.

> To shout to the winds the inspiration of Gracchus
> To wrap oneself in the cloak of Spartacus,
> The serf among the masses;
> Lincoln—a Lazarus wakes up again
> And from the tomb of ignominy raises the people,
> To make of a vermin—a king![121]

Like Castro Alves, many young Brazilian agitators were born to planter families but attended college in the changing Brazilian cities during the 1860s. In the urban centers, these young men engaged in discussions about politics, art, philosophy, and science in ways unthinkable in the rural world where they had been raised. Critical of the old political elite, the students became Tavares Bastos's disciples and a force for social change in Brazil.[122]

In São Paulo, law students and urban professionals got together to create the Radical Club, which congregated around the ex-slave and self-taught lawyer Luiz Gama. Born in Bahia to an African mother who had participated in the Malês Revolt of 1835, Gama had been sold to a man in Lorena, in the coffee-growing Paraíba Valley, but ran away and ended up as one of the most influential abolitionists in Brazil. A hero for an entire generation of Brazilian activists, Gama never hid who his own heroes were: "To the ideology of tender slavery, I counterpose the revolutions of freedom; I want to be a madman like John Brown, Spartacus, Lincoln, Jesus; I hate, however, the pharisaical calm of Pilatus."[123]

The Radical Club organized conferences through which young men could engage in political discussions with Gama and other abolitionist leaders. In 1869, a twenty-year-old law student from Bahia named Rui Barbosa (who would eventually become one of the foremost intellectuals and politicians of Brazil) lectured during a meeting of the Radical Club. "Based on the laws of economic science, illustrated by the history of the American Union before and after 1863," Barbosa argued, it was possible to see "the infinite superiority of free labor to servile labor." He discussed specific examples from American society, pointing out that Virginia, "being until 1787 the pearl of the United States, has been reduced to the fourth place in the federation, having only doubled in population, while Pennsylvania's [population] increased sixfold and New York's tenfold, from 1790 to 1850."[124] Like other antislavery reformers, Barbosa believed that the making of a more modern Brazil depended first and foremost on the adoption of a system of wage labor similar to that of the American North.

While Gama and his radical disciples agitated São Paulo, Tavares Bastos's ally Bocaiuva set up the Republican Club in Rio de Janeiro, which brought together students, journalists, and minor bureaucrats. "After the heroism with which the United States shed the generous blood of thousands of free men to wash away the stain that defaced some of the brightest stars that adorn its flag," Bocaiuva's *A Republica* asked in 1870, "what have the Brazilians done?" The answer was discouraging: "We have discussed and postponed."[125] Praising the antislavery policies of the Union during the American Civil War, the Republican Club scolded the Brazilian political elite for its inaction. In a direct attack to Dom Pedro II and the petty symbols of his power, *A Republica* described Lincoln as a "simple citizen, worker of progress, without garb or fancy hat, without a cloak of stars or toucan craws, without silk trousers or a golden scepter, without ostentation or pomp, the man whose voice moved an entire nation, a people of 32 million souls, who rose, fought for a great idea, spent without hesitation their blood and their treasure." That plebeian, born and raised in the wilderness of the American West, should serve as a model for the pompous Brazilian noble, *A Republica* concluded.[126]

Another radical group was formed in Rio de Janeiro by the followers of a new religion based on orientalist, positivist, and evolutionist fashions. The so-called Espíritas (Spiritists) believed that fighting slavery was a means to reestablish the balance of Brazilian society within the immaterial as well as the material world. One of the founders of this spiritualist movement, Antonio da Silva Neto wrote in 1866 that "the enslavement of the negro in North America was the latent cause of that war of giants between the states of the North and the states of the South. Now, the vanquished lie in disgrace, and the victors are ruined." Yet, Silva Neto enthused, the brave Americans, lovers of democracy, had welcomed such revolutionary change and were now zealously working on reconstructing their society. "A country in which the lumberjack becomes a teacher and a lawyer, and later reaches supreme power," he added in reference to Lincoln, "will not be removed from the position it occupies among the nations by the costs of a war in favor of civilization and humanity. I say more: not even twenty years will pass before North America becomes the power of all powers."[127] In 1869, Silva Neto returned to the topic, maintaining that the struggle between truth and falsehood always produced martyrs. Jesus had been crucified for revealing moral truths, Galileo had been persecuted for revealing scientific truths, and "not long ago, in our continent, John Brown, standing up for four million slaves, was hanged. Nonetheless, Christianity continues to operate its revolution, the sciences have endorsed Galileo, and the freedom of the captives was decreed by the immortal Lincoln shortly after the sacrifice of John Brown!"[128]

The antislavery agitation soon reached Pernambuco, Amazonas, Rio Grande do Sul, and other Brazilian provinces. New abolitionist associations and publications spread like wildfire. Political participation in Brazil widened as people from all classes and ethnicities entered the debate.[129] With the end of the Paraguayan War in 1870, the Brazilian government would move toward reform. To the disappointment of Brazil's democratic forces, however, the Conservatives in power would reject popular demands and implement selective change to protect the planters' interests. The egalitarian vision of radicals like Gama and Silva Neto would never materialize in Brazil. But antislavery reformers would move forward, advancing capitalist development and strengthening the bonds between Brazil and the United States.

The Moderates

In 1870, the Liberal leader José Tomás Nabuco de Araújo urged Dom Pedro II and the governing party to respond to the public outcry: "I deplore the absence of the servile element in the Emperor's speech, in spite of the popular movement, which, like a torrent, uproots everything."[130] The discontented senator had joined the Liberal Center, a coalition of unelected politicians dedicated to pressing the government for reforms. The example of the American Civil War, these reformers thought, loomed large over Brazilian heads. "After the great American republic freed itself from the stain [of slavery] at the cost of blood," the Liberal Center opened its manifesto, "it would be an unacceptable form of blindness not to see that it is time for Brazil to search for a natural and smooth solution to the problem, so we do not risk to see it abruptly untied."[131]

Reformist appropriations of the American Civil War did not, however, go unchallenged. José Martiniano de Alencar, the writer who had praised Fletcher in the 1850s, sought to avert antislavery reform by resurrecting the debate on the Emancipation Proclamation. In a series of open letters to Dom Pedro II written between 1865 and 1868, Alencar—under the pseudonym of Erasmo—warned that "the act of slave emancipation in the South of the [American] confederation, decreed through a violent civil war, cannot be considered consummated yet. Misery and anarchy begin to take the country, which flourished until yesterday; nobody can anticipate the horrific scenes that will unfold in this bloody drama."[132] The recent history of the United States, Alencar contended, should teach his fellow Brazilians that abolitionist agitation would bring nothing but chaos and destruction to their country: "The United States have much to worry about when it comes to the fermentation of their political passions and the deluge of slaves recently liberated, before they can offer the world philanthropic utopias, raptures of idle spirits."[133]

Contradicting Alencar and other reactionaries, yet avoiding the growing radicalism of the abolitionist movement, in May 1871 Prime Minister José Maria da Silva Paranhos—who had recently become the Viscount of Rio Branco—introduced a bill designed to set the stage for a controlled transition from slave to free labor in Brazil. A native of Bahia, Rio Branco moved to Rio de Janeiro a young man, studied at the Military Academy, became a professor and a journalist, and joined the Liberal Party in the 1840s. By the 1850s, however, Rio Branco had come under the influence of the Saquaremas, the major coffee planters of the Paraíba Valley. Chosen by the Conservative Party for a diplomatic mission in the Plata, he performed his duties well and soon became a prominent Conservative politician. He gained notoriety as minister of foreign affairs, handling the implementation of the 1850 ban on the African slave trade. During the Paraguayan War, Rio Branco negotiated with Brazil's allies and organized the provisional government that replaced López.[134]

Although he never publicly defended slavery as a positive good, until the 1860s Rio Branco had sided with reactionary slaveholders in defense of their property rights.[135] In the Plata, however, he learned that slavery made foreigners look down on his country. As he put it before the Chamber of Deputies, "I found myself [in Paraguay] . . . amongst no less than 50,000 Brazilians, who were in touch with neighboring peoples, and I know for myself and through the confession of the most intelligent of them how many times the permanence of this odious institution in Brazil shamed and humiliated us before the foreigners."[136] As prime minister, Rio Branco sought to modernize Brazil from above and obviate more dramatic changes stemming from the radicalization of younger generations and the rise of leaders such as Tavares Bastos.

Rio Branco's bill combined the measures that São Vicente had presented to Dom Pedro II in 1866. Freeing newborns, the law would give the masters a choice of state indemnification or the use of the minors' labor until they turned twenty-one years old. It would also create a public fund for manumission and grant the slaves the legal right to save money in order to buy their own freedom. In cases of conflict over the slave's just price, magistrates would intervene. Additionally, the law would free all the slaves of the state. Finally, it would require masters to register all their slaves in a nationwide inventory; failure to do so within one year would result in loss of slave property.[137]

An apologist for Rio Branco described the path that led him to reform: "Slavery having been extinguished in the United States, only Brazil and the Spanish colony of Cuba formed a woeful exception. The country agitated itself, many emancipation societies were created, many pamphlets and texts appeared."[138] The example of the United States had indeed come in handy for the supporters of Rio Branco. Yet, unlike the radical abolitionists, the last-minute champions of emancipation used the lessons from North America to defend a conservative approach to reform in Brazil. A pamphleteer from Bahia, writing in 1871, declared not to be "an adversary of emancipation; but I want it slow and meditated so that the bloody scenes of the United States do not take place among us; I want emancipation; but protecting the master, less responsible than the society that authorized and encouraged him to acquire such a property."[139] Ultimately, slave emancipation in Brazil would be a measure to protect the interests of the dominant planters and help them gradually become employers of wage labor.

Posing as a wise statesman, Rio Branco spoke to Parliament a few days after introducing his bill, remarking that "we know the history of this question in the United States, we know the reluctance of the southern states, and we know the consequences of not searching for a solution that could conciliate the interests of the [slave] owners and those of society as a whole."[140] Francisco de Paula Negreiros de Saião Lobato, the minister of justice, jumped into the discussion to draw a comparison.

President Lincoln used to say: I do not want, neither do I admit, the emancipation of the slaves of the southern states, I only require that adequate measures be taken to conveniently modify it and bring an end to it in the future. But the slaveholders repelled the fair proposition that was offered, and made a bad demand, which resulted in their complete ruin. Our agriculture will have the same fate if—God shall not allow—we see reluctance from our slaveholders, if they rise and blindly resist. If, on the other hand, they are well directed, if they listen to the advice of prudence, . . . not only will they avoid the cruel fate of the slaveholders of the United States, they will also have their own interests preserved.[141]

Following Saião Lobato's reasoning, a supportive pamphlet urged the Brazilian slaveholders to avoid, whatever the cost may be, the mistake that their American counterparts had committed. "The southern states, which possessed slaves," Rio Branco's apologist narrated, "separated themselves from the northern states, which did not have slaves; a tremendous war broke out between them, and a violent intervention by the government was necessary and total slave emancipation had to be decreed as a compensation for the rivers of blood and wealth that had been squandered, and that could have been spared!"[142] Much blunter, Rio Branco himself remarked that "we should not wait for the solution to come from below, but welcome it from above."[143]

Brazilian elites would not repeat the mistake of Southern slaveholders. In a study that juxtaposes Southerners' experience to that of Brazilian planters and Prussian Junkers, the historian Steven Hahn argues that the slave South paid the price for resisting change: "In comparative perspective, what stands out in the course of emancipation and unification [in the United States] is the swift and dramatic decline in the fortunes of the Southern planter class."[144] Southern planters had their property in slaves suddenly abolished, their region devastated, and their political power in the federal government curtailed. After the war, they became junior partners in a booming industrial economy commanded by the Northern states. In Brazil, things played out differently. Rio Branco and his supporters saw the writing on the wall. At a crucial moment, they reckoned that if the government did not find a solution to the problem of slavery soon, revolutionary social forces would take over the country. The American Civil War showed the Brazilian planter class the advantage of selective change. Seeking to avoid a democratic shift in power, Rio Branco effected a project of conservative modernization.[145]

In spite of Rio Branco's explicit attempt to protect Brazilian slaveholders from a tumultuous transformation, some representatives of the coffee planters of the Paraíba Valley opposed his reform plans. Their reactionary stance notwithstanding, they never defended slavery as a positive good or spoke of secession, as fire-eaters had done in the United States. They even admitted that, in the long run and under the masters' supervision, the end of slavery would be desirable. "We want emancipation," Domingos de Andrade Figueira professed in the Chamber of Deputies, "but conciliating it with the gravest interests of the country, with public order, with economic interests, with the resources of the State. We want emancipation, but not by the means through which you, and the propaganda that you direct, seek to topple the Empire."[146]

The defenders of slavery in Brazil believed that Rio Branco's proposed reform would imperil social order. Paulino José Soares de Souza—the son of the councilor who had opposed Matthew Fontaine Maury's plans to colonize the Amazon—contended that "slavery is an institution that has created roots in our society, attached itself to our way of life, and formed with it a compact whole, being impossible to violently uproot it without making the whole resent and generating perturbations in the things that form with slavery one single body."[147]

Alencar, whose positions in Parliament were even more reactionary than those in his writings, accused the abolitionists of being "emissaries of revolution, apostles of anarchy." The movement, according to Alencar, was on the wrong side of history and, deplorably, the government was following it. "You are the reactionaries," he cried, "who want to pull back the progress of the country, hurting its heart, killing its first industry, agriculture." Alencar claimed that the Brazilian planters, as true lovers of freedom, were patiently preparing their slaves to become useful free laborers and good citizens. The abolitionists and the Rio Branco administration, on the other hand, "believe that to free means only to subtract captivity, and do not remember that freedom conceded to these brute masses is a fatal gift, it is sacred fire handed to the impetus, to the audacity, of a new and savage Prometheus!" The result of hasty emancipation, he feared, would be racial war in Brazil.[148]

But the reactionaries had very weak arguments when confronting the unambiguous example of the United States: most Brazilian politicians knew that slave emancipation had already proven a boon to capitalism in North America. Now, they acted to make sure this process would come gradually to Brazil. A legislative committee charged with studying the Rio Branco bill lamented that "some important members of our respectable agricultural class have been induced to believe that these measures will cause their ruin." The enemies of reform had no reason to worry: "Were not the northern states without slavery more civilized and richer than the southern states of the American Union, when the latter tolerated the institution?"[149]

A member of the committee, Joaquim Pinto de Campos, presented a detailed comparison between the two regions of the antebellum United States to Parliament. In cultivated area, agricultural productivity, commerce, manufacturing, and property value, he argued, "the superiority of the states without slaves to the states with slaves is indubitable." Before the Civil War, Pinto de Campos pointed out, the slave states seemed more like a colony of the free states: "The South sent to the North its raw materials, its coarse products, and got them back manufactured, and consequently having the value many times multiplied." Using quantitative data from *De Bow's Review*—which, Brazilian politicians knew, was anything but an abolitionist publication—Pinto de Campos demonstrated that the free states had proportionally more schools, universities, libraries, and newspapers than the slave states. "Every ten years," he continued, "the census demonstrated to the country and to the whole world the heinous evil that slavery represented. The South had ears but could not hear, to comprehend and to save itself, and it was necessary to wage a tremendous war to convince it of its sin." The message to Brazilian slaveholders was clear: "History and statistics are here. It is our choice now either to ignore this lesson . . . or to take advantage of it, being wise."[150]

Focusing on the discourse of Union leaders and their foreign allies, scholars conclude that the conflict in North America engendered a new era of democratic reform in the Western world.[151] But the American Civil War had another, more consequential, international dimension. The Brazilian political elite pushed aside the democratic message of the Union and instead focused on its economic might. And even those who favored major political change in monarchical Brazil understood that the free North had triumphed because it had an economic system superior to that of the slave South. Rio Branco, Tavares Bastos, and other Brazilians knew very well that an industrial society based on wage labor—and not an egalitarian utopia—had won the war against the rebellion of slaveholders.

In Brazil of the early 1870s, the political elite successfully set their country on the path to adopt the system of labor that had made the American North into a capitalist power. Although they disagreed on how to achieve emancipation, moderates and radicals all looked north to the United States and saw that antislavery reform was a means to insert Brazil in the age of industrial capitalism without causing social disruption. Antislavery reformers all, they spoke the language of progress and sought to tighten bonds with the American North.

Rio Branco's bill was signed into law on September 28, 1871. Celebrations followed, and the streets of Rio de Janeiro were strewn with flowers. According to a local observer, the new US minister to Brazil, James R. Partridge, "present at this splendid celebration of freedom, ordered that some flowers be picked up, saying that he would send them to the United States. Some say that the illustrious diplomat, full of enthusiasm, exclaimed: 'I want people in my country to know that what has cost much spilled blood there, in Brazil only cost flowers.'"[152]

In reality, much more than flowers had been necessary to make Brazilian legislators pass the Law of the Free Womb. For over a decade, Partridge's compatriots had been working alongside Brazilian antislavery forces to push for change in Brazil. Their concerted activism—and their defense of free labor—had sparked the process of emancipation in that country. Although conservative forces had hijacked the radical project, the seeds that the modernizers had planted would continue to germinate. In the wake of the Law of the Free Womb, an intense circulation of people between Brazil and the United States would bring the two countries even closer together. This circulation would allow antislavery Northerners to expand their enterprises in Brazil and help Brazilian elites adapt the postwar American model of development to their own needs.

PART II

The World That Free Labor Made

I looked at the mirror, went from one side to another, took a step back, gesticulated, smiled, and the glass expressed everything. I was an automaton no longer; I was an animated being. From that day on, I was another person.

—MACHADO DE ASSIS, 1882

4

Into the Coffee Kingdom

FOLLOWING THE DOWNFALL of the Confederacy, Joel E. Matthews, an Alabama cotton planter, traveled to Brazil. There, he expected to find "many of the peculiarities of social society which result from the ownership of slaves, which to me are so pleasant and agreeable, and to which I had all my life been accustomed." Matthews indeed found many hospitable Brazilian gentlemen who held slaves. Yet he also found many things that made him anxious. Brazilian society, he noted, "now has paper money, four short railways, wants more of them, and talks much of developing the resources." He warned the Brazilians about the great evils to come if they continued along the road of modernization: "Like all things which come from Satan this is often shown to the world under many pleasing and alluring devices"; soon, however, all innovations would gather under "a blood-red banner, with the words 'Rapine, Robbery and Blood' inscribed on it with letters of fire." Finally, in a stage "no stranger to us of the Rebel States" of the American South, economic development would result in "destruction, desolation and death" in Brazil.[1] Matthews returned to Alabama and stayed there, but many other Americans, from the North and the South, tried their luck in Brazil between the 1860s and the 1870s. Whether they planned it or not, they ended up advancing the very modernization that had terrified Matthews.

The United States experienced tumultuous transformations during the early years of Reconstruction. Benefiting from wartime economic expansion, scientific and technological advancements, and political hegemony, the industrial North thrust forward. Older industries, such as steel, went through a rebirth, while newer ones, such as oil, consolidated. Northern merchants, financiers, and industrialists expanded their influence across the country. There was very little that Northern capital failed to touch.[2] Meanwhile, in the South, planters and yeoman farmers faced hardship. The rebellion cost hundreds of thousands of lives and millions of dollars in property losses, not the least property in slaves. Plantations, farms, and towns were devastated. White Southerners dreaded vengeful freedpeople and invading Yankees. But what really deranged the postwar South were marauding bands and terrorist organizations composed of their own kind.[3] Whether emboldened by success or frustrated by defeat, Americans got on the move. Whereas most moved within the United States, many sought new opportunities abroad.

Brazilian society also faced major changes between the late 1860s and early 1870s. Complications in the Paraguayan War, the emergence of an abolitionist movement, and political reform shook the country. Yet, in the midst of growing agitation, the Brazilian economy received a great boost. Trees of *Coffea arabica* grew at an astonishing rate on the new agricultural frontier of the province of São Paulo. A marginal region surviving on a mixture of sugar and subsistence farming until then, the Oeste Paulista, the plateau northwest of São Paulo City, was on its way to become the leading coffee-producing region in the world.[4] Although slave labor fueled this boom, the *fazendeiros* knew that the termination of the African slave trade in 1850, the low birth rate and the high mortality rate of the slave population, widespread antislavery feelings, and the effects of the Law of the Free Womb would sooner or later bring slavery to an end in Brazil.[5] Furthermore, many of them were convinced that in time the wage system would prove to be more profitable than slavery in coffee agriculture. Hence, they prepared for the transition to free labor by adopting labor-saving machinery and diversifying the economy.[6]

During the coffee boom, the province of São Paulo attracted hundreds of Anglo-Americans. Most of them came from the American South. As soon as the Confederacy was dissolved, a large group of ex-Confederates decided to move to the Oeste Paulista in order to revive a way of life based on slavery and plantation agriculture.[7] But their project clashed with that of the local elite, who planned to transform the newcomers into sharecroppers or smallholders employing free labor. Not long after the ex-Confederates, a man named William Van Vleck Lidgerwood, the machine manufacturer from New Jersey who had served as US chargé d'affaires in Rio de Janeiro, arrived in the Oeste Paulista. Following the coffee money, he first opened an office and, soon after, established a factory in the town of Campinas.

While Lidgerwood Mfg. Co. Ltd. became a powerhouse by producing agricultural machines and setting up textile mills in the Oeste Paulista, the community of ex-Confederates could hardly make ends meet by growing cotton and foodstuffs. As time wore on, they became completely dependent on the

The Province of São Paulo in the 1860s-1870s

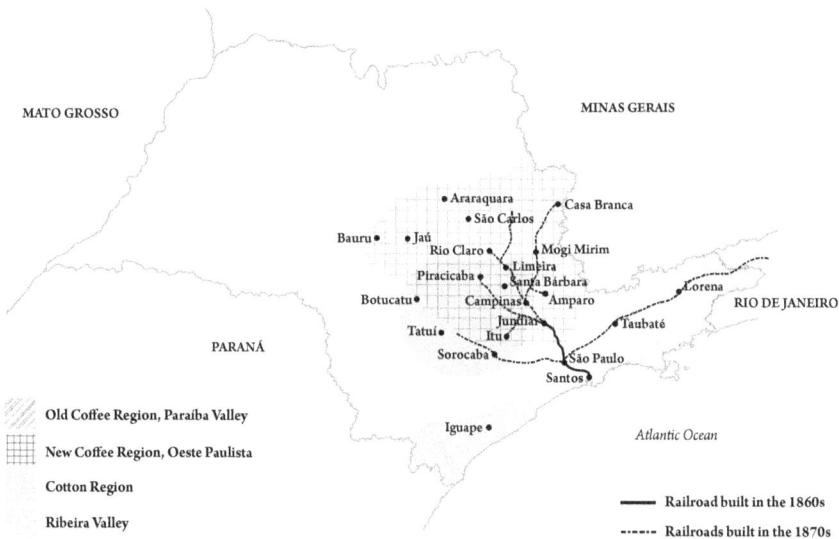

FIGURE 4.1

fazendeiros. Some of them supplemented their income by working on railroad construction and other odd jobs; others, who had the training, found employment as country doctors. The plight of the ex-Confederates, however, did not discourage other Anglo-Americans from trying their luck in the Oeste Paulista. Northern and Southern Protestant missionaries, besides attending to their compatriots, saw an opportunity to establish private schools in the region. Before long, the fazendeiros were sending their children to these institutions, expecting that the American missionaries would prepare them for the new era opening for Brazil.

When surveying shifts in foreign relations during the post–Civil War years, scholars draw a rigid line separating the United States from Latin America. National interests seem to have outdone all other interests, and Americans seem to have embraced the attitudes of Old World empires in relation to undeveloped countries.[8] Yet the rise of the United States to the status of a capitalist power in the late nineteenth century was not a unilateral act. The wealthiest planters in Brazil—one of the most powerful elites of Latin America—actively attracted American men and women to their region in order to modernize production, diversify the economy, and spread formal education. By complying with the projects of the local elite, the newcomers advanced the transition from slave to free labor in the Oeste Paulista. Willingly or not, the Americans contributed to the widening of the divide between the owners of capital and a growing class of impoverished workers in Brazil. What happened in the Oeste Paulista during the 1860s and 1870s was a process of class transformation fueled by American technology and expertise. As they engaged with the fazendeiros, Americans learned invaluable lessons in how to promote the interests of capital on a hemispheric scale.

Cotton and Confederates

In April 1861, John James Aubertin, the superintendent of the São Paulo Railway Co. Ltd., shipped to Manchester a few cotton bolls that he had collected from lands on the shore of the Tietê River, close to São Paulo City. Since 1857, when it was created, the Manchester Cotton Supply Association (MCSA) had been searching for cotton producers who could ease British manufacturers' reliance on cotton planters from the American South. By 1861, as the secession crisis exploded in the United States, the MCSA intensified its search, turning to Egypt, India, Brazil, and other parts of the world. Throughout the 1860s, Aubertin worked for the MCSA distributing cottonseed and cotton gins to São Paulo agriculturalists, who soon began to export cotton.[9]

Even though the MCSA claimed that the "striking success" of cotton cultivation in São Paulo "was mainly attributable to the zealous and persevering exertions of Mr. Aubertin," he had not been acting alone.[10] In fact, Aubertin had been collaborating with Brazilian authorities, who coordinated a campaign to foster cotton cultivation in the region.[11] In his 1862 report to the São Paulo Legislative Assembly, the provincial president remarked that "the recent events in the United States of America, which discontinued the exportation of the cotton that fed the factories in Europe, producing a true crisis there, gave evidence of the great value of this product and convinced us that the farmer who employs himself in this cultivation will not fail to receive good compensation."[12] Already in 1861, the provincial government had created a practical school for cotton cultivation on the *fazenda* of Carlos Ilidro da Silva, an amateur agronomist, in the township of Itu. The region between Itu and Sorocaba, sixty miles distant from São Paulo City, soon became the cotton-growing center of Brazil.[13] By late 1865, a visitor to Sorocaba observed that "one who enters this happy town will soon realize that it is a land of labor and industry. At the entrance, a facility for packing and seeding cotton; ahead, another one, powered by steam; at the center, yet another; not to mention those in the surrounding areas, totaling eighteen to twenty."[14]

While São Paulo cotton was blooming, the cotton kingdom in North America was in upheaval. Immediately following Robert E. Lee's surrender, dozens of white men fled the region in search of a new home for themselves and their kin. Brazil was their primary foreign destination. Their ulterior motives were very clear to contemporary observers. "A pioneer company of planters," a Northern reporter noted, "disgusted with 'free niggers,' the United States Government, the defeat, and everything connected with the country, were about to sail for Brazil, taking with them farming utensils and provisions for six months."[15]

The first visitors from the American South were welcomed by the same people who had been fostering cotton agriculture in São Paulo. Aubertin was responsible for taking three South Carolinians on a tour of the interior in December 1865. Aubertin's guests were James McFadden Gaston, Robert Meriwether, and H. A. Shaw, all of whom had served in the Confederate Army. Shaw and Meriwether had been cotton planters before the American Civil War, and Gaston had dedicated himself to medicine. Aubertin took the South Carolinians to Itu, Sorocaba, and nearby townships, where they enjoyed the hospitality of figures such as Antonio Paes de Barros, the Baron of Piracicaba, one of the richest coffee planters of the Oeste Paulista.[16]

The son-in-law of the Baron of Piracicaba was Antonio Francisco de Paula Souza. The scion of a planter family from Itu, he had studied medicine in Belgium, joined the Liberal Party, entered the Chamber of Deputies, and become a member of the Council of State.[17] In 1865, he ascended to minister of agriculture, commerce, and public works and gave full support for Louis Agassiz's exploration of the Amazon. At the same time, he set to work on attracting ex-Confederates to São Paulo. Upon arrival, Gaston met with Paula Souza, who promised that the Brazilian government was devising "a plan for assisting those who were desirous of coming to Brazil from the Southern States."[18] The Reverend Ballard S. Dunn, former rector of St. Phillip's Church in New Orleans and chaplain in the Confederate Army, also enjoyed the minister's warm welcome soon after he disembarked: "The genial sunshine of generous friendliness, offered by a minister of State, had a singular effect, and I was foolish enough to shed tears."[19] Paula Souza instructed the provincial president to supply the ex-Confederates with everything they needed and hired geographers to accompany the exploration parties.[20]

Local leaders were also excited about the prospects of immigration from the American South. A delegation from the township of Araraquara, located on the farthest agricultural frontier of the Oeste Paulista then, told Gaston to "rest assured that we will receive you as brothers receive brothers."[21] A fazendeiro from Jaú, another distant township of the Oeste Paulista, was glad to inform Paula Souza that "the Americans who have been here thought all was very good and promised to come here and already have land arrangements somewhat set."[22] Richard Gumbleton Daunt, an Irish medical doctor who had been living in Campinas since the 1840s, wrote to Paula Souza that "all the people are profoundly thankful to Your Excellency for the way in which the idea of immigration of the people from the former Confederate States is developing." Daunt further reported that the visitors had been placed in the houses of the richest inhabitants of Campinas.[23]

Returning to North America in early 1866, the Southern travelers published narratives that emphasized the wealth and the friendliness of the fazendeiros. At Joaquim Bonifácio do Amaral's Sete Quedas plantation near Campinas, Gaston was served a banquet. After eating, his host took him on a tour of the fazenda. "Here we saw the coffee trees in full bearing," he recalled, "planted in lines and squares. . . . The appearance of this field gives evidence of much careful attention."[24] Gaston was also impressed by José Vergueiro's Ibicaba plantation in the township of Limeira. Surrounded by blooming coffee trees, Gaston was delighted to observe the lifestyle of his host, who combined "all the various interests that conduce to the comfort of his family and the welfare of the large number of colonists and slaves who are dependent upon his supplies. His extensive fazenda is emphatically a self-sustaining establishment, and he lives within himself to a very large extent."[25]

The Oeste Paulista, the Southern visitors agreed unanimously, offered great incentives to their countrymen willing to grow cotton. Writing for *De Bow's Review* in 1866, Shaw and Meriwether maintained that, while exploring the farmlands of São Paulo, "we saw cotton that would make one thousand pounds an acre, or more. . . . We also saw cotton gins at work, driven by steam, by water and by hand. All the cotton here is of good quality."[26] At Ibicaba, Gaston observed that "the production of cotton here already is stated to reach two thousand pounds of seed cotton to the acre." Gaston thus urged his compatriots to take advantage of the opportunity: "Note this, ye planters of cotton in the Southern States, and think how painstaking you are to develop the growth of cotton in its several stages; yet here, in Brazil, it grows and matures well without culture of any kind."[27] In Sorocaba, Dunn "saw specimens of cotton in the field, equal to any I have ever seen in the United States. This is emphatically the cotton-growing region of Brazil, and only needs the appliances of labor and improved culture to make it profitable indeed."[28] The ex-Confederates believed that Anglo-Saxon cotton planters, who had once expanded from the Carolinas to Texas, could easily convert São Paulo into a new cotton kingdom.[29]

It was not only the prospect of producing cotton, however, that pleased the first ex-Confederates who visited São Paulo. The prospect of growing cotton using slave labor was what truly thrilled them.[30] Gaston observed that, along with the natural advantages that Brazil presented, "the additional element of slave labor here is likely to afford results that cannot be secured by hired labor in the United States."[31] Dunn assured prospective settlers that, in Brazil, "any foreigner, no matter where he may be from, can hold as many slaves as he is able to buy."[32] Shaw and Meriwether thought that, if unable to buy slaves on arrival, their countrymen could at first lease them in Brazil: "Some gangs of negroes, including men, women and children, [are] being offered by the year for fifty dollars each, though the usual price is from sixty to a hundred and twenty."[33]

The Southern visitors trusted that Brazilian elites would not only offer the settlers an opportunity to own slaves but also protect their rights as masters. As Dunn put it, in Brazil, "the rights of property, as guaranteed in the constitution, are carried out to the letter" and no one, not even a man "with the highest title of nobility" would ever "presume to enter the humblest dwelling, without first asking permission; and should permission be withheld, he does not enter, except at his own peril." In Brazil, Dunn exulted, each man was "lord supreme, in his own domicile; however humble or lowly it may be."[34] This idea would resonate with many ex-Confederates who decided to settle in Brazil in the following years. There, they hoped to rebuild a patriarchal society in which the white man was supreme ruler of his land, family, and slaves.[35]

Laying bare the ex-Confederates' plans, in July 1868, "a Southern Gentleman" wrote to the Rio de Janeiro *Anglo-Brazilian Times* that "the Southern slaveholder has eminent executive and administrative qualities that make him an acquisition and an extremely valuable one to any country having analogous conditions." Slave labor, he claimed, had been perfected in the antebellum American South: "As a race, the condition of the negro slaves in the Southern States of the North American Union had steadily and gradually been modified and ameliorated, till they in truth presented to the world the happiest mere laboring community on a large scale that the world has ever seen." If any doubts remained of what kind of service the ex-Confederates could offer Brazil, the proslavery writer clarified that "it is this class of men, men accustomed to such agriculture, possessed of such executive capacities, active and energetic managers of a labor incidentally analogous to what is now and will be for a long time most abundant in Brazil, that I conceive to be most needed in this Empire."[36]

The American Civil War had destroyed slavery in North America. Unwilling to accept defeat, several ex-Confederates visited Brazil in search of lands where their kin could, once again, become plantation owners and slaveholders. In the province of São Paulo, they saw land suitable for cotton cultivation, slaves for sale or hire, and rich coffee planters who had their arms open to foreigners. The ex-Confederates' movement to resettle in Brazil represented an attempt to revive the slave South abroad. Thousands would embark on the adventure; but none would succeed in replicating the slave South in Brazil.

The Clash

In a series of articles published in 1865, the *Diário de São Paulo* speculated that the ex-Confederates would bring "into the midst of our shameful backwardness, their agricultural improvements; into the midst of the traditional darkness that surrounds our agriculture, the light of experience."[37] The rivers of the interior would be "taken by the same small steamers that are used in the United States," the markets of the province would be "enriched by all products necessary to life," "great steam-powered sawmills" would convert local wood into American-style furniture, and "the rich cotton farms" of the ex-Confederates would give birth to textile mills in São Paulo.[38] Communities of Anglo-Saxons would emerge alongside new railroads, "spreading wealth all over the province, covering our frontier with free hands and useful citizens."[39] It became clear from the very beginning that the men who were welcoming the ex-Confederates nurtured plans to use their labor and skills in the process of phasing out slavery and advancing free labor in the Oeste Paulista.

The fazendeiros planned to either sell or lease the uncultivated parts of their own estates to the newcomers who possessed some capital. For those arriving without means, the *Correio Paulistano* suggested employment as sharecroppers. The fazendeiros should understand that "they will gain incomparably more by handing to the immigrants their uncultivated lands than by conserving them under the shadow of primitive forests, as a poorly understood reserve." By employing sharecroppers, the fazendeiro would get "half of what is produced by his new associate—the immigrant." Anyone who inquired "into the balance between the benefits and the costs of American immigration," the *Correio Paulistano* concluded, would easily see that "the profits to be obtained are very significant."[40] Ultimately, the understanding in São Paulo was that the ex-Confederates would occupy marginal—though not isolated—lands of the province either as smallholders, tenants, or sharecroppers, producing crops other than coffee and relying on the goodwill of the local elite.

While the fazendeiros made their plans, Paula Souza acted in the Ministry of Agriculture, Commerce, and Public Works. In October 1865, he wrote to his son, who was studying engineering in Germany, that he was expecting to receive more than fifty thousand immigrants from North America. "We will suddenly have an immense influx of energy, industry, and morality," he envisioned, "and my name may one day be connected to the most beautiful page of our history, if we couple this [immigration] with other reforms."[41] Paula Souza considered establishing communities of ex-Confederates in the Oeste Paulista as part of a comprehensive program to modernize the region. In his 1866 report to Parliament, he spoke of immigration in connection to slave emancipation: "Experience demonstrates that immigration, and the consequent emergence of a market in free labor, will not develop alongside servile labor; when demand [for free labor] does not exist, it cannot emerge." The settlement of ex-Confederates in São Paulo, Paula Souza hoped, would establish "relations of free and industrious labor, which will produce immigration on a scale never seen before."[42]

In June 1866, the editor of the Rio de Janeiro *Anglo-Brazilian Times*, an Irishman named William Scully, lauded Paula Souza for "seeing in servile labor the deepest blot upon the moral and political constitution of this otherwise free and liberally governed country" and for seeking gradual means "to exterminate the evil." Moreover, Paula Souza's effort "to facilitate the settlement of immigrants, whether rich or poor, has been manifested in a most praise-worthy and liberal manner." Two years later, Scully remained hopeful that "although the Southern States of North America will not supply the labor market of the agriculture of the Empire, great results indirectly advantaging the supply may be derived from it, namely valuable examples of labor-saving farming, and numerous experts to direct and utilize the skilled laborers of European immigration."[43]

To the immigration promoters, cotton seemed to be the perfect crop to propel the transition from slave to free labor in Brazil. As Ilidro da Silva observed in 1861, the required capital to start a cotton farm was "of insignificant amount in comparison to what is necessary for the cultivation of coffee and sugar cane."[44] In addition to requiring a modest investment, as Scully put it in 1866, cotton "is a staple which is well adapted to the capabilities of white labor and small proprietorship. . . . Children and women can assist in planting and harvesting without tasking their powers too strongly."[45] A poor man's crop in

the land of coffee, cotton would be fit for foreign farmers who were not supposed to own large estates or many slaves.

The association between ex-Confederate immigration and the advancement of free labor was so clear to elite Brazilians that none other than the abolitionist leader Aureliano Candido Tavares Bastos jumped on the bandwagon.
In 1865, he organized the Sociedade Internacional de Imigração (International
Immigration Society; SII) to assist in the settlement of ex-Confederates.[46] In
his first report, Tavares Bastos noted that Brazil should prepare for "the crisis
that will follow the inevitable abolition of slavery" by attracting immigrants,
who would increase "the number of producers, consumers, and tax-payers,
mitigating the effects of this crisis." Confident as usual, he guaranteed that "the
farmers from the Southern States will meet the need for intelligent and bold
agriculturalists" in Brazil.[47]

Having Paula Souza as an associate, the SII became the unofficial organ of
the Brazilian government to promote the settlement of ex-Confederates.[48]
Tavares Bastos and Paula Souza worked together to obtain free passage for the
exploring parties on river steamships and railroads.[49] Tavares Bastos also mediated an agreement between the Brazilian government and the United States
and Brazilian Steamship Company to subsidize the trip of those interested in
leaving the American South for Brazil.[50] By mid-1866, the SII sent Quintino
Antonio Ferreira de Souza Bocaiuva, the journalist known for his antislavery
stands, to New York City, whence he would promote Brazil as a new home for
ex-Confederates. Paula Souza was pleased and personally wrote to Bocaiuva
asking for books on American monetary policy and "any work on cotton
cultivation, its diseases, and the making of oil from cottonseed and machines for it."[51]

But things did not pan out as Tavares Bastos and Paula Souza had planned.
As soon as Bocaiuva got to New York and spoke with ex-Confederates waiting
for steamship passage to Brazil, he had a change of heart. In an open letter to
Brazilian newspapers, Bocaiuva explained why he decided not to direct ex-
Confederates to his country.

> We want to prepare for the future, and the near future of the country is
> emancipation. God shall permit it to happen soon and without trouble. We
> also want to address the question of the present, and the question of the
> present is the replacement of the slave hand. Thus, here I offer my thoughts.
> The man of the South, ruined landowner who saves from the shipwreck the
> rubble of his fortune, accustomed to servile labor and having, like us

[Brazilians], all the bad habits acquired from this system, will never till the earth and spread the seed himself. He needs and will search for helpers, workers, machine-men, he will be the intelligence and the experience that will direct them. I have learned on my own that all of them hope to find and request slaves for rent. You know that this is impossible in the present situation of our country.[52]

Bocaiuva understood that the ex-Confederates were not planning to change their habits in Brazil. But his warning fell on deaf ears. While he was in New York, Paula Souza died unexpectedly. The new minister of agriculture, commerce, and public works, Manoel Pinto de Souza Dantas, a Liberal senator from Bahia, wrote to Bocaiuva that the Brazilian government was "convinced that the most convenient immigration to this Empire is that composed of individuals accustomed to cultivating the land . . . as the inhabitants of the Southern States are." The new instruction to Bocaiuva was to "immediately transfer residence from New York to New Orleans" and convince cotton planters to move to Brazil.[53]

Unwilling to fulfill his task, Bocaiuva returned bitter and disappointed to Brazil. But, by early 1867, Dantas had elaborated his own immigration scheme, contracting directly with agents from the American South, who would purchase or lease lands in Brazil and bring their own parties of settlers.[54] Unlike his predecessor in the Ministry of Agriculture, Commerce, and Public Works, Dantas planned to scatter the newcomers all over the country. Already in November 1865, he had written to Paula Souza criticizing his exclusive focus on the Oeste Paulista as a destination for the ex-Confederates: "Don't be parochial, see that we [in Bahia] also offer these wonderful American colonists lands in great locations."[55] Sponsored by Dantas, settlements of ex-Confederates emerged in isolated regions of northern and southeastern Brazil.

Charles Grandison Gunter, a cotton planter from Alabama, arrived in Brazil with plans to "buy a place with 50 or 100 slaves if suited in soil and situation, price etc."[56] By August 1866, Gunter had "rented 6000 acres of good land at Linhares on the Rio Doce," province of Espírito Santo, which he planned to distribute among his countrymen. To work his piece of land, Gunter bought forty slaves for "$12,500 half cash and one year without interest—which is considered cheap here."[57] Yet despite Gunter's investment, his settlement would not endure. Julia Keyes, whose family had left Alabama to join the Doce colony, lamented that the first crops all "failed from the unusual drought."

Worse, tropical diseases affected both masters and slaves. "Those who had bought negroes for farming," she narrated, "were most anxious to leave as they were having chills and generally disabled." Soon, the settlers became "nearly all discouraged," and most left the Doce.[58]

Lansford Warren Hastings, a proslavery land surveyor who had plotted to bring New Mexico and Arizona into the Confederacy during the Civil War, planned to establish a settlement in Santarém, in the heart of the Brazilian Amazon. When he advertised his immigration scheme, he highlighted that in Brazil, "considering the comparative scarcity of slaves, they are very cheap; excellent, able-bodied men and women can be purchased at prices ranging from three to six hundred dollars each."[59] By the mid-1870s, when an American naturalist visited the ruins of the Santarém colony, he learned that the settlement had attracted "a rabble of lazy vagabonds, offscourings of the army and vagrants of Mobile, who looked upon the affair as a grand adventure." A settler from Tennessee lamented that, after having "to struggle with utter poverty," the few ex-Confederates who had stayed in the Amazon survived by producing rum, but their product never fetched a good price. He complained that "the Santarem traders take advantage of his helplessness." After years of hard work, the ex-Confederate possessed one slave, a small farm, "a burden of debts that will take him a long time to pay," and "a broken-down body and a discouraged heart."[60]

William Bowen, a cotton planter from Texas, established a settlement in the Ribeira Valley, a region of dense rainforest between southern São Paulo and northeastern Paraná. Bowen acquired slaves and began to cultivate cotton. As early as 1867, though, he started petitioning the provincial government for a road connecting the settlement to larger towns, "as my people have no way to get to market."[61] Besides facing isolation and poverty, the colony became rife with conflict. In a report to provincial authorities, Bowen claimed that some of his countrymen had "left the settlement in account of scarcity of provisions and also on account of efforts made by one G. S. Barnsley at [the township of] Iguape to get into his possession the affairs of the colony."[62]

George Scarborough Barnsley, a physician from Georgia who had served as an assistant surgeon in the Confederate Cavalry, had helped Bowen start the settlement but soon accused him of mismanagement and corruption. In June 1868, Barnsley penned a letter to his father explaining why Bowen's and other colonies of ex-Confederates were facing difficulties in Brazil.

Colonies in unhealthy localities have all failed and all speculations to that end have gone by the board; for very patent reasons: 1st The present age does not permit colonization in bodies for the benefit of one man who becomes a kind of Baron or Feudal Lord; 2nd The Southern people are too poor to settle sickly fertile lands, where they cannot work for themselves; 3rd There must be transportation. . . . The great curse of many of our people is that they come here . . . [and] find that the streets are not paved with gold nor the acute Brazilian ready to open his coffers to every stranger.[63]

The likes of Gunter, Hastings, and Bowen proved Bocaiuva right: most ex-Confederates were indeed moving to Brazil with plans to form their own communities of slaveholders. Yet as Barnsley explained, expensive slaves, isolated settlements, tropical diseases, and lack of resources prevented the emergence of plantation communities ruled by Anglo-Saxon masters in Brazil.

The intentions of the ex-Confederates who resettled in Brazil had clashed with the Brazilian vision of the future. Still, Dantas and others, disagreeing with radical abolitionists like Bocaiuva, insisted on settling Brazilian lands with agriculturalists from the American South who knew how to grow cotton. They made it clear from the outset, however, that Brazil would not extend a helping hand to newcomers who sought to perpetuate the institution of slavery within their enclosed communities. On the contrary, those sponsoring the ex-Confederates wanted them to become small farmers employing the labor of family members or other immigrants. Not surprisingly, the Santarém, the Doce, and the Ribeira colonies crumbled.

Like earlier attempts by proslavery expansionists to establish influence abroad, the ex-Confederates' plan to resurrect the slave South in Brazil was a fiasco. Even after losing the Civil War, old habits endured; and men like Gunter, Hastings, and Bowen were incapable of understanding that the Brazilians wanted nothing to do with proslavery communities. The Santarém, the Doce, and the Ribeira settlements were last-ditch efforts of a project of global dominance that failed time and again to materialize. After all, proslavery expansionism had long been out of touch with a changing world. The Southern proslavery utopia died twice: in the battlefields of North America and in the jungles of Brazil.[64]

Mechanizing the Coffee Kingdom

Not all settlements of ex-Confederates had a catastrophic fate. Struggling immigrants soon heard the news that some of their compatriots were thriving. In December 1866, Gunter's youngest son wrote to his brother in Alabama that he wished their father had "settled on the high lands of S. Paulo instead of the Doce."[65] By June 1868, Barnsley had heard that, "in São Paulo, in the serra-acima country—that is on the great elevated table lands of the interior—the crops have been good and the health excellent."[66] Keyes had also heard about the settlement where the ex-Confederates had "their own schools and churches. In and around Campinas are the points."[67] All three were referring to the settlement of ex-Confederates on the plateau northwest of São Paulo City. At the same time that the immigrants were arriving at the Oeste Paulista, rapid economic development was taking place and new opportunities were emerging for those who would adapt to new demands.

Rich in iron oxide and nitrogen, the *terra roxa* (red soil) of the Oeste Paulista could sustain large coffee crops without much preparation. The global market for coffee was expanding quickly as industrialization made employers seek a stimulant that would keep the proletarian masses working on strenuous and repetitive tasks without becoming rowdy.[68] The American Civil War also had given a great boost to the coffee trade as the Union Army issued an average of thirty-six pounds of coffee per soldier each year.[69] Moreover, the two main competitors of the Oeste Paulista, the British colony of Ceylon and the (not so distant) Paraíba Valley, were facing rapid decline because of pests and soil exhaustion.[70]

Declining competitors, expanding markets, and good soil notwithstanding, a structural impediment haunted the Oeste Paulista: labor shortage. Because the African slave trade to Brazil had ended in the early 1850s, the solution closest at hand was the domestic slave trade. By buying slaves from declining agricultural regions and non-plantation areas of Brazil, the fazendeiros of the Oeste Paulista were becoming the largest slaveholders of the country. Yet they were aware that the slave population was decreasing, abolitionist agitation was starting to pick up steam, and the Brazilian government was moving toward gradual emancipation.[71] Moreover, attentive observers of the world around them, many fazendeiros came to recognize slavery as an element of backwardness that should sooner or later be replaced by free labor. As the historian Barbara Weinstein argues, "For these men, the question was not only whether slavery was profitable, but whether it could form a firm and enduring basis for a prosperous, progressive, and cohesive society. Even before the Rio Branco Law [of the Free Womb] (1871) made abolition inevitable, many of these men would have answered the question in the negative."[72]

It did not take long for fazendeiros like Joaquim Bonifácio do Amaral and José Vergueiro to begin experimenting with free immigrant labor in the Oeste

Paulista. Members of the Liberal Party, they nurtured reformist views similar to those of Paula Souza. As early as the 1840s, the Vergueiro and Amaral families started employing Portuguese, German, and Swiss immigrants at Ibicaba and Sete Quedas. Each family of *colonos*—as rural immigrants were called in Brazil then—was responsible for tending a specific grove of coffee trees. After harvest, they were paid half of the proceeds from sale.[73] But this early experiment in free labor did not bring the expected results. Poorly treated by Brazilian supervisors, feeling cheated by the fazendeiros and the merchants, and unable to accumulate enough money to acquire their own lands, the Swiss and Germans began demonstrating discontent. In late 1856 the Ibicaba immigrants went on strike, which Brazilian authorities repressed with brutality. Only a few hundred colonos remained on the fazendas of the Oeste Paulista thereafter.[74]

Little (if at all) concerned about the welfare of their workers, the modernizers did not feel discouraged by the failure of the first sharecropping experiments in the Oeste Paulista. On the contrary, the fazendeiros soon turned to another means to mitigate their dependence on slave labor: agricultural machinery. When Gaston visited Amaral's fazenda, he saw "all the most recent improvements for treating the coffee." The coffee hulling machines, Gaston learned, received "the coffee directly from the tree, without any preliminary process of drying." Gaston watched the steam-powered revolving cylinders remove the outside hull of the coffee berry and then drop the coffee beans into tanks, which used percolation to remove debris and unripe coffee. The coffee beans were then taken to a cement terrace to dry for a few days. Gaston saw the same coffee hullers at Vergueiro's fazenda. The processed coffee was "entirely free from dust or any foreign matter, and the proprietor states will command from two to five cents per pound more than the rolled or pounded coffee."[75]

Prior to the adoption of coffee hullers, the preparation of the picked coffee was the most labor-intensive stage of production. In order to remove debris, the slaves had first to wash the coffee berries by hand. After washing, they took the berries to dry in the sun. The slaves then had to stir the berries several times a day and store them between dusk and dawn to prevent damage from dew. Depending on the weather, the process could take several weeks, and an unexpected rain could ruin everything. Once both the outer shell and the pulp were dry, the coffee berries were taken to mortars to be pounded. After pounding, the slaves used large manual fans to blow away the shells. Finally, the coffee beans were spread on tables and hand sorted.[76]

Machine-processed coffee required less time drying in the sun, and there was no need for pounding, fanning, or hand sorting it. Thanks to its superior quality, "machine coffee" sold for twice as much as "terrace coffee."[77] More important, the fazendeiros reckoned that, if the heaviest kind of work on the fazendas could be performed by labor-saving machinery, it would be easier to employ free hands in coffee cultivation. In other words, the coffee hullers were integral part of the fazendeiros' movement toward free labor.

The coffee hullers that revolutionized production on the great fazendas were imported by William Van Vleck Lidgerwood from his family's Speedwell Iron Works of Morristown, New Jersey. Although Lidgerwood did important diplomatic work for the US legation during the 1860s, his main occupation was selling agricultural machinery. In July 1862, a few weeks after he arrived in Brazil, Lidgerwood met with Dom Pedro II, who noted that he was a relative of "the owner of a great factory of agricultural implements and requests a privilege for the Walker machine, which cleans coffee beans and was very beneficial in Cuba."[78] Since the 1850s, Speedwell had been manufacturing the improved coffee hullers patented by the New York engineer Robert Porter Walker and selling them to Cuban plantations. It had also supplied Southern planters with implements for cotton cultivation.[79] Now it was Brazil's turn.

In addition to family capital, Lidgerwood counted on the expanding network connecting Brazilian and American interests. On the steamer to Rio de Janeiro, he wrote to his stepfather and business partner Stephen Vail that one of his travel companions was "Mr. Fletcher, the missionary traveler and writer, the one who wrote the book upon Brazil which I bought a couple of years since and which Pa will no doubt remember." A first-rate storyteller, James Cooley Fletcher quickly captivated Lidgerwood: "His society to me has been a great pleasure."[80] The author of *Brazil and the Brazilians* advised Lidgerwood to become a member of the Sociedade Auxiliadora da Indústria Nacional (Auxiliary Society of National Industry; SAIN), through which he applied for the exclusive privilege to import, manufacture, and sell the Walker coffee hullers in Brazil. By the end of 1862, Lidgerwood had acquired that privilege for a period of ten years.[81]

Lidgerwood shared Fletcher's sense of mission, believing that American influence would help Brazil phase out slavery without upheaval. Writing to his stepfather about his first trips to sell machinery in the Paraíba Valley, Lidgerwood confided that "I often compare your trips in those sailing vessels to the [American] South, when it was a comparative wilderness, to my being out here, with the same object, the introduction of machinery."[82] Like the antebellum American South, which had made his stepfather rich, Lidgerwood saw

Brazil as an unimproved agricultural society in need of the civilizing forces of machinery, railroads, and free labor.

At the SAIN, Lidgerwood met the antislavery reformers André Pinto Rebouças and Nicolau Joaquim Moreira, along with whom he created a plowing school at the Botanical Garden of Rio de Janeiro and engaged in other projects to improve Brazilian agriculture. As the historian Teresa Cribelli explains, "The central aim of the Sociedade Auxiliadora [SAIN] was the dissemination of the latest in scientific and technological advances, especially . . . for agricultural improvement and as a way to transition from slave to free labor."[83] Lidgerwood's association with the SAIN unequivocally put him on the side of antislavery reform in Brazil.

In January 1863, Lidgerwood opened a warehouse in Rio de Janeiro so the Brazilian public could see what he had to offer. "We observed with utmost interest," *O Auxiliador da Industria Nacional* reported, "the machines that can be used in this country, and provide a great service to our agriculturalists, always so plaintive about the lack of hands."[84] By September 1865, a *New York Herald* correspondent reported that "Mr. Van Vleck [Lidgerwood] is here looked upon as quite a public benefactor for having introduced so much useful machinery into the country of his adoption. . . . Mr. Lidgerwood is quite a favorite with all, and has become a member of the society for the encouragement and assistance of industry, of which the Emperor is patron."[85]

In his letters to Vail, Lidgerwood celebrated that Brazilians were "getting their eyes opened gradually to the improvements of the age."[86] He became particularly interested in a new railroad being built from the port of Santos to São Paulo City, "where they tell me is one of the most healthy spots in the world (city of about 40,000) and is the center of a large coffee growing region. Therefore, Pa can see that in a few years, or even in two or three years, what an impetus will be given to the agricultural resources and products of the interior of this country." Thrilled about the development of the Oeste Paulista, Lidgerwood told his stepfather that "there is a fine prospect here for business in coffee machinery, water wheels (turbines) for great falls, saw mills and small sugar mills and corn mills."[87]

Prior to the railroad, the cost of transporting coffee from the interior of São Paulo to the port of Santos could reach a staggering 60 percent of the total value of the product. Consequently, regions of good terra roxa too distant from the seacoast simply could not be profitably cultivated with coffee.[88] Railroad expansion transformed everything. In 1865, the São Paulo Railway Co. Ltd., whose superintendent was John James Aubertin, connected the port of Santos

FIGURE 4.2 "The Serra Viaduct, St. Paul's Railroad, Brazil," *Harper's Weekly*,
December 5, 1868. Courtesy of the University of Michigan Library,
Special Collections Research Center, Ann Arbor.

to the provincial capital. In 1868, it arrived in Jundiaí. Then, a group of rich fazendeiros created the Companhia Paulista, which would take the railroad line
to Campinas, Limeira, Rio Claro, São Carlos, and Araraquara before the close
of the 1880s. The new line drastically reduced transportation costs and encouraged the fazendeiros to spread coffee cultivation to new areas.[89]

Before long, the construction of the railroad into the São Paulo interior
made the news in the United States. In December 1868, *Harper's Weekly* published an engraving of an impressive railroad bridge and reported that "the
St. Paul's Railway in Brazil is one of the wonders of modern engineering." It
would soon connect the port of Santos to Campinas, "just in the basin which
is the best coffee-ground in Brazil." Although an English company was in
charge of building the first section, *Harper's Weekly* emphasized, "much of the
actual work was entrusted to the skill of experienced American contractors.
Messrs. D. H. Sampson, Samuel Driesback, O. C. James, and Dr. Reinhart are
among those of our countrymen who have been connected with it."[90]

The Lidgerwood machines arrived in the Oeste Paulista simultaneously with the railroad. In January 1868, the *Diário de São Paulo* applauded the adoption of coffee hullers in Limeira. "The coffee-processing machines from Lidgerwood's factory begin to be introduced among the planters of this township," the newspaper remarked. "Considering the notable economy of time and personnel added to the perfection and cleanliness of the product that comes out after processing," the coffee hullers would bring great benefits to the agriculture of the Oeste Paulista. The fazendeiro would now be able to process over six thousand pounds of coffee per day "with a small number of hands employed." In addition to saving labor, the excellent quality of the product would command high prices. The *Diário* was confident that "time will make the results clear and, in view of them, the planters will seek to equip themselves with these Lidgerwood machines."[91]

In May 1868, Lidgerwood opened an office in Campinas. He was quick to publicize his arrival, buying space in influential newspapers in order to publish statements from fazendeiros who had acquired his coffee hullers. One of them foresaw that, by purchasing Lidgerwood machines, "the planters will acquire several advantages and our agriculture will enjoy a benign influence." Another fazendeiro found the Lidgerwood machine excellent, and thus recommended "it to all planters, with much emphasis, being ready to show its workings on my plantation to whoever wants to see it."[92]

Lidgerwood achieved swift success in the Oeste Paulista. In 1871, the provincial president celebrated "the introduction of the American machines of Lidgerwood, very common in the province, which, despite their elevated price, offer great advantages; in order to understand these advantages one needs only to notice that, in [the port of] Santos, coffee processed by them, known as machine coffee, sells for 200 réis above any other."[93] In 1873, Manoel Ferraz de Campos Sales, a major fazendeiro in Campinas and leader of the local Republican Party, wrote a positive review for the local almanac, noting that "the first machine (Lidgerwood) to appear in the township [of Campinas] to replace the old system was established on the Anhumas plantation, which belonged to Vicente de Souza Queiroz, the Baron of Limeira." Campos Sales was enthusiastic about the widespread adoption of American technology in his region: "Upon the introduction of these new machines, our coffee, which was beginning to suffer in consumer markets because of its poor preparation, reconquered the preference that it deserved thanks to its excellent quality."[94]

But Lidgerwood had done more than bring his own machines to the Oeste Paulista. Campos Sales explained that "until recently, there was no other equipment for coffee processing in this township except the mortar and pestle; today, however, while it still prevails, new devices begin to be introduced, being worthy of note among them, for their degree of sophistication, those of the Lidgerwood system and those of the Conrado system."[95] The German brothers Bierrenbach, established in Campinas as hatmakers since the 1850s, were now manufacturing coffee hullers designed by the German inventor Johan Conrad Engelberg, known as Conrado machines. And they were not modest when it came to these machines, claiming that they were made "by the best system known to date, solid and economic, perfectly finished, and far superior to the American machines."[96] Thirty-three Lidgerwood machines and twenty-six Conrado machines could be found in Campinas by 1872.

Lidgerwood would relentlessly go after smaller manufacturers. From the time of his arrival in the Oeste Paulista, he had made clear that he and his agents were "inventors, proprietors, and the only privileged in the Empire to sell the coffee-cleaning devices known by the name *Lidgerwood Machines*." The competition should know that "any person who might make, sell, or use one of these machines, or counterfeit them, or even parts, without prior authorization from the proprietor or from his agents, will be prosecuted with all rigor of the law."[97] Already in 1868, Lidgerwood sued Engelberg, accusing him of infringing on the privilege obtained in 1862 and renewed, due to improvements, in 1867.

Engelberg defended himself by arguing that Lidgerwood was not the original inventor and did not manufacture his machines in Brazil. He further tried to demonstrate that the Conrado was distinct from the Walker system. After long discussions about cylinders, plates, springs, and screws, in 1871 Lidgerwood obtained a first-instance victory based on the 1830 Brazilian Law of Patents, which protected inventors and introducers alike. The production of the Conrado machines was halted, and the defendant was ordered to pay Lidgerwood for his losses. At the Campinas Courthouse, Engelberg's lawyer offered a sardonic account of Lidgerwood's triumph: "Give passage, interests of agriculture; give way, national conveniences; open the road, public needs; get out: individual rights are advancing; it is William Lidgerwood who goes ahead!"[98] In 1870, Lidgerwood moved against the Bierrenbach brothers and another German inventor, Johan Josef Stirp. In 1877, he sued his former employee, a Scotsman named William Mac-Hardy.[99]

After the first-instance victory against Engelberg, however, Lidgerwood failed to convince Brazilian judges that other manufacturers were infringing on his patent. Based on careful examinations of the machines by designated engineers, local judges concluded that different manufacturers used different mechanisms and that they had only been inspired by Walker's invention. Higher courts overturned the decision of the Campinas Court against Engelberg, and all the other defendants were acquitted.[100] The São Paulo elite chose to foster competition and promote manufacturing in Brazil over protecting an American importer. As influential as Lidgerwood had become in the Oeste Paulista, he had to adapt his enterprise to the fazendeiros' vision of the future.

Unable to defeat his competitors in the Brazilian courts, by the mid-1870s Lidgerwood established his own factory in Campinas—Lidgerwood Mfg. Co. Ltd.—to better meet the demands of the fazendeiros. It was the largest and most advanced machine factory in Brazil, employing over one hundred operatives. He also began to foster closer relationships with the fazendeiros.[101] A man from Casa Branca, a township located eighty miles north of Campinas, thanked Lidgerwood for "your cherished letter including samples of coffee, I will take your good advice with great consideration as to how to improve the processing of my coffee."[102]

Concurrently, Lidgerwood invested in advertising. His ads openly attacked his fastest-growing competitor, Mac-Hardy. In 1877, one of these ads claimed that the Mac-Hardy machines were "simply a regression to the first models introduced by Mr. Lidgerwood 14 years ago and, in any case, made of much inferior materials."[103] A battle that would last for years ensued when Mac-Hardy decided to confront his former employer. "I challenge them to prove what they say," Mac-Hardy wrote to the *Gazeta de Campinas*. "Moreover, I invite whoever wants to examine the quality of the material that I adopt to come see it."[104] Lidgerwood's rejoinder came in the form of dozens of letters from fazendeiros attesting to the superior quality of his machines. "Having examined the different systems of coffee-processing machines used in this province to date," a fazendeiro from Amparo maintained in 1879, "I did not find one that has satisfied me as much as the Lidgerwood system."[105]

Instead of damaging Lidgerwood's reputation, these disputes convinced the fazendeiros that his machines had ushered in a mechanical revolution in the Oeste Paulista. In 1876, a user of the Conrado system recalled that, until the mid-1860s, the only means to process coffee available in São Paulo had been the mortar and pestle, which damaged the coffee beans and left debris mixed in. "Our agriculture understood nine years ago," he continued, "that the Lidgerwood machines—which clean the coffee, presenting few broken beans—were worthy of replacing those [methods] existing up to that point, and the Santos [export] market has contributed much to generalizing the use of these perfected machines." Lidgerwood had not only made coffee from the Oeste

Paulista more desirable but also encouraged other manufacturers in the region to produce their own machines: "Sales, in large scale, of the cylinder-machines of the Lidgerwood system, made the competition offer machines with some modifications, as, for example, those of Conrado."[106]

The more Lidgerwood Mfg. Co. Ltd. grew, the more the fazendeiros saw it as the standard for excellent coffee processing. Planning the participation of São Paulo in the 1878 Paris Universal Exposition, the Campinas Agricultural Club sent a petition to the provincial president containing eighty signatures from the richest men of the Oeste Paulista. The fazendeiros demanded that the types of coffee being sent to Paris should be "those produced with and sorted by the Lidgerwood machines, which are: those known by the names of *moka, large flat,* and *regular flat.*"[107] Agricultural reformers concurred with the fazendeiros about Lidgerwood's positive impact on the Oeste Paulista. His SAIN colleague Nicolau Joaquim Moreira remarked that the Lidgerwood machines were so widespread in the region that its coffee was known in Europe as "machine coffee."[108]

Even the British recognized the excellence of the Lidgerwood machines. Seeking to collect information to help improve coffee production in the colony of Ceylon, a British researcher visited Brazil in the mid-1870s. In the Oeste Paulista, he found out that, after drying, "the coffee berries pass through . . . machines moved by water-power, which process is termed hulling, by which process the skin gets beaten into powder like sawdust." For this operation, the fazendeiros had "excellent machines of American construction."[109]

In 1880, a resident of the distant coffee frontier of São Carlos published an article in the *Gazeta de Campinas* criticizing the coffee planter "who knows that the day when the slave hand will cease wielding the hoe is near, but buys negroes for any price and plants as much coffee as possible." Such an attitude would eventually lead Brazilian agriculture to a catastrophic decline, the writer contended. Yet there was a glimmer of hope on the horizon: "In the middle of this general malaise, indications appear of a truly intelligent work, well-understood efforts, which will in the future replace the current madness, which is reaching the doors of absurdity. We refer here to the useful invention produced by the house of Lidgerwood & C., established in Campinas, named *Huller.*" These machines would "shortly become the most powerful auxiliary in the transition from slave to free labor" in Brazil, the writer from São Carlos predicted. The locals should thank Lidgerwood for the improvements he brought to the Oeste Paulista: "What great results will agriculture obtain, what comforting prospects for those who trust in free labor! This is intelligence defeating old prejudices and erroneous doctrines, while dispelling the crisis that threatens us."[110] There remained no doubt in the minds of modernizing fazendeiros that the Lidgerwood machines—and those of his competitors— were paving the way for free labor in the Oeste Paulista.

In addition to evaluating national interests, historians must survey class relations to explain the rise of the United States as a hemispheric capitalist power in the late nineteenth century.[111] Lidgerwood advanced the interests of the local planter class while promoting American technology. A powerful tool for saving labor, the coffee huller represented an effective means to concentrate capital in the hands of the fazendeiros and make their coffee more appealing to foreign consumers. Slowly but surely, industrial technology that originated in the American North was transforming the fazendeiros from owners of slaves into employers of wage earners. In the Oeste Paulista of the 1860s and 1870s, antislavery reformers—a group that included major slaveholders and a New Jersey manufacturer—were charting a path to free labor that would expand the powers of capitalists from both ends of the hemisphere.

Dependency and Development

In 1868, André Pinto Rebouças reported to the Imperial Institute of Agriculture that his SAIN colleague Lidgerwood had met two farmers from the American South who had purchased twenty-four acres of grassy lands in the province of São Paulo, which locals considered "almost sterile." After burning the grass and plowing the fields, they planted eleven acres of corn and thirteen acres of cotton. When harvest season came, the farmers gathered "12,000 liters of cotton, approximately 4,000 pounds of fiber." Lidgerwood was eager to promote cotton agriculture in the Oeste Paulista, going so far as importing seeds from the United States to be distributed to local farmers.[112] In addition to manufacturing coffee-processing machinery to serve the needs of the fazendeiros, Lidgerwood was providing the structure for the nascent textile industry in the province of São Paulo.

In 1869, two fazendeiros, Luiz Antonio de Anhaia and the Baron of Piracicaba, built a cotton mill close to Itu. A local paper reported that "the machinery will be, in accordance with the contract made with Mr. Lidgerwood, of the most modern and perfect kind known today." The new factory would produce fifteen hundred yards of coarse fabric daily.[113] In 1874, William Pultney Ralston, a Pennsylvania engineer who worked as Lidgerwood's agent in Campinas and married into a planter family from Itu, formed a partnership with two sons of the Baron of Limeira to establish a cotton mill in Piracicaba. "Mr. Antonio de Souza Queiroz, William Ralston, and Luiz [Vicente] de Souza Queiroz," the *Gazeta de Campinas* reported, "propose to establish a great textile factory in that township, similar to others that already exist in this province."[114] Most of the cotton that fed these mills was cultivated by the ex-Confederates who lived nearby.

By the early 1870s, over two thousand ex-Confederates lived in Santa Bárbara, twenty miles north of Campinas and fifteen miles south of Limeira. Between 1865 and 1866, the fazendeiros had worked with Minister Paula Souza to attract settlers from the American South to the Oeste Paulista, paying for their transportation and lodging.[115] Dantas continued to work with them after Paula Souza died. Informed that a group of thirty-one men and women, many accompanied by children, were heading to Santa Bárbara in March 1867, Dantas ordered the provincial president "to provide them the assistance they need to move to that location without delays." He also reimbursed the expenses that José Vergueiro and other fazendeiros had with the immigrants' transportation.[116]

Many ex-Confederates would not have made it to the Oeste Paulista were it not for the assistance that the fazendeiros and the Brazilian government offered. On March 30, 1867, the police chief of Jundiaí communicated to the provincial president that "a number of families of American immigrants, totaling thirty-four people among men, women, and children, presented themselves to me. They are bound for Campinas and require transportation for themselves and their luggage." The police chief lamented that these families were so destitute that they "do not even have resources for their own subsistence."[117]

Initially, most of these impoverished immigrants became tenants or sharecroppers on lands belonging to fazendeiros in and around Santa Bárbara.[118] The ex-Confederates' role as dependent farmers in the Oeste Paulista took root so quickly that, by August 1871, a fazendeiro from Limeira offered "the American immigrants" lands "in excellent condition, close to town, and near the main road for export." Although not good for coffee, the lands were great for sugar, tobacco, grapes, and cotton. "The proprietor," the advertisement made clear, "only requires as compensation half of the gross product of each one of the mentioned crops." For a fee, the sharecroppers would be allowed to use the agricultural machines belonging to the landowner.[119]

Unlike the Swiss and German colonos of the 1850s, who had been channeled to fazendas such as Ibicaba and Sete Quedas, the ex-Confederates would not work in coffee cultivation. In the Oeste Paulista, they would grow cotton on marginal lands. A traveler who visited Santa Bárbara in January 1870 admired "the great cotton farms and the way they are planted by means of the plow." Cotton now grew "on good lands that had been abandoned around here, being most of them taken by tall grass, and for this reason devalued by the Brazilians." The visitor praised the ex-Confederates for reclaiming lands that the locals rejected: "It is undeniable that the North Americans came here to boost this township, which was completely forsaken."[120]

Besides growing cotton for local manufacturers, the ex-Confederates played another very important economic role in the Oeste Paulista. In November 1869, a visitor described how an ex-Confederate in Santa Bárbara "cultivated 14 alqueires [eighty-four acres] of land, having a crop of cotton, and also large quantities of beans, corn, potatoes, etc. etc." The observer was further pleased to learn that "the American agriculturalists have, in addition to their crops, sheep, bees, dairy cows, and everything else that brings abundance and a comfortable domestic life." Another newcomer cultivated cotton on "four alqueires [twenty-four acres] of land having as companions a plow and a mower, in addition to foodstuffs such as corn, beans, etc."[121] At a time when the fazendeiros were concentrating their investments in coffee, the farmers from the American South were employing their implements and their own labor to produce food that would feed the fazendas.

Local observers believed that the mixed commercial farms of the ex-Confederates were setting a positive example for the rest of the population. The editor of the *Correio Paulistano* asserted that "the beneficial influence from the labor and customs of these families . . . reflects itself on the beautification and growth of the township, which in everything resembles a city of the American Union."[122] In June 1869, the provincial legislator João Guilherme de Aguiar Whitaker proposed that the provincial government subsidize the settlement of one thousand more families from the American South in São Paulo. "All territories of the province," he projected, "where lands have stopped producing, not for lack of fertility, but for being exhausted by fire and poor management from backward farmers, will leave the state of abandonment thanks to the arrival of the Americans."[123] In 1872, Campos Sales proclaimed that "the practical and well-trained North Americans showed us the true advantages of their system, demonstrating that each implement did not need more than a man and an animal to carry out its operation. Therein lies the economy of labor, which we so much need." Campos Sales thanked the ex-Confederates for encouraging local agriculturalists to adopt the plow and other tools for cultivating the soil.[124]

The beneficial influence of the ex-Confederates would also help the province to orderly transition from slave to free labor, the fazendeiros reckoned. Whitaker, who was also a prominent landowner in Rio Claro, reasoned that "if there are no more slave hands, our planters will not be able to keep their plantations and will have to sell them, and we will then need men capable of buying and cultivating them." He imagined that as the number of slaves would start to dwindle, large fazendas would be broken up into smaller farms, which the ex-Confederates would purchase and cultivate with their plows and hired hands. "This is why," Whitaker clarified, "it is necessary that we welcome these men who can, as soon as possible, buy the plantations abandoned by the planters because of lack of hands."[125]

In the beginning, the marriage between the fazendeiros and the ex-Confederates satisfied both parties. George Matthews, a medical doctor from Alabama who had become a farmer in Santa Bárbara, was pleased with the land he had leased: "Instead of tall grass you find eight acres around me as red as your chimney and as nicely plowed as your garden, ready to be planted in two or three days in cotton, in my yard some 1/4 acre, you see orange, lemon, sweet lemon, cidra (or citron), one peach tree, two walnuts and several others you are not acquainted with." Cotton grew easily in Santa Bárbara, Matthews told his one son who had stayed in Alabama, and it was grown mostly by the labor of white people. "It has been asserted," he continued, "that cotton couldn't be raised by free labor on account of the miasma of the swamps etc. etc. but here that objection cannot be urged as the health of the white man is not affected by labor in the field." After making six bales of cotton in 1867, Matthews hoped to make fifteen in 1868.[126]

Matthews was happy to be far removed from the postwar American South. He felt relieved to be free from "Yankee oppression" and to have "no election riots, no free nigger excitement, no epidemics, but little sickness, no freeze, cold spells," or any other trouble to worry about. The most pleasing element of life in Brazil, for Matthews, was the respect for a man's domain. "Politeness ramifies through all grades of society, from the lowliest slaves to the highest nabob of the land: No one not even the Emperor will enter your house until invited or will take a seat until asked to do so."[127] Matthews imagined that he had encountered in the Oeste Paulista the patriarchal lifestyle that Northern invaders and rebellious slaves had shattered in the American South.

The unravelling of Matthews's arcadia would not be long in coming, however. "I shall not return to the [United] States this year and can't say when I shall attempt it," he wrote to his son in August 1870, "though it is my intention

at present to do so whenever I shall be able to reach <u>home</u> with means sufficient to give me a little start." Matthews had just finished packing twelve bales
of cotton when he penned this letter. Yet, he regretted, "the present low price
completely knocks down all my calculations as to returning this year."[128] And
the situation went from bad to worse. In January 1871, Matthews's wife Jane
informed their son that "we had bright prospects of being able to get back
home only a few days ago, but I am sorry to say that the great cotton scourge
(the caterpillar) has made its appearance. . . . We may make half a crop or we
may make none."[129]

Worse than being trapped in Brazil growing the poor man's crop, for Matthews, was that he had to offer his medical services to a powerful fazendeiro of
African descent named Francisco Teixeira Vilela. Matthews remarked sarcastically that he had "the honor of dining with this illustrious individual with
another barefoot nigger at the table. The last being far the biggest nigger of the
two." Matthews could not wrap his mind around the fact that "<u>this Gentleman</u>
(of color) owns on his plantation 'Santa Maria' 400 slaves and 800,000 coffee
trees, besides owning another large Fazenda 'Moro Alto,' with 200 more, some
of them much whiter than himself." Matthews observed disparagingly that Vilela
had "a very pretty chocolate color" and kept his hair "trimmed very close to
prevent it curling (kinking)." The fazendeiro offered Matthews well-remunerated
work as a physician on his plantation and even mentioned that he would "build
me a good house anywhere within a mile that I might select." Ashamed of being
dependent on a nonwhite patron, Matthews rejected the offer.[130]

Jane Matthews dreamed of having a dairy cow, eating turkey for dinner,
buying fancy dresses, and employing a domestic slave. Unfortunately for her,
none of these symbols of Southern domesticity were available in the Oeste
Paulista, at least not for the Matthews family.[131] Desperate, George Matthews
elaborated all sorts of plans to make enough money to leave Brazil, from inventing a corn sheller to breeding racehorses. These, however, were all pipe
dreams. Meanwhile, his wife continued her lament, noting that her husband
and their neighbors "have taken a job of work on the railroad, they are not
gradeing, they only cut down and clear it off, it will only take a few days to
accomplish it if they can get hands enough." But hands were hard to come by.

All hands will soon have to be picking cotton, it is opening very fast. Provisions have been scarcer and higher this year than they ever have been since
we have been in Brazil. We have never suffered for anything but there are a
great many that have. . . . We have no school in our neighborhood now,

there are not enough children (that can be spared out of the cotton fields) to justify one to open a school here at present.[132]

It pained Jane Matthews to see her husband and children performing manual labor to make a living in the Oeste Paulista. In August 1872, George Matthews believed he was planting his last crop in Brazil, hoping to realize "my long cherished wish of reaching home again with an ample sufficiency to live under my own vine and fig tree without fear or favor from any man."[133] Nonetheless, the Matthews family had to endure yet another decade of intense toil in Santa Bárbara.

Examining the plight of farmers in the American South, the historian Steven Hahn notes that "the postwar years gave 'hard times' a new and increasingly enduring aspect. . . . Supplying raw materials for Northern factories, the South in particular was relegated to junior partnership—if not colonial status—in a powerful industrializing society."[134] Although the dynamics of power and the political economy differed, ex-Confederates were relegated to junior partnership in the Oeste Paulista as well. Having to work for wages on railroad construction, pick cotton, and exploit the labor of their own children, the ex-Confederates of Santa Bárbara were not much better off than those who had stayed in Alabama, North Carolina, or Georgia after the Civil War ended.

Not all ex-Confederates, however, experienced as much hardship as did Matthews. Hailing from Arkansas, Orville Whitaker (who was not related to the São Paulo legislator of the same surname) abhorred the postwar order of the United States. Writing to a friend in 1874, he lamented that "the Southern states are on the eve of a war of races" and speculated that "the Northern people and the Federal government will ride with the Negro." Whitaker thought Brazil was a safe haven, free from political trouble. More important, he had found a good balance between farming cotton and railroad work, which he performed alongside Matthews and other neighbors.[135]

Although Whitaker managed to acquire one slave, he often made clear that he was positioned nowhere near the fazendeiros. Because cotton had reached a very low price in the early 1870s, he explained, "the Brazilians have most all quit planting it" and had "mostly turned their attention to planting coffee trees." Therefore, he bemoaned, "there has been almost a perfect mania amongst the Brazilians to obtain coffee lands and to buy Negroes, the result is lands that will grow coffee and Negroes have advanced in price quite materially." Whitaker knew that coffee was the best business "that any one can follow in this country," but was also aware that "it will not pay a man of my age to go to planting coffee trees as it takes four years under the most favorable circumstances to realize any crop from them."[136]

Outside visitors concurred with Whitaker. A British correspondent for the *Ceylon Observer* underscored in 1878 that prospects for cotton farmers in the Oeste Paulista were not very promising: "Coffee pays so well that cotton has no chance alongside of the former, and no person who can afford to plant coffee will plant cotton." But starting a coffee plantation, in the age of the Lidgerwood machines and other improvements, was no simple enterprise. Small farmers had to content themselves with cotton. "A poor man with a large family might cultivate it," the British observer continued, "as he could raise all the food for the support of his family whilst the cotton was growing, and along with it, but he would only make a living and no more out of it."[137] The poor men growing cotton by using family labor in the Oeste Paulista were the ex-Confederates.

Nonetheless, Whitaker was hopeful that the rapid development of the Oeste Paulista would end up benefiting his community. In September 1875, he communicated to a friend that the new Santa Bárbara train station was only six miles away from his farm. Even better, Whitaker continued, "in the course of six months there will be seven cotton factories running and the furthest one will not be more than fifty miles from me, some of them are now running, last week I sold sixteen bales of cotton to a factory not more than ten miles from me."[138] The closest and most successful of these factories was the Carioba, established by Ralston and the brothers Antonio and Augusto de Souza Queiroz with equipment supplied by Lidgerwood Mfg. Co. Ltd.

One of the ex-Confederates who took advantage of these changes was William Hutchinson Norris, a former state senator and planter in Alabama. Although Norris moved to Santa Bárbara with enough money to buy a farm, which he named New Alabama, he and his family had to adapt to the demands of the fazendeiros. Norris's son Robert, who had served in Stonewall Jackson's brigade, worked as an overseer on a fazenda forty miles from their home. The pressure to make money also affected the choice of crops at New Alabama. "I do not know how much cotton we will be able to plant," Norris told a son who had stayed in the United States, "but all we can. It is the only produce that brings ready money. Tobacco and cigars don't seem to sell readily, and the Americans have quit raising tobacco, and will plant cotton."[139]

Once New Alabama started producing plenty of cotton, Norris came to believe that in Brazil, "with industry and proper management, any man can make as much as he can possibly house." A dedicated agriculturalist, he was critical of his neighbors. "The Doctor," he censured Matthews, "has recently returned from a trip in the interior of the country where there are plenty of deer, anteaters, tigers and other large game, and I would not be at all surprised if him and Reece move there another year. . . . Neither of them likes to farm and unfortunately for them they don't know how to take care of money."[140]

Perhaps a bit jealous, in 1872 Jane Matthews wrote to her son that "Norris has bought a negro woman, I am truly glad for the old lady's sake." The slave did not understand the language of her new masters, but "the negro boy that they have speaks English as well as he does Portuguese, so I guess he will soon learn her."[141] The presence of black female servants in the household and the challenges of managing them remained an element of mastery as important for the ex-Confederates in Brazil as it had been for planter families in the antebellum South.[142]

The acquisition of two slaves certainly meant a lot to Norris. A proslavery secessionist in Alabama, his decision to rebuild life in Brazil came, above all, from his hatred of abolitionists and freedpeople. "The people of the North imposed slavery upon the people of the South, the North made their fortunes by the operation," he wrote to a friend who had stayed in Alabama. "They abolished slavery in the South, and now they wish to enslave the white people of the South and they will do it, if you of the South do not firmly and boldly take steps under the Constitution to maintain your rights."[143]

Norris often claimed that he had found stability in Brazil, being able to work, feed his family, and prosper without intervention from above or disruption from below. "No government on earth [is] more prosperous, quiet and happy than this," he praised his adopted country in a letter dated 1873. "I came here as poor as the Devil would have me be (it is said he is after the rich) and was compelled to struggle pretty hard for about three years." But now he was "comfortably situated, have plenty of good land, and a beautiful farm. . . . Make heavy crops of cotton, corn, potatoes." While his neighbors complained about hard work and growing debt, Norris had "over forty bales of cotton, plenty of corn, plenty of stock, cows, hogs and horses, etc. I have bought and paid for two negroes and we could pay for six more." He would not exchange his life in Santa Bárbara "for the whole of Alabama."[144]

Although family labor prevailed, one third of the ex-Confederates in Santa Bárbara employed slaves on their farms. Some of these slaves were rented for the cotton harvest only. Those immigrants who were able to buy slaves rarely had more than two or three, and few families managed to live off their farms as Norris did.[145] To supplement their income, the ex-Confederates who

owned slaves put them to work for the fazendeiros. Traveling the Oeste Paulista in the mid-1870s, a British writer noted that "there are a good many Americans in Brazil attracted thither during the war and after the emancipation of
slaves in America, who own small gangs of slaves and a number of mules. With
these they offer their services to the highest bidder for ploughing purposes."[146]
Although slavery persisted, division of labor was becoming a common practice
in the Oeste Paulista. In addition to growing cotton and foodstuffs, the ex-
Confederates were in charge of preparing the land that would bear the fazendeiros' coffee trees.

In order to survive, some ex-Confederates had to go further, combining rural
labor with other activities. In 1867, George Scarborough Barnsley informed his
father that he would leave the Ribeira Valley for the Oeste Paulista, where he
would practice medicine and also farm, hoping to get "all the necessary to
commence moderately."[147] By 1870, Barnsley had moved to Tatuí, near Sorocaba, where he bought a small tract of land with another ex-Confederate:
"Mr. Emerson and I have, jointly, bought a 'chacara' (country-place) near the village and propose living together. By having this place I shall be enabled to plant
grape, keep my horses fat, and have corn and garden. Mr. E will plant cotton."[148]

The farm never thrived and the medical profession became Barnsley's only
viable means to make a living. But it was not easy: "I must confess that the
heavy work I have to do, with exposure, I fear will eventually injure me." In
debt, Barnsley found himself "forced to enter into a contract with the most
influential families of the place to treat [them] for six months, receiving the
money beforehand. This 'partido' [group of people] has been a source of loss
to me and has given arise to much unnecessary labor." Barnsley had to travel
on horseback from one fazenda to the next, serving as doctor to the planters,
their families, and slaves. "Among my 'partido' I have done some very hard
work this past two months," he complained, "having ridden over five hundred
miles in that time."[149]

According to Barnsley, many of his countrymen had moderate success
working as physicians in the Oeste Paulista. Dr. Jones had become a famous
doctor around Santa Bárbara, and "Dr. Crisp practiced some and farmed more
at S. Barbara and did well."[150] Norris's son Robert also became a country doctor. Like Barnsley, he dreamed of farming and, as late as 1885, wrote to his
brother that "with a good pasture my family would be self-sustaining without
any effort of mine."[151] Yet Robert Norris started making ends meet only when
he began practicing the medical profession that he had learned at the Mobile
Medical College at his father's expense. "Robert has kept pretty busy and has

been very successful," Norris observed in 1887, "the typhoid fever is considered almost a new disease in this country, consequently the Brazilian doctors hardly knew how to treat it."[152]

The most successful of these physicians from the American South was James McFadden Gaston. Like Barnsley, Gaston had first settled at the Ribeira but soon started moving around the São Paulo interior. One day, on a road near Tatuí, Barnsley met Gaston traveling with his family. "The four smaller children were put into baskets, two on each side," Barnsley recounted, "and these baskets were tied on to a mule's pack-saddle in the common way. The rest came on horseback."[153] By 1873, the peripatetic Gaston had opened his own clinic in the heart of the Oeste Paulista.

"Dr. Gaston reached Campinas," his son recalled, "just at a time when return for his services was most remunerative. He was well acquainted with the superintendent of the railway, Mr. William J. Hammond, and some of the officials of the telegraph office and the services rendered were well appreciated and well paid for." Gaston specialized in treating the emerging industrial workforce of the Oeste Paulista. "The repair of the many injuries to the fitters, apprentices, and other workmen in the shops," Gaston Jr. continued, "was also part of the business, while the locomotive engineers often met with serious accidents requiring amputation of limbs and relief of pain and suffering." And "there were also more and more large foundries and machine shops springing up in the city of Campinas," which sent several other injured bodies to Gaston's clinic.[154]

In addition to absorbing Northern technology and adapting it to their own needs, Brazilian coffee planters were able to shape the role of impoverished immigrants from the American South. To be sure, neither Gaston nor Norris would be the hands to replace the slaves on the fazendas of the Oeste Paulista. Yet they performed valuable work in the region. Ironically, the expertise of proslavery Southerners ended up enabling the richest Brazilian slaveholders to extricate themselves from the institution of slavery. As the fazendeiros recognized that economic diversification would help Brazil navigate a smooth transition to free labor, they directed the ex-Confederates to occupations that would complement their expanding enterprises. Some immigrants grew cotton for the new textile mills and foodstuffs for the fazendas and towns. Others prepared lands for coffee cultivation and worked on railroad construction. Yet others treated the illnesses of fazendeiros, slaves, and industrial workers. Not all ex-Confederates were happy with their dependent status in the Oeste Paulista. But they did not have many options besides fulfilling the roles that the local elite had reserved for them. This was quite an unequal relationship—one in which Brazilians took advantage of Anglo-American expansionists to refashion capitalist production.[155]

Faith in Education

While American farmers, doctors, and manufacturers helped transform the economy of the Oeste Paulista, American missionaries from both Northern and Southern states helped transform its mind. In 1860, Alexander Latimer Blackford of Ohio moved to Rio de Janeiro to join the newly established mission of the Presbyterian Church in the United States of America (PCUSA), the Northern faction of American Presbyterianism. In 1863, he moved to São Paulo and started to travel around the province, quickly acquiring a significant following.[156]

In 1868, a Catholic mob in the township of Lorena, located in the Paraíba Valley, assaulted Blackford's service. Tavares Bastos intervened immediately, writing to the provincial president demanding protection for the missionary. Fletcher also acted, writing from Boston to Dom Pedro II that episodes like that were doing great damage to Brazil's image in the United States. Always faithful to Brazilian interests, Fletcher did all he could to explain the episode to the American public: "I have excused it by saying that it was far from the capital and a few people, probably mostly low Portuguese rendeiros [tenants] and feitores [overseers], incited to this bloody and cowardly deed by ignorant and fanatical priests; and that I was sure His Majesty did not approve of it."[157]

After the incident in the Paraíba Valley, the Presbyterians concentrated their efforts in the Oeste Paulista. Blackford nevertheless found another impediment to the success of the gospel. Writing to the leader of the PCUSA mission in Brazil, he lamented "the lack of instruction and the weak intellectual development of many people among the most accessible classes, and most inclined to the gospel."[158] Blackford saw the need to educate the local population. But in 1869, before he could go ahead with his new plan, Blackford was called back to Rio de Janeiro.

The PCUSA mission in São Paulo was then transferred to George Whitehill Chamberlain, a native of Pennsylvania and a graduate of the Union Theological Seminary in New York City, who had arrived in Brazil in 1862. In 1871, Chamberlain and his wife, following Blackford's advice, established the Escola Americana in São Paulo City, a day school for boys and girls modeled after New York public schools. The Chamberlains created the first kindergarten in the city and offered previously unavailable classes such as English, German, drawing, music, geography, and astronomy.[159] Moreover, unlike most Brazilian schools, the Escola Americana did not subject students to physical punishment. "One can find there the American ideal," the *Correio Paulistano* celebrated in 1872.[160]

In an advertisement published in 1873, Chamberlain informed the public that, at his institution, "tuition is free or paid in accordance with the conditions of the parents or guardians: no one is excluded for not being able to pay."[161] Chamberlain's charitable intentions notwithstanding, the Escola Americana would end up serving the most affluent residents of São Paulo. The missionary John Beatty Howell, a native of New Jersey and a graduate of the Princeton Theological Seminary, was responsible for turning Chamberlain's school into an elite institution. Appointed school administrator in 1874, Howell decided to make "a change in the terms of registration, requiring from all, with the exception of a few poor members of our church, the payment of tuition." In 1875, he wrote to the Presbytery of Rio de Janeiro that "I believe I can say that these changes made the school better appreciated and attended."[162] The 1878 *Annual Report of the Board of Foreign Missions* described the 125 students of the school as "representing some of the best families in the city."[163]

The local elite heaped praise on the Escola Americana. Francisco Quirino dos Santos, the editor of the *Gazeta de Campinas*, spoke at the 1873 commencement ceremony, "celebrating, with brilliant words, the interesting and imposing spectacle that he was watching."[164] In 1877, the *Diário de São Paulo* remarked that Chamberlain had "spared no sacrifices to take the school to its utmost development, having rendered so many services to public instruction in this capital, taking his dedication so far as erecting at São João Street a beautiful and vast building with all the necessary accommodations to this end."[165] The next year, when a terrible drought afflicted the northeastern provinces of Brazil, Chamberlain organized a festival at the school to collect money for the victims. Present at the event, Eduardo Prado, the son of one of the richest coffee planters of the Oeste Paulista, and Francisco Rangel Pestana, a republican leader from Campinas, both "praised the philanthropic sentiments of the distinguished teachers of the Escola Americana."[166]

In addition to running the school, Chamberlain traveled the province preaching. He made some prominent converts to Protestantism, including Luiz Antonio de Souza Barros, a wealthy fazendeiro from Piracicaba.[167] But the tireless Chamberlain did not restrict his preaching to the planter elite. He visited the settlement of ex-Confederates in Santa Bárbara quite often. During one of his trips, he was invited to preach "at the farm of an influential man close to S. Bárbara and found a rustic audience, children of the countryside and accustomed to labor, who listened with pleasure to the words of salvation."[168]

Stopping in Campinas, Chamberlain met the Reverends George Nash Morton, from Virginia, and Edward Lane, a native of the British West Indies who had relocated to the American South as a young man. They had arrived in 1869 as missionaries of the Presbyterian Church in the United States (PCUS), which had broken with Northern Presbyterians during the secession crisis over the question of slavery.[169] Setting sectionalism aside, Chamberlain became close to Morton and Lane, constantly traveling the Oeste Paulista with them.[170]

The partnership between Northern and Southern Presbyterians soon bore fruit. In December 1871, the *Gazeta de Campinas* reported that Morton and Lane had called a meeting in Campinas "to deliberate on various points concerning the establishment of a school based on the method adopted in many places of the United States." During the meeting, "Mr. Chamberlain, commissioned by Messrs. Morton and E. Lane, read an exposition of the principles of the school that both men seek to establish." Manoel Ferraz de Campos Sales, the influential republican planter, guaranteed unanimous acclaim for the school project from the more than fifty attendees. Wealthy fazendeiros, merchants, lawyers, doctors, and foreign entrepreneurs like William Pultney Ralston gave their blessing to the new school. Under Chamberlain's guidance, Morton and Lane established the Colégio Internacional in Campinas.[171]

In 1874, only one year since its inception, the Colégio Internacional had over one hundred male and forty female students. The *Imprensa Evangélica*— the PCUSA publication in Brazil—recommended it "to parents who desire for their children varied and solid instruction along with a careful moral and religious education."[172] Visiting Campinas in 1874, an American businessman was happy to see that the school was expanding its structure as well as its influence: "Mr. Morton has found it necessary to construct a larger college building, so anxious are the better classes to have their children receive proper instruction and to surround them with refining influences. . . . It is gratifying to our countrymen on entering that city to be told that the conspicuous and prominent building on the hillside is an American college." The demand for the school was so intense, the observer added, that Morton and Lane were compelled to refuse many applicants. The reason behind the popularity of the Colégio Internacional was that it was "non-sectarian, and the training is of the most liberal character"—precisely what the modernizing fazendeiros were looking for.[173]

The Colégio Internacional fascinated reform-minded locals. During a literary festival held in 1875, Clemente Falcão de Souza Filho, a professor at the São Paulo Law School, celebrated that Morton and Lane had brought from the United States the ideal that "citizens must put their talents into the service of their nation, and that the nation, for its part, must give to its children all the means to realize the greatest portion of their possibilities." Such a noble ideal, Souza Filho continued, was the only one compatible with a century in which freedom had triumphed, dogmas had fallen, the telescope and the microscope had expanded human vision, and canals, telegraphs, railroads, and steamships had overcome geographical distance.[174] Contributing to the prestige of the Colégio Internacional, newspaper advertisements stressed that "it prepares students for the academies of the Empire [of Brazil] and also for the universities and polytechnic schools of the United States and Europe."[175] Before long, many Brazilian graduates of American schools would travel to the United States to seek higher education.

Morton and Lane hired prominent intellectuals and reformers to teach at the Colégio Internacional. One of them was Rangel Pestana, who considered the school the best hope for rebuilding Brazilian society: "Since the disappointments of public life began to cloud my heart, I have turned my views to the school as the point from which will spring a generation capable of saving the nation from the evils that are degrading it." He rejoiced that "in this house of education we can already see the shaping of young men who resemble the North-American student, proud and delicate, energetic and respectful of the social laws."[176] Nurturing the same modernizing views, in 1876 the students of the Colégio Internacional created a periodical. In the declaration of principles, they stated that "the Brazilian youth must not continue traditions that are not theirs and that kill the dreams of the most blessed of all lands."[177]

In 1879, Morton left the Colégio Internacional under Lane's supervision and opened another school in the provincial capital, which, he hoped, would be the basis for the first Brazilian university. "There is no reason," Morton maintained, "for the province of S. Paulo, so progressive in material development, not to take the forefront in intellectual and moral development." São Paulo City was home to one of Brazil's two law schools already. "What we need with great urgency now is an academy of arts and sciences," Morton explained. "Later, other colleges will be established. My task is to create the foundation."[178] The plan received enthusiastic support from *A Província de São Paulo*, whose editor in chief in 1879 was none other than Rangel Pestana. The republican publication applauded Morton's "admirable courage," emphasizing that "the idea of the illustrious teacher is magnificent; the province needs an educational institution compatible with the quality of its coffee production and its railroads." But the support came with a warning: the antiquated educational system imposed by the monarchical government would make Morton's endeavor very difficult.[179]

Morton's troubles nonetheless began when he got involved in a controversy with local Positivists.[180] In February 1880, Morton published an article in *A Província de São Paulo* claiming that Auguste Comte's ideas were "fatal, cold, without a soul, without compassion, without life."[181] Articles defending Positivism and attacking Morton appeared subsequently in the same publication.[182] Morton retorted and the controversy became ugly and protracted.[183] Losing supporters and money, he left the country in 1883.[184] But he was not forgotten. Over a decade later, a Brazilian traveler visited Morton in New York City and was pleased to find that he knew all about "the political careers of his former students and friends who had reached the highest positions in the [newly established Brazilian] Republic. He took out of a drawer a collection of postcards, and those from Prudente de Morais, Campos Sales, Bernardino de Campos, and Martinho Campos stood out."[185] Notwithstanding his failings, Morton had contributed to the making of a new elite, mostly men from planter families, who established a new political and social order in Brazil.

While Morton took his own path, the PCUSA continued supporting educational enterprises in the province of São Paulo. Working alongside Chamberlain, João Fernandes Dagama, a Presbyterian missionary born in the Portuguese island of Madeira and educated in the United States, visited fazendas and small towns in the deep Oeste Paulista. In 1874, he heard from the inhabitants of a rural neighborhood in Rio Claro that "nobody there knows how to read, they are desirous of having a school whenever possible so all of them can learn and be instructed in the Gospel."[186] Moved by this and other accounts, Dagama created a school in Rio Claro with plans to "train up a class of earnest, self-denying laborers, who will be fitted to live among the poorer classes in the interior, and lead them in the way of salvation."[187] The PCUSA Board of Foreign Missions reported about his institution in 1885 that "much interest was shown by the public in the annual school examination; not even standing room remained."[188]

Other American Protestant denominations soon joined the Presbyterians in the Oeste Paulista. In 1871, the Southern Baptist Convention (SBC) established a church in Santa Bárbara. Ten years after opening, the head of the SBC mission, a Texan named William Buck Bagby, complained that he was unable to expand his congregation beyond the ex-Confederates, who lacked the money to maintain the church. The solution would be to appeal to the Brazilians. Bagby thus requested funds from the SBC to open a day school in Santa Bárbara, noting that "the Presbyterians have a college at Campinas and another at San Paulo."[189]

The experiences of Chamberlain, Morton, and Lane, Bagby told the SBC, demonstrated that "the conquests of the gospel in papal lands depend much upon the early culture of the inhabitants. . . . The mission school prepares the way for the march of the church." Yet the new Baptist school could not be a strictly religious institution. "The school must be essentially free," he clarified, "otherwise it could not withstand the counter-influence of the free-school system of Brazil that is widely dispersed throughout the Empire. . . . The school, during the regular hours of study, cannot bring in the dogmas of any religion whatever as a subject of instruction."[190] Like the Presbyterians, the Southern Baptists adapted their mission to the demands of the local elite.

During a trip to the provincial capital, Bagby attended a meeting of the PCUSA and had "an opportunity of seeing and consulting with their workers from different localities of the Empire, some of whom have had long, varied, and valuable experience in mission operations in this country."[191] The Escola Americana became a model for the SBC school in Santa Bárbara and Chamberlain a mentor to Bagby. "I am anxious to make a journey in a few weeks to the farther interior with Mr. Chamberlain," Bagby wrote in June 1881. "He speaks Portuguese excellently, and by traveling with him and mingling with the Brazilians I can learn a great deal of their language, manners, and customs, which can never be learned from textbooks."[192]

Not far away from Bagby's day school, the republican leader and fazendeiro Prudente José de Morais Barros and his brother Manoel de Morais Barros became interested in the American model of education. In 1879, the Morais Barros brothers approached the Methodist missionary Junius Newman about establishing a school for girls in Piracicaba. Newman had come from Alabama to Santa Bárbara in 1867 along with his daughter Annie, who had studied at the Colégio Internacional. She established the Colégio Piracicabano in 1881. Soon after, however, Annie Newman got married to a missionary from Tennessee and moved to Rio de Janeiro. In late 1881, with the support of the Woman's Missionary Society of the Methodist Episcopal Church South, Martha Watts of Kentucky arrived in Piracicaba to take charge of the new school.[193]

The network of American missionaries and educators in the province of São Paulo facilitated Watts's adaptation to her new surroundings. "We have had pleasant intercourse with other missionaries," she noted in a letter dated 1881. "We have been invited to visit them at Campinas, and now have a very pressing invitation to go to San Paulo during the sitting of the San Paulo Presbytery—which, no doubt, will be a pleasant meeting of missionaries." Watts was very pleased to meet Chamberlain, who had come to Piracicaba to preach "in Portuguese in our little parlor, one night, to a small congregation," and Bagby, who had "conducted a very successful meeting a few weeks ago, which resulted in quite a number of conversions."[194]

Support from the local elite was even more important for Watts. "I must tell you too," she wrote to the Woman's Missionary Society in 1883, "that the president of the city council is our good friend—Dr. [Manoel de] Morais Barros— also editor of the *Gazette*. He spoke of our school in a very complimentary manner in his paper."[195] Indeed, reporting on the construction of a new school building, the *Gazeta de Piracicaba* celebrated the growth of "an establishment of solid and true education, in accordance with the progress of the century in which we live and, above all, an establishment of solid education for women, which repels old traditions."[196] A few years after opening, the Colégio Piracicabano had more than fifty students, including the daughters of the Morais Barros brothers and other important families from the Oeste Paulista, such as Prado, Penteado, and Pacheco Jordão. Italian, English, German, and American girls attended the school alongside the daughters of the fazendeiros.[197]

The Colégio Piracicabano repeated the success of other American schools in the Oeste Paulista. As Ana Maria de Morais Barros, the daughter of Manoel de Morais Barros, explained in 1883, schools for girls were rare in Brazil and those that existed taught them only "to play the piano and say a few phrases in French." Morais Barros, who was nineteen years old then, criticized the Brazilian woman who only thought of "the flattering phrases directed to her, the envy with which her friends look at her, and believes that everybody admires and courts her." The young reformer nonetheless restricted herself to upholding the patriarchal values of her father and uncle, stating that a woman had to acquire sufficient knowledge of the world to become a good daughter, wife, and mother. She concluded that Brazil should follow the example of the United States, "a nation as young as ours, and one of the happiest in the world, where the true family mother raises sons who make the happiness of the nation; or bravely fulfills, alongside her man, any mission she is charged with, because there she is instructed, educated, and free."[198]

Faithful to the mission that the fazendeiros had bestowed on her, Watts, who never married, was pleased to write to her superiors in July 1889 that "last week I saw another of my 'daughters' married, on her seventeenth birthday; she took upon herself the responsibilities that marriage entails with smiles and joys." The student, Watts rejoiced, had done really well for herself: "Her husband is a nice young man, and industrious, though not poor. He is the second of his family who has chosen a wife from my family."[199] While Watts congratulated herself, the fazendeiros and the women trained at the Colégio Piracicabano were partnering up to reinforce class privilege. Like other American missionaries who worked in the province of São Paulo from the 1860s to the 1880s, Watts advanced the interests of the local elite.[200]

By educating the children of the fazendeiros, the missionaries complemented the work that American capital and, in the case of the ex-Confederates, American labor had begun. Men like Paula Souza, Vergueiro, Campos Sales, and the Morais Barros brothers invited Americans into their region to advance a modernizing project that promised to transform the fazendeiros' class status. Whether they liked the changes taking place in the Oeste Paulista or not, the Americans who lived in Brazil in the age of emancipation were reshaping the role of the United States in the hemisphere. Their interactions with the fazendeiros show that there was more to the American rise to the position of a capitalist power in the late nineteenth century than historians of foreign relations imply when they reflect on changing American attitudes toward Latin America.[201] In slaveholding Brazil, Americans were learning to connect the interests of capital across national borders.

The schools of Watts and Chamberlain, the commercial farms of Norris and Matthews, the medical practices of Gaston and Barnsley, and the factories of Lidgerwood and Ralston formed solid stepping-stones to a more diverse and dynamic social system in the Oeste Paulista. American enterprises accelerated the transition from slave to free labor in the richest slaveholding region of the late nineteenth-century world. In the process, they favored the major fazendeiros, giving them some effective means to concentrate power, expertise, and capital. Now it was time for members of the Brazilian elite to explore the United States and see firsthand what a wholehearted embrace of free labor in the form of the wage system could accomplish.

5

Brave New World

IN 1874, the engineer William S. Auchincloss traveled to Brazil to promote the products of Jackson & Sharp Co. Delaware Car Works. After visiting a fazenda in Campinas, province of São Paulo, he enthused that "much progress has already been made in the introduction of labor-saving machinery and more scientific methods of tillage." Auchincloss was further elated to find that the advancement of Brazilian society bore the mark of the United States. Whereas earlier generations of Brazilian men had pursued their studies in Europe, he observed, the tide was now turning "in favor of America, for each year brings to our shores new students for our colleges and technical schools, who, on the completion of their education, immediately return to their native land. Besides, many of the sons of the gentry pursue practical courses in our cotton mills, laboratories, and machine shops."[1] During the 1870s, members of the Brazilian elite were converging on the United States. They traveled through all sections, visiting factories, farms, mines, universities, and fairs. American entrepreneurs, politicians, and intellectuals hosted them, presenting a reunified and developing nation fueled by the labor of millions of native-born and immigrant wage earners.

Beneath the image of reunification and development, the United States faced growing unrest. The Panic of 1873, corruption scandals, controversial monetary policies, and labor agitation shook American society. The chain of failures initiated in 1873 and capitalists' strategies of vertical and horizontal integration worsened the already shocking concentration of wealth.[2] Whereas the working class pushed the government to curb monopolistic practices and help small producers, capitalists advocated less federal interference in economic and social matters. Pressured from all sides, the Republican Party sided with big capital. By the end of the decade, Reconstruction was buried and the Gilded Age opened.[3]

Brazil also faced unrest in the 1870s. The political elite sought modernization while preserving the status quo. From 1871 to 1875, the Viscount of Rio
Branco implemented a series of reforms, touching on slavery, military recruitment, bureaucratic functions, and laicization, among other things. The government also expanded access to higher education, invested in railroads, and
established telegraphic communication with Europe and North America.[4]
Nonetheless, the more the Conservative government reformed, the more
insurgent groups cried for an overhaul of Brazilian institutions. Young men,
some hailing from the nascent middle class and others from rich planter
families, lambasted the slow pace of reform. They wanted to stimulate rapid
economic growth, liberate capital, and submit the country to the rule of engineers and entrepreneurs.[5]

A Brazilian journalist named José Carlos Rodrigues became a link between
these two troubled societies. From 1870 to 1879, he lived in New York City,
associated with Liberal Republicans, and published Portuguese-language periodicals, which he shipped to Brazil. Rodrigues's main contention was that
free labor in the service of big capital had successfully rebuilt the United States
after the Civil War. Sharing Rodrigues's worldview, two Brazilian engineers
from influential families toured North America—one in 1869 and the other in
1873—researching transportation systems, factories, large-scale agriculture,
and mining operations. Regardless of the widespread corruption, racial inequality, and class conflict fracturing American society then, Brazilian observers concluded that the universalization of wage labor had given the United
States the perfect formula for national advancement. And they believed that
the same could be done in Brazil.

Taking advantage of the growing network connecting the two countries,
young Brazilians flocked to Northern universities during the 1870s. Most were
the sons of the wealthy fazendeiros of the Oeste Paulista, who sought to acquire scientific and practical training. In institutions like Cornell, they got in
touch with the newest production and transportation technologies in the
world, thus identifying material improvement with the prevalence of free
labor. Older Brazilians came to the same understanding in 1876, when they
participated in the Centennial Exhibition in Philadelphia. Scientists, planters,
and politicians used the opportunity to travel around the United States, going
from New England to the Mississippi Valley and the Pacific coast. They were
fascinated by how quickly the postwar United States had managed to rebuild
itself on the basis of free labor.

The Brazilian observers concluded that the victory of antislavery forces in the United States had given rise to an unmatched capitalist economy. When surveying the political struggle that overthrew New World slavery, scholars underscore that the main legacies of antislavery were the expansion of the public sphere and the emergence of a human rights discourse.[6] Although there is no denying that antislavery had the potential to expand political participation and foster humanitarian ideals, it did something that had even more profound consequences in the modern world: it normalized and entrenched wage labor. From the perspective of visitors from the only remaining independent slave society in the Western world, the downfall of slavery and the triumph of free labor in the United States had opened opportunities for capitalists to multiply railroads, expand manufacturing, modernize agriculture, and build a powerful financial machinery. The Brazilians understood that free labor in the form of the wage system was the force quickly integrating a war-ravaged country and transforming it into a capitalist power. While celebrating wage labor, the enthusiasts of the Gilded Age overlooked flagrant problems affecting American society. It became clear then that antislavery reformers favored fast economic development and territorial integration over social justice and political equality. Hence, the postemancipation United States, regardless of its iniquities, consolidated itself as a model of capitalist development for Brazil.

The Journalist

José Carlos Rodrigues was born into a planter family from Cantagalo, northeastern Rio de Janeiro. In the early 1860s he moved to São Paulo to study law. There, he frequented radical circles and established a close relationship with Luiz Gama, the ex-slave turned into lawyer and abolitionist leader.[7] In 1862, he joined his classmate Francisco Rangel Pestana to create a student newspaper titled *O Futuro*.[8] In his first writings, Rodrigues assailed slavery, the Catholic Church, and the monarchy. He also commented on the most dramatic event of the decade, the American Civil War, attacking Southern secessionists and their supporters: "The majestic edifice of democracy collapses. The apologists of slavery, the despots of all nations, sing Hosanna and continue their work of destruction. The United States, the land made sacred by the blood of the free, is the victim of a civil war, which sucks its life and threatens the cause of the republic."[9] However outraged, Rodrigues was confident that the cause of freedom would prevail and set an example to the rest of the world. "Today," he proclaimed in September 1862, "the nations, submerged in the shadows of despotism, turn their eyes to the North, hoping that a star will shine on the horizon, which will guide them through the desert."[10]

After graduation, Rodrigues moved to Rio de Janeiro and started working at the Ministry of Finance. He also took English lessons with the Presbyterian missionary George Whitehill Chamberlain and converted to Protestantism. When, in 1867, an accusation of embezzlement cut his public career short, he moved to the United States, first settling in Lowell, Massachusetts. Soon, the networks that American missionaries had established came in handy. Chamberlain found him work translating pamphlets for the American Tract Society and American schoolbooks for the Escola Americana in São Paulo. James Cooley Fletcher, who lived in Newburyport, Massachusetts, then, also became Rodrigues's close friend, introducing him to prominent American intellectuals and entrepreneurs.[11]

In 1870, Rodrigues rented an office in the *New York Times* building. On October 24 of the same year, the first edition of *O Novo Mundo* came out. A monthly publication in Portuguese, it was sent to Brazil by the New York–Rio de Janeiro line of steamers. Rodrigues modeled his illustrated review on American publications like *Harper's Weekly* and *Frank Leslie's Illustrated Newspaper*. *O Novo Mundo* would run for almost a decade and reach more than ten thousand subscribers, a remarkable achievement for the time. In the first edition, Rodrigues announced the objectives of the new publication: "After the domestic war in the United States, Brazil and South America have sought to carefully study the things of this country. *O Novo Mundo* proposes to contribute to this study, not only by providing news from the United States but also by exposing the principal manifestations of its progress and by discussing the causes and tendencies of this progress."[12]

Rodrigues's descriptions of the postwar United States emphasized economic prosperity and technological advancement. "A few years ago," he wrote in May 1875, "the farmer of the great West spent his hot summer days cutting hay and grain with the reaper or the sickle: now he does the same work in a few hours by means of one of those American harvesters drawn by the horse; and the farmer, wearing gloves and sitting down, finds great fun in what recently used to be a heavy task." The same advancement could be observed in industrial enterprises: "In leather shoe manufacturing, three men can now, with the aid of machinery, work as much as six did fifteen years ago." Transportation had also been revolutionized, and the United States now had forty thousand more miles of railways than it had ten years earlier, which cut freight

FIGURE 5.1 Railroad station in Upstate New York. *O Novo Mundo*, April 24, 1871.
Courtesy of the Fundação Biblioteca Nacional, Rio de Janeiro.

costs in half. Material improvement, he rejoiced, seemed inexhaustible: "Large, heavy, and expensive devices are everywhere being replaced by smaller, compact, and inexpensive machines."[13] Rodrigues celebrated that the Northern model of development, with its constant improving of production and complex interdependencies, had expanded to all regions of the country after the Union victory in the Civil War. The countryside and the city had become cogs of one single engine in the reborn nation.[14]

As much as he sang the praises of free labor, the heroes of *O Novo Mundo* were not the laborers themselves. Rodrigues described Cyrus West Field, the founder of the Atlantic Telegraph Company, as "a great inventor, of those to whom we owe the greatest conquests of civilization."[15] *O Novo Mundo* also praised Oliver Dalrymple, a Pennsylvania land speculator who pioneered large-scale wheat agriculture in the Dakota Territory, where he managed thousands of acres of land. "To produce and reap the grains," Rodrigues explained, "Mr. Dalrymple employed 500 horses and mules, 80 seed-sowers of 8 ½ feet, 160 plows of 14 inches, 250 steel-pointed harrows, 15 threshers and cleaners of 40-inch cylinders, 15 steam engines of 10 horse-power, 80 reapers, and a workforce of 400 men."[16] Another capitalist who received the admiration of *O Novo Mundo* was Edward Cooper, a steel magnate, who "quickly acquired perfect and complete scientific knowledge, which allowed him to perfectly understand all operations in their smallest details."[17]

FIGURE 5.2 Dalrymple Farm in the Dakota Territory. *O Novo Mundo*, November 1878.
Courtesy of the Fundação Biblioteca Nacional, Rio de Janeiro.

For Rodrigues, no one embodied American greatness better than Cornelius Vanderbilt, who had started his business at age sixteen piloting a small ferry from New York City to Staten Island. "Sixty years later," Rodrigues exulted, "Vanderbilt dies leaving nothing less than one hundred twenty thousand contos de réis! How it is possible in one life to accumulate such capital is something impossible to explain to someone who does not know the value of indomitable energy allied to the good fortune of an American."[18]

An enthusiast of powerful capitalists, Rodrigues often sided with capital against labor. Reporting on a strike of Pennsylvania coal miners in December 1870, he questioned "if the condition of the working classes is so awful that it justifies their general discontent or the concept of enmity that they have little by little formed against capital, the inquietude that they always show, suspicious of those who are their natural allies."[19] A critic of unions and socialists, Rodrigues littered *O Novo Mundo* with maxims such as "labor—even arduous labor—is our duty; and for being so, it is our glory and salvation."[20] All men, he preached, should value "independence of character; the innate aversion to any form of tutelage; the sublime aspiration of being what the

Yankees style—*self-made man*—a man made by himself; without patrons or protectors."[21]

Rodrigues's analysis of Reconstruction in the American South was consistent with his laissez-faire ideals. He saw corruption all around and singled out Radical Republicans as the root of all evil.

> First, the states that had seceded were placed under military and dictatorial rule, not as lost brothers, but as desolate strangers. Second, the negro, still a brute because of enslavement, was given the right of suffrage—that is, he was made into a desirable tool. Third, the war having created large pecuniary needs, it was necessary to raise money by customs tariffs, which unevenly affected different industries. All these reforms grew along with staggering corruption.

Rodrigues also despised the so-called carpetbaggers, "these adventurous vultures from the North who were quick to fall on the corpse of the South. The ignominies that these men practiced are unprecedented in the history of the most corrupt eras of human society."[22]

Rodrigues aligned himself with sections of the New York elite who disapproved of the military occupation of the Southern states, high tariffs, monetary inflation, the income tax, labor organizations, and machine politics. He echoed Liberal Republicans such as Carl Schurz and Charles Sumner, who had turned against President Ulysses S. Grant. Like these dissidents, Rodrigues subscribed to the ideas of the political economist Richard Cobden, advocating free trade and minimal government intervention in economic and social matters. He also shared with the Liberal Republicans an antislavery background and an antislavery language, which they used to justify their views.[23]

The editor of the *New York Tribune* and Liberal Republican leader Horace Greeley became Rodrigues's role model. When Greeley ran against Grant in 1872 promising to end Reconstruction, Rodrigues offered his support.[24] The historian Sven Beckert explains that to the New York elite who rallied behind Greeley freedom "meant first and foremost self-ownership and the right to participate in markets, both of which seemed to have been accomplished in the states of the former Confederacy" by the 1870s.[25] Rodrigues concurred with this idea: Reconstruction should guarantee political stability in the South, which meant returning major planters to power, and secure the exslaves' right to freely and individually establish labor contracts. Nothing more. He went so far as to argue that the Radicals had "invented or exaggerated the horrors committed in the South by white people against the negroes, and with this system Grant got what he wanted, more power, more centralization."[26] Rodrigues spread the Liberal Republican contention that, if left alone, race relations would improve in the South: "The masters or former masters continue saying that the negroes are the best rural workers of the world and, in general, good relations exist among them."[27]

Despite the many evils that he saw in Reconstruction, Rodrigues was convinced that slave emancipation had been a blessing for the South, especially in economic terms. "The work of Reconstruction in the South is complete," he wrote in December 1870. "The negro is not only a free man, he is a citizen; and the material wealth of the country is recovered under the wise and peaceful administration of those who forever crushed the terrible hydra of slavery."[28] Rodrigues was delighted to learn that cotton planters were now able to see the advantages of free labor. In October 1872, *O Novo Mundo* quoted one of them at length. "Free labor costs much less than slave labor used to cost us," the Southern planter explained. The cost of owning a slave used to be about twenty-five to thirty dollars per month, he continued, "if we calculate the costs of taxes, medicine, interest, feeding, and maintaining him as a child and after old age." Now cotton planters were able to hire "the same negro for ten or fifteen dollars per month, in addition to home and food." To be sure, there were some drawbacks: "It is true that negroes now do not work as much as before; but, in any case, their proportional labor is much cheaper." This cotton planter, one of the richest in the South according to Rodrigues, believed that wartime destruction—and not slave emancipation—caused difficulties for some of his neighbors. Nonetheless, he concluded, the planter who employed agricultural tools and fertilizers was making "more money planting cotton with free labor than he would with the slave's sweat."[29]

Rodrigues acknowledged that freedom caused labor shortages, especially in the cotton areas, because ex-slaves could now pack and leave.[30] But, true to his liberal beliefs, he did not see it as a problem: "The difficulty caused by lack of hands has made agriculture more careful and scientific, and many negroes, who have not emigrated from the South, now find more incentive in free labor than they found under the lash of the overseer." Progress, Rodrigues added, was evident in the fact that by the late 1870s "the cotton crop in the states of the South has reached a number of bales superior to any year when the fiber was produced by slave hands."[31] Rodrigues celebrated that, in the American South, the sudden liberation of four million slaves had created a rational system of labor exploitation from which the planters could reap great profit.

In addition to the recovery of cotton production, Rodrigues was thrilled that slave emancipation had brought economic diversification to the American

FIGURE 5.3 Port of New Orleans, Louisiana. *O Novo Mundo*, January 23, 1875.
Courtesy of the Fundação Biblioteca Nacional, Rio de Janeiro.

South. "Another result of the war and the consequent ruin it caused is the increase of manufacturing in the South," he observed in October 1871. Southerners had learned that "instead of sending cotton to Europe or the northern states to be woven, it is better to weave it at home and save in brokerage, freight, and other expenses."[32] And there was more: "Turpentine, yellow pine, grains, precious minerals, excellent and rich layers of phosphates and fossil bones, not to forget about the already extensive manufacturing. The manufacture of natural fertilizers from these phosphates is already most important, and cotton manufacturing is prospering more than in the North."[33] Northern capital, Rodrigues explained, was fueling the industrial boom of the South. Near Aiken, South Carolina, "a capitalist from New York, Mr. W. C. Langley, has a factory with 15,000 spindles, recently established there, and going very well."[34] This kind of investment, he speculated, was strengthening the bonds between the sections.[35]

Rodrigues never hid his goal when describing the progress of the postwar United States in *O Novo Mundo*. He sought to inspire his Brazilian readers to embrace antislavery reform. "Let this eloquent example serve to calm the fears of those who worry about the future of agriculture in case of immediate slave emancipation," he wrote as early as January 1871, "and we shall soon have in the

FIGURE 5.4 Bird's-eye view of St. Louis, Missouri. *O Novo Mundo*, March 23, 1872.
Courtesy of the Fundação Biblioteca Nacional, Rio de Janeiro.

Empire [of Brazil] a great material prosperity such as the one we have here demonstrated to our readers!"[36] One year later, after discussing the labor of the ex-slaves in the South, he reiterated that "this example shall serve to strengthen the courage of those Brazilians who, worried about the interests that surround them, fear a change that is now highly necessary, not only in regard to the great moral interests of humanity, but also to their own material interests, and those of the country."[37] As late as 1879, Rodrigues emphasized that "the complete cessation of slavery is our greatest ambition. On the day no more slaves exist, our agricultural industry will begin its first era of true prosperity."[38]

Like other modernizers of his generation, Rodrigues was convinced that slavery bred backwardness.[39] Hence, he had no doubt that slave emancipation would bring economic development to Brazil in the same way that it had done for the American South: "The freedmen of Brazil will continue to grow coffee, as those of the United States continued to grow cotton. In a few years the cultivation of coffee and other products, stimulated by freedom and the consequent breakup of enormous rural properties, will be done on a much larger scale and in a more rational and productive way."[40] With the "inglorious and degrading" institution of slavery gone, free Brazilians would "take the plow and embrace rural work; then we will see Brazil doubly prosper: by the excess of production of the freedmen in relation to the slaves and by the fruits of the labor of millions of unfortunate people who have been obstructed by slavery from working in agriculture."[41] Rodrigues envisaged Brazil's slaves and free poor becoming wage earners. They would not work for themselves but seek employment on coffee plantations, converting them into agroindustrial enterprises.

When Prime Minister Rio Branco set to work on the Law of the Free Womb, Rodrigues backed him and forcefully attacked the critics of reform. "The system of slavery died a disgraceful and ridiculous death in the United States, thanks to its own madness," he charged, "and it will die in the same way in Brazil if its supporters do not understand the spirit and the forces at work in the times they live in."[42] As early as November 1871, however, Rodrigues started pressing for new measures to expedite the end of slavery in Brazil. By the mid-1870s, he had joined those who criticized the Law of the Free Womb as slow and incomplete.[43] In addition to a forceful enforcement of the law, he demanded legislation guaranteeing the education of slave children and abolishing corporal punishment.[44]

Rodrigues foresaw that as the country entered the path of reform and agriculture received "the electrifying touch of free labor," Brazil would "attract to its shores the superabundant population of Europe." Inspired by the Homestead Act of 1862, which made provisions for the distribution of public lands to farmers in the American West, and the Pacific Railroad Act of 1862, which authorized land grants to railroad companies willing to connect the West Coast to the Midwest, Rodrigues suggested that the Brazilian government should "slice up its public lands, not only directly for the immigrants but also indirectly through concessions to railroads and other progressive institutions willing to help."[45] The editor of *O Novo Mundo* looked to the American West as a source of inspiration. The immigrant pioneer would open up the way to the interior for the railroad corporations in Brazil. The great planters would follow, acquiring and developing the new lands with wage labor.

Rodrigues coupled his effort against slavery with a campaign to improve Brazilian agriculture. He often celebrated that over two-thirds of all coffee consumed in the United States came from Brazil. He nevertheless warned his readers that Brazilian export duties were too high and that Brazil's competitors were expanding production and improving cultivation techniques. "You must not only manage to produce large quantities of coffee," he advised the planters in 1877, "but also improve it, because if we now have access to all the markets of the world, we will only be able to secure them through the quality of our product, not its quantity."[46]

According to Rodrigues, American technology had the potential to improve Brazilian agriculture, making it compatible with the age of industry and concentrating capital in the hands of the coffee planters. Thus, he set out to open Brazilian markets for American capital goods. Editors of American periodicals helped in this endeavor. In November 1870, the Nation informed its readers that O Novo Mundo "will be a valuable medium for spreading still further knowledge in Brazil of the products of American invention and skill, already so popular there."[47] O Novo Mundo advertised American locomotives, agricultural implements, steel structures, and steam-powered machines, among many other things.

Similar to what James Cooley Fletcher and Aureliano Candido Tavares Bastos had done before, Rodrigues championed Americans with established business interests in Brazil. He praised the "beautiful ferry boat line" that Thomas Rainey had established in Rio de Janeiro.[48] He noted that the Botanical Garden Rail Road Co. had revolutionized the habits of the people of Rio de Janeiro and called it a "true blessing brought about by the streetcar pioneer in Brazil, Mr. C. B. Greenough."[49] Rodrigues described George Nash Morton, the founder of the Colégio Internacional in Campinas, as "a very well educated North American whose mission is to develop his students intellectually and morally."[50]

Rodrigues took his project of channeling American products and expertise to Brazil one step farther in July 1877, when he created another monthly periodical titled Revista Industrial. Seeking to attract American advertisers, Rodrigues published notes in English indicating that "the Revista Industrial, as its name implies, has for its principal aim: to disseminate among the planters and farmers, the railroad, industrial, and commercial classes of Brazil, the latest movements of invention and industry in the United States, and to make known in the United States the resources and progress of Brazil."[51] In support of Rodrigues's new enterprise, a group of Philadelphia manufacturers, which included Baldwin Locomotive Works, pointed out that they had long advertised in O Novo Mundo and were excited about the Revista Industrial. "From our knowledge of the standing of these periodicals with the Brazilian public, and their circulation in that country," Rodrigues's sponsors asserted, "we believe them to be valuable means of advertising the business of American manufacturers and merchants in Brazil."[52]

The Revista Industrial reiterated the tenets of O Novo Mundo. In 1877, it condemned the Great Railroad Strike, which was shaking the United States:

"The discontented railroad workers were joined in the cities by the scum of the population and also the immense class of unemployed who, under a system of complete political freedom, have acquired the conviction that the Government must provide for their livelihood, which the rich steal from the poor—all these axioms from the Commune."[53] Drawing on John B. Jervis's *Question of Labor and Capital* (1877), Rodrigues argued that "the workers have no just cause to antagonize the capitalist, because it is he who, with his money, provides the instruments, machines, and tools that are indispensable to labor."[54] A simple relation of trade, the encounter between labor and capital should be regulated by free-market laws, and strikes should be banned. Like in the issue of Reconstruction, Rodrigues aligned with the New York elite when it came to labor activism. Like in the issue of slave emancipation, he worked to normalize and entrench wage labor.[55]

The *Revista Industrial* carried on the antislavery arguments of *O Novo Mundo*, identifying slavery as the main cause of Brazilian backwardness. Unfree labor, the editorial of the first volume posited, was responsible for "maintaining us enslaved to antiquated and obsolete processes."[56] In the new publication, Rodrigues was even more emphatic than in *O Novo Mundo* when expressing his contempt for the social order that slavery engendered: "If it were necessary to present patent proof of the cancer that now takes Brazil, . . . it would be enough to point to the immense territories never surveyed, latifundia surrounded by miserable tenants, henchmen, parasites, and political firebrands, and worked by unfortunate and ignorant slaves."[57] The *Revista Industrial* singled out slavery as the cause of irrational and destructive economic practices, contending that "the nefarious abundance of slaves inevitably perpetuates the barbarous routines of ax and fire."[58]

Before long, Rodrigues's views made him a favorite among Brazilian modernizers. Antislavery reformers such as Nicolau Joaquim Moreira and Cristiano Benedito Ottoni often contributed to *O Novo Mundo*.[59] The Liberal leader Tavares Bastos developed a very cordial relationship with him, constantly praising his work. "Go on, my friend," Tavares Bastos wrote a letter to Rodrigues in 1872, "rendering services to our Brazil through your beautiful publication, which every day becomes more popular here."[60] When Tavares Bastos died of pneumonia in 1875 at the age of thirty-six, many saw Rodrigues as the man to assume the leadership role in efforts to modernize Brazil.

The majority of Rodrigues's admirers lived in the Oeste Paulista, where he had his largest readership. The *Correio Paulistano* used his writings as sources for discussing antislavery legislation, agricultural improvement, immigration policy, railroad construction, manufacturing enterprises, and educational reform, among other things. "Occupying himself assiduously with Brazil in brilliant articles, written within the intense glow coming from the place where he lives," an editorial praised Rodrigues in 1874, "our illustrious and solicitous countryman has become an independent thinker and journalist, impartial and profoundly judicious, and day to day offers invaluable services to our land through his wise observations."[61] When the *Revista Industrial* came out, the *Correio Paulistano* welcomed it with joy: "No doubt, the new periodical will render an invaluable service to the progress of the country, . . . especially to our countrymen who dedicate themselves to agriculture, because they will find in the *Revista Industrial* a powerful tool always providing useful and beneficial information."[62] The contributors to the *Gazeta de Campinas* also drew inspiration from Rodrigues. In 1871, Manoel Ferraz de Campos Sales, the fazendeiro and republican leader of the Oeste Paulista, used articles he found in *O Novo Mundo* to criticize the "the fatal belief, very common among our agriculturalists, that the free hand is absolutely impotent and unable to cultivate coffee."[63] Rodrigues's publications reinforced among the richest coffee planters the idea that the future of Brazilian agriculture lay in free labor in the form of the wage system.

Rodrigues reciprocated the admiration from the Oeste Paulista. In 1875, he sponsored the establishment of a school in Itu, christened Instituto do Novo Mundo. "The illustrious editor of *O Novo Mundo* had a very felicitous idea," *A Província de São Paulo* rejoiced; "his act is inspired by this noble sentiment that makes the North Americans so admired and esteemed by other peoples: to love one another."[64] Rodrigues shipped over one thousand books from New York to Itu, along with desks, a printing press, and innovative didactic materials. The new school would admit two hundred students. As a contribution to the school's maintenance, Rodrigues would make monthly donations of one hundred copies of *O Novo Mundo*, whose sale, he calculated, could pay for the salary of a librarian in addition to rent. George Nash Morton joined the school board along with some of the wealthiest men of the Oeste Paulista.[65]

Rodrigues portrayed the fazendeiros as the great entrepreneurs and modernizers of Brazil. In the Oeste Paulista, he enthused, "there is *self-help*; there is self-consciousness; there is individual initiative; there is trust in personal effort; there is unshakable certainty of the success of perseverance and labor."[66] Upon receiving a report on São Paulo railroads in 1875, he proclaimed that it was no exaggeration calling that province "the Brazilian Pennsylvania."[67] When Antonio Paes de Barros, the Baron of Piracicaba, died in 1876, Rodrigues described him as a trailblazer, responsible for starting coffee cultivation, introducing the plow, projecting the first turnpikes and railroads, and building the first textile mill in the Brazilian interior.[68]

Rodrigues also opened his publications to fazendeiros seeking to promote their region. In 1875, João Guilherme de Aguiar Whitaker, the provincial legislator and landowner in Rio Claro, wrote to *O Novo Mundo* about the "multiplicity of enterprises and industrial associations through which [São Paulo] contributes to the common good." He mentioned the proliferation of railroads, plows, and steam-powered machines, which would help in the transition to free labor: "All around we see the agriculturalist trying to alleviate labor through the assistance of new implements and understanding well that to invest in production is to sow capital that will produce advantageous fruits."[69]

Feeling that he had accomplished his mission of bringing Brazil closer to the United States, Rodrigues left New York City in 1879. He first went to the Colombian state of Panama to work as a correspondent for American newspapers, investigating the French attempt to build a canal there. He criticized the French and became an early supporter of American takeover.[70] Then he moved to London, where he became a financial advisor for entrepreneurs seeking to invest in Latin America. By the late 1880s, he returned to Brazil a rich man and bought the *Jornal do Commercio*.

Emphasizing the egalitarian features of the struggle against slavery, historians go so far as claiming that antislavery bolstered an international campaign against capitalist exploitation.[71] In a country that still held nearly two million slaves, however, another attitude prevailed. For Rodrigues and for the admirers of his writings in Brazil, antislavery had recast the United States as a capitalist power. Northern victory in the Civil War, Brazilian antislavery reformers rejoiced to find out, had spread wage labor and subjected the United States to the rule of major capitalists, who created unprecedented economic growth and integrated the disjoined parts of the nation. The message was clear: if Brazilians were planning to enter the capitalist race of the late nineteenth century, they should overthrow slavery and adopt the postwar American model of development. The Oeste Paulista, Rodrigues and his readers believed, was on the right track.

The (White) Engineer

While Rodrigues was still taking his first steps in the United States, a member of a prominent planter family from the Oeste Paulista arrived in the country to work as an engineer. Antonio Francisco de Paula Souza was the eldest son of his namesake and Maria Rafaela Aguiar de Barros, a daughter of the Baron of Piracicaba.[72] The elder Paula Souza, a Liberal leader, had served as minister of agriculture, commerce, and public works during the 1860s, supporting the Thayer Expedition and attracting ex-Confederates to Brazil. At the time, the young Paula Souza was studying engineering abroad, first in Zurich and later in Karlsruhe. From the time he arrived in Europe, he started planning a new journey. "I would like to go to the United States," the son wrote to the father in May 1861, "because, as soon as the [civil] war is over, or even now, when works are being conducted during the war, there will be a lot to do there."[73] The father thought it was a wonderful idea, but suggested that the son finish his studies first.[74]

The outcome of the American Civil War made the young Paula Souza all the more determined to visit North America. "A trip to the United States," he told his father in January 1866, "is not only advantageous from a technical perspective; there I can also understand the results of slave emancipation. I do not believe that Brazil can advance while maintaining this plague, which demoralizes everything, and which damages all true liberties."[75] Yet because his father died shortly after receiving this letter, Paula Souza decided to postpone his trip and return to Brazil.

On arriving, in 1867, Paula Souza got involved in the emerging abolitionist movement, seeking to "extirpate this cancer that lacerates us." In his spare time, he read about the United States: "Tocqueville, 'Démocratie en Amérique.' Then Michel Chevalier, 'Voyage aux États Unis.' I was so interested in reading about the history and institutions of this country that I was not satisfied before reading Laboulaye, 'Paris en Amérique,' and Astie, 'Histoire des États Unis.'"[76] Counting on influential friends and family members, Paula Souza was named general inspector of public works in his province. But the job did not bring him joy. Frustrated with the local reality and inspired by his readings on the United States, in 1869 he expressed his reformist views in a pamphlet. "Agriculture in Brazil," he asserted, "should have freed itself from this fatal inheritance from colonial times, slave labor; because slavery is incompatible with freedom and the rights of man."[77] Paula Souza also attacked the Brazilian monarchy, accusing it of fostering corruption and incompetence. As a result, his position as a public employee became untenable and he quit.

In April 1869, Paula Souza left Brazil for the United States in search of new professional experiences. In New York City, he spoke to the director of the United States and Brazilian Steamship Company, who directed him to St. Louis, Missouri. After a few weeks looking for a job there with no success, Paula Souza followed a few men to northwestern Missouri, where he found employment as a mapmaker at the Chillicothe-Brunswick Railroad Company.[78]

In September 1869, one month after his arrival, Paula Souza wrote to *O Ypiranga*, a São Paulo newspaper connected to the Liberal Party, describing Chillicothe: navigable rivers, water power for mills, good wood for construction, coal for steam engines, and fertile lands. "All the necessary elements for great prosperity are present here." But something had gone wrong in Chillicothe's recent past. "Why was this county," he inquired, "poor, very poor, until recently, until 1866? What satanic power prevented education, industry, and commerce from entering this portion of the blessed soil of the United States?" Paula Souza had the answer to his own questions: "Slavery! The eternal law could not be disavowed here. Slavery prevented the development of public education, the diffusion of wholesome moral principles, and consequently nothing advanced." To illustrate his point, Paula Souza narrated the story of a railroad project that had been stalled for almost twenty years because Chillicothe landowners feared that "the Yankees would come inhabit the region with their schools and their strange ideas, making it easier for the slaves to escape."[79]

The dawn of progress in Chillicothe came after the American Civil War. "Slavery ended: a new and amazing spectacle began," he exulted. "In these very fields, which some used to say only Africans could work, the men from the North produce twice, three times, as much as slave labor used to produce." According to Paula Souza, Chillicothe represented undeniable proof of the superiority of free to slave labor.

> The locals are the first to question their old inertia and lament how much time they wasted. . . . There is no mourning or pain in these fields; there is only the perpetual feast of free labor. It is really admirable, my friend, the development that has taken this town since emancipation. . . . All this movement, all this feverish activity, only took Chillicothe after slavery was gone. Banks, schools, newspapers, new buildings, a growing city, everything resulted from the transformation of labor. The magic wand of free labor, one of the Yankee fairies, created all this almost overnight, because about two years ago the beehive was silent and muffled under the malefic breath of slavery.[80]

Paula Souza saw new technology applied where only brute force had worked before: "Replacing the hoe and the overseer's lash, an elegant and modern equipment pulled by a horse, driven by a man comfortably placed on a comfortable seat." Paula Souza could not hide his astonishment before the spectacle of free labor revolutionizing a former slave state. "Slavery had precluded local elements from becoming productive," he continued. "Slavery now disappeared and things changed character, progress is the natural consequence."[81] Wage labor was an expansionist force, Paula Souza understood, which had made the free North the richest part of the Union before the Civil War and was now improving the South and the West.[82] He hoped it would soon expand to Brazil as well.

Paula Souza's objective was to inform his "province of everything that shows the inevitability of slave emancipation and the exigency of doing it without wasting time, because the difference in civilization that already exists between our country and others may increase to such a proportion that we will, for a long time, be seen as the orphans of progress." His fellow countrymen, Paula Souza advised, had much to learn from the American postwar experience: "I wish we could copy them! And erase the old and corrupt formulas that subjugate us, making us forget that we live in the American continent!"[83] There was no doubt in Paula Souza's mind: wage labor had to prevail.

If, in a public letter to his countrymen, Paula Souza painted Chillicothe in vibrant colors, his work experience there was far from vivid. "I vegetate, don't live," he wrote in his diary. After producing sixteen maps, which he valued between seventy-five and one hundred dollars, Paula Souza asked the railroad manager for fifty dollars. "But he had the imprudence of offering me 10 dollars! I told him to give the money to the poor and left."[84] Personal humiliation led the antislavery Paula Souza to reflect on the harsh reality of wage labor in the postwar United States: "It is a curious and perhaps inevitable thing in this world! Someone in need arrives and the employer throws him a crumb for a job that he would never perform for ten times more money. The capitalist not only takes advantage of the abundance of labor but also considers himself a protector, telling his workers that they would starve to death were it not for him."[85]

A few days after quitting his job, however, Paula Souza gave more thought to the problem of free labor, writing that "the political economy axiom of supply and demand is real, just like the axioms of the hard sciences. . . . Every man attends first to his own interests, only after can he attend to the interests of others." Reducing labor exploitation to scientific laws, Paula Souza convinced himself that the wage system was the most rational labor arrangement of all. Accordingly, he ended up regretting his earlier rebellion: "I did not need to go too far with the consequences to see how wrong and imprecise my premises were."[86] Like Rodrigues and other Brazilian and American antislavery reformers, Paula Souza normalized the exploitation of free but destitute workers by those who owned the means of production.

Soon, Paula Souza got a new job in Chillicothe. Try as he might, he could not live up to his own ideals. "The General Inspector of Public Works of the heroic province of São Paulo," he remarked sarcastically, "is now measuring assistant, carrying measuring chains, levels, etc.!!!" Making matters worse, he thought his new boss was "a great ignoramus" who could mechanically measure angles but knew next to nothing about physics or mathematics. Yet, once again, Paula Souza took a moment to reflect and saw that he could learn something from the experience: "Is it necessary that all engineers and assistants be scientific authorities? No. If this were the case, the progress of the world would be very slow." He came to the conclusion that it was practical knowledge that drove progress in the United States. "It is exactly in this point," he noted, "that the Americans are more advanced than any other nation. Here, no one expects a man to become a luminary in his field. What they want is a punctual execution of each one's duty. . . . Whether he does it mechanically or knows the principles governing methods and theories, it makes no difference."[87]

Nonetheless, the practical system of railroad building failed to guarantee stability for workers in the United State. Three months after Paula Souza's arrival in Chillicothe, financial difficulties struck the railroad company, which laid off the workers. Once again, he reflected on the hazards of free labor: "There are men here who are very poor and depend on daily manual labor, and by this act of the company they will go without the daily bread and will have to search for a new occupation, but they do not complain!" Paula Souza felt bad for complaining about his own difficulties as he realized that "I am not so poor to need to live off daily labor."[88] A member of a wealthy planter family, Paula Souza was positioned above the employment problems of common railroad workers in the United States. Yet, from his privileged position, he apprehended that the system of labor that he so vigorously defended did not offer a secure livelihood for the proletarian masses.

As he prepared to return to St. Louis, another engineer told Paula Souza to go to northwestern Illinois as the Rockford, Rock Island, & St. Louis Railroad Company needed engineers. Paula Souza's work experience there lasted only one month. Yet it confirmed one valuable lesson about the burgeoning transportation system of the United States. "The method of building American railroads (on the western prairie)," he observed, "consists of drawing a line avoiding the expensive properties. Then they check how many cubic yards of earth and the landfills, how many pillars and bridges, and go on doing every-thing blindly with the highest speed possible. There is no calculation; there is only action." He could not get over the fact that American engineers knew so little about theoretical matters: "Even the chief engineers, I am convinced, would not pass a preparatory exam in Zurich or Karlsruhe, even on the easiest subjects." But, all things considered, Paula Souza came to admire this system. "There is no need to be rigorous with theories," he argued, "and even when they are left out it is possible to execute works for the general good, as long as the time of execution can be shortened by such lack of attention."[89]

Although Paula Souza was sometimes concerned about the problems that this construction system might entail, he concluded that, by swiftly extending railroads across the continent, American engineers were successfully integrat-ing and developing a nation that not long ago had been devastated by a bloody separatist war. Speaking from the perspective of someone who had lived in Europe and South America, Paula Souza understood that the railroads existed to expand and integrate production. The western railroads, he believed, em-bodied the relentless logic of capitalist development and national integration of the postwar United States.[90]

After quitting his third job in the United States, Paula Souza decided to make the best of his stay and go on a tour. His first stop, right next to Rock Island, was the town of Moline, where he met a man named John Deere. "Thanks to his activity and intelligence," Paula Souza observed, "he ascended from mere laborer to owner of a great establishment in which more than 100 agricultural implements are made per day and hundreds of men find employ-ment." Deere seemed to embody the character traits of "the most energetic men of the country." Paula Souza considered his host a visionary for leaving Vermont for northwestern Illinois during the 1840s, anticipating that "several systems of communication, by land and water, would meet there or in the sur-rounding areas." Starting out as a blacksmith with a small workshop, Deere rendered invaluable services to the Northeastern farmers who were migrating west. By manufacturing plows adapted to the soil of the Midwest, Deere & Co. had become a giant of American capitalism.[91]

Yet, according to Paula Souza, good location and good products alone did not explain Deere's success. Because salaries were high in Illinois, Deere had to "introduce in his workshop machines that expedited labor and therefore decreased the price of the manufactured goods." In short, wage labor encour-aged the manufacturer to improve production. "Every year he enriches his workshop with a new labor instrument: now scissors to cut steel sheets, now a mallet to shape certain pieces, now a mechanical saw or jointer which increases production tenfold, etc." Deere employed steam-powered machines for all sorts of activities. "All these means of production," Paula Souza remarked, "were directed by very well-trained and well-paid operatives."[92]

Paula Souza grasped that free labor in the form of the wage system created a virtuous circle for capitalists: Deere, who owned a factory in Illinois, employed wage earners to produce plows; because the wage earners could come and go, searching for better employment, Deere had to save as much labor as possible, adopting production technologies that enhanced the quality of his plows. Under such a labor system, Paula Souza could see with his own eyes, the overwhelming majority of wage earners would never achieve an autonomous existence in the United States. Deere and his fellow employers, on the other hand, would accumulate more and more capital.

Still in Moline, a town of no more than ten thousand people, Paula Souza visited a bucket manufacturer who adopted the assembly line. "Like in John Deere's factory, I observed there a complete division of labor," he rejoiced. "Each operative executed one single task, and as a consequence the quantity of manufactured items each day was stupendous." At the Mississippi River, Paula Souza inspected the installation of turbines that would produce great amounts of energy and bring even more companies to Moline. He was astonished that "in one town we see more factories than in whole Brazilian provinces." He was further dazzled to think that "there are dozens of towns like Moline and thousands of men like John Deere in the American Union."[93]

From Illinois, Paula Souza took a southbound train. Crossing Tennessee, he observed that "between Decatur and Nashville it is possible to see a country similar to Rio Claro and Limeira: red soil, grass, some cotton and corn farms." When he arrived in Nashville, Paula Souza thought that "it is just like S[ão] Paulo. The view of the plains that on the horizon elevate into mountains, the river, the steep streets, everything is very similar to S. Paulo. The population is almost the same as that of S. Paulo, but commerce, construction, etc. are more intense here." The postemancipation Upper South, with its new railroads and steamers, gave Paula Souza hope for the future of his province. Nashville was "already an important point, and will continuously grow in importance: navigation on the Cumberland, railroads to all points." Paula Souza made detailed notes and drawings as he planned to apply what he learned to his native region.[94]

From Tennessee, Paula Souza went to Kentucky: "The country you cross is more populated; the small villages quickly succeed one another and the farms seem very well managed." Louisville was a pleasant surprise, making Paula Souza feel "in a civilized country: 150,000 inhabitants, rich, commercial, becoming a manufacturing, or, rather, an industrial center. It possesses many factories of machines, railroad equipment, bridges." From Kentucky to Ohio, Paula Souza reached "the queen of the West. Cincinnati is in fact a magnificent city: rich, industrial, full of magnificent buildings, and a large commerce. It is here that innumerable railroads converge."[95]

From Cincinnati, Paula Souza headed to Chicago. Nothing fascinated him more than the stockyards. He marveled at the railroads delivering cattle and grains, the speed with which the livestock moved from one place to the next, the fast processing of paperwork, the banks located nearby, the grain elevators storing corn to feed the yards, and the railroads exporting the processed meat to other states. Paula Souza saw firsthand what the historian William Cronon describes as "a new corporate network that gradually seized responsibility for moving and processing animal flesh in all parts of North America." The Chicago meatpacking industry, according to Cronon, fostered "a growing interpenetration of city and country. With it, seemingly, came an increasing corporate control over landscape, space, and the natural world."[96] Paula Souza, like other Brazilian visitors who came before and after him, felt exhilarated watching the spectacle of corporate capitalism. At every turn, he celebrated the exploitation of wage earners by those who owned the most sophisticated production and transportation technologies.

Paula Souza described the working of the slaughterhouses in detail: the hogs were taken from the pens and forced to go up an inclined plane that took them to the fifth floor of the building. There they were inserted into "a small compartment in which they are tied, killed, skinned, and gutted." All was done "with speed and cleanliness thanks to several ingenious machines used." From the upper to the ground floor, the carcasses went through different processes, which never disrupted one another. "Thanks to this division of labor and the improved machinery, in one day a slaughterhouse can buy a large number of living hogs and ship them to states of the South as cured meat."[97] Paula Souza was thrilled to see that, in the United States, labor-saving machinery and expert management had reached far beyond manufacturing. Fueled by free labor, industrial production had revolutionized something as ancient as slaughtering and butchering pigs.

After weeks exploring the Upper South and the Midwest, Paula Souza left for Europe and returned to Brazil a few months later. Back home by 1871, he started promoting American practices and institutions in his articles.

Writing on agricultural production, Paula Souza remarked that American farmers always adopted scientific methods of cultivation and processed all they produced in "appropriate machines: ventilators, dryers, threshers, etc." Referring to Lidgerwood Mfg. Co. Ltd. of Campinas, he pointed out that "we can understand the degree of perfection of these mechanisms by reminding ourselves that our best coffee-processing machines are of American invention." Comparing political structures, Paula Souza argued that businesses had more incentives to grow in the United States than in Brazil. "Instead of putting obstacles to private enterprise," he prescribed based on what he had seen, "general laws must foster it, not by trying to determine its activities with the excuse of protecting it, but setting it free, only regulating with clarity the rights of property."[98] Curiously, Paula Souza left out of his published works the bitter experiences that he had while laboring in North America. He also remained silent about the suffering of wage earners in railroad construction and other enterprises. All he could—or chose to—remember was the astonishing economic development of the postwar United States. A development propelled by wage labor and managed by engineers. A model that he would try to replicate in Brazil.

The (Black) Engineer

André Pinto Rebouças was Paula Souza's peer. Even though he did not belong to the planter elite, his family held slaves as domestic servants, and his father was Antonio Pereira Rebouças, a respected jurist and politician in the monarchical period. The young Rebouças earned the degree of military engineer from the Central School of Rio de Janeiro. After an educational trip to Europe, he started working with his brother, who was also an engineer, on port improvements. In 1865, Rebouças served in the Paraguayan War. Back in Rio de Janeiro in 1866, he became a well-known figure among the urban elite, joined the Sociedade Auxiliadora da Indústria Nacional (Auxiliary Society of National Industry; SAIN), and engaged in rebuilding the docks and the water supply system of the capital city. In 1871, Rebouças designed a railroad line in the southern province of Paraná. Unlike Paula Souza, however, Rebouças was a person of African descent.[99]

In 1872, Rebouças went on another foreign trip, this time to Europe and then the United States. In London, the American investor Charles J. Harrah, former partner of William Milnor Roberts in the construction of the Dom Pedro Segundo Railroad, handed Rebouças two letters of introduction.[100]

Arriving in New York City on June 9, 1873, he went straight to the luxurious Fifth Avenue Hotel. Yet, to his surprise, "I was told that they had no more rooms and directed me to another hotel. After a few attempts, I understood that the problem of color was the cause of the rejections." Rebouças then went to the Brazilian Consulate. The consul general did all he could to fix the situation but could get a room for Rebouças at the Washington Hotel only under the condition that he did not dine at the restaurant. "The first room I got was a very dirty little room on the 3rd floor," he wrote in his diary. "Later they gave me a bedroom with a living room on the ground floor, n. 43, with a direct exit to the public square where Broadway begins." Direct access to the street kept Rebouças out of the common areas of the hotel.[101]

An avid reader of *O Novo Mundo*, Rebouças set up a meeting with José Carlos Rodrigues. The two men bonded immediately. But Rodrigues's company did not make things much easier for Rebouças: "I spent the evening with Mr. Rodrigues. The prejudice of color prevented me from watching the spectacle at the 'Grand Opera House.'"[102] Passionate about opera, Rebouças never had a problem going to opera houses in Paris or Milan. Rodrigues, the great enthusiast of American society, felt deeply embarrassed about what was happening and tried to alleviate his friend's distress: "Rodrigues informed me yesterday that the mulatto [Frederick] Douglass, an old friend of President Grant and very influential in his reelection, was recently rejected by hotels in Washington. This fact created great controversy in newspapers and a motion in the Senate."[103] Rebouças learned that the color line was an inescapable reality in the United States, affecting even someone as famous as Douglass, whom Rebouças included in the Brazilian racial category of mulatto.

If Rebouças's visit was not as miserable as racist Americans were willing to make it, it was because he could rely on the expanding networks connecting Brazil to the United States. "I presented Harrah's letter at the [office of] Engineer [William] Milnor Roberts, director of the New York-Pacific Railway." Because Roberts was out of town, his secretary hosted Rebouças "with much kindness," taking him to the Cooper Institute, the Astor Library, the Seventh Regiment Armory, and the construction grounds of the Brooklyn Bridge.[104] Observing the building materials, Rebouças noticed that "Americans have unreserved trust in their steel, which they consider much superior to the European. They use it in their locomotive wheels, the walking beams of their steamships, etc."[105]

Rebouças also rejoiced to find a fellow member of the SAIN in New York: "At around one o'clock I had the pleasure to embrace at his office—165 Park Street—my old friend and colleague [William Van Vleck] Lidgerwood and get to meet his older brother John H. Lidgerwood."[106] The Lidgerwood brothers took Rebouças to the New York Department of Docks. The three men then headed to the construction grounds of the post office building. The mobile scaffolding system, Rebouças thought, was "recommendable for its elegance and economy."[107] They also visited the workshop of John Stephenson, a streetcar manufacturer who often advertised in Rodrigues's *O Novo Mundo*. "Philanthropist, free trader, a specialist and a lover of his business," the manufacturer delighted Rebouças.[108] In the workshop, he saw "good order and excellent machinery performing prodigious work. It is a true beehive."[109] Like Paula Souza, Rebouças was mesmerized by the world that wage labor had created.

After a few days, Rebouças informed his friends that he would go on a railroad journey. "John Lidgerwood offered to accompany me in the excursion in order to avoid difficulties caused by the prejudice of color."[110] The two men took the Fall River line of steamers from New York City to Providence. Then, they traveled by train through Rhode Island, Massachusetts, Upstate New York, Pennsylvania, and New Jersey, making several stops on the way. The color line followed Rebouças around. At a train station in Utica, New York, "a restaurant owner complained about my color, and it was necessary for John Lidgerwood to mention my nationality: my friend intentionally repeated the title 'Doctor.'" The same thing happened time and again. Although people of African descent could not travel or eat peacefully in the United States, Rebouças bumped into them everywhere: "In the trains as in the hotels the service is performed by blacks and mulattos."[111] In the brutal racial order of the post–Civil War United States, people of African descent had been incorporated to the ranks of wage earners. Rebouças witnessed how capitalist exploitation coexisted with racial segregation.

Setting the color line aside as much as he could, Rebouças concentrated on the economic organization of the American Northeast. He admired the very transportation system in which he suffered from racism, taking notes about everything he saw: tracks, bridges, canals, steamships, locomotives, and more. "The American wagons are much superior to the European kind," Rebouças registered in his notebook, "more room, more light, more air; individual safety, cold water, water closet, lighting, refreshments, newspapers, books and novels, sweets and fruits."[112]

In Lowell, Rebouças visited the Tremont Mills, in which he saw one "500 H.P. machine from Corliss Steam Engines Co.—Providence, Rhode Island. 4 turbines of 190 H.P. each. Good order and great hygiene everywhere.

Similar disposition at Suffolk Mills."[113] He also went on a tour of the Lowell Carpet Mills, "which employs steam and hydraulic engines of 250 H.P." The city of Lowell charmed Rebouças: "How beautiful this little town is; how different from the manufacturing towns of old Europe."[114] From Lowell, he headed to Cambridge to visit the Massachusetts Institute of Technology. Being himself an engineer, Rebouças delighted in inspecting the modern buildings, hallways, classrooms, chairs, desks, and lighting systems. He was also excited to see steam-powered engines and other advanced devices at the students' disposal.[115]

In northern New York, the Niagara waterfalls did not impress Rebouças as much as the local tourism industry, which he considered more developed than that of the Roman ruins in Italy. The cable car over the falls, he remarked, "is certainly characteristic of Yankee audacity." The new suspension bridge was "one of the most beautiful things engineering has ever produced."[116] In Buffalo, Rebouças admired the steamers on Lake Erie and "the Erie Canal, the first of a series of great works of public utility that made her [the United States] surpass Europe in prosperity."[117]

Pennsylvania steel also made an impression on Rebouças. In Pittsburgh, he inspected the American Iron Works Co. and observed that "the mill employs 2500 workers." In Philadelphia, he stopped by the shipyard of William Cramp & Sons. One of the Cramp brothers showed him around the facilities. Rebouças made a long list of all the machines he saw and paid close attention to a "large steamship of 1800 H.P. under construction." As in most manufacturing facilities he visited, he found "good order, good hygiene, much room around the establishment." He then went to Wilmington to inspect the luxurious cars of Jackson & Sharp Co. Delaware Car Works.[118] Finally, Rebouças visited Baldwin Locomotive Works, which was "preparing ten locomotives, out of a purchase of twenty, for the Dom Pedro Segundo Railroad."[119]

Nothing impressed Rebouças more, however, than the nascent oil industry of northwestern Pennsylvania. Near the town of Titusville, he reached "the shore of a marvelous stream; black from the petroleum extracted here!" In the middle of "a true forest of derricks," containing no fewer than sixty, Rebouças found himself in ecstasy: "At 10 P.M., the spectacle became marvelous. At the bottom of the Oil Creek Valley, the petroleum stream reflecting, at intervals, the flames of the gas pipes; . . . trees projecting fantastic shadows under the glow of a cyclopean light." The age of industry opened itself before Rebouças as he listened to "the hum of the steam engines burning natural gas, the grind of the wooden derricks; the blows of the mining bars perforating new wells;

the panting of the locomotive on the railway parallel to the river." The discovery of petroleum in Oil Creek, Rebouças learned, dated from 1858, but it was during the Civil War that this industry boomed. He reflected on the deeper meaning of the spectacle before his eyes: "In the times of Moses, God made water come out of rocks to free the people of Israel; in order to free the slaves of America, God made even more: He made oil emerge from the earth of Pennsylvania! When God works for liberty He is capable of producing wonders!"[120] For Rebouças, the oil of Pennsylvania represented more than just wealth that made the Union richer than the Confederacy; it represented, first and foremost, the power of industrial capitalism, capable of accomplishing things unimaginable in slave societies.[121]

Rebouças closed his wanderings at Lidgerwood's estate in Morristown, New Jersey, where the first coffee hullers that had been transforming Brazilian agriculture were produced. He was delighted to learn that, "in the garden of this residence, [Samuel] Morse worked with the help of the Lidgerwood family, inventing here the electric telegraph."[122] Rebouças also visited the Boonton Iron Works and the Grant Locomotive Works nearby.[123] Back in New York City, he heard that Rodrigues wanted to publish an article about his journey titled "Mr. Perpetual-Motion Rebouças." Shy, he declined the tribute. After buying some books, he left for Rio de Janeiro on June 23, 1873.[124]

Like Paula Souza, Rebouças was very selective in regard to what he publicized about the United States in the Brazilian press. He hardly mentioned anything about the color line. Instead, he lauded the American government for fostering private enterprise: "In the United States, a country in which *self-help* and the spirit of association are more vigorous than in England even, it is common practice for the federal or state government to provide 6% interest guarantee and direct pecuniary relief for canal and railroad companies."[125] Rebouças was also interested in the way American agriculture expanded westward, noting that, "in North America, the sons of the New World, the *Yankees*, prepare the lands and sell them in condition to be cultivated to European colonists." But this system was only possible, he added, under free labor: "Colonization and slavery, it must not be forgotten, are always in mortal struggle, in perfect antagonism. The great example of the United States clearly demonstrates that colonization is only possible after emancipation."[126]

During the 1870s, Rebouças's and Paula Souza's influence grew in Brazil. Both became important agents of infrastructural expansion. In their projects, they drew inspiration from the postwar United States. Only by submitting to the rule of engineers and capitalists, they preached, could a large nation develop its full potential and integrate its different parts. Rebouças's praise for how American society rebuilt itself after the Civil War made this point clear.

> The deadly North American war revealed to the world that it was not only in the length of its railroads that the United States was superior to France and England combined, but also that this unmatched republic was far ahead of the European nations in the arts of war as well as peace! Today, the United States is a very rich country of 40,000,000 inhabitants. Today, the great North American republic attends to all its national demands: it rebuilds New York, once made of wood, using porphyry, marble, and granite! Today, the engineer Pullman is invited to England to teach how to build palace-cars for railroads! Today, Americans can be proud of having river steamers unmatched in Europe, true floating palaces of indescribable luxury and elegance such as the *Providence* and the *City of Bristol*! Today, the prodigious nation can build in Philadelphia a monument to celebrate the centennial of its independence which will cast a shadow over the marvelous palaces of the London, Paris, and Vienna expositions![127]

Both Rebouças and Paula Souza knew well that economic inequality, corruption, and racism plagued the postwar United States. But they chose not to mention these problems. They did not waver over their commitment to free labor, which they saw as a transformative force. The United States was the land of the future, and the future, they trusted, would take care of all problems.

Modernizing members of the Brazilian elite, Rebouças and Paula Souza selected the characteristics of the American postwar experience that would better serve their own projects and interests. The great legacy of antislavery, they concluded, was a new capitalist world power, an economic system unmatched by any other country.[128] The only remaining independent slave society in the Western world and the world's leading coffee producer, Brazil would rebuild its plantation agriculture by adopting a system based on the concentration of capital in the hands of very few and the exploitation of formally free but destitute workers. Together, Brazilian observers and their American hosts were making wage labor into the universal formula of development.

The Students

Thanks to a geologist named Charles Frederick Hartt, more Brazilian engineers would come to think like Paula Souza and Rebouças. Born and raised in Atlantic Canada, Hartt joined Louis Agassiz at the Harvard Museum of Comparative

Zoology in the early 1860s. In 1865, he visited Brazil as a member of the Thayer Expedition; two years later, funded by the Cooper Institute, he returned to Brazil to continue his research. In 1868, thanks to Agassiz's recommendation, Hartt became chair of geology at the recently established Cornell University, and the following year he finished writing *Geology and Physical Geography of Brazil*, which was published along with Agassiz's *Scientific Results of a Journey in Brazil*.[129] A few months later, Hartt organized a new expedition to Brazil funded by Edwin Barber Morgan, a banker from Upstate New York.[130]

José Carlos Rodrigues did not miss the chance to praise *Geology and Physical Geography of Brazil*: "In an agricultural country, in which industry still needs to be developed, a work like the one we analyze here cannot be underestimated. It is impossible to create a rational and practical agricultural system without knowing nature or the composition of the mass that sustains the plant."[131] *O Novo Mundo* also published Hartt's biography and portrait. During the second visit of the Morgan Expedition to Brazil, in September 1871, Hartt was struck by the reach of Rodrigues's work. "I feel deeply indebted for what you have done for me in Brazil, I find I am known everywhere," he wrote to the editor while traveling the Amazon. "What is more, many persons who can't for the life of them see what is the use of my work think it must amount to something because the *Novo Mundo* says so."[132]

Personal friends, Hartt and Rodrigues worked together on attracting Brazilian youths to American universities. Brazilians had been studying abroad since the early nineteenth century, when the University of Coimbra, in Portugal, became a popular destination for the sons of the ruling elite seeking juridical education. By the middle of the century, as engineering became more popular, Brazilian youths chose French, German, Belgian, and Swiss institutions. During the 1870s, thanks to Rodrigues and Hartt, the United States became their primary destination. These men carried out the plan that antislavery reformers like Aureliano Candido Tavares Bastos and James Cooley Fletcher had made when they promoted a steamship line connecting New York City to Rio de Janeiro.[133]

In June 1871, *O Novo Mundo* presented a long article about Cornell. It described the beautiful campus, mentioned that Hartt was a member of the faculty, and explained its origins in the Land-Grant College Act of 1862. Rodrigues supported government grants for higher education as an efficient means to create large research institutions. But, consistent with his laissez-faire, he stressed that land-grant colleges were free from government intervention. All they had to do was to use government resources for the advancement of agriculture and the mechanical arts. Rodrigues grasped that the mission of such institutions was to promote capitalist development.[134] And this was precisely what Cornell was doing. As proof of its immediate impact, Rodrigues noted that Cornell had its own farm and workshops, in which students worked, and "all the roads and bridges close to the university were built by the students."[135]

Although located in Upstate New York, Cornell seemed well suited to Brazilian students willing to acquire knowledge applicable to their own country. Among its collections in natural history, the university had the Brazilian Collection in Archeology and the Brazilian Collection in Botany.[136] In 1874, with the help of his students, Hartt organized the Geological Survey of Brazil, which received support from the Brazilian government. Modeled after the surveys of the American West being conducted at the time, this project sought to research and publicize Brazil's natural resources, in addition to studying "the agriculture of the country, including the products of each agricultural region, the methods employed in cultivation, etc."[137]

Thrilled about the resources for Brazilian students available at Cornell, Rodrigues highlighted that "the costs here are not higher than in [the] São Paulo or Pernambuco [law schools]; and Brazilian parents will do well to send their sons to receive practical education in the United States." By mid-1871, the editor of *O Novo Mundo* reported that "a few days ago a Brazilian youth, Mr. E. F. Pacheco Jordão, arrived from Itu, São Paulo."[138] Elias Fausto Pacheco Jordão was the son of a wealthy fazendeiro. Thanks to the networks Rodrigues had established, he soon adapted to the American university. "Jordão is well and contented," Hartt informed Rodrigues, "he is a nice filho [son], I think he has come to the best place he could himself find."[139]

Other students from São Paulo soon followed Pacheco Jordão. Writing in 1874, Tomás de Aquino e Castro narrated how the network connecting Cornell to Brazil functioned. On arriving in New York City by steamship, Aquino e Castro and his cousin "went searching for the office of *O Novo Mundo* in order to visit the illustrious editor Mr. J. C. Rodrigues," who had acquired a reputation as "the patron of the Brazilian students in the United States." Rodrigues accompanied the two young men to Ithaca, introducing them to Hartt, who, "affable and kind, welcomed us with deference and consideration." At the hotel, "we received the joyful visit of the students Elias [Fausto Pacheco] Jordão, [Luiz de] Souza Barros, [Carlos] Paes de Barros, [Antonio de] Queiroz Teles Neto, Bento [de Almeida] Prado, and José Prado, who until then were the only Brazilians living there and who were enthusiastic about the growing community. We were eight then—and how odd!—all from the heroic province of São Paulo."[140]

In 1878, at the age of thirty-seven, Charles Frederick Hartt died of yellow fever while conducting research in Brazil. Yet Brazilian students kept enrolling at Cornell. Out of the thirty-four Brazilian students enrolled at the university during the 1870s and 1880s, twenty-three were from the province of São Paulo. Like Pacheco Jordão, most were children of the fazendeiros of the Oeste Paulista and most studied engineering.[141] Since the American Civil War, São Paulo had been the Brazilian province with the closest ties to the United States. The most successful colony of ex-Confederates in Brazil was situated in Santa Bárbara, William Van Vleck Lidgerwood had established his factory in Campinas, and American missionaries had opened schools all over the province. Writing in 1875 for O Novo Mundo, João Guilherme de Aguiar Whitaker, the fazendeiro from Rio Claro, took pride in seeing one more element tying his region to the United States: "Around fifty men from São Paulo crossed the ocean to study in that country. Thankfully! Let us pray that they come back strengthened by example, by education, and capable of sowing the seeds that will fertilize our soil already so inclined to adopt North American uses and customs."[142]

Reinforcing these networks, the Brazilian students created a monthly publication titled Aurora Brasileira: Periodico Litterario e Noticioso—Orgão dos Estudantes Brasileiros nos Estados Unidos.[143] They made clear from the outset who their mentor was, emphasizing that "the coming of so many Brazilians to this university happens thanks to that gentleman, who has shown the advantages of education in this country through the civilizing pages of O Novo Mundo and has welcomed all Brazilians in New York, advising that they come to this university, one of the best in the country. The creation of the Aurora is, therefore, a triumph of O Novo Mundo."[144]

Like O Novo Mundo, the Aurora Brasileira portrayed São Paulo as the motor of Brazilian progress. In April 1874, it reminded its readers that "long ago, through independent initiative, the province of São Paulo first considered replacing the slave hand, and this happened well before the law . . . that put a definitive end to the trade in Africans to Brazil." Moreover, São Paulo agriculture, "diverse and abundant as it is, has long rejected the old routine." Private enterprise had brought railroads, factories, and schools to the province. "The Massachusetts of Brazil," São Paulo was destined for great things, according to the Aurora Brasileira.[145]

Also like O Novo Mundo, the Aurora Brasileira drew inspiration from American antislavery forces. The son of a fazendeiro from the township of Brotas, located fifty miles northwest of Rio Claro, Francisco de Assis Vieira Bueno was an enthusiast of the American Republican Party. "In the midst of the horror of a civil war, when all attentions converged to it," he wrote in reference to the Land-Grant College Act, "the representatives of the American Union discussed, and A. Lincoln sanctioned, laws that provided industrial education to the people, to all the people. In this act we find the greatness of the Americans."[146]

The fazendeiros and their sons knew well what kind of institution Cornell was. Before the Civil War, Ezra Cornell, the university founder, had declared his detestation of slavery and concluded from his visits to Virginia that it bred ignorance and poverty. In 1871, the university librarian reported that the abolitionist Samuel Joseph May had "generously presented to this Library his collection of books and pamphlets relating to the Slavery and Anti-Slavery contest in this country." Responding to the librarian's request, other abolitionists donated materials to the collection, making Cornell a center for the study of slavery and its pernicious effects.[147]

Vieira Bueno and his fellow Cornell students believed that if Brazilian legislators followed the example of American Republicans, adopting measures similar to the Land-Grant College Act, the backward practices of Brazilian agriculture would soon disappear.

> The farmer who understands a little about physics, instead of prayer and vows, will employ his time in saving the plants of his garden by irrigation; instead of having four rifle shots on each corner of his cotton farm, maybe he will find in chemistry the means to extinguish the caterpillar; veterinary seems less open to error than the often brutal practices of the witch-doctor; mechanical engines might replace the pestle and improve the mortar; botany might teach many things that can be useful in gardens and orchards.[148]

The Brazilian students at Cornell became agricultural modernizers: "The progress of agriculture requires the assistance of machines, means of communication, railroads, bridges, dams, docks, the opening of ports, the destruction of reefs." Full of optimism, they asserted that "the time that dawns now in Brazil is that of Engineering. The movement begins: on all steamships young Brazilians depart for the United States, seeking to study the sciences—confident that they will render great services to their country: fifteen came to Cornell alone, and many others are on their way."[149]

The time at Cornell represented a transformative experience for the sons of the fazendeiros. Aquino e Castro described the positive surprise he had when he first arrived on campus: Pacheco Jordão "worked with his own hands, spiking the soil of the Union with several miles of railway"; Souza Barros "breathed an atmosphere of acids in the chemistry laboratory"; Paes de Barros

TABLE 5.1 Theses Produced by Brazilian Students at Cornell University (1870s–1880s)

Author	Thesis title	Degree	Year
Carlos Paes de Barros	"Review of the Works at the Mont Cenis Tunnel"	Civil Engineering	1876
Francisco de Assis Vieira Bueno	"The Theorem of Three Moments and Its Application to Bridge Building"	Civil Engineering	1876
Antonio Epaminondas de Maria Frota	"Studies and Investigations on the Harbor of Ceará, Brazil and a Plan of Its Improvement"	Civil Engineering	1877
Domingos Correia de Morais	"East Tarrytown Viaduct"	Civil Engineering	1877
Joaquim Viegas Muniz	"Foundations on Water"	Civil Engineering	1877
Bento de Almeida Prado	"Rotation of Crops"	Agriculture	1878
Augusto Cezar de Vasconcelos	"Warming and Ventilation"	Mechanical Engineering	1878
Quintiliano Nery Ribeiro	"Swiss Architecture"	Architecture	1878
José Tibiriçá Piratininga	"Boiler Explosions"	Mechanical Engineering	1879
Anastacio Rodrigues de Aquino Coimbra	"Iron, Steel and Their Manufacture"	Mechanic Arts	1884
Casimiro Eugenio Amoroso Lima	"Food and the Physiology of Digestion"	Agriculture	1885
Arão Ferreira de Ávila	"Conservation of Energy"	Electrical Engineering	1885
Bento de Barros	"The Effect of Nitrogenous and Non-Nitrogenous Foods, on the Fat and Lean Meat of Sheep"	Agriculture	1888

Source: Kroch Library of Rare and Manuscript Collections, Cornell University.

"surveyed university lands"; Vieira Bueno studied bridge building; and Almeida Prado "trained by moving agricultural implements on the American soil." Aquino e Castro was confident that his friends' training represented more than individual efforts: "It was Brazil that had come here to remake itself, undressing the dull cloak of the royalty and taking the garments of the humble worker of the century!"[150] Rodrigues went further, connecting these efforts to the end of slavery in Brazil. "They want to learn," he proclaimed, "they see on the walls of the near future the 'mene, mene, tekel, upharsin' of slavery; and through this sentence they see their country in need of all the energy from the men who will found the new order. . . . Never before have young Brazilians dedicated themselves so much to natural sciences and mathematics as now."[151]

The positive experience of the Brazilian students at Cornell led *O Novo Mundo* and the *Aurora Brasileira* to expand their promotion of American higher education. They wrote about Lehigh University, in Pennsylvania, explaining that it provided hands-on experience for engineering students at its two foundries.[152] They pointed out that Lafayette College, also in Pennsylvania, was a center of excellence in the study of mining.[153] They also advertised the University of Cincinnati, the Massachusetts Agricultural College, and the Rensselaer Polytechnic Institute. Dozens of Brazilian youths joined these and other American institutions of higher education in the 1870s and 1880s.

In 1875, José Custódio Alves de Lima, the son of a fazendeiro from the township of Tietê, located fifty miles west of Campinas, transferred from Cornell to Syracuse University and took with him the Brazilian students' publication. He renamed it *Aurora Brazileira: Engenharia, Mechanica, Sciencia, Agricultura, Artes e Manufacturas*. Inspired by publications such as *Scientific American*, Alves de Lima sought to make the journal into a guide for Brazil's progress: "If there is a country in need of periodicals dealing with mechanics applied to industry and agriculture, this country certainly is Brazil. True, we are a rich country, but we are very poor at the same time; we certainly have inexhaustible treasures, but we have not used them yet. Our people still has very deficient ideas about mechanics, engineering, agriculture, etc."[154] The new *Aurora Brazileira* (now with a "z") would "familiarize the Brazilian people with the scientific progress made here [in the United States] from a material and a moral perspective."[155]

Alves de Lima's central goal was the improvement of Brazilian agriculture. "We understand," he announced in October 1877, "that the time is arriving when no one will be a good agriculturalist without knowledge, even if superficial, about the principles of chemistry, geology, and botany." According to Alves de Lima, scientific knowledge applied to agriculture automatically led to mechanization. He preached that "on a farm, economy basically consists of performing labor with the least cost, the least waste, in the best way possible." Only by "applying modern agricultural machines and using steam-power" would the agriculturalist reach this goal.[156]

Like Rodrigues, Alves de Lima was invested in introducing American technology into Brazil. He often announced, in English, that "parties who would like to have their goods known and introduced in Brazil, principally those manufacturers of engines, bridges, agricultural implements, locomotives, rolling stock, etc., will find at once that it pays to advertise in the *Aurora Brazileira*, which is the only organ of men of progress in Brazil."[157]

Alves de Lima hoped that by introducing American capital goods into Brazil, his periodical would help eradicate what he identified as the main cause of

Brazilian backwardness: slave labor. Work that could be performed by machines, he observed, "is done in Brazil by slaves, who, we must admit, are always sluggish. Why should Brazil not imitate the United States at least in material improvements?"[158] Like other antislavery reformers of his generation, Alves de Lima saw industrial technology as a force opposed to slavery. He contended that the Law of the Free Womb would "only attain the beneficial results that our legislators envisioned if, from now on, we promote the complete revolution in our system of rural labor, replacing manual work with machines, creating a reasonable economy of time and money."[159] Technology would help Brazil substitute the immigrant for the slave: "The German, Portuguese, Italian, or American colonists will work better if they have in hand a plow or an improved machine to cut grass, rice, etc. . . . Thus, Brazilian agriculture needs to adopt machines, just like the United States did after slave emancipation."[160] An agricultural modernizer, Alves de Lima concluded that the concentration of capital in the hands of the planter class was the key factor in fostering wage labor and creating capitalist development in Brazil.

Alves de Lima's approach to slave emancipation was based on that of André Pinto Rebouças, whom the *Aurora Brazileira* often praised as one of the most brilliant minds in Brazil. When, in 1877, Rebouças presented at the SAIN a project "to provide technical education to the people and prepare them in arts and industry," Alves de Lima applauded with enthusiasm. He stressed that Rebouças was tackling the most important challenge that Brazil would face in the near future: "Will the Brazilians be prepared to receive with courage the shock that, sooner or later, will come? Are the planters working on improving agricultural labor so, when they have no more slaves, the work on their plantations will not be disturbed?" The Brazilian government should follow Rebouças's lead and tell the planters that "their capital will not be affected by slave emancipation *if they adopt* the agricultural machinery used in this country [the United States] and in others."[161]

Alves de Lima chided Brazilian planters who invested in slaves instead of machines. "They consider expensive a machine that does the work of ten slaves and still do not hesitate to pay ten times more for one slave!"[162] What these benighted planters needed was "practical knowledge to calculate with precision if it is advantageous to buy three or four slaves to obtain a certain quantity of labor that we could easily obtain through a machine that costs half, a third, or a quarter of the capital immobilized."[163] The adoption of machinery would help planters free themselves from the burdensome slave property and employ wage earners. Alves de Lima looked down on the followers of Senator Bernardo Pereira de Vasconcelos, a spokesman for the Paraíba Valley, who had insisted in the 1840s that "our civilization came from Africa." These were men fighting the spirit of the age: "The tortoise-statesman (as everyone knows) alluded to the benefit of importing more slaves to Brazil, the greatest error that our ancestors bequeathed to the present generation."[164]

But there were signs of progress among Brazilian planters. Like Rodrigues and the Cornell students, Alves de Lima admired the fazendeiros of his native province. "There is no Brazilian who is not ecstatic about the progress that S[ão] Paulo has made in such a short time," he wrote in May 1877. "While in other regions of the Empire individual energy obtains nothing, in S. Paulo capital is raised in order to build railroads that carry life and light everywhere." New schools emerged throughout the Oeste Paulista. And now, Alves de Lima exulted, "we are proud to say that here [in the United States] we find young men from Campinas, Piracicaba, Tietê, Capivari, Tatuí, Jundiaí, Santos, Itu, and other towns, who decided to come on their own or through advice from their parents. Some study engineering, others mechanics, agriculture, or medicine." These young men had the potential to transform their country: "Our readers from other provinces will be surprised to learn that the students from São Paulo are the children of wealthy planters, who see in the education of their sons a great investment not only useful to themselves but also to society and their birthplace."[165]

Along with knowledge, São Paulo was absorbing technology from the United States. Alves de Lima noted that "the Porter Manufacturing Company, which has always advertised in the *Aurora*, is presently building several steam-powered machines to be used in the townships of Tietê and Capivari in the province of São Paulo."[166] Moreover, Luiz de Souza Barros, a student at Columbia University and a contributor to the *Aurora Brazileira*, sent "one hay-cutting machine, three different harvesters, one corn-planting machine, one grain-processing machine, one alfalfa-planting machine, several cultivators, and other implements to the plantation of Mr. José de Souza Barros, a planter from Araraquara." Alves de Lima extolled "the progressive spirit of the Souza Barros family."[167]

Brazilian young men attended American universities in the 1870s and 1880s to learn how to rebuild a national economy and integrate a territory of continental dimensions on the basis of free labor. They learned in the United States that applied scientific knowledge could help major planters efficiently put freedpeople and the free poor to work for them. Their vision of the future entailed the overthrow of slavery and the adoption of wage labor.[168] After graduation, they would return home to create enterprises that would bring São Paulo closer to American economic standards.

The Guests

While Brazilian youths studied hard at institutions like Cornell, some of their most prominent countrymen went on a tour of the United States. On April 15, 1876, none other than Dom Pedro II landed in New York City. James O'Kelly, a *New York Herald* reporter who covered the visit, noted that "the Emperor of Brazil wins favor at every step. His Majesty pleasantly represents himself as a student, eager to be instructed and willing to avail himself of knowledge that subsequently may be put into practical operation in his own domain, and may redound to the advantage of the empire of which he is the benign ruler." Pleasing American sycophants, Dom Pedro II self-identified as "the Yankee Emperor."[169]

On May 10, 1876, Dom Pedro II joined Ulysses S. Grant for the opening ceremony of the Centennial Exhibition in Philadelphia. Together, they started the Corliss Engine, which supplied energy to the main building. The Brazilian monarch of Habsburg, Bourbon, and Braganza lineage was the most celebrated of the two. Americans were so enamored of Dom Pedro II that the *Phrenological Journal and Science of Health* published a special article about his physical features. "The contour of his forehead shows excellent memory, and his eyes indicate ability to talk with precision and clearness." A striking body accompanied such a magnificent head: "Over six feet by three inches in height, and possessing an athletic frame, with a face whose expression is gentle and winning, and manners that are simple and dignified, he reminds an observer of the knightly kings of romance."[170]

However flattered Dom Pedro II felt, such praise had more to do with American politics than with his own aptitudes as a statesman. By 1876, the Grant administration was facing charges of corruption and abuse of power. The day after Dom Pedro's arrival, the *New York Herald* discussed what he might observe during his stay: "If he looks to Washington he will see a strange flowering of the centennial period—a House of Representatives so busily engaged in ferreting out corruptions that it has no time to pass the bills necessary to supply the public buildings with gas and coal."[171] Distilling their irony, the critics of Reconstruction projected onto the Brazilian monarch the qualities that they found lacking in American politicians. "Dom Pedro is the first Emperor we have seen on this imperial soil, where all are emperors," the *New York Herald* taunted. "How much better our Yankee Emperor behaves than some of his foreign cousins! . . . When he goes home he will know more about the United States than two-thirds of the members of Congress."[172] Elite New

Yorkers, who had earlier co-opted José Carlos Rodrigues to the opposition to Reconstruction, now manipulated the Brazilian monarch. Unwittingly, "the knightly king of romance" offered a precious opportunity to those who were pushing back against social and political reform in the United States.

That Dom Pedro II was the ruler of a slave empire did not escape American observers. Yet they were quick to transform shame into honor. The *New York Evangelist* claimed that Dom Pedro II favored emancipation. "But wisely mindful of the prejudices as well as interests which time had established among his wealthier subjects," he enacted piecemeal liberation and encouraged free immigration. "By these means he gradually demonstrated the superiority of free labor, and so prepared the public mind for a degree of total, though gradual, emancipation, which was promulgated in 1871."[173] Similarly, the Philadelphia *Friends' Intelligencer* highlighted that "the total abolition of slavery in Brazil is believed to be, now, the desire and intent of the Emperor, and he ardently cherishes the hope of accomplishing the work 'without causing convulsions, or reducing to misery both the planters and their former slaves.'"[174] Echoes of anti-Reconstruction propaganda were more than evident in articles like these. As white Americans grew hostile to admitting black people as full citizens of the United States, attacks on immediate slave emancipation became common.[175] The slow transition that Dom Pedro II seemed to encourage in Brazil thus appeared as wise policy making.

The admirers of Dom Pedro II suggested that the American people could see the results of his enlightened rule in the Brazilian section of the Centennial Exhibition.[176] The popular *Frank Leslie's Illustrated* declared that "Brazil is justly credited with making one of the finest and most interesting displays, embracing all the varied products of the country and its provinces."[177] Brazil mounted the largest foreign exhibition in Philadelphia, containing raw materials, handcrafts, paintings, publications, weapons, and agricultural implements, among many other items.[178] Fascinated by the Brazilian section and celebrating the friendship between the two countries, *Lippincott's Monthly Magazine* proclaimed that "Brazil, the great power of South—as the Union is of North—America, possesses nearly half of the accessible virgin territory of the tropics. Our interest joins hers in retaining this vast endowment as far as possible for the benefit of the Western World."[179] As usual, Dom Pedro II received praise for the work of other people. An official committee of seven members had set up the Brazilian section. Servants, managers, secretaries, diplomats, and students assisted the committee. Rodrigues provided crucial advice and services to all.[180]

The Brazilian committee's main goal was to publicize that "coffee is actually esteemed as the best product and as the first cause of the public wealth in Brazil." Nicolau Joaquim Moreira, the prominent agricultural reformer at the SAIN and a member of the committee, prepared a pamphlet in English titled *Brazilian Coffee*, which Rodrigues published, to be distributed to the American public. Referring to the contribution of his SAIN associate William Van Vleck Lidgerwood, Moreira remarked that São Paulo planters used modern machinery to ensure the best quality. "For hulling, screening, selecting and polishing coffee," he explained, "the more advanced farmers employ the most improved machinery, conspicuous among which are the American machines of Lidgerwood & Co." The New Jersey manufacturer had "rendered great services to the cultivators of this product, especially in S. Paulo, whence the coffee known in the market as *machine coffee*, comes."[181] On the fazendas of the Oeste Paulista, the *Catalogue of the Brazilian Section* stressed, coffee was "gathered in sieves, sun dried, decorticated, and polished by American machines." It further emphasized that "the coffee of S. Paulo (which is exported through Santos) enjoys the best reputation in foreign markets, and there are few farmers of S. Paulo who do not employ machinery for improving coffee."[182]

The Vergueiro, Paula Souza, Souza Queiroz, Pacheco Jordão, Paes de Barros, and other powerful planter families sent samples of their coffee to Philadelphia. The fazendeiros of the Oeste Paulista had been preparing their participation for a long time. By 1874, local authorities had organized a provincial exhibition to gather the best coffee of the province. The president of São Paulo had instructed municipal councils and police chiefs to "invite the largest number possible of producers to submit specimens of industry and agriculture to the exposition."[183] The coffee was subsequently sent to a national exhibition organized by the Ministry of Agriculture, Commerce, and Public Works in 1875. There, specialists selected the cream of the crop to be sent to Philadelphia.[184]

On April 2, 1876, the Brazilian committee wrote to the director of the Centennial Exhibition that Brazil had "a quantity of coffee which is to be distributed gratuitously in order to convince Americans that our coffee is the best."[185] Moreira was confident that Brazilian coffee would be "distinguished in the great and pacific competition which is going to take place in the country which was so fortunate as to be the home of Washington, Franklin, Lincoln and Johnson."[186] Brazilian coffee samples received several prizes in Philadelphia. The Caffé do Brazil became a very popular spot of the Centennial Exhibition by selling cups of Brazilian coffee to the visitors wandering around Fairmount

FIGURE 5.5 Caffé do Brazil at Fairmount Park, Philadelphia, 1876.
Courtesy of the Free Library of Philadelphia.

Park. Rodrigues believed that the café would teach "the great mass of visitors to the Exposition" to appreciate "a good cup of coffee." On opening day, Dom Pedro II took President Grant there to enjoy the beverage.[187]

But the Brazilians were not in the United States only to promote their coffee. They also wanted to observe the wonders of American development, which extended far beyond Philadelphia. Dom Pedro II, the committee members, and other Brazilian visitors spent several weeks exploring the country. From Massachusetts mill towns to Louisiana sugar plantations, from Pennsylvania oil fields to California fruit farms, they were pleased to witness what free labor could do for a country so recently devastated by a civil war.

The sprawling transportation infrastructure was the first thing that caught the Brazilians' attention on their tours. Dom Pedro II, who wrote a detailed journal of his trip, joked that soon Americans would "build a Yankee Tunnel underneath the Bering Strait. And it will be possible to go by train from N.Y. to Lisbon. And maybe South America."[188] Traveling west with the monarch,

Luís Pedreira do Couto Ferraz, the Baron of Bom Retiro, remarked that "the movement on these railways is astonishing. People outside have no correct idea of it. There are railways everywhere. It is a wonder collisions do not occur more frequently."[189] The Cornell student Vieira Bueno traveled alongside João Martins da Silva Coutinho, the Army engineer who had guided Louis Agassiz through the Amazon in the 1860s. They rejoiced to see Buffalo and realize that it had become "the commercial hub between East and West, formed by the great railroad lines, Lake Erie, and the canals."[190]

Through the train windows, the Brazilian visitors saw a nation becoming unified and an industrial economy flourishing. They marveled at how quickly the railroad and other means of transportation had encouraged the settlement and development of the North American hinterlands, expanding the power of both capital and the state.[191] According to O'Kelly, from New York to Illinois, Dom Pedro II "did not cease to admire the small, growing towns, so thickly scattered along the line of the railway, and the frequent occurrence of splendid public buildings in situations where they could scarcely have been expected, giving proof of the energy, self-reliance and industry of the inhabitants." On arriving in Chicago, the Brazilian monarch found "it truly wonderful that such a magnificent city could have been built up in a few years, but, important as are the buildings and splendid streets, the public improvements, like the water works and the tunnels, are still more worthy of attention and praise."[192]

Chicago, more so than any other American city, dazzled the Brazilian observers. The committee member Pedro Dias Gordilho Paes Leme, a coffee planter from the Paraíba Valley, took a tour of the Chicago stockyards and was impressed that "all these pens combined can house 60,000 animals!" He inspected the slaughterhouses, attentively observing "the bleeding, skinning, opening, and separating in four parts of five hogs per minute; within just ten minutes the hog reaches the tables for salting."[193] Vieira Bueno and Coutinho regarded Chicago as the new center of world: "I do not know if it is its large streets full of mansions, the Palmer Hotel by itself, the fifteen railroad lines that arrive there, Lake Michigan with myriad steamers, the commerce of wheat and flour, or the unmatched fire department. I do not know what makes me repeat—to see Chicago and then die! What frenzy, what activity, what luxury!"[194]

From Chicago Dom Pedro II headed to Omaha and stopped by smelting works, observing "the powerful machinery and arrangements for rolling and working the metal." According to O'Kelly, Dom Pedro II was "very well satisfied with the examination of this specimen of our industrial enterprise."[195]

Passing through Cheyenne, Wyoming, "the Emperor was surprised to see a city so far West, where he had expected to meet only buffaloes and Indians."[196] On his way back east, Dom Pedro II was pleased to see mining enterprises, extracting not only gold and silver but also iron, coal, lead, and copper. He was also surprised to see thriving factories of sewing machines and plows in cities like Des Moines, Iowa.[197]

Arriving in Pennsylvania, Dom Pedro II decided to visit the oil fields. "His Majesty proceeded to inspect the Imperial Petroleum Works," O'Kelly narrated, "where he had an opportunity of acquainting himself with the various processes through which the oil passes during its preparation for the market. The Emperor was deeply interested in all that he saw." In Pittsburgh, Dom Pedro II made a stop at "the American Iron Works, where 3,000 men are employed, and, having carefully inspected the works, he paid the manager the compliment of saying that in some of the departments the works were more complete than any he had seen in Europe."[198] Coutinho and Vieira Bueno also enjoyed exploring the "City of Smoke": "Never before, my friend, have I experienced similar sensation as seeing through the dense night such a beautiful spectacle of innumerable forges throwing in the atmosphere smoke and blazes of fire as if they were the volcanos of the Andes. It is beautiful to see those men there in the glowing heat of the red hot iron, working for the progress and the comfort of those whom Fortune has chosen."[199]

True, mining and manufacturing made the country pulsate; but the Brazilian explorers understood that agriculture was its lifeblood. Thus, they set to inspecting the works of agricultural machinery manufacturers. In Syracuse, José Custódio Alves de Lima took Moreira and Paes Leme to the workshop of Bradley & Co., which advertised in the *Aurora Brazileira*.[200] In St. Louis, Vieira Bueno and Coutinho visited "the warehouse of agricultural implements of Semple, Birge & Co., a great establishment in which the farmer finds the ax, rake, plow, oxbow yoke, corn thresher and mill, animal-powered machines, steam-powered machines, and hundreds of other things that are the secret of the agricultural prosperity of this country."[201] In Moline, Illinois, Paes Leme visited the most famous manufacturer of agricultural implements of all. "Mr. [John] Deere gave us a warm welcome in his house, where we dined. In the afternoon we went to the fields to see the work of the gang plows. The work is excellent and performed with economy of time and labor, and the machine responds with ease to every movement of the farmer as I could see for myself while controlling one of them." A few miles from Deere's factory, Paes Leme visited two other establishments that also produced plows and harvesters.

"One hundred forty thousand precious implements a year," he marveled, "come out of this small corner of the state, in which 8,000 souls live."[202]

In central Illinois, the Brazilians stopped by the Burr Oak Farm, which Paes Leme described as "an ocean of corn!" The owner, M. L. Sullivant, welcomed the visitors with joy, took them on a tour, and invited them to dine and sleep at his house. The forty-thousand-acre farm, entirely enclosed and divided into fifty-acre plots, employed three hundred workers, five hundred mules, "200 plows, 150 cultivators, 45 seeders, 25 harrows, and a large number of carts." Paes Leme saw black and white workers toiling side by side, all receiving fifteen dollars a month plus food and shelter. The reason the operation worked, he concluded, was that "the whole property is cut by a railroad line built in the American style. . . . Everything is light and inexpensive, and this way the bushel of corn reaches Atlantic ports at 12 cents after traveling more than 1,000 miles."[203] Vieira Bueno and Coutinho deplored that there were not many men like Sullivant in Brazil: "Go tell a Brazilian planter that the cultivation of corn can generate a great fortune, . . . go tell him and he will laugh at your face or will come up with the trite idea—this is not for Brazil."[204] But the Brazilian observers trusted that the time would come when, by employing labor-saving machinery, Brazil's coffee plantations would extract more profit from wage earners than Burr Oak did.

Irrigated farming in California also impressed the Brazilian visitors.[205] Paes Leme rejoiced to find one of "the curiosities of this country of fairy tales, . . . the great labor and extreme care at the cultivation of precious fruits from the European Mezzogiorno." On visiting a fair exhibiting the produce of Santa Clara Valley, he noted that "the dry climate of California and its deep and rich soil are excellent for such crops, but the cultivation would not be profitable were it not for the railroads which take the vegetables and fruits to the markets of New York and other cities." Paes Leme emphasized that the railroad made California bloom: "Affordable transportation transforms the character of a country!"[206]

However, a good transportation system had to be coupled with a good labor system so that the American West could flourish. According to the Brazilian observers, free labor was the force behind rapid development. High salaries in California, Paes Leme argued, led agriculturalists "to acquire improved implements such as gang plows, mowers, and other machines to process cereals. These powerful assistants and the fertility of the soil have sustained cultivation for more than twenty years, producing such good wheat that it now competes with Russia and Turkey, where salaries are almost nonexistent, and builds

FIGURE 5.6 Five years before the Centennial Exhibition, Rodrigues had published a special report on Burr Oak, which kindled the interest of many Brazilian readers. "Cultura em Grande Escala nos Estados Unidos," *O Novo Mundo*, October 24, 1871.

Courtesy of the Fundação Biblioteca Nacional, Rio de Janeiro.

fortunes for the farmers of the West."[207] Paes Leme, himself a slaveholder from the Paraíba Valley, could not help but conclude that free labor produced better results than unfree labor. After all, he tirelessly repeated, American agriculture was now the most efficient in the world. "The average productivity of a worker here is 400 dollars, reaching a maximum of 1,000 dollars in California." In slaveholding Brazil, he lamented, it did not surpass fifty dollars.[208] Paes Leme reached the same conclusion that Antonio Francisco de Paula Souza had reached seven years earlier: wage labor created a virtuous circle that led to technological improvement and the accumulation of capital.

Like Paes Leme, Nicolau Joaquim Moreira wanted to understand how free labor thrust the postwar United States forward. He therefore decided to study immigration during his trip. In a report to the Brazilian Ministry of Agriculture, Commerce, and Public Works, Moreira explained that foreigners migrated to the United States because they could find well-paying employment there. Based on his observations, he proposed measures to be adopted in Brazil such as civil marriage, an easy road to citizenship, and a homestead act based on the one Lincoln had signed in 1862. But none of these reforms would be effective, he advised, without "the complete abolition of slavery, which has contributed to our contempt for work and our preference for inertia instead of activity. The existence of slavery or serfdom in manufacturing and farming, instead of dignifying labor, degrades it."[209]

Buying into the myth of the American frontier, the Brazilian explorers tried to demonstrate how native-born and immigrant workers integrated a coherent system of economic expansion.[210] Paes Leme explained that the Anglo-American pioneer, after cutting trees and creating a profitable lumber industry, "begins the economic labor of the plow, as we can observe on the western prairies." Once production began to decline, the pioneer moved onto "new adventures and new lands, selling the small property to European immigrants, who then establish a new agricultural system, suitable for the needs of manufacturing, which makes the country advance. Following this march, the Americans establish great cities which become, in a short time, production centers of all articles necessary for men."[211] Moreira added that "immigrants only enjoy true stability when they live close to consumer markets and means of transportation, maintain their religion, educate their children, and acquire useful knowledge: thus, *the railroad, the telegraph, the church, the school, and the newspaper* are the five indispensable elements of American immigrant colonies."[212] These elements, he believed, could take root only where free labor prevailed.

Inspired by the panorama of American progress, the Brazilian visitors went shopping. They purchased locomotives from Baldwin and wagons from Jackson & Sharp and Pullman Palace Car Works.[213] The Brazilian committee also made a large purchase of American agricultural machinery to serve as samples for Brazilian importers, inventors, manufacturers, and planters.[214] Paes Leme attended a special demonstration in Philadelphia, observing how "Buckeye, McCormick & Co., Russell & Co., Rochester Works, and others engaged in combat with great gallantry, presenting excellent and ingenious machines." He trusted that the dissemination of American agricultural technology in Brazil would constitute "the shortest and safest way of transforming our agricultural labor." Paes Leme was confident that "the plow and the horse ... will be the emancipators of the rural worker in Brazil."[215] The Brazilian observers had figured out the formula of American development: concentrate capital to exploit free labor to concentrate more capital and so on and so forth. Their goal now was to replicate this formula in their own country to eliminate slavery.

Attentive observers, the Brazilian visitors noticed that not all sections of the United States developed at the same pace. When traveling south on the Mississippi, Dom Pedro II remarked that "I have not seen as many churches and even fewer schools than in the North and West."[216] He soon got annoyed by listening to what Southerners had to say: "Their tone is that of people who have not yet resigned themselves to the consequences of their imprudence and, above all, of their evil and selfish cause. For now, I cannot say much besides that the North has pleased me much more than the South."[217] On the steamer, Dom Pedro II even had a small altercation with a Southern woman who had lost her husband and son in the Civil War. "She told me that she had no nation and was surprised that I had visited the prevaricator Grant. I responded kindly and she agreed with me that the principle of slavery had made the cause of the South unlikable." At last, Dom Pedro II argued that, "for our world, the result [of the Civil War] was very positive and it was necessary to submit to it, having as consolation the country united again, forming a great nation. To this point she responded with two emphatic <u>nevers</u>."[218]

When Dom Pedro II arrived at his destination, he found out that the Lost Cause affected both the mind and the body of the South. "The impression made on His Majesty by New Orleans," O'Kelly reported, "has not been favorable. He finds a noticeable difference between the energy and bustle of the Northern and Western cities and the easygoing aspect of the Creole population."[219] Yet Dom Pedro II soon came to the conclusion that the Lost Cause was already yielding to progress. He was glad to see plowed fields close to

Natchez, Mississippi, and bales upon bales of cotton in Southern ports. In New Orleans, while inspecting new railroads and streetcar lines, he met cotton planters who were sending their sons to study at Northern universities.[220] As surprised as the emperor with the transformation of the postwar South, Paes Leme celebrated that "today, thanks to rising sugar prices, northern capital begins to explore the rich resources of the great [Mississippi] valley."[221]

On the sugar plantations of Louisiana, Dom Pedro II gazed in wonder at the horse-drawn plows cutting the earth and the transformed organization of labor. "The blacks work well under a year-long contract," he noted, "which they often renew, making from 13 to 18 dollars per month—depending whether they get food or not—but in both cases they get housing, which does not seem bad."[222] The dynamics of wage labor, Vieira Bueno and Coutinho observed during their visit to the South, had forced sugar planters to adopt a rational system of cultivation. "The unreliable labor of the black free hand makes agriculture in Louisiana so uncertain in its results that the planter cannot foresee with any precision what his next crop will be," Vieira Bueno expounded. Seeking a remedy for uncertainty, the Louisiana sugar planters used bagasse and bean stems as fertilizers and applied mule-drawn plows imported from Kentucky to the soil. "You see, my friend," Vieira Bueno concluded, "that the difference between sugarcane cultivation in Brazil and in Louisiana is that, in the latter, the work is expeditious thanks to the use of improved agricultural implements."[223]

In the United States of the 1870s, Brazilian visitors understood that the destruction of slavery had brought about unpreceded economic growth. Scholars must grapple with this transformation to understand why an institution that lasted for over three centuries vanished from the western hemisphere in the second half of the nineteenth century.[224] A capitalist giant had emerged from the ashes of a war that destroyed slavery. The triumph of the free North had resulted in a well-integrated national transportation system, a great influx of immigrant workers, vigorous research and learning institutions, unprecedented urban growth, large-scale mining enterprises, large-scale agricultural enterprises, efficient and widespread manufacturing facilities, revolutionary labor-saving machinery, and expanding commercial networks. Thereafter, no one—in Brazil, in the United States, or anywhere in the Americas—seriously considered rebuilding or forever preserving chattel slavery. The post–Civil War United States proved antislavery reformers right: by the 1870s, all knew that slave labor was no match for the wage system.

After witnessing the transformation of the Southern states, the Brazilian explorers returned to the Northeast. Closing his journey, Dom Pedro II went to Massachusetts. He first visited his friend Louis Agassiz's grave: "I took some flowers that grew close to it and sent one to Mrs. Agassiz." The monarch then met John Greenleaf Whittier, whose embrace he was delighted to feel. Whittier introduced Dom Pedro II to other American admirers: Henry Wadsworth Longfellow, Ralph Waldo Emerson, Wendell Phillips, and George Bancroft.[225] From Massachusetts, he returned to Philadelphia for the Fourth of July. A few days later, the monarch and the Brazilian committee left the United States with "the best wishes of a free people for the future of the great Empire of Brazil."[226] The Centennial Exhibition had consummated a transnational alliance of antislavery reformers that had begun to emerge two decades earlier. And it would not be long before these modernizers would finalize their transformative project.

6

The Triumph of Free Labor

ON MAY 17, 1888, only four days after Princess Regent Isabel signed the Golden Law, the *Boston Daily Advertiser* drew a parallel between the processes of emancipation in the two largest slave societies of the Western world. In the United States "slavery was overthrown by a war begun in order to maintain it," whereas in Brazil "the same end has practically been reached by peaceful means." Different paths to emancipation generated different outcomes: "The republic is still suffering, and seems likely to suffer for years to come, from the bitterness of spirit engendered by the strife. The empire has reached a condition in which public sentiment seems to be all in accord as to the evils of slavery and eager to erase the blot upon the nation." The *Boston Daily Advertiser* then explained how progressive coffee planters willingly accepted gradual emancipation in Brazil, something that reactionary cotton planters had refused in the United States. Elite Brazilians had learned from the American experience: "Another curious fact in this connection is that one great means used in Brazil to secure emancipation is the same that President Lincoln proposed, without avail, to the South."[1] Northerners celebrated that, unlike Southern planters, the Brazilian fazendeiros had accomplished a transition to free labor that preserved their power and wealth.

For the powerful and wealthy in the United States, the 1880s were years of optimism. Reconstruction officially ended in 1877 when Ulysses S. Grant left office. By 1880, the economy had overcome the crisis dating back to 1873. As confidence resurged in the Gilded Age, employers sought to make employees work longer hours, adopted new managerial strategies to speed up production, and acquired new technologies to replace skilled workers.[2] In rural areas, falling commodity prices and monopolistic practices enriched corporations and impoverished farmers.[3] The gap between rich and poor grew wider. In response, organizations such as the Knights of Labor sprang into action to protect producers and attack speculators. Capital and the state coalesced to protect the privileged few, using brute force against organized labor when they saw fit.[4]

Although coffee continued its relentless expansion in Brazil of the 1880s, the country was far from enjoying a reign of tranquility and understanding. Competing projects on how emancipation should be enacted clashed in Parliament and on the streets.[5] A group composed mostly of members of the Liberal Party and new professional classes created the Sociedade Brasileira Contra a Escravidão (Brazilian Antislavery Society; SBCE) and the Associação Central Emancipadora (Central Emancipation Society; ACE), which advocated a fixed date—no later than the end of the nineteenth century—for emancipation. Another group, closer to the Conservative Party and the planters of the Paraíba Valley, wanted to sit back and wait for the Law of the Free Womb to run its course, avoiding any shakeup of the political system.[6] Yet another group, connected to the fazendeiros of the Oeste Paulista and the Republican Party, was more concerned about securing means to increase the size of the workforce, thus depressing wages and making slavery unnecessary.[7]

The 1880s were a defining moment for Brazilian and American antislavery reformers. Curiously, Henry Washington Hilliard, a former brigadier general in the Confederate Army, helped ignite the final discussion on slave emancipation in Brazil. Turned into a Republican after the Civil War, Hilliard was nominated minister to Brazil in the late 1870s. When the Brazilian abolitionists approached him, he had no qualms about supporting their cause. Ironically, as American public opinion applauded Hilliard's antislavery initiative, slave-grown coffee from Brazil was inundating American markets, serving as fuel for overworked wage earners. Coffee enthusiasts in the United States, however, justified consumption of the Brazilian product by pointing out that modernizing coffee planters were advancing toward free labor.

As the fazendeiros grew richer, the Brazilian abolitionists radicalized and the slaves rebelled en masse. Although frightened by the prospect of social revolution, the fazendeiros were ready to act. Relying on new technologies and government subsidies, they succeeded in transforming their plantations into agroindustrial enterprises moved by free workers. All the while, they pushed aside possibilities of more comprehensive reforms. As slavery withered and died, a few disillusioned activists denounced the failure of free labor to create social justice in Brazil. But neither the Brazilian fazendeiros nor American public opinion took heed. After all, for most antislavery reformers, the transition from slave to free labor had never been about creating an egalitarian society.

Unlike the planters from the American South, who had insisted on preserving and expanding chattel slavery, the richest slaveholders in Brazil were able to shape the great structural transformation of the age: the relentless expansion of free labor in the form of the wage system. By associating with American capital and adapting the lessons from the postwar United States to their needs, the fazendeiros transformed their own class and expanded their powers. The study of American influence on Brazilian emancipation contributes to a long-standing scholarship that traces how a mode of production based on wage labor rose from the ashes of slavery in the western hemisphere.[8] Instead of serving the needs of the working majority, Brazilian and American antislavery reformers forged a postemancipation arrangement that ended up concentrating wealth in the hands of very few. The triumph of free labor in Brazil brought immediate results: booming agroindustry and expanding coffee yields. It also resulted in the brutal exploitation of an emerging rural proletariat. The fazendeiros' allies in the United States felt elated, however. Without the upheaval that had occurred in the American South, Brazilian planters had placed themselves alongside American capitalists.

The Banquet and the Battle

Born in North Carolina, raised in South Carolina, and educated at South Carolina College, Henry Washington Hilliard set up as a lawyer in Montgomery, Alabama. He then joined the Whig Party, served as a state representative, and was elected to the House of Representatives in 1845. Deeply frustrated by the growing sectionalism of the time, he decided not to run again in the 1850s.[9] When Abraham Lincoln was elected, Hilliard wavered for a moment. But when the Confederate government gave him the mission to persuade Tennessee to secede, Hilliard fulfilled his duty obediently. In 1862, he became a brigadier general in the Confederate Army and fought under General Braxton Bragg. Hilliard's service lasted only six months, however. Feeling unfit for military duty, he spent the remaining war years writing a novel.[10]

After the Civil War, Hilliard resumed his law practice in Alabama and joined the Republican Party, becoming a (so-called) scalawag. According to the historian Eric Foner, men like Hilliard believed that "they stood a greater chance of advancing their interests in a Republican South than by casting their lot with Reconstruction's opponents."[11] Hilliard ran again for the House in 1876, but suffered a bitter electoral defeat. His commitment to the Republican Party bore fruit, however. Rutherford Hayes approached him with a diplomatic mission. "As a large number of Southern men had gone to Brazil at the close of the war," Hilliard recalled, the newly elected president told him that he "might render important service to the country by accepting the mission to Rio."[12] Hayes's politics of sectional appeasement included a sympathetic gesture toward the ex-Confederates who had migrated to Brazil. Ignored by Grant until 1876, distressed émigrés had been relying on individual charity. Hilliard received orders to use US Navy vessels to transport ex-Confederates who wished to return to the United States.[13]

In Brazil, Hilliard established close ties with members of the Liberal Party. In a letter to the US secretary of state, he painted a flattering portrait of these men: "There is a strong party in this country favorable to liberal institutions; a party of progress; a party that will yet make itself felt in reconstructing the political system of Brazil." An influential Liberal had told Hilliard that Brazilians "should take our civilization from the United States and not from Europe." Hilliard had been attentively observing the relations that American entrepreneurs such as his personal friend Charles B. Greenough had established with the Liberals, and was "much gratified to know that they are regarded with respect and confidence. Their influence must be felt not only upon the commerce of the country but upon public opinion."[14] In early 1878, Hilliard rejoiced that Dom Pedro II substituted the Liberals for the Conservatives in the executive branch of government.[15]

As he became closer to the Brazilian Liberals, Hilliard soon understood that there were rifts within the party: "Some of these leaders are extreme in their opinions; others are more moderate. But they all desire progress."[16] Hilliard, always a moderate in his country, would energize the most radical faction of Brazilian Liberalism. He met Joaquim Nabuco, the son of Senator José Tomás Nabuco de Araújo, in Petrópolis: "Young, thoroughly educated, already acquainted with Europe, . . . and a statesman of high promise, he bestowed attentions upon me which were appreciated. In the whole course of my life I had met no one whose future seemed brighter."[17] A founding member of the SBCE alongside André Pinto Rebouças, Nabuco had entered the Chamber of Deputies in 1878 and presented a bill to have slavery abolished by 1890. Despite being rejected, the project gained him notoriety.[18]

On October 19, 1880, Nabuco wrote to Hilliard asking his "enlightened opinion upon the results which the immediate and total substitution of slave labor by free labor has produced, and still promises to produce, in the Southern States of the Union." But Nabuco already had an answer to his inquiry: "There can be no doubt, after the late harvests, regarding the wisdom of emancipation as an economic measure for the reconstruction of the Southern States." Even former slaveholders acknowledged that their wealth had "considerably augmented in the hands of free laborers, and that from this standpoint, abolition has been a great benefit to that section of territory where it threatened to become a catastrophe and permanent ruin."[19]

A movement drawing on a number of traditions, Brazilian abolitionism adopted arguments ranging from romantic views of human virtue to geopolitical considerations.[20] Yet the astonishing recovery of the postemancipation South made the economic argument—that is, the idea that free labor was more productive than slave labor—the most prominent of all. Hence, the duty of the abolitionist movement, Nabuco informed Hilliard, was "to enlighten the opinion of the [Brazilian] agriculturists themselves, by the experience of free labor in other countries, and to demonstrate to the country that only with emancipation can it trust its future to agriculture." He thanked the American diplomat in advance for "a service rendered to a million and a half of human beings whose liberty is solely dependent upon their masters becoming convinced that free labor is infinitely superior in every respect to forced and unremunerated labor."[21]

Earlier, in September 1880, Nicolau Joaquim Moreira, the longtime member of the Sociedade Auxiliadora da Indústria Nacional (Auxiliary Society of National Industry; SAIN) and now president of the ACE, had published a study of the benefits of slave emancipation. Moreira, who had been a member of the Brazilian committee at the Centennial Exhibition, opened his study by commenting on the "disgraceful position of the slave states of the American Union" in the antebellum period. Plagued by illiteracy, backward economic practices, and widespread poverty, the slave South had fallen far behind the free North. But emancipation, he remarked, had changed the region for the better. Now, textile mills flourished in the South, "manufacturing the cotton that at the time of slavery was sent to Lowell or England." Agricultural output diversified and increased. And the ex-slave "now serves as a free worker, making 15 dollars, tripling his labor and improving his products." No crisis had resulted from emancipation in the American South as freedom "does not sterilize the soil, but fertilizes it; does not kill labor, but improves it; does not decrease production, but doubles it; does not degrade man, but ennobles him."[22]

Moreira argued that Brazil would follow the same path after emancipation. To prove his assertion, he pointed out that since the Law of the Free Womb, as the slave population declined in Brazil, coffee exports had doubled because "the machines came to save time, spare hands, decrease worker mortality, and increase the value of the product."[23] Like Nabuco, Moreira saw slave emancipation as a step toward a more efficient system of production, which would serve the interests of the great planters above all others. Informed of the transformation of American society in the post–Civil War era, Brazilian abolitionists sought to shape free labor into a tool for capitalist accumulation in their country.

Over seventy years old and having experienced uncountable political troubles in his life, Hilliard did not hesitate to reinforce the Brazilian abolitionists' economic argument. On October 25, 1880, he sent an extensive reply to Nabuco. Accepting the role bestowed on him, Hilliard identified as "a native of the South, brought up and educated there, a slave-holder, representing for a number of years in Congress one of the largest and wealthiest planting districts and a section where slave labor was exclusively employed." For decades, Hilliard had heard that cotton could not be grown with free labor as "contracts would be disregarded, disputes would spring up, and at critical times work would be abandoned, bringing irreparable disaster." Recent events, however, proved all these predictions wrong: "Never were the States of the South so prosperous as they are to-day." Freedpeople continued to work the cotton fields, and "the results are far more satisfactory than under the old system of compulsory labor." To support his contention, Hilliard emphasized that "the largest cotton crop ever made in the South, estimated at 6,000,000 bales, has been produced this year chiefly by the labor of freedmen."[24] Indeed, as the historian Sven Beckert notes, "Reconstruction resulted in a rapid, vast, and permanent increase in the production of cotton for world markets in the United States. American rural cultivators recovered, despite all predictions to the contrary, their position as the world's leading producers of raw cotton. By 1870 their total production had surpassed their previous high, set in 1860."[25]

Hilliard exposed his distaste for Radical Reconstruction, complaining about "the anomalous spectacle" of black men "suddenly elevated to office" and Northern adventurers seeking "for their own advantage to control the freedmen." Still, the American South had been able to not only recover but expand production after a destructive war and years of occupation. Based on the Southern experience, Hilliard maintained that Brazil—a land free from the evil of sectionalism—"need not hesitate to commit itself to the policy adopted in the United States. With the extinction of slavery, free labor will develop its immeasurable resources." Hence, he suggested that a period of "seven years might be fixed as the term in Brazil for holding the African race still in bondage."[26]

Thrilled by Hilliard's response, the SBCE did not waste time, forwarding his letter to the principal newspapers of Rio de Janeiro and publishing it in the form of a pamphlet. All this noise excited Andrew Jackson Lamoureux, the editor of the *Rio News*, an English-language newspaper published in Brazil's capital city. Born in Iosco, Michigan, Lamoureux had entered Cornell University in 1870. In 1877, he accompanied two friends on a journey to Brazil. After working as a clerk at the US legation, he created the *Rio News* with the objective of reaching foreigners with business interests in Brazil.[27] Lamoureux identified with men like Rebouças and Moreira, describing them as "individuals who believe that the most productive soil is that worked by the proper owner; who wish to improve man by the earth and the earth by man; and who seek to distribute property among the masses as to render man completely free and independent."[28] In 1883, Lamoureux's printing office published Rebouças's *Agricultura Nacional: Estudos Economicos. Propaganda Abolicionista e Democrática.*[29]

In 1880, Lamoureux not only translated and republished Hilliard's and Nabuco's letters but also forwarded the texts to American and British newspapers. A firebrand, he opined that "instead of protracting the transition period for an indefinite time as in the law of 1871, or until 1890 as proposed by Deputy Joaquim Nabuco, or until 1887 as suggested by Minister Hilliard, or to any time in the future whether near or remote, we believe that the great evil should be abolished now and forever." Incorporating the economic argument against slavery, Lamoureux asserted that Brazil could not afford to live one more day under the scourge: "The plain economic facts of the case teach that as long as slavery exists just so long will there be stagnation in industry, decadence in business, uncertainty in enterprise, checks in national development, and that when it shall be abolished then and not until then will there come that true and permanent prosperity which the country so much needs."[30]

Whereas Lamoureux produced a radical response to Hilliard's initiative, a Brazilian planter who had been to the United States for the Centennial Exhibition tried to counteract his proposition. On November 5, 1880, the *Jornal do Commercio* published an open letter by Pedro Dias Gordilho Paes Leme, who told Hilliard that "I had the good fortune of traveling your country, admiring its greatness." Paes Leme contended that, unlike the North and the West, which had advanced after the Civil War, the South still suffered the effects of emancipation: "Since 1864, a battle between the two races emerged, being the colored people encouraged by the infamous *carpetbaggers* who still ruled in 1876. Property had to be defended by gunmen. Crimes and pauperism developed in a noticeable way."[31] Manipulating some statistics, he argued that, because emancipation came suddenly, Southern agriculture had declined after the war. In Brazil, he speculated, the consequences of freeing the slaves ahead of what the Law of the Free Womb prescribed would be even more devastating. Paes Leme wanted indefinite time to "organize labor in the country so that, by enlarging the circle of [private] manumissions, the transition can be made without a shock."[32]

Paes Leme's open letter only emboldened the abolitionists. On November 20, 1880, fifty of them came together for a banquet in honor of Hilliard. On the wall of the dining room, they hung a picture of Lincoln signing the Emancipation Proclamation. Rebouças opened the ceremony. "The American Minister," he praised the guest of honor, "once a slaveholder, once a Southerner, performed an act of abnegation by advising the Brazilians to free themselves as soon as possible from the nefarious institution of slavery, which caused the worst disgrace that his great and beloved nation ever suffered." Nabuco spoke after Rebouças, comparing Hilliard's role in Brazil of the 1880s to that of Benjamin Franklin in France of the 1780s. Hilliard's speech was exactly what the abolitionists wanted to hear. "The experience of all nations," he uttered, "teaches us that no country can enjoy the highest prosperity and happiness attainable, where slavery exists." All attending the banquet rejoiced.[33]

Reactionaries were outraged. Two days after the banquet, Antonio Moreira de Barros, who represented the interests of the coffee planters of the Paraíba Valley in the Chamber of Deputies, fumed before his peers: "What does the clear and manifest intervention of a representative of another country in our entirely domestic issue mean?" Nabuco did not miss the chance to provoke. "You do not want to know what the foreigner thinks," he interrupted Barros, "but when the British government speaks loudly you know how to keep quiet." In uproar, deputies exchanged accusations while Barros challenged Hilliard's argument: "Mr. Paes Leme has demonstrated through indisputable data the opposite of what the American Minister has argued."[34]

Attentive to decorum, Hilliard simply ignored Barros. But the plucky Lamoureux did not. He considered that Barros's attack, "which was as weak as it was unwarranted, was simply a secondary consideration; but as it offered a tangible excuse for bringing the question before the government, it was seized upon with all the avidity that a drowning man grasps a straw." After Prime Minister José Antonio Saraiva declared that Hilliard had not broken any diplomatic rule, Lamoureux laughed at the "drowning man" Barros: "In declining to consider the matter Counselor Saraiva very effectively crushed one of the most childish ventures which the pro-slavery party has thus far undertaken."[35]

When it came to Paes Leme's open letter, Lamoureux wrote that he had shown "so much misplaced knowledge and so little familiarity with the real factors in the discussion that an answer was wholly unnecessary." Nonetheless, he would have one. To the point that slave emancipation had caused economic decline in the American South, Lamoureux retorted that it was all nonsense. During the Civil War, plantations were destroyed, railways were torn up, cities were plundered, ports were blockaded, and enormous debts were contracted. "And yet all these sad results of a most destructive war Mr. Paes Leme ascribes to the immediate abolition of slavery—and that, too, in the face of repeated assertions of prominent Southern statesmen to the effect that the negro has developed into an orderly and industrious citizen." Emancipation, in fact, had saved the Southern economy. Lamoureux presented statistics showing that, in spite of a destructive war, the South had produced thirty-one million bales of cotton in the decade following emancipation compared to thirty-two million in the decade preceding it. From 1875 to 1880 alone, it had produced twenty-four million bales, far surpassing the average of antebellum years. By arguing that emancipation had ruined the American South, Paes Leme had made a fool of himself. Lamoureux concluded that "it is the unanimous testimony of all well-informed men that the South was never more prosperous than today, and that this happy result is owing to the substitution of free for slave labor."[36]

The reactionaries had selected their spokesman poorly. After all, writing for publications such as *O Novo Mundo* after his stay in the United States in 1876, Paes Leme had sung the praises of free labor.[37] As Moreira reminded the Brazilian public, "Mr. Paes Leme became full of admiration upon seeing the extensive estate of Mr. Sullivant in Burr Oak, where four square leagues of soil are cultivated, employing some 300 workers, making a yearly profit of 160 contos de réis from a total of 300 [initially] invested." If troubled by the antislavery argument, Moreira advised, "the planters should address the distinguished agriculturalist whose name I just mentioned, and not the abolitionists."[38] In the end, Paes Leme's attempt to disprove Hilliard seemed quite absurd.

While Paes Leme and Barros were trounced in Brazil, Hilliard was applauded in his own country. The *New York Times* reported that Nabuco had called forth from Hilliard "a long statement as to the industrial result of emancipation in this country, and his able and temperate letter, coming from a Southern man who was engaged in the rebellion, has greatly encouraged the friends of immediate emancipation in Brazil, while it has somewhat offended the Brazilian Bourbons."[39] The Philadelphia *North American* ridiculed Hilliard's foes, noting that "there are some very sensitive patriots in the Brazilian

Chamber of Deputies." But they should not worry: "Much as we would like to see slavery abolished, not only in Brazil, but in every other country where it is practiced, it is not our policy to interfere under any circumstances with the internal administration of any foreign nation."[40] The United States would not force Brazilians to let go of slavery. Yet Americans like Hilliard and Lamoureux were already working alongside Brazilian antislavery reformers to entrench the wage system on coffee plantations.

No reproach to Hilliard came from the American government. And he received praise even in his native South. The *Georgia Weekly Telegraph* explained that Hilliard would be retained in office by President-Elect James Garfield as "his recent action on the slavery question has rather helped the influence with the present administration and is the best introduction he could have had to that which is to come."[41] Lamoureux was delighted with such an accolade, informing his readers that Hilliard's "course here with relation to the question of emancipation was warmly approved at home." Hilliard had been proved right in his belief that the exercise of his private influence on behalf of Brazilian antislavery "could not possibly offend a government which had just liberated four millions of slaves at so great a cost." After all, "in the United States the evils of slavery and the benefits of free labor have been practically and thoroughly tested."[42]

For Lamoureux, Hilliard had adopted "a course which reflects the highest credit upon him both as a man and as the representative of a great nation."[43] Praised for his decisive support for Brazilian abolitionism, Hilliard left Brazil at his own request in June 1881. After a frustrating political career in the United States, Brazil had offered him an opportunity to shine. Hilliard had, at once, placed the Brazilian abolitionists under the spotlight and legitimized their contention that slave emancipation had been an economic blessing for the American South. The former Confederate achieved the boldest feat of his political career as he sided with antislavery reform in Brazil.

Fuel

With a few exceptions, Americans agreed with Hilliard that, despite all troubles of Reconstruction, the economy of the American South advanced after slave emancipation.[44] Yet the problem of slavery continued to be debated as Americans realized that enslaved people still produced some essential items in their daily lives. In a series of articles published in *Scribner's Magazine* in 1878 and one year later as a book titled *Brazil: The Amazons and the Coast*, the naturalist Herbert Huntington Smith revealed to the American public "The Story of Coffee."[45] Born in Manlius, New York, Smith had studied at Cornell and accompanied Charles Frederick Hartt on his expeditions to Brazil. Traveling the Brazilian interior in the mid-1870s, Smith had visited a plantation in the Paraíba Valley belonging to a man whom he called Sr. S.

Smith pointed to the good management of the plantation. "The negroes are kept under a rigid surveillance," he observed, "and the work is regulated as by machinery." At four in the morning all were awakened. Meals were "served in the field, with the slightest possible intermission from work." At seven in the afternoon, the slaves left the fields to do "household- and mill-work until nine o'clock; then the men and women are locked up in separate quarters, and left to sleep seven hours." Precise labor management was coupled with efficient machinery: "Sr. S., ever ready to seize modern improvements, is adopting the new system of drying [coffee] by steam." Labor-saving technologies made coffee production into a modern enterprise. "The large number of machines secures, not only nicety in the result," Smith added, "but a greater capacity for work, to meet the wants of an extensive plantation."[46]

Good labor management and new technologies, however, were not enough to overcome the immanent irrationality of slavery, according to Smith. On large plantations, with hundreds of slaves, "the planters work their negroes as they would never work their mules, yet complain that they reap no profits." Reflecting on the system in place at the plantation of Sr. S., Smith remarked that "he is growing richer by unjust laws and unrighteous, tyrannical institutions; witness the neglected grounds of his poorer neighbors, and the smileless faces of his slaves." Worse than brutalizing the workers, for Smith, was that unfree labor impaired the economy of the Paraíba Valley as a whole. The railroad brought only a few luxury items to the planter family and almost nothing to the two hundred slaves as "their food is furnished by the plantations, and their clothes are few and scanty." Meanwhile, "an equal population in the United States would necessitate shipments of coal, provisions, cloths, and a thousand articles of luxury; all this would be clear gain to a railroad, and no slight addition to the outgoing freights." Carrying very little besides coffee, railroads in the Paraíba Valley were financially inviable. Slavery hindered commercial activity, precluded diversification, and slowed down the expansion of the very coffee economy that it was supposed to fuel. Observing the stagnant region, Smith contended that "this want of growth is due, no doubt, to the ruinous system of cultivation, robbing the ground without enriching it; and to the high freight tariffs, and consequent uselessness of the interior lands."[47]

Like other Northerners who had visited Brazil since the 1850s, Smith took a critical albeit patient approach to the problem of slavery.

> I came to Brazil, with an honest desire to study this question of slavery in a spirit of fairness, without running to emotional extremes. Now, after four years, I am convinced that all other evils with which the country is cursed, taken together, will not compare with this one; I could almost say that all other evils have arisen from it, or been strengthened by it. And yet, I cannot unduly blame men who have inherited the curse, and had no part in the making of it. I can honor masters who treat their slaves kindly, albeit they are owners of stolen property.

Drawing on racist ideas common among nineteenth-century white intellectuals, Smith claimed that, in material terms, "no doubt many of the negroes are better off than they were in Africa," having learned in Brazil "some lessons of peace and civility; even a groping outline of Christianity." Yet, he continued, bondage had made the slave "dependent, like a child, on his master, and utterly unused to thinking for himself." Much worse, in Smith's opinion, was the effect of the institution on the prospects of attracting free workers to Brazilian agriculture: "'Laborers!' cries Brazil. 'We must have labor!' and where will she get honest workmen, if honest work is a degradation? Slavery has made it so."[48] As he contemplated the problems of the Paraíba Valley, Smith joined the conversation on how to replace slavery with wage labor.

Notwithstanding the permanence of slavery in Brazil, American consumers were drinking more and more Brazilian coffee. An Englishman who had immigrated to New York City in the 1840s contributed to popularizing coffee consumption through a simple though effective invention. Working as a bookkeeper for a coffee importer, Jabez Burns had patented a coffee roaster in the 1850s. In the early 1860s, he improved his device and was able to sell it in great numbers thanks to the conflict raging between North and South. More so than in any other times, he reflected, in times of war "necessity is the mother of invention." During the Civil War the needs of the troops were many and urgent: "Rifles and cannons, ships and monitors, clothing and equipment, transportation and provisions, rations, and not the least of these was coffee, which had to be supplied at short notice." It was under these circumstances, according to Burns, that his attention was called to the necessity of improving the method of roasting coffee.[49]

Burns's Patent Coffee Roaster was a commercial success, reaching large and small towns across the United States by the late 1870s. Instead of buying green beans and then using cooking pans to roast them at home, now consumers could buy coffee properly roasted in grocery stores.[50] Burns further influenced the coffee trade by publishing a monthly journal titled *The Spice Mill*. In 1880, he remarked that "our people are using many articles that they feel they could not get along without that never would have had a place, and never would have been missed, but for the tact and ingenuity displayed in the method of their introduction." Burns explained that industrial technology had given rise to mass production and wide distribution of goods, making coffee into an integral part of American life. "We do not intend to treat coffee as a useless article by any means," he continued, "but it never would have risen to the enormous consumption it has attained in this country but for the mechanical improvements to facilitate the manufacture and the convenient, attractive and enticing style in which much of it has been presented to the consumer."[51]

Necessity was the mother of invention; but inventions also created new necessities. The historian Steven Topik estimates that, by the end of the nineteenth century, the United States was consuming an annual average of thirteen pounds of coffee per capita and importing 40 percent of the world's production.[52] Americans consumed large amounts of coffee because it was made available to them through new machines, packaging, and distribution systems.[53] As a New York wholesaler named Francis Beatty Thurber put it in 1881, "The revolution which has taken place in the coffee trade of the United States during the last twenty years is a striking confirmation of the principle that work can be done in the best and cheapest manner on a large scale, where machinery is employed that is controlled by the best available skill."[54]

John Arbuckle, the son of a woolen mill owner from Pennsylvania, reaped massive profits from the marriage between industry and coffee. In 1859, he started a wholesale grocery business in Pittsburgh. Specializing in coffee, Arbuckle acquired roasters from Burns and employed dozens of women to pack and label roasted coffee in one-pound paper bags commonly used for peanuts at the time. Sales rocketed, and Arbuckle soon acquired a machine capable of performing the work of five hundred human packers. In 1873, he created a brand name for his coffee: Ariosa. Although the origin of the name was never explained, some speculated that "A" came from Arbuckle, "rio" from Rio de Janeiro, and "sa" from Santos. Whether accurate or not, the speculation connected Arbuckle to mass-produced Brazilian coffee. Packets of Ariosa coffee spread like wildfire. The brand soon became associated with the American West, where coffee beans in bulk were hard to come by.[55]

Arbuckle was no innovative genius. Others were packing coffee and selling it at the same time that he was building his company. What distinguished Arbuckle were his aggressive advertising campaigns and his early effort to vertically integrate the coffee business. In 1881, he moved his headquarters from Pittsburgh to Brooklyn, New York, greatly expanding his operations in coffee and entering the sugar business. He now had over one hundred warehouses all over the United States and had established offices in Rio de Janeiro and Santos. Arbuckle also owned a shipping fleet and a barrel factory. His plant in Brooklyn had a stable with nearly two hundred horses, shops for repairing machines and wagons, a printing shop, a first-aid clinic, a powerhouse with twenty-six large steam boilers, and much more.[56]

Arbuckle's success attracted major entrepreneurs to the coffee business. An Irish immigrant who arrived in the United States in 1832, John Roach had made a fortune during the Civil War by manufacturing marine engines. After buying out many of his competitors, in 1871 he acquired a shipyard in Chester, Pennsylvania. When, in 1875, the binational subsidy to the United States and Brazilian Steamship Company expired and the line was discontinued, Roach set out to rebuild the service. "The chief product which we buy from Brazil, coffee, is one that we must have, but cannot raise in any part of our own territory," he explained. Brazilians liked to get paid in gold for their coffee, but Roach was hoping to induce them to accept something else in exchange. He knew that "Brazil wants, in turn, our bread, lard, ham, and other food, as well as clothing and all lines of manufactures." However, for this change to take place, it was necessary to take trade away from the hands of British intermediaries and carry American goods directly to Brazil.[57]

Hoping to repeat the formula that had made him rich, Roach sought a subsidy from the American government. An ally of Republican politicians, he faced the opposition of the Democrats, who had obtained control of the House of Representatives in the elections of 1874. Since the scandals of the Grant administration, favors to steamship and railroad companies had become synonymous with corruption. Roach's projected line of steamers to Brazil therefore became a target for Democrats trying to pose as enemies of greed and fraud.[58]

Regardless of his failure to acquire a subsidy from the American government, Roach mustered powerful allies in Brazil. In September 1877, José Carlos Rodrigues described Roach as "one of the richest and most enterprising industrialists of this country," who possessed "one of the best shipyards in this Republic, and who has sent to sea the magnificent steamers of the Pacific Line."[59] In November of the same year, Henry Washington Hilliard reported to the US Department of State that he had done what he could "to influence the [Brazilian] government to entertain with favor the proposal submitted to it by our enterprising countrymen."[60] In 1878, the Brazilian government approved an annual subsidy of a hundred thousand dollars for Roach's line.

Roach launched the *City of Rio de Janeiro*, a large new steamer, on March 8, 1878. One month later, Roach launched the *City of Para* before a fifteen-thousand-strong crowd, which included President Rutherford Hayes, Secretary of War George W. McCrary, and Secretary of the Interior Carl Schurz. When the first of Roach's steamers arrived in Rio de Janeiro, Dom Pedro II inspected it alongside Hilliard.[61] On June 5, 1878, the *City of Rio de Janeiro* left Brazil carrying thirty-five thousand bags of coffee, the largest single coffee shipment to that date.[62]

Smith joined the chorus singing Roach's praises: "Once a month, we can see the United States flag flying over the finest steamers that enter the port of Rio de Janeiro. I am not acquainted with Mr. John Roach, but I heartily admire the plucky spirit he showed, in building three such magnificent ships for the Brazilian trade." Smith usually opposed government aid to private enterprises, but he made an exception for Roach. Great Britain, France, and Germany subsidized their steamship lines, providing advantages to their trading houses. Moreover, the commerce of Brazil presented great potential for American merchants, manufacturers, and farmers. "Ever since the John Roach line was established," Smith observed, "our trade with Brazil has been increasing, slowly and steadily; just as it should in a healthy growth. So I believe that the line ought to be encouraged."[63]

To the regret of his admirers, unable to secure the subsidy from the American government and facing competition from smaller vessels and British shippers, Roach suffered losses and shut down operations in 1880. Nonetheless, one year later he joined Collis Potter Huntington to organize another steamship line to Brazil. Roach served as the company's president while Huntington became vice president; investors in the new line included the former US secretary of the treasury Hugh McCulloch, the shipping entrepreneur Charles R. Flint, the railroader and banker Edward H. Ripley, and the wholesaler Horace K. Thurber.[64] Horace happened to be the brother and business associate of Francis Beatty Thurber, author of *Coffee: From Plantation to Cup*, which was published in 1881 to promote coffee consumption in the United States.

In early June 1882, the press reported that the first steamship of the new line had been launched at Roach's works in Pennsylvania, and two others were under construction. "The vessels are to be built of iron," the *New York Daily Tribune* announced, "with water-tight compartments, and are to be of about 3,500 tons capacity, with excellent accommodations for saloon passengers."

The semimonthly steamers would go from New York to Rio de Janeiro, with stops in Newport News (Virginia), Saint Thomas (Danish West Indies), Belém (Pará), Recife (Pernambuco), Salvador (Bahia), and Santos (São Paulo).[65]

Roach's insistence and the other capitalists' gamble were justified. The coffee market in the United States was expanding rapidly thanks to temperance advocates' promotion of the beverage as a remedy for alcoholism. "Yes, far better than the Bacchanalian cup of old," a coffee enthusiast wrote in 1872, "is this non-inebriating draught, since it may be indulged with impunity; for while it refreshes and stimulates, it does not stultify the mind."[66] During the 1870s, the Woman's Christian Temperance Union established Temperance Coffee Houses all over the United States. The popularity of coffee among temperance advocates kept growing, especially in American industrial centers. In 1880, *Harper's Weekly* reported on the work of Dr. Kennion, who preached "to the neglected and outcast population of New York," including people "from the very lowest orders of humanity." This activist had become very popular among the poor because "in his efforts to reclaim the drunkard he soon found that something more was necessary than the mere advice to him not to drink. If he must not take whiskey, he must have something else, and Dr. Kennion gives him good warm coffee and nice fresh bread."[67]

Burns, who had been a devout temperance crusader since a young age, used the *Spice Mill* to advance the cause. He went so far as propagating the myth that "in Brazil, where great quantities of coffee are used and where all the inhabitants take it many times a day, alcoholism is completely unknown." He further noted that "the immigrants arriving in that country, though beset with the passion for alcohol, contract little by little the habits of the Brazilians, acquiring their fondness for drinking coffee and their aversion of liquors."[68] Like most upper-class temperance advocates, Burns preached that native and foreign workers in industrial American cities suffered because of their own dissipation.[69] An enemy of unions and socialists, he sought to educate the masses for hard work and resignation. "There always has been hewers of wood and drawers of water," he claimed, "and there always will be; and these very classes are a necessity to our highest civilization, for the good of all there must be work done." If the poor wanted to be useful members of society, Burns advised, they should just stop drinking alcohol and have more coffee. In his *Spice Mill*, along with his praise for coffee, he offered a passionate defense of corporate capitalism. "There must be minds to direct, and there must be concentrated capital," Burns professed, "the judicious circulation of which is the wealth and health of every nation."[70]

FIGURE 6.1 "Dr. Kennion's Street Coffee-Urn Cart—A Good Temperance Movement,"
Harper's Weekly, November 20, 1880. Courtesy of the University of Michigan Library,
Special Collections Research Center, Ann Arbor.

For American capitalists, coffee acquired the status of a magic potion, capable of making men and women work at the pace of machinery. They claimed, in concert with coffee enthusiasts such as Thurber, that "it exhilarates, arouses, and keeps awake. It counteracts the stupor occasioned by fatigue, by disease, or by opium; . . . while it makes the brain more active, it soothes the body generally, makes the change and waste of tissue slower, and the demand for food in consequence less."[71] A beverage combining such essential qualities, Thurber believed, would naturally become "a sine qua non with multitudes, who, while they would seek the stimulant, would also avoid the penalty of the intoxicating draught." Coffee, he proposed, was a great auxiliary to temperance "since its use tends largely to supersede that of spirituous liquors."[72]

Coffee was associated with energy in the rapidly industrializing United States. For the mass of people engaged in the repetitive and exhausting tasks of factory work, construction sites, or agroindustrial enterprises, coffee promised to remove "all sense of fatigue and disposition to sleep." Better yet, "it also excites the vascular system, and renders more powerful the contractions of all the muscles."[73] At a time when men felt that proletarianization could undermine their manliness, coffee promised to revive masculinity.[74] Coffee even seemed to have a heroic side to it. In *The Temperance Reform and Its Great Reformers* (1878), the Methodist reverend William H. Daniels claimed that "our American soldiers (during the late war) found that good food, good sleep, and good coffee were better than all the 'fire-water' of the rum-casks. A pilot on our wild Atlantic coast once told me that when he drank brandy he could not stand severe exposure as well as when he used only hot coffee."[75]

Brazilian antislavery reformers rejoiced to learn what purpose coffee served in the United States. Rebouças wrote in 1883 that Americans craved "a tonic which morality and hygiene proclaim to be the best replacement for alcoholic beverages." He concurred with American temperance advocates that coffee made better workers and better men. "The women of the United States have lately engaged in a bold campaign to abolish the sale of alcoholic beverages," Rebouças told his Brazilian readers, "which brutalize their children and husbands, and cause so many domestic scandals. May Brazilian coffee help the intelligent daughters of the North American Republic in their holy mission of extirpating from America the vice that degrades the Anglo-Saxon race!" Rebouças felt honored that "the most prosperous nation in the world is the one that buys the most Brazilian coffee. It is impossible to have a better customer." He thanked some of his close friends for informing the American public about the quality of Brazilian coffee: "We shall remember that this promotion began in 1876 through the venerable agronomist Mr. Nicolau Joaquim Moreira, then a member of the Brazilian Committee at the International Exhibition of Philadelphia; subsequently, it was carried forward on the pages of *O Novo Mundo* by Mr. José Carlos Rodrigues and his faithful collaborators."[76]

If, on the one hand, Rebouças was proud that Brazilian coffee helped American workers to free themselves from alcoholism, on the other, he thought it disgraceful that another, even greater evil subjugated coffee workers in Brazil: slavery. And the question was not only a moral one: "It is necessary to apply *human* freedom, the foremost and most energetic agent of human progress, to the production and preparation of coffee; to provide capital and science to this industry so it can increase its *productive capacity*, actively and efficaciously contributing to the wealth and prosperity of Brazil and, simultaneously, augmenting the wellbeing of all humankind."[77] Adapting American coffee enthusiasts' language of energy and regeneration, Rebouças declared that only free labor would realize Brazil's full potential in coffee production.

For their part, American observers were confident that, before long, Brazil would embrace free labor. One year after the Law of the Free Womb was ratified, an American coffee specialist maintained that, in Brazil, "the ultimate extinction of slavery generally will be accomplished when the existing slaves shall have passed away, since their children are born free. When the swift railroad shall have wholly superseded the slow mule conveyance, commerce will proportionally increase, because capitalists and free labor will yield a more profitable return."[78] Technology would form the shortest path to slave emancipation in Brazil, American coffee enthusiasts believed. Thurber acknowledged that some Brazilian planters feared that emancipation would ruin their business, but he thought otherwise: "The power of machinery can be utilized, and history will record of its adaptation in Brazil a story similar to that it has written respecting the United States." According to Thurber, labor-saving machinery could augment production tenfold, thus making the use of wage labor viable. The good news, he concluded, was that "Brazil has already begun to use new machinery and adopt improved processes of cultivation and preparation upon the plantations."[79]

Smith was also hopeful about the Brazilian willingness to change, pointing out that "Brazil should have a certain credit above other slaveholding countries, present and past; for she alone has voluntarily set herself to getting rid of her shame." American observers like Smith felt better believing that the more coffee they consumed, the faster Brazil would transition to free labor.

> Now, as I sip my morning coffee and pen these concluding lines, my thoughts go back to the bright hill-sides, the tired slaves, the busy Rio streets, the good and evil of this great industry. From great to small; it is a little matter, this cup of coffee, but the prosperity of a great empire depends on it. So here I drink to the health of Brazil, to her political and social and commercial welfare, to the downfall of evil and the growth of all good, all noble impulses that are buried in noble hearts. *Viva o Brasil!*[80]

Nurturing similar hopes, by the mid-1880s Burns published articles in the *Spice Mill* celebrating that "the time is not far distant . . . when slavery will become extinct in Brazil and the American continent be wholly freed from the blight of involuntary human servitude except in the punishment of crime."[81]

Of course, men like Burns, Thurber, Arbuckle, and Roach cared little about the plight of the working class in Brazil or the United States. But they cared much about consolidating wage labor and increasing production and trade. Coffee, in addition to amassing profits for American businessmen, helped them foster temperance among American workers and improve Brazilian agriculture. Working in concert with antislavery reformers such as Smith and

Rebouças, these entrepreneurs made coffee into the fuel powering capitalism at both ends of the hemisphere. While attacking slavery and promoting coffee, they helped bring into existence mass production, mass consumption, and sophisticated new forms of labor exploitation. These changes impacted workers who toiled in factories in New York as well as those who grew coffee in the Oeste Paulista.

The Brazilian West

While American coffee enthusiasts advertised the benefits of the beverage, one specific region of Brazil was coming to dominate the global coffee market. As the *Spice Mill* observed in 1884, "Within recent years, the coffees of this province were little known, and speculators usually passed them off under names indicative of coffees of greater repute. This has now changed, and the berries from the province of San Paulo, known in the trade as 'Santos,' can at present fight their own battles against competitors, and proclaim their origin with a warrant of success."[82] The Oeste Paulista transformed the global coffee market, and coffee transformed the Oeste Paulista.

By the mid-1880s, an American visitor had a pleasant surprise to see that "the San Paulo of today has an air of dignity and wealth. Many of the coffee-nobles of Brazil have palaces here." Previously known for its modesty, São Paulo City had become "the center of a country abounding in picturesque scenery and great coffee plantations, the owners of which are among the richest people in the world."[83] The railroad connecting the port of Santos to the interior crossed the provincial capital and permitted the fazendeiros to reside there. As the historian Warren Dean explains, "The larger plantations were put in the hands of hired administrators. The richest planters came to own strings of estates, all supervised from their mansions in São Paulo [City]. The administrator mailed daily reports to the owner, in a form that appears to have been standardized."[84]

The residence of the rich fazendeiros, São Paulo City had become a commercial hub and an administrative center. In the mid-1880s, it had eight different banks, ten railroad headquarters, ten insurance companies, and a dozen steamship line agencies, in addition to gas, water, telegraph, and telephone companies.[85] An army of professionals and workers powered the growing city: from lawyers to coachmen, from engineers to bricklayers, from physicians to butchers. Manufacturers produced everything from cast iron and wagons to soda and pasta. Streetcars took urban dwellers from their homes to factories, offices, shops, restaurants, libraries, parks, theaters, and many other places.[86]

The US consul general Christopher Columbus Andrews got interested in São Paulo upon "hearing people speak of its capital as being the most American of any city in Brazil."[87] A native of New Hampshire, Andrews had reached the rank of major general of the Union Army and served in occupied Texas during Reconstruction. Visiting São Paulo in 1884, the first American he met was George Whitehill Chamberlain, who took him to the newly erected Presbyterian church. "Mr. Chamberlain, who has been a missionary in Brazil fifteen or twenty years," Andrews recalled, "preached an extemporaneous sermon in the Portuguese language to a respectable and devout congregation of about two hundred, nearly all white Brazilians." The building could hold nearly one thousand worshippers. "Its ceiling is very high," Andrews continued, "and it has a new, fresh, and pleasant appearance. . . . It is of wood, and the material was brought from the United States."[88]

The next day, Chamberlain showed Andrews the Escola Americana, established in 1870, which now had one hundred forty students. "It appeared to be a very well managed school," Andrews remarked. In the evening, he dined at Chamberlain's house with "a party of about thirty ladies and gentlemen who are residents of São Paulo." Andrews was pleased to learn that his compatriot had made a name for himself among the local elite: "I would here say that Mr. Chamberlain is known in São Paulo as the *Padre Americano*, or American priest. He is an energetic, active, and effective man, highly respected by all classes, and exerts a large influence."[89]

At twenty-five hundred feet high, São Paulo City is located on the eastern edge of a plateau extending west to the interior. Some fifty miles downhill to the southeast is the seaport of Santos. Attentive to the growing importance of Santos to the coffee trade, in 1879 Brazilian authorities commissioned the best engineer they could think of to design an improvement plan for its harbor.[90] Having built a section of the Dom Pedro Segundo Railroad in the early 1860s and returned to the United States to serve as chief engineer of the Northern Pacific Railroad and president of the American Society of Civil Engineers, William Milnor Roberts would now modernize Santos.

On arriving at his new job, Roberts learned that the commerce of Santos had recently gone through a major expansion. "Since the opening of the São Paulo railway in 1867," he noted, "deeper-draught steamers and sailing vessels have been patronizing this port mainly on account of the annually increasing quantities and superior quality of coffee brought in by the railway from the interior of the rich province of São Paulo." From twenty-seven thousand tons in 1867, coffee shipment had increased to sixty-eight thousand tons in 1878.

Nonetheless, most of the coffee had to be carried on the heads and shoulders of stevedores. "These men labor hard," Roberts observed, "and do their work with energy; but the system involves a tax upon the producer, and upon the vessel, which a more modern arrangement would avoid."[91] Port improvements would make the dockworkers' labor more rational in order to increase profits for the fazendeiros and the merchants.

Roberts devised improvements to secure a sufficient depth of water for large steamers, make piers and quays more efficient, provide direct access to trains, satisfy sanitary needs, and offer suitable grounds for private contractors to establish warehouses near the harbor. He worked alongside coffee merchants to better attend to their needs: "At the office of the [building] 'commission,' in Santos, every facility was afforded to all who were disposed to take an interest in the proposed improvement, to examine the plans, and to offer any suggestions that might occur to them."[92] Local figures approved Roberts's plan, and in March 1881 the provincial government of São Paulo provided funds for the works.[93] The remodeling of the port would go on during the 1880s and 1890s, transforming Santos into the main coffee mart of the world.

As dynamic as the emporiums of Santos and São Paulo City had become, foreign visitors to the province were surprised to discover what existed beyond the narrow strip close to the ocean. Unlike most Brazilian provinces, São Paulo stretched its enterprises deep into the interior. In the early 1860s, when he first worked in the country, Roberts had glimpsed the possibility of developing the interior of Brazil in the same way that the American Midwest had been developed. In 1879, he was glad to see the transformation of the Oeste Paulista. São Paulo City, he noted, "has become the center for a growing and already extensive railway system, which accommodates a considerable portion of the province. This system must continue to advance, and spread its branches farther into the interior, along with the augmenting population." At the time of Roberts's visit there were 669 miles of railroad lines up and running in the province, with many more under construction. "Most of these lines have been extended into the coffee-growing regions," he exulted, "which, in consequence of the improved facilities of transportation thus afforded, have been cultivated to a much greater extent than they could have been without the railways."[94] By the mid-1880s, over 1,300 miles of railroads crisscrossed the province and the system continued to expand. During his visit, Andrews rode the Paulista Railroad, the new line connecting São Paulo City to the interior, built with local capital from the coffee industry.[95] He found the trip quite pleasant: "The railway-car in which we went was comfortable and neat." Observing the scenery, he thought it resembled "the western part of the United States, except for occasional banana-trees."[96]

A three-hour railroad journey to the northwest of São Paulo City took the traveler to Campinas, the heart of the coffee-producing Oeste Paulista. In the mid-1880s, Campinas had three daily newspapers, a water supply company, streetcars, gas lighting, theaters, six private schools, a racetrack, several clubs and associations, four banks, ten breweries, three hat factories, two steam-powered sawmills, four coach manufacturers, several shops, hotels, and so on. More important, six foundries produced agricultural machinery and implements in Campinas.[97]

The largest factory in Campinas, Lidgerwood Mfg. Co. Ltd., employed nearly two hundred workers. Besides producing his famous coffee-hulling machines, William Van Vleck Lidgerwood worked with local inventors to expand his supply. In October 1881, two Brazilian engineers announced that "the trustworthy house of Lidgerwood & Comp., whose norm has always been to offer the best possible service to agriculture, has just given us proof of their esteem for our invention, offering to manufacture and sell the Taunay-Telles machines, designed to dry coffee."[98] Lidgerwood Mfg. Co. Ltd. now turned out steam engines, turbines, waterwheels, sawmills, cotton mills, hydraulic pumps, plows, reapers, water pipes, faucets, fences, gates, sugar mills, distillers, corn threshers, bread-making machines, tobacco-cutting machines, bottling machines, packing machines, and much more.[99]

In his 1883 *Agricultura Nacional*, Rebouças declared that "we owe to the son of the great Republic, the tireless mechanical engineer William Van Vleck Lidgerwood, the beginning of all improvements introduced, in recent years, to the mechanisms of processing coffee." Rebouças, who had worked with Lidgerwood at the SAIN, guaranteed that his agricultural machines were the best available in Brazil: "Numerous and various machines have been invented and patented for the preparation of coffee, in Brazil as well as in Europe and the United States; here, though, no one has been able yet to surmount, in more than twelve years of experience, the machines of William Van Vleck Lidgerwood."[100] In 1885, the Lidgerwood coffee huller got the highest prize at the Provincial Exposition of São Paulo. Although he had already received medals at exhibitions in Amsterdam, Nice, and Antwerp, it was significant that Lidgerwood now won before a jury of fazendeiros.[101]

Adding to Lidgerwood's fame, Dom Pedro II honored him with the title of *comendador* (commander) of the Imperial Order of the Rose. Proud of his countryman, Andrews noted that "his machinery is acknowledged in Brazil to

FIGURE 6.2 "Lidgerwood Manufg. Company Limited. Campinas Railway Station.
Showing L. M. Co. Workshop on the Right," Campinas, 1901.
Courtesy of Historic Speedwell, Morristown.

have caused an important saving, not only of labor, but of life. The title of *commandador* [*sic*], conferred upon him by the Brazilian Government, was certainly a very slight recognition of the great service he has rendered to the industry of the country."[102] When Dom Pedro II visited Campinas in 1886, he stopped by Lidgerwood's workshop, where he received the Brazilian coat of arms made of cast iron in that very location.[103]

Lidgerwood's influence had increased to such an extent that, in 1885, his attorney petitioned the Campinas municipal council requesting the purchase of public grounds close to the train station. Lidgerwood was looking for a larger and more convenient location for his factory, and he wanted it quickly. He hoped that the local authorities would disregard the usual procedure for selling public property—that is, public auction—and transfer it through private sale. "Now, to avoid false and misplaced modesty," the petitioner advanced, "it seems that the establishment of a new foundry and machine factory, considering all that it can offer, would not be an insignificant addition to the township."[104] Seeking to strengthen the position of Campinas as an industrial center, the municipal council conceded, and soon Lidgerwood opened his new manufacturing plant.[105]

In 1887, Lidgerwood opened an office in São Paulo City. Shortly after, he opened a factory there. By then, Lidgerwood had resettled in London and expanded his business from agricultural machinery to heavy machinery for mining, fishing, shipping, lumbering, and the construction of docks, dams, canals, railroads, bridges, and ships. By the 1900s, machines made by Lidgerwood Mfg. Co. Ltd. could be seen at work in major enterprises such as the Panama Canal, the New York City subway, a port on the Amazon River, railroads in the American West, coaling stations at the Baltic Sea, and dams in Australia, South Africa, and California.[106] The experience modernizing Brazilian coffee agriculture had prepared the New Jersey businessman to become a capitalist with global influence.

Whereas Lidgerwood became a successful entrepreneur, other Americans scraped by in the Oeste Paulista. Riding the train northwest from Campinas, Andrews arrived at "the station where one stops who wishes to visit the American colony—the settlement of farmers who emigrated to Brazil from the Southern States of the United States soon after the civil war. They live on a tract of moderate but not first-rate fertility, surrounding the village of Santa Barbara, about ten miles south from the station."[107] On their farms, the ex-Confederates grew corn, rice, beans, and potatoes. "I have rarely seen finer hogs than are to be found in this community," the US consul Henry Clay Armstrong remarked after visiting the community in the mid-1880s.[108]

A former aide-de-camp to General Wirt Adams in the Confederate Army and member of the Alabama legislature, Armstrong took personal interest in the plight of the ex-Confederates living in Brazil. What he saw deeply concerned him. Foodstuffs alone could not provide a comfortable life in the Oeste Paulista. Even William Hutchinson Norris, always so sanguine about life in Brazil, sounded rather gloomy in 1886, when he wrote to his son in Alabama that "I know of but few farmers that will make more corn than it will require to run them another year."[109]

Although cotton prices were plummeting, it brought instant cash. According to Armstrong, a portion of the crop was exported to Liverpool via Santos. But the bulk of the ex-Confederates' cotton was sold to the textile mills located in the Oeste Paulista.

These factories are owned mainly by Brazilians. One, called the Carioba Factory, was founded by Americans, but was afterwards sold to an English

FIGURE 6.3 In June 1888, Lidgerwood's factory in Brooklyn, New York, was featured on the cover of *Scientific American*. Private collection.

company. It is situated at the junction of the Quilombo and Piracicaba Rivers, two miles from the station of Santa Barbara. It employs from sixty to seventy hands, and turns out from 1,000 to 1,200 yards of cloth per day. Only the coarser goods are as yet made. The efficient manager of this enterprise is Mr. W. P. Ralston, Jr., of Pennsylvania.[110]

The textile industry of the Oeste Paulista thrived because the ex-Confederates continued performing the task that the local elite had assigned them. Some of the factories they supplied had been set up by Lidgerwood. By 1884, his company had built no fewer than fifteen cotton mills in Brazil.[111] Moreover, the Pennsylvania entrepreneur William Pultney Ralston, a former agent of Lidgerwood Mfg. Co. Ltd., had become a prominent manufacturer in the region.

In addition to cotton, some ex-Confederates cultivated sugarcane to make rum. Charles M. Hall of Georgia had the most successful distillery in the region. "This rum, or pinga, as it is now commonly called here," Armstrong observed, "is barreled and sent to the village of Santa Barbara and the city of Campinas, where it meets with a ready sale at an average price of $40 per pipe, equivalent to about 25 cents per gallon."[112] Hall was an exception, though. "Where the plow is used," Andrews reported on the sugarcane farms of Santa Bárbara, "farmers cultivate six or seven acres to the hand, and subsistence crops—corn, beans, etc.—enough to sustain the farm." The workforce was composed of family members since "labor, and very unreliable, costs forty cents per day for about ten hours' work, by one hand, or about ten dollars a month, food included."[113] Therefore, sugarcane, a very labor-intensive crop, did not pay what the ex-Confederates expected.

In 1885, Norris's son noted that "melons are generally planted early and watered by hand to come on soon—this crop is very remunerative—early melons bring prices ranging from 50c to 75, and good melons—(40 or 50 pounds) $2.00 to $2.50 a piece readily."[114] Armstrong explained that, considering the relatively small amount of labor required, the new means for prompt shipment to city markets, and the favor that the ex-Confederates' melons received among consumers, "this industry should and no doubt will be brought to a large development, and made to contribute no little to the prosperity of the community." Although droughts sometimes ruined crops, melons had "the advantage of bringing in money at a season of the year when it is often badly needed and can be profitably used in defraying the expense of gathering the cotton crop."[115] The fruit became so vital to the ex-Confederates that in 1896 they addressed desperate petitions to the São Paulo government after it

TABLE 6.1 Textile Mills in the Oeste Paulista and São Paulo City (1884–1885)

Location	Name	Spindles	Looms	Cloth produced annually (meters)	Capital (milréis)	Operatives	Proprietors
Santa Bárbara	Carioba		40		200,000		Clement Wilmot and George Wilmot
Itu	Salto	1,600	50–60		250,000	100	Francisco Fernandes de Barros
Jundiaí	Industrial Jundiaiana		25–40		140,000–200,000		Antonio Lemos da Fonseca
Cachoeira do Votorantim	Cachoeira do Votorantim				100,000		Stock Company
São Paulo	Major Barros		60	720,000	240,000–300,000	93	Diogo Antonio de Barros
Itu	São Luiz		20–24	450,000	100,000–150,000		Antonio de Souza Queiroz and William Pultney Ralston
Piracicaba	Piracicaba		80–100	800,000	300,000–400,000	180	Luiz Vicente de Souza Queiroz
Sorocaba	Sorocaba	1,500	40–50		250,000		Manoel José da Fonseca
Tatuí	Tatuí	3,530	54–80	900,000	400,000	124	Manoel Guedes Pinto de Melo

Sources: William T. Wright, "Cotton-Mills in Santos," in Reports from the Consuls of the United States on the Manufactures, Commerce, Etc. of Their Consular Districts (Washington: Government Printing Office, 1884); John Casper Branner, Cotton in the Empire of Brazil (Washington: Government Printing Office, 1885).

banned melon sales because of a cholera epidemic.[116] In the end, the immigrants from the American South had contributed to diversifying the Oeste Paulista, even if reluctantly.

The ex-Confederates were not the only foreigners farming in the Oeste Paulista. The same year that Andrews explored the region, a Dutch researcher named C. F. Van Delden Laërne visited farms and plantations there. Close to Santa Bárbara, he met a Swedish immigrant. "According to Mr. Magnussen a colonist can get on very well in Brazil," Laërne reported, "if he is willing to work briskly." After working for eleven years as a sharecropper for a fazendeiro, Magnussen had been able to acquire a farm with eight thousand coffee trees. "Now he works his lands himself, with two of his sons and a daughter," Laërne continued, "besides one camarada, an American, to whom he pays only one milreis per day with board." Very likely an ex-Confederate, the *camarada* (associate) helped the Swede maintain the coffee trees and grow foodstuffs. According to Magnussen, food crops were a good supplement to coffee as they could "speedily and readily be disposed of at the neighboring market of Campinas."[117]

Magnussen was an exception, however. Most immigrants in the Oeste Paulista worked for the fazendeiros. Laërne visited several fazendas that, while preserving slavery, experimented with free labor. At Joaquim Bonifácio do Amaral's Sete Quedas plantation in Campinas, he saw immigrants employed as sharecroppers, receiving "free lodging in stone houses with tiled roofs." At the Monte Alverne plantation in São Carlos, he saw slaves toiling alongside free workers, who "keep and dress a small portion of the plantations, receiving an annual payment of 100 réis per tree." At the Montevideo plantation in Araras, each immigrant family received lodging, pasture for three or four cattle, provision grounds, fruit-bearing coffee trees, and five hundred réis per alqueire (approximately fifty liters) of coffee they gathered. The Bom Retiro plantation in Amparo impressed Laërne: "With an eye to the ultimate substitution of slaves by colonists, the owner has had the old senzalas or slaves-quarters broken down, and handsome rows of cottages built on each side of the mansion house." Thirty-eight cottages had been built, and twelve more were under construction.[118]

Laërne also visited the Santa Veridiana plantation in the township of Casa Branca, which belonged to the richest fazendeiro of the Oeste Paulista, Antonio da Silva Prado. In 1882, Santa Veridiana employed forty-nine German and Italian families, amounting to over two hundred people: "They did not work here on parceria [sharecropping], but for a settled sum or wages for picking." Each family also received free housing, free schooling for their children, pasture for two animals, and provision grounds. "Senhor Prado seems however in the beginning of 1883," Laërne continued, "to have had reason . . . to reduce the price [of the picked alqueire] from 600 réis to 500." Dissatisfied, more than half of the workers left Prado's plantation.[119]

Immigrant dissatisfaction was an old problem in the Oeste Paulista. In late 1856, a sharecroppers' uprising shook the pioneering Ibicaba plantation in Limeira and dozens left. The immigrants who remained became a headache for the fazendeiros as they wanted to grow more foodstuffs than coffee.[120] Nonetheless, the experiment continued, and by the 1880s antislavery reformers saw Ibicaba as a model for the future of Brazilian agriculture. "The cultivation of coffee by free hands, by immigrants and settlers," Rebouças declared in 1883, "is an accomplished fact, since many years, in the province of S. Paulo. This distinguished province and Brazil owe such a great deed to Senator Nicolau Pereira de Campos Vergueiro, who established in 1847 on his Ibicaba plantation, a league and a half from the city of Limeira, the colony Senator Vergueiro."[121] The senator's son, José Vergueiro, took over the property and, after the uprising, made adjustments to the sharecropping system. Visiting Ibicaba, Laërne had the impression that "the colonists here were very well contented. In the landlord they saw not only their master but their friend."[122] To be safe, however, Vergueiro held on to his slaves, some four hundred of them.[123]

Andrews also made sure to visit Ibicaba, located only half an hour by train from Santa Bárbara. There he met Chamberlain again. "The Rev. Mr. Chamberlain arrived from São Paulo before dinner," Andrews narrated, "and was received by Mr. Vergueiro as an old friend." The fazendeiro and the missionary "passed the evening in an animated and friendly conversation on religious and other questions." This interaction gave Andrews the impression that Vergueiro was a truly progressive man. This idea was strengthened when Vergueiro showed him Ibicaba's immigrant village, brickyard, lumberyard, hospital, chapel, warehouses, vegetable gardens, and sprawling coffee fields, amounting to over one million fruit-bearing trees. What impressed Andrews most, however, were the machines that Vergueiro applied to coffee processing: "We first visited the mill, steam-engine, water-tanks, and machinery for cleaning the coffee; also the machinery for filling sacks. There was a large stock of superior coffee on hand, and the machinery and works for cleaning and preparing it were of a character calculated to excite wonder and admiration."[124]

Like other American observers, Andrews saw mechanization as a decisive step in the steady march of the fazendeiros toward free labor. The employment of machinery in coffee processing, he noticed, was forcing the sharecroppers to grow as much coffee as they could in order to make a living. "The machinery for cleaning coffee and putting it in its most attractive condition for the market is expensive," Andrews remarked. The newcomers could not afford to buy machines, and "many immigrant coffee farmers are consequently obliged to send their coffee to market in a crude condition, and to submit to a heavy deduction in price on that account." As an alternative, they could use the fazendeiros' mills "and get it hulled at about half a cent per pound."[125] Either way, sharecroppers were now losing their long-coveted autonomy.

Laërne also understood that mechanization concentrated capital in the Oeste Paulista, making small-scale coffee production an onerous task. He visited a coffee farm belonging to a German immigrant named Detlef Brune Schmidt, who had married José Vergueiro's adopted daughter Catherina, a German-born woman whose biological mother had died right after arriving in Brazil to work at Ibicaba. Contributing to his father-in-law's experiment, Schmidt employed only free workers, a total of forty-eight adults and twenty-six minors.[126] He had been taking his coffee to be processed at Ibicaba, but now he was setting up his own machinery. He soon found himself in debt. As Laërne observed, "Mr. Brune acknowledged that coffee-planting can yield no profit whatever if the planter works with borrowed capital."[127]

What Andrews and Laërne saw in the Oeste Paulista was that coffee production now required large investments, well beyond the means of most immigrants. Because the global market—and especially the American market—now demanded coffee processed by machines, the immigrants' options shrank: they could either submit to deductions by using the fazendeiros' machines, try to purchase their own and fall into debt like Schmidt, try their luck with mixed commercial farms like Magnussen and the ex-Confederates, or work for wages on the large fazendas. Needless to say, the fazendeiros welcomed this new form of concentrating capital with great joy.

After leaving Ibicaba, Andrews took the train to Jundiaí, whence he entered another branch of the São Paulo transportation network, the Ituana Railroad. On the train, he met the president of the railroad company, Rafael Tobias de Aguiar Paes de Barros, the second Baron of Piracicaba, "who with his family was going to his plantation at Itu." Noticing that Andrews was enjoying the landscape, the fazendeiro informed him "that the soil in that neighborhood was called massapé, and that it was good for growing coffee, cotton, and cane."[128]

After a four-hour journey, Andrews arrived in Piracicaba, where he had another pleasant surprise: "Miss Watts had her school of young misses, mostly Brazilians, paraded in two lines in the front yard and on the steps, and as we passed up between them they shook hands with each of us and presented flowers."[129] After the ceremony at the Colégio Piracicabano, Martha Watts took Andrews on a tour of Piracicaba, a town which she was proud of.

> Since we came here the street has been leveled, and pavements laid, and street lamps placed at convenient distances, the old houses are undergoing repairs, and it is becoming one of the promenades of the city. The city is improving generally, and has more inhabitants; before, only those remained in town who were obliged to, or who had no country house to go; but now parents stay in town to keep their children at school. One such case resulted in the starting of a soap and candle factory. The dry goods shops are enlarging their stocks and houses also. Thus you see that we have helped in the improvement of the place.[130]

After seeing the town, Andrews rode on horseback to the Piracicaba River to visit the textile mill of Luiz Vicente de Souza Queiroz. The American diplomat was impressed: "We there saw a new embroidery-machine doing the work which a hundred operatives would do by hand. The proprietor has a handsome new villa not far from the river, and from which there is a splendid view of the falls and rapids. . . . I should say the Piracicaba River is larger there than the Merrimack at Lowell."[131]

The influence of local entrepreneurs was growing in the Oeste Paulista. "Several American as well as English civil engineers have gained well-merited distinction by their services in Brazil," Andrews observed, "but the field now appears to be almost wholly occupied by native talent."[132] Andrews himself had ridden railroads designed by Antonio Francisco de Paula Souza. After the work experience in Missouri and Illinois, Paula Souza had returned home to become chief engineer of the Ituana Railroad and the Paulista Railroad. In the late 1870s and early 1880s, he had established a water supply system and a streetcar line in Campinas, surveyed lands and designed turnpikes all over the Oeste Paulista, and further extended the railroad system to the interior.[133]

But Paula Souza was just one of the several sons of the fazendeiros who had returned from the United States and engaged in modernizing their province. Cornell graduates assumed prominent roles in São Paulo during the 1880s. Elias Fausto Pacheco Jordão taught at the Escola Americana and established a newspaper in the town of Itu before serving the provincial government as assistant engineer of Public Works and becoming superintendent of the Ituana Railroad. José Tibiriçá Piratininga first worked at the Mogiana Railroad, then became provincial engineer of traffic, and by the late 1880s served as general inspector of the Ituana Navigation Company. Domingos Correia de Morais worked as assistant engineer of water works in São Paulo City and, in 1888, became president of the São Paulo Streetcar Company.[134]

Graduates of other American universities also contributed to developing infrastructure in São Paulo. José Custódio Aves de Lima, a Syracuse graduate and former editor of the *Aurora Brazileira*, served as assistant engineer of Public Works and later worked as an inspector at the Mogiana Railroad and the Sorocabana Railroad. Eduardo de Andrade Vilares, another Syracuse graduate, worked as an assistant engineer at the Mogiana Railroad and superintendent of the Ituana Railroad.[135] Tomás de Aquino e Castro, who had begun his studies at Cornell but transferred to the University of Cincinnati, became assistant engineer of Public Works.[136] José Nabor Pacheco Jordão, a Columbia alumnus, and Eugenio de Lacerda Franco, a Rensselaer graduate, worked as assistant engineers at the Paulista Railroad.[137] Luiz Gonzaga da Silva Leme, another Rensselaer graduate, first worked as an assistant engineer at the Paulista Railroad and later as chief engineer and general manager of the Bragantina Railroad.[138]

Besides working on transportation infrastructure, graduates of American universities returned to their families' fazendas to transform production. According to Laërne, José Tibiriçá Piratininga made systematic use of the plow on his land in Mogi Mirim, where "houses are being built for the reception of colonists."[139] In December 1880, the *Cornell Daily Sun* reported that Augusto Cezar de Vasconcelos, class of 1878, had "taken charge of a large coffee plantation."[140] The Cornell graduates Carlos Paes de Barros and Bento de Almeida Prado also established themselves as planters in the Oeste Paulista.[141] A British researcher of the coffee industry who visited São Paulo in the late 1870s admired the spirit of enterprise of the new generation: "The young Brazilian engineers, nearly all of whom have been trained in the United States, go at their work with a heartiness unknown to the fazendeiro."[142]

Other Brazilians who graduated from American universities engaged in commerce, extractive industries, and manufacturing. Fernando de Albuquerque, a Lafayette graduate, partnered with an American classmate and established an agency in Santos to import agricultural machinery and railroad supplies from the United States.[143] A Cincinnati alumnus, Joaquim da Silveira Melo, established a lumber company and a coffee mill in the township of Pirassununga.[144] Fernando Paes de Barros, a Syracuse graduate, built a steam-powered sawmill in Itu. Antonio de Queiroz Teles Neto, also a Syracuse graduate, set up a cotton mill in Jundiaí. Two other Syracuse graduates, Francisco Fernando Paes de Barros Jr. and Otaviano Abdon Pereira Mendes, entered a partnership to establish a cotton mill near Itu with five thousand spindles.[145]

The graduates of American universities were part of a modernizing process that integrated coffee planters like Vergueiro, machine manufacturers like Lidgerwood, foreign engineers like Roberts, farmers like the ex-Confederates, missionaries like Chamberlain, and the mass of landless workers. In the 1880s, American technology and expertise, mediated by a multitude of Brazilian and American modernizers, were transforming a largely unimproved slave economy into an agroindustrial power moved by free labor. To the advantage of great planters, merchants, and manufacturers, American and Brazilian antislavery reformers had successfully widened the gap separating those who possessed capital from those who owned nothing but their own labor power in the Oeste Paulista. Visitors from abroad saw precisely that when they explored the region. The fazendas, railroads, piers, machines, mills, and schools they inspected convinced them that a new birth of capitalism was about to take place in Brazil.[146] All that was needed now was a final push.

The Final Push

On May 31, 1883, André Pinto Rebouças published an article titled "The Province of S. Paulo after Emancipation" in the *Gazeta da Tarde*. He opened by stating that "no other province is better prepared for immediate and uncompensated emancipation than the province of S. Paulo." Sprawling railroads, manufacturing enterprises, mechanized agriculture, and many other factors made São Paulo the perfect candidate to lead the way to free labor in Brazil. "On the day the [London] *Times* announces that the fertile territory of this rich province is free," Rebouças envisaged, "thousands upon thousands of immigrants will take steamers to Santos." He looked to the example of the American South to foresee the future of the province: "On the day after emancipation, the highlands of S. Paulo will follow the path of the Mississippi Valley after the war of freedom in the United States. The production of coffee will increase just like the production of cotton increased there." The fertile soil of the Oeste Paulista, "tilled by free men," would produce ten times more than "now when it is still watered by the tears and the sweat of miserable slaves." Rebouças dreamed of the day São Paulo would overthrow slavery and enter the modern age. He went so far as speculating that, "had the province of S. Paulo the courage to decree emancipation now, in a few years it would surpass, in wealth and prosperity, the richest states of the North American Republic."[147] For a moment, however, it seemed that São Paulo would fail him.

In 1884, the abolitionist movement had succeeded in pushing their agenda into the executive branch of government. Prime Minister Manoel Pinto de Souza Dantas, the Liberal from Bahia who had promoted ex-Confederate immigration to Brazil, presented a bill that would, among other things, free all slaves who reached the age of sixty without compensating masters, fix prices for slaves to be freed by the government emancipation fund, enlarge the same fund through a tax on property in slaves, and terminate the interprovincial slave trade.[148] Reactionary forces immediately cried foul. The opposition to Dantas became so rabid that Andrew Jackson Lamoureux drew a parallel with what had happened in the United States a few decades earlier: "The protests of our [Brazilian] planters' clubs are nothing more nor less than the threats of the pro-slavery party in the United States to break up the Union if their views were disregarded."[149]

After a vicious battle in Parliament and the press, Dantas fell and José Antonio Saraiva took his place. Known for his pragmatism, Saraiva submitted the bill to a conservative overhaul: slaves who reached sixty would have to work three more years to compensate their masters; slave values for government manumission were set above market prices; the emancipation fund was divided in thirds in order to free older slaves, reimburse planters willing to convert to free labor, and pay the fare for immigrants willing to work on plantations; last but not least, the government would fine people for aiding fugitive slaves. The final text of the law turned the fine into imprisonment.[150]

Saraiva stepped down before his bill was submitted to the Senate. Dom Pedro II then named a Conservative from Bahia as the new prime minister. João Maurício Wanderley, the Baron of Cotegipe, ensured the ratification of the Law of the Sexagenarians. He also named Antonio da Silva Prado as minister of agriculture, commerce, and public works. "The new minister of agriculture is one of the most progressive planters of São Paulo and is a warm friend of a more liberal immigration policy," Lamoureux remarked in August 1885. "Unhappily, however, he is equally friendly to the converse policy of retaining slavery as long as possible and indemnifying planters to the last penny."[151] On June 12, 1886, Prado presented the regulations of the already infamous Law of the Sexagenarians, adopting a draconian reading of the fugitive slave clause. He determined that not only those who helped fugitive slaves but also those who failed to report runaways to the authorities would be sent to jail.[152]

The abolitionist movement immediately organized demonstrations against what they called Prado's "Black Regulations." The most dramatic events unfolded in his own province. With Luiz Gama's death in 1882, a man named Antonio

Bento had become the leader of the São Paulo abolitionists. Unlike Gama, Bento was a white man, a member of a planter family, a judge, a devout monarchist, and a zealous Catholic. But just like Gama, he was an admirer of John Brown. Bento's tall and slender body, long beard, and self-denial evoked frequent comparisons to the American abolitionist. He recruited a group of black and white activists who became known as the Caifazes. Like the followers of John Brown, these men repudiated any law that upheld slavery and were ready to use force. The Caifazes infiltrated fazendas and helped the slaves escape, leading them to a fortified community in Santos through the Brazilian underground railroad.[153]

The Oeste Paulista was in disarray. Confrontations between runaways and the police multiplied.[154] Some slaveholders became hysterical. But the Caifazes had urban professionals, manual workers, and even the sons of the fazendeiros on their side. In July 1887, Lamoureux rejoiced that a new movement had "sprung into existence among the young men in various parts of the province, which is nothing less than assisting slaves to escape. The two thousand odd fugitives in and about Santos are the results of their work, and hardly a day passes that they do not help others to escape." Many of these activists, Lamoureux explained, were "young men of position and influence, not to be scared by threats or police interference."[155]

However raucous, the reactionaries were few and powerless in São Paulo. Soon, the mass flights led the members of the Brazilian Republican Party to turn their backs on the defenders of slavery. Whereas Republicans like Antonio Francisco de Paula Souza had disavowed slavery long ago, until the mid-1880s the party leader Manoel Ferraz de Campos Sales had been afraid of alienating slaveholders from his cause. Although Campos Sales supported the Dantas bill, he preached that slavery was an economic question that should be solved by society, not the government. Now facing a general uprising, he instructed the fazendeiros to free their slaves.[156]

To everyone's surprise, Prado yielded to social pressures. In September 1887, he resigned his position as minister and denounced in the Senate a petition from some Campinas fazendeiros who were asking for energetic measures against fugitive slaves. According to Lamoureux, Prado and his allies had realized that "if the new order of things must come and free labor must be employed, then the quicker the change is made, the better. Waiting for an inevitable crisis is painfully trying business for a man of life and energy, and it is a losing business besides."[157]

In November 1887, Prado and Campos Sales gathered a group of twenty influential fazendeiros in São Paulo City to discuss how to rearrange plantation

labor in the midst of chaos. Campos Sales proposed immediate and unconditional freedom. To his disappointment, however, most fazendeiros followed
Prado, who had proposed to pay salaries but under the condition that the
freedpeople remain on their masters' fazendas for three more years. The fazendeiros also decided to approach Antonio Bento, offering to hire the slaves he
had been sheltering. The leader of the Caifazes, worried about holding onto
thousands of refugees, did not object.[158]

Not all coffee planters in Brazil were prepared for the end of slavery though.
As 1888 approached, the declining Paraíba Valley still resisted. "The planters
of the province of Rio de Janeiro seem determined to show their contempt for
law and humanity," Lamoureux raged.[159] They clung as hard as they could to
the status quo, arguing that the Law of the Sexagenarians—which they had
vehemently opposed earlier—should be the last word on slave emancipation in
Brazil. Comparing the planters of the Oeste Paulista with those of the Paraíba
Valley, Lamoureux saw a split between two class attitudes: "The almost simultaneous action of the provinces of S. Paulo and Rio de Janeiro relative to the
agricultural labour question will to most foreigners present a comparison of
energy and conscious strength on the one side, to one of confessed weakness
and timidity, strongly mixed with stubbornness on the other."[160]

While the Paraíba Valley stalled, the Oeste Paulista moved on. The fazendeiros found in Prado's younger brother, Martinho da Silva Prado Junior, the
practical man they needed. A member of the Republican Party, Prado Junior was
known as a progressive fazendeiro.[161] For decades, São Paulo provincial legislators had been discussing ways to encourage mass immigration, but most plans
required the fazendeiros to take the risk of advancing money to immigrants and
making them pay their debts. In 1885, Prado Junior proposed that the provincial
government, now very affluent thanks to coffee, pay private companies for the
transportation and the placement of immigrants. Lamoureux offered a candid
analysis of the new scheme, pointing out that "the government of the province
being an oligarchy of planters, and these planters feeling that their prosperity
depends upon a new class of laborers to take the place of the slave, their only
object and desire is to turn the stream of European emigration this way and to
use the resources and influence of the province for that purpose."[162]

Though the first contracting companies failed and accusations of embezzlement surfaced, Prado Junior soon came up with a corrective. In 1886, along
with Nicolau de Souza Queiroz and the Baron of Piracicaba, he created the
Sociedade Promotora de Imigração (Society for the Promotion of Immigration; SPI). The new association received full support from Provincial

President Antonio Queiroz Teles, a fazendeiro from Jundiaí who had been experimenting with immigrant labor since the 1850s. The minister of agriculture, commerce, and public works—Prado Junior's older brother—also directed lavish resources to the SPI. With government funds, Prado Junior published pamphlets and maps, built a hostel for the newcomers, contracted with the Paulista Railroad to transport the immigrants from Santos to the interior, and established a branch of the SPI in Genoa, Italy.[163]

Between 1887 and 1888, the SPI succeeded in attracting over 120,000 European immigrants to São Paulo, making the fazendeiros less apprehensive about the 100,000 slaves who had left the plantations. Of all immigrants reaching São Paulo, over three-fourths were Italian. At the time, Italy had been suffering from economic stagnation, and masses of peasants were struck by extreme poverty.[164] Whereas Italians with a little money to spare preferred to migrate to the United States or Argentina instead of Brazil, free transportation proved to be enticing to the poorest members of Italian society.[165] As Prado Junior acknowledged, "Only those individuals without resources, attacked by necessity in all its forms, emigrate to Brazil, and they do it by seeking free or reduced passage."[166]

Overnight, poor peasants from Italy became the rural proletariat of the Oeste Paulista. Lamoureux lamented that "neither the Sociedade Promotora de Imigração, nor the province of São Paulo, nor the Empire of Brazil wants immigrants which shall become citizens and small proprietors; they simply want laborers for the great plantations, a class to take the places made vacant by slave emancipation."[167] A supporter of the SPI addressed an angry letter to Lamoureux. The attack nonetheless confirmed the plans of the fazendeiros. "Too much is made of this citizenship, this proprietorship," the writer charged. The half-starved immigrants from Europe would willingly sacrifice "all the doubtful pleasures of proprietorship and citizenship for the certainty of two good meals a day for their children, which this country offers to all who are willing to work." As to the labor they would perform in Brazil, Lamoureux's critic questioned, "is there any farm-work much more pleasant and easy than the carrying on of an already formed coffee plantation in the province of São Paulo? I know of no family who has suffered in the work, not one."[168]

The fazendeiros' plan succeeded. By enlarging the pool of workers, they managed to depress wages and make free labor a viable system for large-scale agriculture in the Oeste Paulista. By April 1888, Lamoureux observed that "the large number of immigrant laborers which have settled in this country during the past year, and the large number of slaves liberated in São Paulo but kept on the plantations as paid laborers, has largely and suddenly increased the number of wage-earners."[169] A few months later, a member of the Chamber of Deputies maintained that the introduction of new workers served to "increase the competition among them and in that way salaries will be lowered by means of the law of supply and demand."[170] In Brazil, immigrants and ex-slaves could aspire to very little beyond working for wages. "Desirable lands," Lamoureux regretted, "are held in large estates, and [Brazil's] provisions for the sale of its public lands to immigrants are illiberal and onerous."[171] Meanwhile, the government offered the fazendeiros all they asked for: "We have repeatedly called attention to the facts that the planters pay no [land] taxes, railways are built for their accommodation, immigrants are imported at public cost to labor for them, and finally the Treasury lends them money, at reduced interest."[172]

Speaking to the São Paulo Legislative Assembly in 1887, Provincial President Queiroz Teles celebrated the new arrangements, congratulating the provincial legislators who, setting aside radical projects, had acted "in accordance with our circumstances." The progress of São Paulo, he believed, depended on the maintenance of concentrated wealth. "Without large property its territory would not be crossed by railroads now and its rivers would not be navigated," Queiroz Teles argued. "The application of science to agriculture led to the recognition of the importance of preserving large property, because the new processes that came to replace primitive labor depend on large capital and intelligent management, which small enterprises cannot attain."[173]

Based on an enlarged workforce, concentrated property, and mechanization, a wage system emerged on the fazendas. The care of a certain number of coffee trees through the annual cycle accounted for one-half to two-thirds of a worker's payment. The harvest, which required intensive labor and extended from May to August, paid a fixed sum for each alqueire of coffee picked. Occasional day labor for the fazendeiro in processing or transporting coffee and other odd jobs were less frequent, but supplemented the income. The workers received free housing in villages within the fazendas called *colonias*. Most workers were allowed to produce some food on provision grounds, a job that usually fell on women and took place outside harvest season.[174]

Regardless of his objections to the means and ends of the fazendeiros, Lamoureux thought that they would gain much by the new system. Like all other antislavery reformers, he insisted that "experience has proved over and over again that slave labor is the most expensive in world; and we are likely to see this proof capitally shown by the increase of agricultural production in

S. Paulo."[175] The radical Lamoureux could not hide his admiration for the fazendeiros' achievement.

> A steady stream of immigrants has been pouring into S. Paulo, the slaves have been liberated by hundreds and thousands, the coffee plantations are being largely and rapidly extended, the railways are prospering, new industries are springing up, the towns and cities of the province are increasing in population and trade, the freedmen—to everybody's surprise—are settling down contentedly on the plantations to the life of free, paid laborers, and everywhere are seen the signs of enterprise and prosperity.[176]

With such a system up and running, most fazendeiros welcomed emancipation. In March 1888, Cotegipe fell from power. With the support of Antonio da Silva Prado, who became minister of foreign affairs, the new prime minister and Parliament took the definitive step. On May 13, 1888, Princess Regent Isabel—Dom Pedro II was in Europe—signed the Golden Law freeing all Brazilian slaves unconditionally and without compensation. Blissful, Lamoureux wrote that "the work thus so happily accomplished on the 13th instant, was pre-eminently popular in character, and was forced to its conclusion by popular movements and influences." He thanked Bento, "the John Brown of Brazilian emancipation," and Prado, "a warm advocate of the substitution of free for slave labor."[177]

Scholars of slavery can learn much about how capitalism evolved by studying the case of the Oeste Paulista. It provides an example of class transformation. As Florestan Fernandes put it in a sociological study written in the 1970s, "The coffee planter ended up representing in Brazilian history the rural lord who was compelled to accept and identify himself with the bourgeois dimension of his interests and social status."[178] The study of US-Brazilian relations in the age of emancipation shows that such a process took place in a transnational context. Attentive to the transformations of American society and broader trends in the world capitalist system, the fazendeiros of the Oeste Paulista saw that, however profitable, slavery had no viable future. For decades, they had been building a more dynamic labor system on their plantations. The fazendeiros completed the process of modernization in the late 1880s and created an agroindustrial order that no slave society had ever matched. They succeeded where proslavery Southerners had failed because they were willing to absorb technology and expertise promoted by a transnational coalition of antislavery reformers. Learning from the American North, the fazendeiros set up an efficient system to exploit a multiethnic proletariat that allowed them to hold on to power for several decades thereafter.

Brave New World

As usual, change generated discontent. Two ex-Confederates, James Ox Warne and John Jackson Clink, were responsible for turning lynching into a tool for the defense of slavery in São Paulo. In February 1888, they urged slaveholders in the township of Penha do Rio do Peixe, fifty miles northeast of Santa Bárbara, to take revenge on the local police chief, who had refused to act as a slave catcher. A mob broke into his house with the excuse that a runaway had been hiding there and assassinated him. Lamoureux explained that Warne and Clink had "incited the Brazilian planters to the deed by telling them they 'had only cockroach blood,' and that a revolution would have occurred before this in any other country."[179] The lynching shocked public opinion. Lamoureux later reflected that, at least, this horrific crime had contributed to clinching the question of emancipation in the Oeste Paulista: "From that moment, the fate of slavery in S. Paulo was sealed. The sympathies of moderate men everywhere were irretrievably lost, and the government found it impossible to stem the tide of popular indignation against the authors and abettors of so monstrous a crime."[180]

Not all ex-Confederates responded violently to the coming of emancipation in Brazil, but few were happy. Already by the early 1880s, James McFadden Gaston, then a famous surgeon in Campinas, had become terrified of "the evident tendency toward a revolution in Brazil." As abolitionism turned into a mass movement, Gaston feared that slave rebellion would threaten white people's lives in the Oeste Paulista. According to his son, he "could not see that the Brazilian government would take the wise course of paying owners for their slaves and by using this means of freeing the negroes avoid civil war." Dreading another bloodbath, Gaston had made up his mind. "It is to be hoped that they will stave off the issue [of emancipation]," he wrote to a relative in early 1883, "until we can get out of the country, which I am expecting to realize in March or April at the farthest."[181] Before the end of that year, Gaston returned to the United States. With the money and experience he had gathered in the Oeste Paulista, he opened a clinic in Atlanta, Georgia.

In 1885, another ex-Confederate, George Matthews, made his way back. William Hutchinson Norris, who had always been critical of Matthews, condemned his decision to leave Santa Bárbara. Referring to a neighbor who had left with Matthews, Norris wrote to his son that "he is not making anything in Florida. The last word I said to him when he left was 'show yourself a man,' you know what that means, I fear he did not."[182] Penniless and lonely in Florida, Jane

Matthews looked at her husband and realized that "he is still dissatisfied though, and says he intends going somewhere else when he sells his land here." But, she clarified, "we never had the least idea or wish to go back [to Brazil]."[183]

Too proud to return, Norris preferred to face hardship in Brazil than give up his dream of patriarchy in the United States. When slave emancipation finally came, however, he reconsidered his situation. Writing a letter twelve days after the Golden Law had been signed, Norris lamented that "this is the gloomiest period of my life." His dream of patriarchy, it became clear then, had always been intertwined with slavery. "I am nearly 88 years of age," he continued commiserating, "and not able to perform any labor and by the laws of Brazil all our Negroes are free, and I have no labor to make or attend to my farm. . . . What will become of my dependent children and grandchildren, I do not know, but I will not fret about it." Yet Norris could not help but fret: "I do not believe any man can farm here with free negro labor and make any money. I will not attempt it. I must try to make provision to live on. This whole country is in a demoralized condition."[184] Norris, who had already lived through a process of emancipation in his native country, had to witness another one in his adopted land. He nonetheless remained in Santa Bárbara until he died in 1893.

From a completely different standpoint, Lamoureux and Rebouças also revealed misgivings about the postemancipation order. Now fighting for land reform, they exposed the process of proletarianization in São Paulo. Lamoureux pointed to the conditions at the immigrant hostel: "The poor overcrowded wretches are clamoring to be sent to the plantations of the interior, but as the demand for laborers has come to an end, they have been kept in the station at São Paulo, in the heat and discomfort of an over-crowded building."[185] The fazendeiros had formed a reserve army of labor that they could exploit at will. Rebouças, who had sung the praises of free labor after visiting the United States in the 1870s, quickly became disappointed by what he saw in Brazil. "The province of S. Paulo is already saturated with laborers," he raged. "As great as the planters' resources are in that extraordinary region, it is necessary to confess that 150,000 immigrants, introduced from 1886 to 1888, have already produced a plethora of rural wage earners."[186]

It did not take long for working-class movements to surface. But the fazendeiros had the authorities on their side. As soon as immigrants spoke out at a Campinas plantation, in August 1889, a police force of thirty men was sent to suppress their demonstration. "A conflict ensued," Lamoureux protested, "which resulted in the killing of one and the wounding of three Italians."[187] The immigrants were not the only victims. That same month, a police force marched to the township of Boituva, forty miles west of Itu, where freedpeople had settled on an abandoned farm. Following orders from a local fazendeiro, the policemen kicked the squatters out, killing two and wounding three. The authorities subsequently burned their shacks and destroyed provisions. Five days later, the police assassinated eight ex-slaves twenty miles from there, in Tatuí. Rebouças was outraged: "It has been reported that on arrival they killed a couple of blacks and shot many others who, later, were found dead. Among the victims there are two children who were burned inside a barn!!!"[188]

According to the historian Steven Hahn, "Like all categories and ideal types, 'free labor' embodied many complexities and contradictions. Its focus on voluntary exchange in the marketplace obscured the historical process that required people to seek work from someone else rather than to work for themselves."[189] Rebouças and Lamoureux were among the few antislavery reformers to denounce such historical process in postemancipation Brazil. In utter despair, they witnessed impoverishment, displacement, and brutal repression become part of workers' daily life in the Oeste Paulista after the enactment of the Golden Law.

However disgruntled, Rebouças and Lamoureux admitted that the new system had maximized the potential of the coffee economy. In July 1888, Rebouças pointed out that "the numbers of the coffee trade surpass by millions those of 1887."[190] In April 1889, Lamoureux quoted from a Paulista Railroad report indicating that "not only was the passenger movement largely increased over the preceding year, which is proof of business activity and the possession of a fair amount of ready cash among the people, but the freight traffic, both in imports and exports, was also very largely expanded." Far from hurting the Oeste Paulista, emancipation had revitalized it. "The planter has had his new difficulties to contend with of course," Lamoureux observed, "but if the free laborer has increased trade in manufactured and other goods, and has added so considerably to the traffic of the railways—and all this without decreasing the exportable products of the country—then the general result must be considered good."[191]

American observers rejoiced to hear the news from the Oeste Paulista. As early as January 1888, Jabez Burns's *Spice Mill* was predicting that slave emancipation in Brazil would cause no coffee famine. In fact, coffee production was expanding as the fazendeiros were taking the final step to fully rationalize production. Burns concentrated on the experiments of Martinho da Silva Prado Junior. After purchasing "land in the then almost unknown district of Ribeirao Preto for a coffee plantation," this visionary fazendeiro "at once began clearing the land, procuring free labor for the service." In less than a decade, the results were astounding: "A railway has reached that locality; the plantation possesses about 500,000 bearing trees, and a large number of new trees and the present coffee crop is estimated at from 60,000 to 70,000 arrobas [approximately from 1,920,000 to 2,240,000 pounds]." The fazenda had a capacity for about 600,000 more trees, and Prado Junior continued to open new coffee plantations along the railway line.[192]

Lamoureux's countrymen did not share his criticism of the fazendeiros. Much to the contrary, less than a week after Princess Isabel signed the Golden Law, the *St. Paul Daily Globe* reported that "Brazil has been fortunate in extinguishing the institution of slavery by peaceful methods and without disturbing the business condition of the Empire." The Minnesota newspaper applauded the fazendeiros, who, long since, "realizing that it was only a question of time when the institution of slavery would entirely disappear, at once began to set their houses in order for the change that was inevitable, and thus helped to speed it along. Last year a number of the largest slave owners in the Empire, including Minister [Antonio da Silva] Prado, manumitted their slaves." Although Brazilian emancipation had been unconditional, production was not suffering as "the coffee planters had already provided for the introduction of imported labor in sufficient numbers to take the place of the negroes who were expected to quit work when their freedom was gained."[193]

For American observers, the heroes of emancipation in Brazil were neither Rebouças nor Nabuco, let alone the Caifazes or the fugitive slaves. On June 30, 1888, the Chicago *Daily Inter Ocean* published a portrait of Prado and placed him at center stage. "Antonio da Silva Prado, Senator of the Empire from Sao Paulo, retired from the late Ministry in the spring of 1887 because his associates in the government would not second his proposal to hasten emancipation." Prado, his brother, and their allies then began "setting free their slaves and making contracts with them as freemen." Success was immediate as these fazendeiros cultivated their coffee "more successfully and economically than they had ever been able to do with slaves. Their example was contagious. The movement for immediate emancipation ran over the province as waves of religious excitement sometimes sweep over communities." In the months leading up to the Golden Law, slavery dissolved and a vigorous wage system emerged in the Oeste Paulista. "It was evident to every one," the *Daily Inter Ocean* rejoiced, "that the movement for immediate abolition was irresistible."[194]

Americans gazed in awe at the group of landowners who had proactively transformed their own class. Even observers from the Southern states lauded the fazendeiros. In January 1889, the *Macon Telegraph* reported that "the large crop of 8,000,000 bags of coffee has been secured, the freedmen working, it is true, a little sluggishly and picking negligently, many of them, yet the work has been performed." As an antidote to the ex-slaves' (alleged) sluggishness, the ingenious fazendeiros had taken measures to "procure immigrants from Europe by the hundreds of thousands, and since August last Italian laborers are pouring into Brazil." The Georgia newspaper concluded that "the planters thus fully gain their point; whether the former slaves work with a will or not, they will have no lack of white labor as good or even more reliable."[195]

Reflecting on the broader meaning of slave emancipation, the Chicago *Daily Inter Ocean* commented that "much the greater proportion of the coffee and sugar of the world now is grown by free labor, and it is beyond question that the production of these articles has increased vastly and their quality undergone improvement since the time, still within the memory of men who are not very old, when they were all but entirely the products of slave labor." Proslavery advocates had been wrong in relation to sugar in the Caribbean and cotton in the American South. Now they were completely disproved by coffee in Brazil: "Already the tide of immigration is flowing with a hitherto unknown strength toward the free Empire. Foreign capital is seeking investment there. Machinery and enterprise are taking the formerly slave-cursed acres for their own. The empire which Dom Pedro transmits to his heirs will be more prosperous than that which he inherited."[196] In short, Brazilian emancipation had once and for all vindicated the antislavery reformers. The exponential growth of coffee exports from the port of Santos in the decades following slave emancipation left no doubt that free labor had made the Oeste Paulista into an agroindustrial behemoth. By the early twentieth century, Brazil produced over three-fourths of all the coffee in the world.[197]

The successful transition from slave to free labor in Brazil had been so momentous that the American Republican Party celebrated it in their platform for the 1888 presidential election. After invoking the names of Abraham Lincoln and Ulysses S. Grant, the Republicans praised their Brazilian friends: "In the spirit of those great leaders and of our own devotion to human liberty, and with that hostility to all forms of despotism and oppression which is the fundamental idea of the Republican Party, we send fraternal congratulations to our fellow Americans of Brazil upon their great act of emancipation, which completed the abolition of slavery throughout the two American continents."[198] The party that had crushed a slaveholding aristocracy in the

TABLE 6.2 Receipts of Coffee at the Port of Santos (1880–1902)

Year beginning July 1	Pounds	Year beginning July 1	Pounds
1880–1881	148,931,532	1891–1892	447,897,647
1881–1882	227,955,463	1892–1893	424,120,904
1882–1883	260,303,427	1893–1894	222,892,335
1883–1884	247,556,651	1894–1895	530,079,668
1884–1885	277,081,315	1895–1896	409,202,155
1885–1886	220,765,999	1896–1897	675,200,990
1886–1887	341,729,491	1897–1898	813,840,524
1887–1888	148,168,300	1898–1899	736,731,023
1888–1889	348,546,731	1899–1900	755,525,062
1889–1890	247,382,840	1900–1901	1,054,656,125
1890–1891	390,521,345	1901–1902	1,345,500,361

Source: Harry Crusen Graham, *Coffee: Production, Trade, and Consumption by Countries* (Washington: Government Printing Office, 1912).

American South two decades earlier now exalted the fazendeiros of Brazil for finalizing the work of antislavery modernization in the western hemisphere.

The effort to promote free labor in the age of emancipation had been a well-planned collaboration connecting Brazil to the United States. It had emerged during the secession crisis, grown during the American Civil War, strengthened after Lincoln's Emancipation Proclamation and Rio Branco's Law of the Free Womb, consolidated as Americans settled in Brazil and Brazilians explored the United States, and triumphed in 1888. In both countries, the privileged classes gained much from the triumph of free labor: more railroads, more machines, more coffee, more cotton, more everything. In both countries, the working class, now free from human masters but subjected to poverty, had no choice but to continue to struggle.

Epilogue

ONE YEAR AND A half after Princess Isabel signed the Golden Law, a coalition of generals, planters, and urban professionals overthrew the monarchy and established a republican regime in Brazil. Joaquim Nabuco immediately joined the ranks of the dissatisfied as the militarization of politics and the newfound power of money displeased his aristocratic sensibilities. But as time went by, he changed his mind and became a faithful servant of the Republic. From 1905 to 1910, Nabuco served as Brazilian ambassador in Washington, D.C. In 1908, two decades after the Golden Law, he received an invitation to lecture at the University of Wisconsin. Although Nabuco could not attend because he fell ill, a surrogate speaker delivered his lecture, which the *American Historical Review* published in 1909. The title of Nabuco's lecture was "The Share of America in Civilization." In dialogue with authors such as W. T. Stead, who had published *The Americanization of the World: or, The Trend of the Twentieth Century* in 1902, Nabuco discussed what he thought was the distinctive contribution of the United States to the modern world.[1]

A system of spontaneous immigration, Nabuco told his audience, was the quintessential American accomplishment. In his words, "Choosing one's own country is a right that would not be generally acknowledged before this country created it and made it acceptable to the world." Nabuco's abolitionist background came to the fore as he posited that immigration was the antithesis of slavery: "Before the American spirit started immigration, the greatest human migration was the slave-trade, the covering of America by man-stealth with African slaves. The contrast between immigration and the slave-trade is enough to show what a regenerating part the American spirit has had in the march of civilization."[2]

Although Europe did not admit human bondage in its own national territories, Nabuco continued, "slavery was her colonial policy; in the New World slavery marked the period of European colonization and continued as a legacy from the colonial times after the Independence." Nabuco acknowledged that the British had started the campaign against slave labor in the nineteenth century. Yet they had failed to offer an adequate replacement for it. For Nabuco, "what killed the slave-trade and slavery was immigration." While slavery persisted in the Southern states of the Union, the Yankee spirit perfected the system that eventually rendered slave labor obsolete. Civilization advanced in the United States because Northern society created a much more efficient form of recruiting laborers than the slave trade. "Immigration, not slavery," Nabuco reiterated, "represents the true American sap."[3]

The revolutionary force of spontaneous migration not only defeated slavery in North America but also transformed Europe. As Nabuco put it, the attraction of the United States "broke in Europe the old stratifications; created centrifugal forces. . . . It destroyed what remained of a dungeon-like character in the old national barriers, by making country a wholly voluntary allegiance; in a word, it upset forever the foundations of despotism, of practical serfdom, by rendering the people everywhere free to move away from it." Echoing some optimistic modernizers of the pre–World War I period, Nabuco claimed that immigration bred cosmopolitanism. And he thanked the United States for it: "I consider immigration the greatest force in modern civilization, and there is no doubt that it is an American force."[4]

However fascinated by the openness of American society to newcomers, Nabuco rejected the naïve view of the United States as an egalitarian republic of smallholders and shopkeepers, where everyone had equal chances to succeed. He knew quite well that the opening of the twentieth century marked a new era. He knew that the American dream had changed character.

> The idea of civilization has been up till now associated with individual initiative; in landed property, with the system of small estates, more than with the *latifundia*; in trade and industry, more with competition than with concentration. But there is evidently now in progress an evolution, in the sense of unification, that can be called American. Great nationalities, cosmopolitan trains, fast boats, aeroplanes, cables, wireless telegraph, Hague Conferences, all seem to announce that the new tendency of mankind, in every direction, is the "merger." In theory, centralization seems to assure the better service of so many millions of people, just as the cold storage assures

their better feeding, by saving incalculable quantities of food which formerly would decay in the same day; but there are too many points to be considered in centralization, political and social, and only experience will shed any light over them. For the moment no one can say whether the new American political economy is or is not one of the great contributions of this country to civilization.[5]

Nabuco was unsure about what the concentration of capital and political centralization would do to the modern world. But he was confident that the United States would play a central role in a global civilization of large-scale industry, powerful corporations, shortening distances, expanding empires, scientific discoveries, and constant technological innovation. After all, he saw these changes as consequences of the Americanization of the world.

Six years after Nabuco's lecture was published, George Scarborough Barnsley wrote about his own experience. Unlike most migrants of that era, he had moved out of the United States. And he did it twice. After serving as an assistant surgeon in the Eighth Regiment of the Georgia Confederate Cavalry during the Civil War, Barnsley migrated to Brazil. He had frustrating experiences trying to cultivate cotton and eventually became a country doctor in the province of São Paulo. The routine of going from one fazenda to the next treating the fazendeiros and their dependents was exhausting and poorly remunerated.

Following some of his countrymen who decided to return to the American South after slavery ended in Brazil, Barnsley tried a new beginning. But what he found in his native land during the 1890s disappointed him: "The trees seemed so much smaller apparently; through East Tennessee the country looked so desolate, and woebegone, while the railroad depots were mere shacks to ours in Brazil, which most always have a small flower garden, some trees or vines, an earthen jar or pot with good water to drink. My old home was as beautiful as ever, but it too looked shriveled up somehow." While living in Georgia, Barnsley was criminally charged for sharing his wine with a neighbor and fishing on Sundays. "The impression took hold of me," a weary Barnsley noted, "that I had gotten into a country where people were prejudiced, narrow-minded, and selfish. I was glad to get back to Brazil where I could do as I pleased and [had] perfect freedom to think as it suited me."[6]

By the 1900s, Barnsley had moved back to Brazil and established a clinic on the outskirts of São Paulo City. Much had changed since Barnsley and his compatriots had first seen that place. São Paulo City, which had fewer than thirty thousand inhabitants in the 1860s, had grown to nearly half a million people by the 1910s. All kinds of industries were at work in the new metropolis, "from glass tumblers and bottles etc. to mending an electrical motor. There are thousands of factory people and mechanics." Paved streets, streetcars, beautiful houses, and large flower gardens made daily life very pleasant for Barnsley. "If you have money in your pocket," he remarked, "you can buy pianos, pianolas, automobiles, Edison gramophones, and all kinds of machinery etc. If you have only moderate sums to spend there are the numerous cinematographs, theaters, musical concerts, galleries, football, ping-pong, four o'clock teas, regattas on the Tiete [River] or Santos, public and private parks, reading rooms with current literature in many languages."[7]

The signs of an improving civilization were not restricted to the capital of the state, however. "This same change," Barnsley continued, "which in [the] last 25 years had been made [in the state capital], has taken hold in the interior towns and villages wherever in contact with the railroad." The wealth of São Paulo was based on a modern economic complex extending deep into the hinterland.

What was when we came a virgin forest, with savage indians, only partially known, is now dotted with populous thriving towns and cities, covered with a sea of coffee bearing trees. Electricity is used for lighting towns, transportation, and power for manufactories, mills. Great cotton weaving factories are at work all over the state, railroads are made [in] every direction, and on the main are Pullman cars etc. . . . The State which once imported rice from U.S. and India—now exports. The banana business is growing up to be a competitor of cotton and sugar. Fruits and vegetables of all kinds, of temperate and tropic climates, are in the markets all the year round. Scientific fishing on the coast furnishes great quantities of delicious fish, brought on ice or refrigerated air cars from Santos.

Barnsley looked around him and conjectured that "all vestiges of old slavery times are gone, even to most of the negroes." Moreover, European immigrants offered a valuable contribution to the development of São Paulo. "The great changes in architecture, horticulture, vegetable and fruit culture, manufactures" were all encouraged by the newcomers, according to Barnsley. "The foregoing," he wrapped up his description of his adopted country, "will enable to get at an opinion of the changes since the Republic got into existence, and the slavery [question was] settled forever."[8] Brazil too had entered the modern age.

Different backgrounds and life experiences notwithstanding, neither Nabuco nor Barnsley had difficulty in understanding what free labor in the form of the wage system had accomplished. Once the two largest slave societies in the Western world, Brazil and the United States thrived after slavery was gone. By the early twentieth century, as the Old World plunged into a catastrophic war, the United States was about to become the richest and most powerful nation in modern history. Although far from American standards, Brazil—and especially the state of São Paulo—boasted one of the most advanced capitalist economies south of the equator.

In addition to transforming each one of these two nations, free labor had brought them together. In their relationship with Brazil, American antislavery reformers were able to refashion their national image, at once spreading the labor system triumphant after the Civil War and presenting the United States as a progressive alternative to European empires. By attracting American capital and expertise to their country, Brazilian antislavery reformers were able to accomplish a relatively peaceful transition to free labor and bring about the fast modernization of the Brazilian economy. By the early twentieth century, this transnational alliance of reformers had given rise to profitable commercial ties and a stable diplomatic partnership. Americans and Brazilians had come a long way since the antebellum era, when questions pertaining to the reproduction and expansion of slavery created thorny conflicts between them.

In spite of all changes, by the early twentieth century the legacies of slavery were still alive in the United States and Brazil. As hard as certain ideologues tried to exclude the problem from public debates, writers such as Machado de Assis and W. E. B. Du Bois made sure that the history of slavery continued to be discussed, influencing generations of thinkers in these two countries. Moreover, in the rural areas and the cities of Brazil and the United States, people of African descent continued to struggle for civil rights and better living conditions. They knew all too well that the triumph of free labor had engendered new forms of inequality.

Ultimately, the end of slavery refashioned labor exploitation in both countries. A new era opened for Brazil and the United States as massive contingents of people were set free and, at the same time, were kept destitute by those who concentrated capital and political power. Simultaneously, millions of human beings were leaving the Old World in search of better opportunities or just survival. Capitalists in Brazil and the United States made the most of their need to work for wages.

This was the era of "great nationalities, cosmopolitan trains, fast boats, aeroplanes, cables, wireless telegraph, Hague Conferences," which fascinated Nabuco. This was the era of "pianos, pianolas, automobiles, Edison gramophones, and all kinds of machinery," which enthralled Barnsley. This brave new world had very little to do with the world of masters and slaves of the antebellum American South or monarchical Brazil. The new order would create its own challenges: total wars, hypernationalism, overproduction, explosive population growth, rural flight, consumerism, and environmental degradation, among other things. These problems remain with us today because we still live in the world that free labor made.

ACKNOWLEDGMENTS

WHILE WRITING THIS BOOK, I received precious support from institutions that foster the study of history. It all began at the University of Pennsylvania, where I was a graduate student from 2011 to 2017. The Benjamin Franklin Fellowship, the School of Arts and Sciences Dissertation Research Fellowship, and the School of Arts and Sciences Dissertation Completion Fellowship gave me the means to conduct the research that makes up the bulk of this study. At Penn, I was able to participate in enriching academic activities. Above all, the Workshop in the Global Nineteenth Century was a formative experience for me.

Between 2017 and 2018, my home was the American Antiquarian Society. As a recipient of the Hench Postdoctoral Fellowship I was able to fully dedicate myself to transforming a dissertation into a book manuscript. Also in 2017–2018, I participated in the Global History Seminars at Harvard's Weatherhead Center, where I engaged with great scholars interested in transnational topics. From 2018 to 2020, I worked at Saint Michael's College. As the Henry G. Fairbanks Visiting Humanities Scholar-in-Residence, I had the opportunity to conduct more research and revise the manuscript. Finally, as I worked on the finishing touches in this book, I was being welcomed to Wesleyan University, where I work as Assistant Professor of American Studies. As a new member of the faculty, I look forward to many more academic endeavors at Wesleyan.

Books like this only come to life thanks to academic presses. I'm very proud that Princeton University Press accepted to publish my work. The raw material that allowed me to craft this book came from many libraries and archives, in the United States and Brazil, that generously opened their doors to my research: Alabama Department of Archives and History; American Antiquarian Society; Arquivo da Câmara Municipal de Campinas; Arquivo do Estado de São Paulo; Arquivo Edgard Leuenroth, Unicamp; Arquivo Histórico do Museu Imperial; Biblioteca Brasiliana Mindlin, USP; Biblioteca Municipal Mário de Andrade; Centro Cultural Martha Watts; Centro de Memória Arquivos Históricos, Unicamp; David M. Rubenstein Library, Duke University;

Department of Records, City of Philadelphia; Durick Library, Saint Michael's College; Free Library of Philadelphia; Fundação Biblioteca Nacional; Fundação Getulio Vargas; Fundação Joaquim Nabuco; Hagley Museum and Library; Hargrett Rare Books and Manuscripts, University of Georgia; Historic Speedwell Archives; Houghton Library, Harvard University; Indiana Historical Society; Kroch Library of Rare and Manuscript Collections, Cornell University; Loja América; Louisiana State University Library; Merrill G. Burlingame Special Collections, Montana State University Library; Morristown and Morris Township Library; Museu da Imigração, Santa Bárbara; Museu Presbiteriano Reverendo Júlio Andrade Ferreira; Museu Republicano de Itu; Oliveira Lima Library, Catholic University of America; Southern Historical Collection, Wilson Library, UNC; Special Collections Research Center, University of Michigan; Sterling Memorial Library, Yale University; Van Pelt Library, University of Pennsylvania.

———

As I tried to map the networks that connected people between the United States and Brazil in the nineteenth century, I created my own (twenty-first-century) transnational network. And I was very fortunate to meet wonderful people in the process. I'm thankful to many people, in two countries, who often went out of their way to help me write this book.

First and foremost, I'd like to thank Steven Hahn. He welcomed me to American academia in 2011 and has offered his untiring support since. A considerate advisor, stimulating professor, generous reader, brilliant writer, and inspiring public intellectual, he is and will always be a model for me. He was there for me at every turn, encouraging my academic work and other intellectual and political endeavors. Having Steve as a mentor and a friend was the best thing about the journey that culminated in the publication of this book.

As a graduate student, I received invaluable guidance from some amazing scholars, who continued to shape this work after I graduated. Stephanie McCurry's enthusiasm for my research gave me confidence to go against the flow and create something bold. Within my limitations, I tried to emulate her provocative take on classic topics and her sharp challenges to mainstream ideas. Eiichiro Azuma does the kind of work I want to do in my career. During the time we spent together, he showed me the challenges of transnational history and inspired me to explore its potentials. Angela Alonso has been an inspiration for a long time, well before I started my doctoral studies. She first told me to go for this topic and has always encouraged me to cross academic and geographic borders. I can't thank these professors enough for everything they have done for me.

I also had the great privilege to work with Sven Beckert in this project. His enthusiasm for pushing the boundaries of history is contagious and his support for innovative work tireless. He not only welcomed me to the Global History Seminar in 2017–2018 but also read my manuscript, made brilliant suggestions, and invited me to publish in the America in the World Series of Princeton University Press. Since 2018, I've been working alongside great editors at PUP. I'd like to give special thanks to Jeremi Suri (coeditor of the America in the World Series alongside Sven Beckert), Eric Crahan, Thalia Leaf, Priya Nelson, Jenny Wolkowicki, Joseph Dahm, and the excellent (anonymous) outside readers.

At the University of Pennsylvania, I had the opportunity to work with many intelligent and kind intellectuals who made graduate school a superb experience. I am thankful for the insights I received from Warren Breckman, Kathy Brown, Roger Chartier, Sally Gordon, Amy Offner, Vanessa Ogle, Kathy Peiss, Eve Trout Powell, Dan Richter, Robert St. George, and Tamara Walker. During my years at Penn, I had the privilege to rely on three generous graduate chairs: Antonio Feros, Peter Holquist, and Benjamin Nathans. I also appreciated very much the work of the department's staff members Joan Plonski, Octavia Carr, and Bekah Rosenberg. At Van Pelt, John Pollack showed me how to get the best out of archives and libraries.

Back in Brazil, four people have encouraged me to go along this path since the time I was an undergrad. Miriam Dolhnikoff taught me the historian's craft. She introduced me to the profession I love so much. Monica Dantas has also been a great professor and now has become a collaborator in research. Rogério Baptistini Mendes and Grácia Fragalá are more than friends, they are family now. I'm deeply grateful for their support since we met in 2005 and the way they remind me of my origins and my values.

I spent six fantastic years among friends in Philly. From day one, Emma Teitelman and Kevin Waite were there for me. I was so lucky to have these two by my side every time I needed them—and there were many. I admire their intelligence and cherish their friendship very much. My dear friends Adam Goodman, Caleb Knedlik, Janine Van Vliet, Alex Ponsen, and Evgenia Schneider Schoop were so generous in so many ways. We experienced delightful moments together, and they offered me brilliant ideas on how to proceed with this and other projects.

All the staff at the American Antiquarian Society is so amazing that I would have to list all their names here, but it would not be enough to express how grateful I am for their support. I'd like to give special thanks to Nan Wolverton, who, among many other things, organized a colloquium that shaped this book. She gathered a "dream team" of scholars—Christopher Clark, Teresa Cribelli, Thavolia Glymph, and Barbara Weinstein—whose masterful insights transformed this book into something much better than it would have been. I was also very lucky to work alongside Peter Onuf at the AAS. In all his kindness, he not only read and reread my work but also organized a workshop with fellows and staff members. Ashley Cataldo, Kate Grandjean, Sarah Schuetze, and Adrian Weimer read my work closely and gave me very productive feedback. Reeve Huston and Samantha Harvey, in addition to offering many thoughtful comments on my manuscript, were very good friends when I needed most.

At Saint Michael's College, I worked alongside generous colleagues who made me feel valued for what I do and taught me much about the academic world. I was delighted to spend two years with George Dameron, Kathryn Dungy, Susan Ouellette, Jennifer Purcell, and Doug Slaybaugh in the History Department. Saint Michael's staff offered me invaluable support. I'd also like to thank Christina Root and Jeffrey Trumbower for coordinating the Humanities Program and the Fairbanks. Moreover, I'm grateful to Brian Lacey for his support of the scholarship and his enthusiasm for the liberal arts.

My colleagues at Wesleyan, in addition to giving me superb insights to finalize this book, welcomed me to their institution with utmost kindness. I'm very fortunate to work at the American Studies Department with scholars who are always willing to break intellectual barriers and challenge academic conventions. Their fascinating works inspire me to expand my thinking about the United States in the world and the world in the United States. I'm very grateful to Matthew Carl Garrett, Megan Glick, Laura Grappo, Indira Karamcheti, J. Kehaulani Kauanui, Joel Pfister, Amy Cynthia Tang, and Margot Weiss. I'd also like to thank Laura Borhman for her vital support for the American Studies Department. Moreover, I'm delighted to work alongside historians such as Demetrius Eudell, Ethan Kleinberg, and Valeria López Fadul at Wesleyan.

Many people read parts of my work or otherwise engaged with it, providing invaluable ideas on how to move forward. As the research and writing processes unfolded, I was very lucky to cross paths with Jeremy Adelman, Juan Pablo Ardila, Fernando Atique, Roderick Barman, Matt Barton, Peter Beattie, Pepijn Brandon, Alexis Broderick Neumann, Vincent Brown, Steve Bullock, Ema Camillo, Cristina de Campos, Celso Thomas Castilho, Claudia Chierichini, Teresa Davis, Jeremy Dell, Rosana Dent, Greg Downs, Roquinaldo Ferreira, Harold Forsythe, Zephyr Frank, Reinaldo Fuentes, Antonio Carlos

Galdino, Naomi Glascock, Lesley Gordon, Keila Grinberg, Anne Hanley, Robert Hegwood, Katie Hickerson, Kathleen Hilliard, Tom Holloway, Dani Holtz, Richard Huzzey, Tina Irvine, Justin Jackson, Matt Karp, Andrew Kirkendall, Hendrik Kraay, Sam Lacy, Elaine LaFay, Mollie Lieblich, Virginia Ling, Noam Maggor, Hope McGrath, José Juan Pérez Meléndez, Rachel Miller, Max Mishler, Salar Mohandesi, Alexandra Montgomery, Isadora Moura Mota, Tore Olsson, Patrick O'Connor, Stephen Ortega, Gabriel Raeburn, Jessie Regunberg, Andrés Reséndez, Judith Ridner, Gabriel Rocha, Sarah Rodriguez, Marlen Rosas, Brian Rouleau, Melike Sayoglu, John Shufelt, David Silverman, Iuliia Skubytska, Alexandra Stern, Camille Suarez, Kristian Taketomo, Kristin Waters, Joel Wolfe, and Andrew Zimmerman.

———

I grew up listening to the women in my family tell stories about my ancestors: impoverished migrants from all over the place, people without roots, but brave people. And I used to wonder about the mysterious confluence of forces that made them come together and form my family. I still wonder, every single day. My dead family members are my inspiration, and so are my living father, mother, brother, sister, in-laws, nephew, nieces, uncles, aunts, and cousins. I think of them all, of how our lives are connected. They are my people, and they make me very proud.

To close these acknowledgments, I'd like to thank the person who has been by my side for well over a decade and never doubted that it would all work out—my best friend, my partner in life, my wife Livia. She is the light of my days. She reminds me every day of what really matters. She makes me aware that all we got is the here and now, and we must make the best of it. I'm very fortunate to share life with her. Her strength and her love carried me all the way. This work is as much mine as it is hers. I thank her for being part of this journey and all journeys that are to come.

ABBREVIATIONS AND ARCHIVAL COLLECTIONS CONSULTED

Manuscripts

ALABAMA DEPARTMENT OF ARCHIVES AND HISTORY, MONTGOMERY (ADAH)

Charles G. Gunter Family Papers
William H. Norris Family Papers

AMERICAN ANTIQUARIAN SOCIETY, WORCESTER, MA (AAS)

American Broadsides and Ephemera
American Slavery Collection

ARQUIVO DA CÂMARA MUNICIPAL DE CAMPINAS (ACMC)

Petições

ARQUIVO DO ESTADO DE SÃO PAULO (AESP)

Secretaria da Agricultura

ARQUIVO HISTÓRICO DO MUSEU IMPERIAL, PETRÓPOLIS (AMIP)

Arquivo da Casa Imperial do Brasil

BIBLIOTECA MUNICIPAL MÁRIO DE ANDRADE, SÃO PAULO (BMA)

Arquivo Paula Souza

CENTRO CULTURAL MARTHA WATTS, PIRACICABA (CCMW)

Acervo do Colégio Piracicabano

CENTRO DE MEMÓRIA ARQUIVOS HISTÓRICOS, UNIVERSIDADE
ESTADUAL DE CAMPINAS (CMAH-UEC)

Tribunal de Justiça de São Paulo, Comarca de Campinas

DAVID M. RUBENSTEIN RARE BOOKS AND MANUSCRIPT LIBRARY,
DUKE UNIVERSITY (DMR-DU)

Godfrey Barnsley Papers

DEPARTMENT OF RECORDS, CITY OF PHILADELPHIA (DRPHI)

United States Centennial Commission

FUNDAÇÃO BIBLIOTECA NACIONAL,
RIO DE JANEIRO (FBN)

Coleção Tavares Bastos

FUNDAÇÃO GETULIO VARGAS, RIO DE JANEIRO (FGV)

Coleção Quintino Bocaiuva

FUNDAÇÃO JOAQUIM NABUCO, RECIFE (FJN)

Arquivo Joaquim Nabuco

HARGRETT RARE BOOKS AND MANUSCRIPTS LIBRARY,
UNIVERSITY OF GEORGIA (HRB-UG)

Howell Cobb Family Papers

HISTORIC SPEEDWELL ARCHIVES ROOM, MORRISTOWN, NJ (HSAR)

Lidgerwood Manufacturing Company
Stephen Vail Family Correspondence

HOUGHTON LIBRARY, HARVARD UNIVERSITY (HOL-HU)

Louis Agassiz Correspondence and Other Papers

INDIANA HISTORICAL SOCIETY, INDIANAPOLIS (IHS)

Calvin Fletcher Papers

KROCH LIBRARY OF RARE AND MANUSCRIPT COLLECTIONS, CORNELL UNIVERSITY

Academic Theses

LOUISIANA STATE UNIVERSITY LIBRARIES, BATON ROUGE (LSUL)

Israel L. Adams and Family Papers

MERRILL G. BURLINGAME SPECIAL COLLECTIONS, MONTANA STATE UNIVERSITY LIBRARY (MGB-MSU)

William Milnor Roberts Papers

MORRISTOWN AND MORRIS TOWNSHIP LIBRARY (MMTL)

Morristown Manuscript Collection
Stephen Vail Journals

MUSEU PRESBITERIANO REVERENDO JÚLIO ANDRADE FERREIRA, CAMPINAS (MPRF)

Relatórios dos Campos de Trabalho

SOUTHERN HISTORICAL COLLECTION, WILSON LIBRARY,
UNIVERSITY OF NORTH CAROLINA
AT CHAPEL HILL (SHC-CH)

George Scarborough Barnsley Papers
James McFadden Gaston Papers

STERLING MEMORIAL LIBRARY, YALE UNIVERSITY (SML-YU)

James Watson Webb Papers

Periodicals

AMERICAN ANTIQUARIAN SOCIETY

American Missionary (New York)
Liberator (Boston)
Littell's Living Age (Boston)
Railroad Gazette (Chicago)

ARQUIVO EDGARD LEUENROTH, UNIVERSIDADE
ESTADUAL DE CAMPINAS

Gazeta de Campinas

CENTRO CULTURAL MARTHA WATTS, PIRACICABA

Gazeta de Piracicaba

CHRONICLING AMERICA,
HTTP://CHRONICLINGAMERICA.LOC.GOV

Charleston Courier
Fremont Journal
Memphis Daily Appeal
New York Daily Tribune
New York Herald
St. Paul Daily Globe

CORNELL DAILY SUN ARCHIVES,
HTTP://CDSUN.LIBRARY.CORNELL.EDU

Cornell Daily Sun (Ithaca, NY)

FUNDAÇÃO BIBLIOTECA NACIONAL, RIO DE JANEIRO

Aurora Brazileira (Syracuse)

GOOGLE BOOKS, HTTP://BOOKS.GOOGLE.COM

Revista Industrial (New York)

HAGLEY MUSEUM AND LIBRARY, WILMINGTON

Spice Mill (New York)

HARP WEEK, HTTP://HARPWEEK.COM

Harper's Weekly (New York)

HATHITRUST DIGITAL LIBRARY, HTTP://HATHITRUST.ORG

Atlantic Monthly (New York)
Lippincott's Monthly Magazine (Philadelphia)
Phrenological Journal and Science of Health (New York)
Railway World (Philadelphia)
Southern Quarterly Review (Charleston)

HEMEROTECA DIGITAL BRASILEIRA,
HTTP://BNDIGITAL.BN.GOV.BR/HEMEROTECA-DIGITAL

A Actualidade (Rio de Janeiro)
Anglo-Brazilian Times (Rio de Janeiro)
O Auxiliador da Industria Nacional (Rio de Janeiro)
Bazar Volante (Rio de Janeiro)
Cidade do Rio (Rio de Janeiro)

Correio Mercantil (Rio de Janeiro)
Correio Paulistano (São Paulo)
Correio da Tarde (Rio de Janeiro)
Diário de Pernambuco (Recife)
Diário do Povo (Rio de Janeiro)
Diário do Rio de Janeiro
Diário de São Paulo
O Futuro (São Paulo)
Gazeta da Tarde (Rio de Janeiro)
A Immigração (Rio de Janeiro)
Imprensa Evangélica (Rio de Janeiro)
Jornal do Commercio (Rio de Janeiro)
O Novo Mundo (New York)
Opinião Liberal (Rio de Janeiro)
Radical Paulistano (São Paulo)
A Republica (Rio de Janeiro)
Revista de Engenharia (Rio de Janeiro)
Revista Illustrada (Rio de Janeiro)
A Revolução Pacífica (Rio de Janeiro)
Rio News (Rio de Janeiro)
Semana Illustrada (Rio de Janeiro)
Sentinella da Monarchia (Rio de Janeiro)
A Vida Fluminense (Niterói)
O Ypiranga (Itu)

INTERNATIONAL MISSION BOARD, PERIODICALS DATABASE,
HTTPS://WWW.IMB.ORG/RESEARCH/ARCHIVES/

Foreign Mission Journal (Richmond)

KROCH LIBRARY OF RARE AND MANUSCRIPT COLLECTIONS,
CORNELL UNIVERSITY

Aurora Brasileira (Ithaca, NY)

MAKING OF AMERICA JOURNALS,
HTTP://QUOD.LIB.UMICH.EDU/M/MOAJRNL/

De Bow's Review (New Orleans)

THE NATION ARCHIVE,
HTTP://EBSCOHOST.COM/ACADEMIC/THE-NATION

Nation (New York)

NINETEENTH-CENTURY US NEWSPAPERS,
HTTP://GALE.COM/C/19TH-CENTURY-US-NEWSPAPERS

Boston Daily Advertiser
Charleston Mercury
Daily Inter Ocean (Chicago)
Georgia Weekly Telegraph (Macon)
North American (Philadelphia)

NYS HISTORIC NEWSPAPERS,
HTTP://NYSHISTORICNEWSPAPERS.ORG/NEWSPAPERS/

Daily Journal (Ithaca, NY)

PROQUEST HISTORICAL NEWSPAPERS,
HTTP://PROQUEST.COM/LIBRARIES/ACADEMIC/NEWS
-NEWSPAPERS

Friends' Intelligencer (Philadelphia)
Methodist Quarterly Review (New York)
National Era (Washington, DC)
New York Evangelist
New York Observer and Chronicle
New York Times
Saturday Evening Post (Philadelphia)

READEX AMERICA'S NEWSPAPER ARCHIVE, HTTP://READEX.COM
/CONTENT/AMERICAS-HISTORICAL-NEWSPAPERS

Daily Age (Philadelphia)
Macon Telegraph

READEX WORLD NEWSPAPER ARCHIVE,
HTTP://READEX.COM/CONTENT/WORLD-NEWSPAPER
-ARCHIVE

A Província de São Paulo

NOTES

Introduction

1. E. P. Thompson, *The Making of the English Working Class* (New York: Pantheon Books, 1963), 445.

2. Eric Hobsbawm, *The Age of Capital, 1848–1875* (New York: Scribner, 1975), 4. For a similar, but more recent, historical analysis of this transformation, see Jürgen Osterhammel, *The Transformation of the World: A Global History of the Nineteenth Century* (Princeton: Princeton University Press, 2014). For the concept of modernization, see Vladimir I. Lenin, *The Development of Capitalism in Russia: The Process of the Formation of a Home Market for Large-Scale Industry* (Moscow: Progress Publishers, 1964 [1899]); Joseph A. Schumpeter, *Capitalism, Socialism, and Democracy* (New York: Harper, 1947); Barrington Moore Jr., *Social Origins of Dictatorship and Democracy: Lord and Peasant in the Making of the Modern World* (Boston: Beacon, 1966); Eugen Joseph Weber, *Peasants into Frenchmen: The Modernization of Rural France, 1870–1914* (Stanford, CA: Stanford University Press, 1976); Marshall Berman, *All That Is Solid Melts into Air: The Experience of Modernity* (New York: Viking Penguin, 1980); David Harvey, *The Condition of Postmodernity: An Enquiry into the Origins of Cultural Change* (Cambridge, MA: Blackwell, 1990).

3. James McPherson quantifies the economic disparity between the regions in the antebellum era, concluding that "the North—along with a few countries in northwestern Europe—hurtled forward eagerly toward a future of industrial-capitalism that many Southerners found distasteful if not frightening; the South remained proudly and even defiantly rooted in the past." *Drawn with the Sword: Reflections on the American Civil War* (Oxford: Oxford University Press, 1996), 22.

4. Thomas C. Holt, *The Problem of Freedom: Race, Labor, and Politics in Jamaica and Britain, 1832–1938* (Baltimore: Johns Hopkins University Press, 1992), 50.

5. Edward B. Rugemer, *The Problem of Emancipation: The Caribbean Roots of the American Civil War* (Baton Rouge: Louisiana State University Press, 2008); Matthew Pratt Guterl, *American Mediterranean: Southern Slaveholders in the Age of Emancipation* (Cambridge, MA: Harvard University Press, 2008); Brian Schoen, *The Fragile Fabric of Union: Cotton, Federal Politics, and the Global Origins of the Civil War* (Baltimore: Johns Hopkins University Press, 2009); Walter Johnson, *River of Dark Dreams: Slavery and Empire in the Cotton Kingdom* (Cambridge, MA: Belknap, 2013); Joshua D. Rothman, *Flush Times and Fever Dreams: A Story of Capitalism and Slavery in the Age of Jackson* (Athens: University of Georgia Press, 2014); Matthew Karp, *This Vast Southern Empire: Slaveholders at the Helm of American Foreign Policy* (Cambridge, MA: Harvard University Press, 2016); Edward E. Baptist, *The Half Has Never Been Told: Slavery and*

the Making of American Capitalism (New York: Basic Books, 2016); Caitlin Rosenthal, *Accounting for Slavery: Masters and Management* (Cambridge, MA: Harvard University Press, 2018); Sven Beckert and Seth Rockman, eds., *Slavery's Capitalism: A New History of American Economic Development* (Philadelphia: University of Pennsylvania Press, 2018).

6. Rafael de Bivar Marquese, *Feitores do Corpo, Missionários da Mente: Senhores, Letrados e o Controle dos Escravos nas Américas, 1660–1860* (São Paulo: Companhia das Letras, 2004); Gerald Horne, *The Deepest South: The United States, Brazil, and the African Slave Trade* (New York: New York University Press, 2007); Ricardo Salles, *E o Vale Era o Escravo. Vassouras— Século XIX. Senhores e Escravos no Coração do Império* (Rio de Janeiro: Civilização Brasileira, 2008); Mariana Muaze and Ricardo Salles, eds., *O Vale do Paraíba e o Império do Brasil nos Quadros da Segunda Escravidão* (Rio de Janeiro: Faperj, 2015); Dale W. Tomich, ed., *The Politics of the Second Slavery* (Albany: SUNY Press, 2016); Márcia Regina Berbel, Rafael de Bivar Marquese, and Tâmis Parron, *Slavery and Politics: Brazil and Cuba, 1790–1850* (Albuquerque: University of New Mexico Press, 2016); Dale W. Tomich, ed., *New Frontiers of Slavery* (Albany: SUNY Press, 2016); Rafael de Bivar Marquese and Ricardo Salles, eds., *Escravidão e Capitalismo Histórico no Século XIX: Cuba, Brasil, Estados Unidos* (Rio de Janeiro: Civilização Brasileira, 2016); Dale W. Tomich, ed., *Slavery and Historical Capitalism during the Nineteenth Century* (Lanham, MD: Lexington Books, 2017).

7. Seymour Drescher, *Abolition: A History of Slavery and Antislavery* (Cambridge: Cambridge University Press, 2009); Maria Helena P. T. Machado, *O Plano e o Pânico: Os Movimentos Sociais na Década da Abolição* (São Paulo: Edusp, 2010); Robin Blackburn, *The American Crucible: Slavery, Emancipation and Human Rights* (London: Verso, 2011); Brent E. Kinser, *The American Civil War in the Shaping of British Democracy* (Farnham: Ashgate, 2011); John T. Cumbler, *From Abolition to Rights for All: The Making of a Reform Community in the Nineteenth Century* (Philadelphia: University of Pennsylvania Press, 2013); David Brion Davis, *The Problem of Slavery in the Age of Emancipation* (New York: Vintage, 2014); Andre M. Fleche, *The Revolution of 1861: The American Civil War in the Age of Nationalist Conflict* (Chapel Hill: University of North Carolina Press, 2014); Angela Alonso, *Flores, Votos e Balas: O Movimento Abolicionista Brasileiro, 1868–1888* (São Paulo: Companhia das Letras, 2015); Don H. Doyle, *The Cause of All Nations: An International History of the American Civil War* (New York: Basic Books, 2015); W. Caleb McDaniel, *The Problem of Democracy in the Age of Slavery: Garrisonian Abolitionists and Transatlantic Reform* (Baton Rouge: Louisiana State University Press, 2015); Celso Thomas Castilho, *Slave Emancipation and Transformations in Brazilian Political Citizenship* (Pittsburgh: University of Pittsburgh Press, 2016); Manisha Sinha, *The Slave's Cause: A History of Abolition* (New Haven, CT: Yale University Press, 2017).

8. William Appleman Williams, *The Tragedy of American Diplomacy* (Cleveland: World, 1959); Walter LaFeber, *The New Empire: An Interpretation of American Expansion, 1860–1898* (Ithaca, NY: Cornell University Press, 1963); William Appleman Williams, *The Roots of the Modern American Empire: A Study of the Growth and Shaping of Social Consciousness in a Marketplace Society* (New York: Random House, 1969); William Appleman Williams, *Empire as a Way of Life: An Essay on the Causes and Character of America's Present Predicament, along with a Few Thoughts about an Alternative* (New York: Oxford University Press, 1980); Walter LaFeber, *The Cambridge History of American Foreign Relations. Volume 2: The American Search for Opportunity, 1865–1913* (Cambridge: Cambridge University Press, 1993).

9. David M. Pletcher, *The Diplomacy of Trade and Investment: American Economic Expansion in the Hemisphere, 1865–1900* (Columbia: University of Missouri Press, 1998); Fareed Zakaria, *From Wealth to Power: The Unusual Origins of America's World Role* (Princeton: Princeton University Press, 1998); Thomas F. O'Brien, *Making the Americas: The United States and Latin America from the Age of Revolutions to the Era of Globalization* (Albuquerque: University of New Mexico Press, 2007); George C. Herring, *From Colony to Superpower: U.S. Foreign Relations since 1776* (New York: Oxford University Press, 2008); Frank Ninkovich, *Global Dawn: The Cultural Foundation of American Internationalism, 1865–1890* (Cambridge, MA: Harvard University Press, 2009); Richard H. Immerman, *Empire for Liberty: A History of American Imperialism from Benjamin Franklin to Paul Wolfowitz* (Princeton: Princeton University Press, 2010); Jay Sexton, *The Monroe Doctrine: Empire and Nation in Nineteenth-century America* (New York: Hill & Wang, 2011); Elizabeth Cobbs Hoffman, *American Umpire* (Cambridge, MA: Harvard University Press, 2013); A. G. Hopkins, *American Empire: A Global History* (Princeton: Princeton University Press, 2018); Marc-William Palen, *The "Conspiracy" of Free Trade: The Anglo-American Struggle over Empire and Economic Globalization, 1846–1896* (New York: Cambridge University Press, 2016).

10. On British influence in Brazil during the nineteenth century, see Richard Graham, *Britain and the Onset of Modernization in Brazil 1850–1914* (Cambridge: Cambridge University Press, 1968); Leslie Bethell, *The Abolition of the Brazilian Slave Trade: Britain, Brazil and the Slave Trade Question, 1807–1869* (Cambridge: Cambridge University Press, 1970); Robert Edgar Conrad, *World of Sorrow: The African Slave Trade to Brazil* (Baton Rouge: Louisiana State University Press, 1986); Manolo Florentino, *Em Costas Negras: Uma História do Tráfico Atlântico de Escravos entre a Africa e o Rio de Janeiro, Séculos XVIII e XIX* (Rio de Janeiro: Arquivo Nacional, 1995); Peter Rivière, *Absent-Minded Imperialism: Britain and the Expansion of Empire in Nineteenth-Century Brazil* (New York: St. Martin's, 1995); Jaime Rodrigues, *O Infame Comércio: Propostas e Experiências no Final do Tráfico de Africanos para o Brasil, 1800–1850* (Campinas: Editora Unicamp, 2000).

11. On the persistence and expansion of unfree labor in the modern world, see Willemina Kloosterboer, *Involuntary Labour since the Abolition of Slavery: A Survey of Compulsory Labour throughout the World* (Leiden: Brill, 1960); Tom Brass, *Towards a Comparative Political Economy of Unfree Labour: Case Studies and Debates* (London: F. Cass, 1999); Richard B. Allen, *Slaves, Freedmen, and Indentured Laborers in Colonial Mauritius* (Cambridge: Cambridge University Press, 2006); Madhavi Kale, *Fragments of Empire: Capital, Slavery, and Indian Indentured Labor in the British Caribbean* (Philadelphia: University of Pennsylvania Press, 2010); Robin Law, Suzanne Schwarz, and Silke Strickrodt, eds., *Commercial Agriculture, the Slave Trade and Slavery in Atlantic Africa* (Rochester, NY: Boydell & Brewer, 2013); Alessandro Stanziani, *Bondage: Labor and Rights in Eurasia from the Sixteenth to the Early Twentieth Centuries* (New York: Berghahn Books, 2014).

12. Eric Williams, *Capitalism and Slavery* (Chapel Hill: University of North Carolina Press, 1944); Manuel Moreno Fraginals, *El Ingenio: Complejo Económico Social Cubano del Azúcar* (Havana: Comisión Nacional Cubana de la Unesco, 1964); Emília Viotti da Costa, *Da Senzala à Colônia* (São Paulo: Editora Unesp, 1998 [1966]); Eric Foner, *Free Soil, Free Labor, Free Men: The Ideology of the Republican Party before the Civil War* (New York: Oxford University Press, 1970); Florestan Fernandes, *A Revolução Burguesa no Brasil: Ensaio de Interpretação Sociológica* (Rio de Janeiro: Zahar Editores, 1974); David Brion Davis, *The Problem of Slavery in the Age of*

Revolution: 1770–1823 (Ithaca, NY: Cornell University Press, 1975); Warren Dean, *Rio Claro: A Brazilian Plantation System, 1820–1920* (Stanford, CA: Stanford University Press, 1976); Eric Foner, *Nothing but Freedom: Emancipation and Its Legacy* (Baton Rouge: Louisiana State University Press, 1982); Steven Hahn, *The Roots of Southern Populism: Yeoman Farmers and the Transformation of the Georgia Upcountry, 1850–1890* (New York: Oxford University Press, 1983); Steven Hahn, "Class and State in Postemancipation Societies: Southern Planters in Comparative Perspective," *American Historical Review* 95, no. 1 (February 1990): 75–98; Holt, *Problem of Freedom*; Julie Saville, *The Work of Reconstruction: From Slave to Wage Laborer in South Carolina, 1860–1870* (New York: Cambridge University Press, 1994); Rebecca J. Scott, *Degrees of Freedom: Louisiana and Cuba after Slavery* (Cambridge, MA: Harvard University Press, 2005); Sven Beckert, *Empire of Cotton: A Global History* (New York: Knopf, 2014).

13. "A Educação do Engenheiro Civil," *Aurora Brazileira*, January 1878.

14. Richard Franklin Bensel, *The Political Economy of American Industrialization, 1877–1900* (Cambridge: Cambridge University Press, 2000), 4.

15. For works of transnational history that address questions of political economy, see Eiichiro Azuma, *Between Two Empires: Race, History, and Transnationalism in Japanese America* (New York: Oxford University Press, 2005); Julie Greene, *The Canal Builders: Making America's Empire at the Panama Canal* (New York: Penguin, 2009); Katherine Benton-Cohen, *Borderline Americans: Racial Division and Labor War in the Arizona Borderlands* (Cambridge, MA: Harvard University Press, 2009); Andrew Zimmerman, *Alabama in Africa: Booker T. Washington, the German Empire, and the Globalization of the New South* (Princeton: Princeton University Press, 2010); Beckert, *Empire of Cotton*; Tore C. Olsson, *Agrarian Crossings: Reformers and the Remaking of the US and Mexican Countryside* (Princeton: Princeton University Press, 2017); Andrew Offenburger, *Frontiers in the Gilded Age: Adventure, Capitalism, and Dispossession from Southern Africa to the U.S.-Mexican Borderlands, 1880–1917* (New Haven, CT: Yale University Press, 2019).

16. Karl Marx and Friedrich Engels, *Manifesto of the Communist Party* (New York: Penguin, 2011 [1848]), 67.

Chapter 1

1. John C. Calhoun to Henry A. Wise, Washington, May 25, 1844, in *Diplomatic Correspondence of the United States, Inter-American Affairs, Volume 2, 1831–1860*, ed. William R. Manning (Washington: Carnegie Endowment for International Peace, 1932), 127.

2. Robert E. May, *The Southern Dream of a Caribbean Empire, 1854–1861* (Baton Rouge: Louisiana State University Press, 1973); David M. Potter, *The Impending Crisis, 1848–1861* (New York: Harper & Row, 1976), 90–328; William W. Freehling, *The Road to Disunion, 1776–1854, Volume II: Secessionists Triumphant* (New York: Oxford University Press, 2007), 25–201; Adam Rothman, *Slave Country: American Expansion and the Origins of the Deep South* (Cambridge, MA: Harvard University Press, 2007).

3. Eric Foner, *Free Soil, Free Labor, Free Men: The Ideology of the Republican Party before the Civil War* (New York: Oxford University Press, 1970).

4. Leslie Bethell, *The Abolition of the Brazilian Slave Trade: Britain, Brazil and the Slave Trade Question, 1807–1869* (Cambridge: Cambridge University Press, 1970), 62–266; Richard Huzzey, *Freedom Burning: Anti-Slavery and Empire in Victorian Britain* (Ithaca, NY: Cornell University

Press, 2012), 40–74; Beatriz G. Mamigonian, *Africanos Livres: A Abolição do Tráfico de Escravos no Brasil* (São Paulo: Companhia das Letras, 2017).

5. Wilma Peres Costa, *A Espada de Dâmocles: O Exército, a Guerra do Paraguai e a Crise do Império* (São Paulo: Hucitec, 1996), 16–102; Thomas Whigham, *The Paraguayan War, Volume 1: Causes and Early Conduct* (Lincoln: University of Nebraska Press, 2002), 48–73.

6. The foundational works in this tradition are Gilberto Freyre, *Casa-Grande e Senzala: Formação da Família Brasileira sob o Regimen de Economia Patriarchal* (Rio de Janeiro: Maia & Schmidt, 1933); Eric Williams, *Capitalism and Slavery* (Chapel Hill: University of North Carolina Press, 1944); Eugene Genovese, *The Political Economy of Slavery: Studies in the Economy and Society of the Slave South* (New York: Vintage, 1967).

7. Edward B. Rugemer, *The Problem of Emancipation: The Caribbean Roots of the American Civil War* (Baton Rouge: Louisiana State University Press, 2008); Matthew Pratt Guterl, *American Mediterranean: Southern Slaveholders in the Age of Emancipation* (Cambridge, MA: Harvard University Press, 2008); Brian Schoen, *The Fragile Fabric of Union: Cotton, Federal Politics, and the Global Origins of the Civil War* (Baltimore: Johns Hopkins University Press, 2009); Walter Johnson, *River of Dark Dreams: Slavery and Empire in the Cotton Kingdom* (Cambridge, MA: Belknap, 2013); Joshua D. Rothman, *Flush Times and Fever Dreams: A Story of Capitalism and Slavery in the Age of Jackson* (Athens: University of Georgia Press, 2014); Matthew Karp, *This Vast Southern Empire: Slaveholders at the Helm of American Foreign Policy* (Cambridge, MA: Harvard University Press, 2016); Edward E. Baptist, *The Half Has Never Been Told: Slavery and the Making of American Capitalism* (New York: Basic Books, 2016); Caitlin Rosenthal, *Accounting for Slavery: Masters and Management* (Cambridge, MA: Harvard University Press, 2018); Sven Beckert and Seth Rockman, eds., *Slavery's Capitalism: A New History of American Economic Development* (Philadelphia: University of Pennsylvania Press, 2018).

8. Rafael de Bivar Marquese, *Feitores do Corpo, Missionários da Mente: Senhores, Letrados e o Controle dos Escravos nas Américas, 1660–1860* (São Paulo: Companhia das Letras, 2004); Gerald Horne, *The Deepest South: The United States, Brazil, and the African Slave Trade* (New York: New York University Press, 2007); Ricardo Salles, *E o Vale Era o Escravo. Vassouras—Século XIX. Senhores e Escravos no Coração do Império* (Rio de Janeiro: Civilização Brasileira, 2008); Mariana Muaze and Ricardo Salles, eds., *O Vale do Paraíba e o Império do Brasil nos Quadros da Segunda Escravidão* (Rio de Janeiro: Faperj, 2015); Dale W. Tomich, ed., *The Politics of the Second Slavery* (Albany: SUNY Press, 2016); Márcia Regina Berbel, Rafael de Bivar Marquese, and Tâmis Parron, *Slavery and Politics: Brazil and Cuba, 1790–1850* (Albuquerque: University of New Mexico Press, 2016); Dale W. Tomich, ed., *New Frontiers of Slavery* (Albany: SUNY Press, 2016); Rafael de Bivar Marquese and Ricardo Salles, eds., *Escravidão e Capitalismo Histórico no Século XIX: Cuba, Brasil, Estados Unidos* (Rio de Janeiro: Civilização Brasileira, 2016); Dale W. Tomich, ed., *Slavery and Historical Capitalism during the Nineteenth Century* (Lanham, MD: Lexington Books, 2017).

9. For a biographical account, see Craig M. Simpson, *A Good Southerner: The Life of Henry A. Wise of Virginia* (Chapel Hill: University of North Carolina Press, 1985).

10. Leonardo Marques, *The United States and the Slave Trade to the Americas, 1776–1867* (New Haven, CT: Yale University Press, 2016), 139–184.

11. Henry A. Wise to John C. Calhoun, Rio de Janeiro, February 18, 1845, in *Correspondence between the Consuls of the United States at Rio de Janeiro, etc., with the Secretary of State, on the*

Subject of the Slave Trade. Thirteenth Congress—Second Session. Ex. Doc. No. 61. House of Representatives (Washington: US House of Representatives, 1849), 70.

12. Dale T. Graden estimates that some 800 to 1,000 vessels built in the United States engaged in the traffic of enslaved Africans to Brazil and Cuba during the nineteenth century, transporting over one million human beings. *Disease, Resistance, and Lies: The Demise of the Transatlantic Slave Trade to Brazil and Cuba* (Baton Rouge: Louisiana State University Press, 2014), 39, 217–232.

13. On American views of the Haitian Revolution, see Ashli White, *Encountering Revolution: Haiti and the Making of the Early Republic* (Baltimore: Johns Hopkins University Press, 2010).

14. On Virginians' fear of slave rebellion, see Alan Taylor, *The Internal Enemy: Slavery and War in Virginia, 1772–1832* (New York: Norton, 2014).

15. On the domestic slave trade in the United States, see Walter Johnson, *Soul by Soul: Life inside the Antebellum Slave Market* (Cambridge, MA: Harvard University Press, 1999); Steven Deyle, *Carry Me Back: The Domestic Slave Trade in American Life* (New York: Oxford University Press, 2005).

16. Henry A. Wise to John C. Calhoun, Rio de Janeiro, January 12, 1845, in *Correspondence between the Consuls of the United States at Rio de Janeiro*, 45–46.

17. Henry A. Wise to John C. Calhoun, Rio de Janeiro, February 18, 1845, 72.

18. Henry A. Wise to John C. Calhoun, Rio de Janeiro, February 18, 1845, 75.

19. Henry A. Wise to John C. Calhoun, Rio de Janeiro, February 18, 1845, 78.

20. Bethell, *Abolition of the Brazilian Slave Trade*, 242–266.

21. *Relatório da Repartição dos Negócios Estrangeiros Apresentado à Assembléa Legislativa, na Terceira Sessão da Sexta Legislatura* (Rio de Janeiro: Typographia Imperial e Constitucional de J. Villeneuve, 1846), 9.

22. Um Brasileiro, "Correspondencia," *O Mercantil*, November 17, 1846.

23. Henry A. Wise to James Buchanan, Rio de Janeiro, November 16, 1846, in Manning, *Diplomatic Correspondence of the United States, Inter-American Affairs*, 366–367.

24. Henry A. Wise to James Buchanan, Rio de Janeiro, December 9, 1846, in Manning, *Diplomatic Correspondence of the United States, Inter-American Affairs*, 370.

25. Henry A. Wise to Hamilton Charles James Hamilton, Rio de Janeiro, July 31, 1846, *British and Foreign State Papers, Volume 35, Part 1, 1846–1847* (London: Harrison and Sons, 1960), 505.

26. Henry A. Wise to Hamilton Charles James Hamilton, Rio de Janeiro, July 31, 1846, 508.

27. Henry A. Wise to Hamilton Charles James Hamilton, Rio de Janeiro, July 31, 1846, 515.

28. "Negócios Internacionaes.—Questão Americana," *Sentinella da Monarchia*, April 7, 1847.

29. Gabriel Francisco Junqueira, speech at the Brazilian Chamber of Deputies, May 28, 1847, in *Annaes do Parlamento Brazileiro, Câmara dos Srs. Deputados, Quarto Anno da Sexta Legislatura, Sessão de 1847, Volume 1* (Rio de Janeiro: Typographia de H. J. Pinto, 1880), 176.

30. Henry A. Wise to James Buchanan, Rio de Janeiro, April 12, 1847, in Manning, *Diplomatic Correspondence of the United States, Inter-American Affairs*, 380–381.

31. Antonio Pereira Rebouças, speech at the Chamber of Deputies, May 28, 1847, in *Annaes do Parlamento Brazileiro*, 184–185. For Rebouças's biography, see Keila Grinberg, *A Black Jurist in a Slave Society: Antonio Pereira Rebouças and the Trials of Brazilian Citizenship* (Chapel Hill: University of North Carolina Press, 2019).

32. "Conflicto com o Gabinete de Washington," *O Mercantil*, April 21, 1847.

33. Gabriel José Rodrigues dos Santos, speech at the Chamber of Deputies, May 29, 1847, in *Annaes do Parlamento Brazileiro*, 201–202.

34. Urbano Sabino Pessoa de Melo, speech at the Chamber of Deputies, May 28, 1847, in *Annaes do Parlamento Brazileiro*, 187.

35. Simpson, *Good Southerner*.

36. Matthew Karp, for example, argues that "Wise denounced the Brazilian slave trade but never said a word against Brazilian slavery. Indeed, he probably believed that his battle against the former was indispensable to the preservation of the latter. To protect African slavery inside Brazil, the African slave trade had to be eliminated." *This Vast Southern Empire*, 75.

37. Jaime Rodrigues explains that "the threat to the [Brazilian] nation coming from British pressure was becoming stronger than the diffuse threat of labor shortage. It was urgent to evaluate the concrete necessity of maintaining the traffic in Africans and whether, at that moment, it provided any guarantee to the maintenance of sovereignty or, on the contrary, it threatened it." *O Infame Comércio: Propostas e Experiências no Final do Tráfico de Africanos para o Brasil, 1800–1850* (Campinas: Editora Unicamp, 2000), 114–115.

38. Bethell, *Abolition of the Brazilian Slave Trade*, 331–332.

39. Graden, *Disease, Resistance, and Lies*, 178–188.

40. José Maria da Silva Paranhos, *Relatório da Repartição dos Negócios Estrangeiros Apresentado à Assembléa Geral Legislativa na Quarta Sessão da Nona Legislatura* (Rio de Janeiro: Typographia Universal de Laemmert, 1856), 21.

41. Graden, *Disease, Resistance, and Lies*, 188–191.

42. José Maria da Silva Paranhos, *Relatório da Repartição dos Negócios Estrangeiros Apresentado à Assembléa Geral Legislativa na Primeira Sessão da Décima Legislatura* (Rio de Janeiro: Typographia Universal de Laemmert, 1857), 20.

43. Matthew Fontaine Maury, "Great Commercial Advantages of the Gulf of Mexico," *De Bow's Review*, December 1849.

44. On the navigation policies of monarchical Brazil, see Vitor Marcos Gregório, *Uma Face de Jano: A Navegação do Rio Amazonas e a Formação do Estado Brasileiro, 1838–1867* (São Paulo: Annablume, 2012).

45. Susanna B. Hecht, *The Scramble for the Amazon and the "Lost Paradise" of Euclides da Cunha* (Chicago: University of Chicago Press, 2013), 142–152.

46. "Letter of Matthew Fontaine Maury to William Lewis Herndon, April 20, 1850," *Hispanic American Historical Review* 28, no. 2 (May 1948): 217. Susanna B. Hecht points out that, for Maury, "a Confederate tropical Manifest Destiny would be beneficial in many ways. Maury, like many other Southerners, feared a Malthusian crisis in a South overrun with black slaves, leading to problems of race war and miscegenation. Since slave systems could not expand on the North American continent, they needed a dumping ground for 'excess' population. The Amazon would be the salvation of American slavery. . . . If Amazonia was colonized, the tensions between the Northern and Southern states would be significantly reduced." *Scramble for the Amazon*, 145–146.

47. "Letter of Matthew Fontaine Maury to William Lewis Herndon," 217–218. On the process of Anglo-American conquest of Mexican Texas, see Gary Clayton Anderson, *The Conquest of Texas: Ethnic Cleansing in the Promised Land, 1820–1875* (Norman: University of Oklahoma Press, 2005).

48. William Lewis Herndon, *Exploration of the Valley of the Amazon, Part I* (Washington: Robert Armstrong, 1853), 236.

49. Lardner Gibbon, *Exploration of the Valley of the Amazon, Part II* (Washington: A. O. P. Nicholson, 1854), 273.

50. Herndon, *Exploration of the Valley of the Amazon*, 251, 277.

51. Sérgio Teixeira de Macedo to Paulino José Soares de Souza, Washington, November 14, 1850, in Arthur Cezar Ferreira Reis, *A Amazônia e a Cobiça Internacional* (São Paulo: Companhia Editora Nacional, 1960), 81–86. For a comprehensive analysis of American expansionism in this era, see Steven Hahn, *A Nation without Borders: The United States and Its World in an Age of Civil Wars, 1830–1910* (New York: Viking, 2016), 114–191. For an analysis of popular attitudes concerning territorial expansion, see Amy Greenberg, *Manifest Manhood and the Antebellum American Empire* (New York: Cambridge University Press, 2005).

52. Sérgio Teixeira de Macedo to Paulino José Soares de Souza, Washington, November 14, 1850.

53. Luis Cláudio Villafañe Gomes Santos, *O Império e as Repúblicas do Pacífico: As Relações do Brasil com Chile, Bolívia, Peru, Equador e Colômbia* (Curitiba: Editora UFPR, 2002), 68–71.

54. Demétrio Magnoli, *O Corpo da Pátria: Imaginação Geográfica e Política Externa no Brasil, 1808–1912* (São Paulo: Editora Unesp/Moderna, 1997), 180–181.

55. Matthew Fontaine Maury, *El Río Amazonas y las Comarcas que Forman su Hoya: Vertientes hacia el Atlántico* (Lima: J. M. Monterola, 1853); Matthew Fontaine Maury, *O Amazonas e as Costas Atlânticas da América Meridional* (Rio de Janeiro: Typographia de M. Barreto, 1853); Matthew Fontaine Maury, *El Rio Amazonas, las Regiones que Forman su Hoya y las Vertientes Atlánticas de Sud-América* (La Paz: E. Alarcon, 1854).

56. Matthew Fontaine Maury, *The Amazon, and the Atlantic Slopes of South America: A Series of Letters Published in the National Intelligencer and Union Newspapers, under the Signature of "Inca"* (Washington: F. Taylor, 1853), 21, 54–55.

57. James Henry Hammond, "Maury on South America and Amazonia," *Southern Quarterly Review*, October 1853. For an analysis of Hammond's worldview, see Drew Gilpin Faust, *James Henry Hammond and the Old South: A Design for Mastery* (Baton Rouge: Louisiana State University Press, 1982).

58. Hammond, "Maury on South America and Amazonia."

59. On filibustering and nineteenth-century American imperialism, see Robert E. May, *Manifest Destiny's Underworld: Filibustering in Antebellum America* (Chapel Hill: University of North Carolina Press, 2004).

60. Francisco Inácio de Carvalho Moreira, "Nota da Legação Imperial em Washington ao Governo dos Estados-Unidos," Washington, August 15, 1853, in *Relatório da Repartição dos Negócios Estrangeiros Apresentado à Assembléa Geral Legislativa na Segunda Sessão da Nona Legislatura, Anexo D* (Rio de Janeiro: Typographia Universal de Laemmert, 1854), 4.

61. Gomes Santos, *Império e as Repúblicas do Pacífico*, 68–71.

62. William Trousdale, "Minute of Interview of October 28, 1853," in Manning, *Diplomatic Correspondence of the United States, Inter-American Affairs*, 442.

63. William Trousdale, "Note of an Interview with Dom Pedro II, Emperor of Brazil, at the Imperial Palace of Petropolis," February 26, 1855, in Manning, *Diplomatic Correspondence of the United States, Inter-American Affairs*, 471.

64. William Trousdale to José Maria da Silva Paranhos, Rio de Janeiro, November 21, 1855, in Manning, *Diplomatic Correspondence of the United States, Inter-American Affairs*, 491.

65. "Memorandum of a Conversation between William Trousdale, United States Minister to Brazil, and Visconde de Maranguape," December 6, 1855, in Manning, *Diplomatic Correspondence of the United States, Inter-American Affairs*, 494.

66. Trousdale, "Note of an Interview with Dom Pedro II," 472.

67. João Batista de Castro Morais Antas, *O Amazonas: Breve Resposta à Memória do Tenente da Armada Americana-Inglesa F. Maury sobre as Vantagens da Livre Navegação do Amazonas* (Rio de Janeiro: Fundação Alexandre de Gusmão, 2013 [1854]), 11, 24, 84.

68. Pedro de Angelis, *De la Navigation de l'Amazone: Réponse a un Mémoire de M. Maury, Officier de la Marine des Etats-Unis* (Montevideo: Imprimerie du Rio de la Plata, 1854), 93–94, 204–205, 214.

69. Paulino José Soares de Souza, "Ata de 1º de Abril de 1854," in *Atas do Terceiro Conselho de Estado, 1850–1857* (Brasília: Centro Gráfico do Senado Federal, 1978).

70. Soares de Souza, "Ata de 1º de Abril de 1854."

71. Soares de Souza, "Ata de 1º de Abril de 1854."

72. Walter Johnson considers Maury responsible for outlining the "expansionist agenda of pro-slavery political economy for the 1850s." In Maury's vision, Johnson explains, "the Mississippi and the Amazon were united and the course of history changed; . . . Anglo-Saxon civilization and African labor transformed wilderness into empire." *River of Dark Dreams*, 296, 302. See also Guterl, *American Mediterranean*, 19–20.

73. James Cooley Fletcher to Calvin Fletcher, Rio de Janeiro, July 28, 1852, Calvin Fletcher Papers, Box 6, Folder 7, IHS.

74. James Cooley Fletcher to Calvin Fletcher, Tijuca, March 22, 1853, Calvin Fletcher Papers, Box 7, Folder 2, IHS.

75. James Cooley Fletcher to Calvin Fletcher, Rio de Janeiro, January 10, 1854, Calvin Fletcher Papers, Box 7, Folder 5, IHS.

76. Daniel Parish Kidder and James Cooley Fletcher, *Brazil and the Brazilians: Portrayed in Historical and Descriptive Sketches* (Philadelphia: Childs & Peterson, 1857), 239.

77. Kidder and Fletcher, *Brazil and the Brazilians*, 242.

78. James Cooley Fletcher to Dom Pedro II, Rio de Janeiro, July 14, 1855, Arquivo da Casa Imperial do Brasil, Documento 6082, AMIP.

79. Kidder and Fletcher, *Brazil and the Brazilians*, 246.

80. "Panorama," *Diário do Rio de Janeiro*, May 16, 1855.

81. "Notícias Diversas," *Correio Mercantil*, May 17, 1855.

82. José de Alencar, "Ao Correr da Penna," *Correio Mercantil*, May 20, 1855.

83. Kidder and Fletcher, *Brazil and the Brazilians*, 246.

84. "Notícias Diversas," *Correio Mercantil*, January 1, 1857.

85. On the authorship of the text, a passage in the introduction clarifies that "although the present volume is the result of a joint effort, the desire for greater uniformity caused the senior author to place his contributions in the hands of his junior colleague (J. C. F.) with the permission to use the name of the former in the third person singular." Kidder and Fletcher, *Brazil and the Brazilians*, 4. See also Daniel Parish Kidder, *Sketches of Residence and Travels in Brazil: Embracing Historical and Geographical Notices of the Empire and Its Several Provinces* (Philadelphia: Sorin and Ball, 1845).

86. Kidder and Fletcher, *Brazil and the Brazilians*, 4.

87. Kidder and Fletcher, *Brazil and the Brazilians*, 77–78.

88. Kidder and Fletcher, *Brazil and the Brazilians*, 132–133.

89. Fletcher manipulated facts that, for long, Brazilian planters had been manipulating to uphold their interests. As Barbara Weinstein notes, "In contrast to the U.S. South, there was never any significant effort in Brazil to restrict or roll back the process of manumission. Whereas free blacks increasingly signified a potential challenge to the political order in the South, as well as an implicit criticism of slavery, manumission was perfectly compatible with a defense of slavery as a 'necessary evil.' Furthermore, steady rates of manumission helped to bolster the Brazilian slave-owners' claims that theirs was a moderate and humane form of slavery." "The Decline of the Progressive Planter and the Rise of the Subaltern Agent: Shifting Narratives of Slave Emancipation in Brazil," in *Reclaiming the Political in Latin American History*, ed. Gilbert M. Joseph (Durham, NC: Duke University Press, 2001), 90.

90. Kidder and Fletcher, *Brazil and the Brazilians*, 406–407. The immigrant colonies that existed in the province of São Paulo were private enterprises, not to be confused with government colonization projects, which sought to attract foreign settlers to marginal regions of the Brazilian territory in order to develop unexplored resources and prevent threats of foreign occupation. On these differences, see Giralda Seyferth, "The Slave Plantation and Foreign Colonization in Imperial Brazil," *Review (Fernand Braudel Center)* 34, no. 4 (2011): 339–387.

91. Kidder and Fletcher, *Brazil and the Brazilians*, 412–413, 138.

92. Kidder and Fletcher, *Brazil and the Brazilians*, 411.

93. Emília Viotti da Costa, *The Brazilian Empire: Myths and Histories*, rev. ed. (Chapel Hill: University of North Carolina Press, 2000), 110.

94. According to Barbara Weinstein, "The 'weak' defense of slavery [in Brazil] also created a political climate in which experiments with sharecropping and other non-slave-labor arrangements could be applauded rather than denounced for encouraging abolitionist sentiment. Senator Nicolau Vergueiro's efforts to substitute immigrant workers for slaves on his coffee estates in São Paulo, beginning in the 1840s, might have proved unsuccessful but were generally met with praise and occasional public subsidies. These failures may well have reinforced the 'necessary evil' argument, as planters concluded that free immigrant brokers were less adaptable to the plantation work routine than slaves, but they did not foreclose all discussion of alternative sources and forms of labor." "Decline of the Progressive Planter," 90. On the conditions of life and labor at Ibicaba, see Felipe Landim Ribeiro Mendes, "Ibicaba Revisitada Outra Vez: Espaço, Escravidão e Trabalho Livre no Oeste Paulista," *Anais do Museu Paulista: História e Cultura Material* 25, no. 1 (2017): 301–357.

95. Kidder and Fletcher, *Brazil and the Brazilians*, 413–414.

96. Kidder and Fletcher, *Brazil and the Brazilians*, 578–581.

97. James Cooley Fletcher to Calvin Fletcher, Rio de Janeiro, October 16, 1853, Calvin Fletcher Papers, Box 7, Folder 4, IHS.

98. David Gueiros Vieira, *O Protestantismo, a Maçonaria e a Questão Religiosa no Brasil* (Brasília: Editora Universidade de Brasília, 1980), 105–110.

99. Thomas Rainey, "The Commerce of Brazil with the United States and Great Britain, Considered in Its Bearings on the Establishment of Mail-Steamship Communication between

the United States, the West India Islands, and Brazil," in Kidder and Fletcher, *Brazil and the Brazilians*, Appendix H, 609–612.

100. Thomas Rainey, *Ocean Steam Navigation and the Ocean Post* (New York: D. Appleton, 1858), 29.

101. Rainey, "Commerce of Brazil."

102. "Brazil and the Brazilians," *Littell's Living Age*, October 1, 1859.

103. *Saturday Evening Post*, September 5, 1857.

104. "Brazil and the Brazilians," *National Era*, November 5, 1857.

105. "Brazil and the Brazilians," *Methodist Quarterly Review*, January 1859.

106. J. D. B. De Bow, "The Empire of Brazil—Its History, Statistics, and Future," *De Bow's Review*, January–June 1858.

107. "Fletcher's Second Lecture—Abolitionism," *Memphis Daily Appeal*, December 18, 1858.

108. "American Policy on the American Continent," *Charleston Mercury*, April 15, 1857.

109. "Our Minister to Brazil," *Fremont Journal* (quoting the *New York Tribune*), February 26, 1858.

110. "Telegraphic Intelligence," *Charleston Mercury*, June 25, 1858.

111. "The News," *New York Herald*, February 16, 1858.

112. "Slavery and Foreign Relations," *National Era*, February 18, 1858.

113. "7 de Dezembro," *Diário do Rio de Janeiro*, December 7, 1857.

114. "Rio, 7 de Dezembro," *Correio Mercantil*, December 7, 1857.

115. "Rio, 7 de Dezembro de 1857," *Correio da Tarde*, December 7, 1857.

116. "Ministério dos Negócios Estrangeiros," *Jornal do Commercio*, December 7, 1857.

117. According to Rafael de Bivar Marquese and Tâmis Parron, "The nature of proslavery discourse in the South and the projection of the United States into the international arena through its successful annexation of other North American territories produced a space of relative autonomy in the interstate system that was vital to the survival of slavery in peripheral countries such as Brazil and the Spanish Empire." "International Proslavery: The Politics of Second Slavery," in Tomich, *Politics of the Second Slavery*, 49–50. In reality, in the 1840s and 1850s, Brazil felt pressured from all sides, having to stave off the advances of Southern proslavery expansionists, who were becoming ever more aggressive, and British abolitionists, who did not want to see slaveholders expand their powers.

118. *New York Daily Tribune*, February 16, 1858.

119. "Our Minister to Brazil," *Liberator*, February 26, 1858.

120. "Interesting from Brazil—Direct Trade with the South," *Charleston Mercury*, June 25, 1858.

121. Richard Kidder Meade to Howell Cobb, Rio de Janeiro, December 31, 1860, Howell Cobb Family Papers, Box 44, Folder 26, HRB-UG.

122. According to part of the scholarship, Southerners' opposition to tariffs and interest in exporting cotton made them the great foreign traders of the antebellum period. But these works generally overlook trade with Latin America and other predominantly rural societies. See Schoen, *Fragile Fabric of Union*, 100–145; Baptist, *Half Has Never Been Told*; Johnson, *River of Dark Dreams*, 280–302.

123. James Cooley Fletcher, *Lyceum Lectures by Rev. J. C. Fletcher: Address Care of Ticknor & Fields, Boston, Mass. or to the Lecturer at Newburyport, Mass.* (1859), American Broadsides and Ephemera, AAS.

124. "Lecture on Brazil by Rev. J.C. Fletcher," *New York Times*, November 15, 1860.

125. "Rev. Mr. Fletcher's Lectures on Brazil," *New York Times*, February 28, 1863.

126. "Notícias Diversas," *Correio Mercantil*, October 24, 1863.

127. As Stephanie McCurry points out, "The Confederate States of America was a proslavery nation. Founded in defiance of the spirit of the age, it aimed to turn back the tide of abolition that had swept the hemisphere in the Age of Revolution. Trusting that major powers had had their fill of the failed experiment in emancipation, Confederate founders proposed instead to perfect the slaveholders' republic and offer it to the world as the political form best fitted to the modern age." *Confederate Reckoning: Power and Politics in the Civil War South* (Cambridge, MA: Harvard University Press, 2010), 310. Interestingly, from the outset of the conflict in North America, the other major independent slave society in the Western world understood that the Confederate attempt to make slavery the foundation of a new nation was a losing proposition.

Chapter 2

1. "South America," *New York Times*, November 26, 1865.

2. For the varied responses that British society formulated to the American Civil War, see R. J. M. Blackett, *Divided Hearts: Britain and the American Civil War* (Baton Rouge: Louisiana State University Press, 2001).

3. Dean B. Mahin, *One War at a Time: The International Dimensions of the American Civil War* (Washington: Brassey's, 1999), 23–256; Don H. Doyle, *The Cause of All Nations: An International History of the American Civil War* (New York: Basic Books, 2015), 106–130.

4. Jay Sexton, *The Monroe Doctrine: Empire and Nation in Nineteenth-Century America* (New York: Hill & Wang, 2011), 123–158.

5. Richard Graham, *Britain and the Onset of Modernization in Brazil 1850–1914* (Cambridge: Cambridge University Press, 1968), 160–186; Leslie Bethell, *The Abolition of the Brazilian Slave Trade: Britain, Brazil and the Slave Trade Question, 1807–1869* (Cambridge: Cambridge University Press, 1970), 242–387; Jaime Rodrigues, *O Infame Comércio: Propostas e Experiências no Final do Tráfico de Africanos para o Brasil, 1800–1850* (Campinas: Editora Unicamp, 2000), 97–125.

6. William Appleman Williams, *The Tragedy of American Diplomacy* (Cleveland: World, 1959); Walter LaFeber, *The New Empire: An Interpretation of American Expansion, 1860–1898* (Ithaca, NY: Cornell University Press, 1963); William Appleman Williams, *The Roots of the Modern American Empire: A Study of the Growth and Shaping of Social Consciousness in a Marketplace Society* (New York: Random House, 1969); William Appleman Williams, *Empire as a Way of Life: An Essay on the Causes and Character of America's Present Predicament, along with a Few Thoughts about an Alternative* (New York: Oxford University Press, 1980); Walter LaFeber, *The Cambridge History of American Foreign Relations. Volume 2: The American Search for Opportunity, 1865–1913* (Cambridge: Cambridge University Press, 1993).

7. David M. Pletcher, *The Diplomacy of Trade and Investment: American Economic Expansion in the Hemisphere, 1865–1900* (Columbia: University of Missouri Press, 1998); Frank Ninkovich,

Global Dawn: The Cultural Foundation of American Internationalism, 1865–1890 (Cambridge, MA: Harvard University Press, 2009); Sexton, *Monroe Doctrine*; Elizabeth Cobbs Hoffman, *American Umpire* (Cambridge, MA: Harvard University Press, 2013); Marc-William Palen, *The "Conspiracy" of Free Trade: The Anglo-American Struggle over Empire and Economic Globalization, 1846–1896* (New York: Cambridge University Press, 2016).

8. For Webb's biography, see James L. Crouthamel, *James Watson Webb: A Biography* (Middletown, CT: Wesleyan University Press, 1969).

9. James Watson Webb to William Henry Seward, No. 17, Legation of the United States, Petrópolis, May 20, 1862, in *Message of the President of the United States to the Two Houses of Congress at the Commencement of the Third Session of the Thirty-Seventh Congress, Volume I* (Washington: Government Printing Office, 1862), 704–710. For more details on the colonization scheme, see Nicia Vilela Luz, *A Amazônia para os Negros Americanos: As Origens de uma Controvérsia Internacional* (Rio de Janeiro: Editora Saga, 1968); Maria Clara Sales Carneiro Sampaio, "Não Diga que Não Somos Brancos: Os Projetos de Colonização para Afro-Americanos do Governo Lincoln na Perspectiva do Caribe, América Latina e Brasil dos 1860" (PhD diss., Universidade de São Paulo, 2014).

10. James Watson Webb to William Henry Seward, No. 17. Webb's justification for his Brazilian scheme paralleled the justification that the promoters of Liberia adopted in the antebellum years. Nicholas Guyatt shows how their idea of benevolence operated: "Unable to explain why free blacks should be denied the privileges of citizenship, colonization proponents sought to uphold their 'dearest political principles' by imagining the redemption of Africa. Instead of expulsion from the United States, benevolent colonization was presented as an opportunity for blacks to create their own America, with the development of the English colonies as both the inspiration and the guarantor of African success." "'The Outskirts of Our Happiness': Race and the Lure of Colonization in the Early Republic," *Journal of American History* 95, no. 4 (March 2009): 1000.

11. "Concession to General J. Watson Webb of the United States of America, July 8, 1862," James Watson Webb Papers, Box 8, Folder 102, SML-YU.

12. William Henry Seward to James Watson Webb, No. 33, Department of State, Washington, July 21, 1862, in *Message of the President of the United States to the Two Houses of Congress*, 713.

13. Marquis of Abrantes to James Watson Webb, June 24, 1862, James Watson Webb Papers, Box 8, Folder 100, SML-YU.

14. On Raphael Semmes's role in the Confederate Navy, see Stephen R. Fox, *Wolf of the Deep: Raphael Semmes and the Notorious Confederate Raider CSS Alabama* (New York: Vintage Civil War Library, 2008).

15. Benvenuto Augusto de Magalhães Taques, "Nota do Governo Imperial à Legação dos Estados Unidos," Rio de Janeiro, December 9, 1861, in *Relatório da Repartição dos Negócios Estrangeiros Apresentado à Assembléa Legislativa, na Segunda Sessão da Décima Primeira Legislatura, Anexo I* (Rio de Janeiro: Typographia Universal de Laemmert, 1862), 11–14.

16. James Watson Webb, "Nota da Legação dos Estados Unidos ao Governo Imperial," Rio de Janeiro, November 1, 1861, in *Relatório da Repartição dos Negócios Estrangeiros*, 3.

17. Doyle, *Cause of All Nations*, 30.

18. Raphael Semmes, *The Cruise of the Alabama and the Sumter* (New York: Carleton, 1864), 36.

19. Raphael Semmes, *Memoirs of Service Afloat: During the War between the States* (Baltimore: Kelly, Piet, 1869), 619, 211.

20. Semmes, *Memoirs of Service Afloat*, 617.

21. Some scholars point out that the slave South formulated an effective foreign policy to defend its interests. See, for example, Gerald Horne, *The Deepest South: The United States, Brazil, and the African Slave Trade* (New York: New York University Press, 2007); Edward B. Rugemer, *The Problem of Emancipation: The Caribbean Roots of the American Civil War* (Baton Rouge: Louisiana State University Press, 2008); Matthew Pratt Guterl, *American Mediterranean: Southern Slaveholders in the Age of Emancipation* (Cambridge, MA: Harvard University Press, 2008); Walter Johnson, *River of Dark Dreams: Slavery and Empire in the Cotton Kingdom* (Cambridge, MA: Belknap, 2013); Rafael de Bivar Marquese and Tâmis Parron, "Proslavery International: The Politics of the Second Slavery," in *The Politics of the Second Slavery*, ed. Dale W. Tomich (Albany: SUNY Press, 2016), 25–56; Matthew Karp, *This Vast Southern Empire: Slaveholders at the Helm of American Foreign Policy* (Cambridge, MA: Harvard University Press, 2016). In the case of Brazil at the time of the American Civil War, however, Confederate proslavery foreign policy estranged a potential ally.

22. James Watson Webb to the Marquis of Abrantes, Rio de Janeiro, May 21, 1863, in *Message of the President of the United States, and Accompanying Documents, to the Two Houses of Congress, at the Commencement of the First Session of the Thirty-Eighth Congress, Part II* (Washington: Government Printing Office, 1863), 1271.

23. João Pedro Dias Vieira, "Atentado do Vapor de Guerra 'Wachussett' dos Estados Unidos no Porto da Bahia," in *Relatório da Repartição dos Negócios Estrangeiros Apresentado à Assembléa Legislativa, na Terceira Sessão da Décima Segunda Legislatura* (Rio de Janeiro: Typographia Universal de Laemmert, 1865), 41–42.

24. Semmes, *Memoirs of Service Afloat*, 619.

25. James Watson Webb to William Henry Seward, Petrópolis, November 5, 1862, James Watson Webb Papers, Box 9, Folder 109, SML-YU.

26. James Watson Webb to William Henry Seward, Petrópolis, November 5, 1862.

27. James Watson Webb to William Henry Seward, Petrópolis, April 21, 1863, James Watson Webb Papers, Box 10, Folder 116, SML-YU.

28. "From Rio de Janeiro: A Difficulty between the English and American Ministers—Gen. Webb's Conduct Vindicated—His Popularity—Miscellaneous News," *New York Times*, January 9, 1863; "Our Minister at Rio de Janeiro: His Quarrel with the British Resident," *New York Times*, January 23, 1863.

29. James Watson Webb to William Henry Seward, Petrópolis, April 21, 1863.

30. William Dougal Christie, *Notes on Brazilian Questions* (London: Macmillan, 1865), 12.

31. Richard Graham notes that "the end of the slave trade [in 1850] did not mark the end of British interest in ending Brazilian slavery. It was not until Brazil gave evidence of a firm commitment to end the institution itself that Great Britain ceased to exert pressure." *Britain and the Onset of Modernization in Brazil*, 167. American support for Brazil during the Christie affair contributed to diminishing British pressure.

32. Richard Graham, "Os Fundamentos da Ruptura de Relações Diplomáticas entre o Brasil e a Grã Bretanha em 1863. A 'Questão Christie,' Parte I," *Revista de História* 49 (January–March 1962): 117–137.

33. Richard Graham, "Os Fundamentos da Ruptura de Relações Diplomáticas entre o Brasil e a Grã Bretanha em 1863. A 'Questão Christie,' Parte II," *Revista de História* 50 (April–June 1962): 379–400.

34. Graham, "Fundamentos da Ruptura, Parte II," 394–400.

35. "Um Diplomata Modelo," *A Actualidade*, January 8, 1863.

36. "Revista Diária," *Diário de Pernambuco*, March 9, 1863.

37. James Watson Webb to Thomas Rainey, June 6, 1863, *Diário do Rio de Janeiro*, June 12, 1863; "Miscellaneous News," *New York Herald*, August 3, 1863.

38. "Extract from a Letter Addressed to Hon. S. P. Chase, Secretary of the Treasury of the United States, by James Monroe U.S. Consul to Rio de Janeiro; Date March 30, 1863," James Watson Webb Papers, Box 10, Folder 115, SML-YU.

39. J. B. Bond to James Watson Webb, Pará, June 20, 1863, James Watson Webb Papers, Box 11, Folder 120, SML-YU.

40. "Interior," *Jornal do Commercio*, November 19, 1864.

41. William Van Vleck Lidgerwood to José Antonio Saraiva, Rio de Janeiro, January 29, 1866, William Van Vleck Lidgerwood Letterbook, Microfilm 0045–31, Reel 31, Morristown Manuscript Collection, MMTL.

42. William Van Vleck Lidgerwood to William Henry Seward, Rio de Janeiro, April 3, 1866, William Van Vleck Lidgerwood Letterbook, Microfilm 0045–31, Reel 31, MMTL.

43. William Van Vleck Lidgerwood to William Henry Seward, Rio de Janeiro, April 3, 1866.

44. James Watson Webb to William Henry Seward, Petrópolis, April 21, 1863.

45. Jay Sexton, for example, argues that the Republican Party saw Great Britain as a potential ally and a model in the 1860s: "With the resources of the Union being consumed on Civil War battlefields, it is not surprising that the Lincoln administration sought British assistance in its foreign policy. But these policies also reflected the willingness of Republicans to work alongside Old World powers, particularly Britain. When Republicans looked across the Atlantic in the 1860s, they saw much that they liked." *Monroe Doctrine*, 149–150.

46. William R. Summerhill, *Order Against Progress: Government, Foreign Investment, and Railroads in Brazil, 1854–1913* (Stanford, CA: Stanford University Press, 2003), 45.

47. Cristiano Benedito Ottoni, *Autobiographia, Maio 1870* (Rio de Janeiro: Typographia Leuzinger, 1908), 107–108.

48. Ottoni, *Autobiographia*, 106.

49. Edward Price apud Ottoni, *Autobiographia*, 119.

50. Edward Miller to All Whom It May Concern, St. Louis, October 31, 1857, William Milnor Roberts Papers, Box 2, Folder 1, MGB-MSU.

51. Adeline de Beelen Roberts, "An Obituary Notice of William Milnor Roberts (Furnished by Mrs. W. Milnor Roberts, and Read before the American Philosophical Society, by Frederick Fraley, January 6, 1882)," *Proceedings of the American Philosophical Society* 20, no. 111 (January–June 1882): 199–202.

52. William Milnor Roberts, "Autobiography," ca. 1866, William Milnor Roberts Papers, Box 1, Folder 2, MGB-MSU.

53. "Interesting from Brazil," *New York Times*, July 12, 1858.

54. "Affairs in Brazil," *New York Times*, June 8, 1860.

55. "Affairs in Brazil," *New York Herald*, September 29, 1859.

56. "South America," *New York Times*, July 20, 1858.

57. Roberts, "Autobiography."

58. William Milnor Roberts, "Dom Pedro 2° Railroad for Mr. Fletcher," 1864, William Milnor Roberts Papers, Box 6, Folder 2, MGB-MSU.

59. Roberts, "Dom Pedro 2° Railroad for Mr. Fletcher."

60. *History of the Baldwin Locomotive Works from 1831 to 1897* (Philadelphia: J. P. Lippincott, 1897), 57–58.

61. "Railroads in Brazil," *Railroad Gazette*, September 29, 1876.

62. *Railway World*, February 25, 1888.

63. John Casper Branner, *The Railways of Brazil, a Statistical Article* (Chicago: Railway Age, 1887), 21–22.

64. Gilberto Freyre, *Ordem e Progresso: Processo de Desintegração das Sociedades Patriarcal e Semipatriarcal no Brasil sob o Regime de Trabalho Livre* (Rio de Janeiro: José Olympio, 1959), 147.

65. William Milnor Roberts, "Dom Pedro 2° Railroad Report," 1862, William Milnor Roberts Papers, Box 6, Folder 1, MGB-MSU.

66. Roberts's vision is compatible with Teresa Cribelli's contention that, by the middle of the nineteenth century, "the railroads did more than move freight and people; they became crucial for narratives of progress in the United States and Brazil, nations linked by the desire to incorporate enormous stretches of unsettled territory into the national body." *Industrial Forests and Mechanical Marvels: Modernization in Nineteenth-Century Brazil* (New York: Cambridge University Press, 2016), 151.

67. Roberts, "Dom Pedro 2° Railroad Report."

68. On the Northern vision of westward expansion and its clash with Southern proslavery expansionism, see Steven Hahn, *A Nation Without Borders: The United States and Its World in an Age of Civil Wars, 1830–1910* (New York: Viking, 2016), 78–113.

69. Roberts, "Dom Pedro 2° Railroad Report."

70. "Festa Industrial," *A Revolução Pacífica*, June 15, 1862.

71. *As Estradas de Ferro do Brazil em 1879. Estradas de Ferro nas Provincias do Rio de Janeiro, Minas Geraes e S. Paulo. Informações Colligidas pela Administração da Estrada de Ferro D. Pedro II* (Rio de Janeiro: Typographia Nacional, 1880), 7.

72. Andrew Jackson Lamoureux, *The Rio News Handbook of Rio de Janeiro* (Rio de Janeiro: A. J. Lamoureux, 1887), 194.

73. Roberts, "Obituary Notice of William Milnor Roberts."

74. "South America," *New York Times*, November 26, 1865.

75. "Launch of a Steamer for Brazil," *New York Times*, September 10, 1860.

76. "Launch of a Steamer for Brazil."

77. "News from Brazil and La Plata," *New York Herald*, February 16, 1861.

78. "Noticiario," *Diário do Rio de Janeiro*, June 30, 1862.

79. *A Vida Fluminense*, October 17, 1868.

80. "El Mariscal" is in Spanish in the original. *A Vida Fluminense*, October 24, 1868.

81. Thomas Rainey, "O Diario do Rio de Janeiro," *Jornal do Commercio*, February 17, 1868.

82. Rainey, "O Diario do Rio de Janeiro."

83. "Notícias Diversas," *Correio Mercantil*, June 16, 1863; "Companhia Ferry, Festa em Paquetá," *Diário do Rio de Janeiro*, September 9, 1866; "Theatros," *Jornal do Commercio*, August 29, 1866; *Correio Mercantil*, January 10, 1866; "Agradecimentos," *Jornal do Commercio*, June 13, 1867; "Voluntários da Pátria," *Diário do Rio de Janeiro*, April 30, 1870; "Paço Imperial," *Diário do Rio de Janeiro*, September 29, 1873; "Socorros a Buenos-Ayres," *Diário do Rio de Janeiro*, April 23, 1871; "Escola Normal da Provincia do Rio de Janeiro," *Diário do Rio de Janeiro*, January 31, 1874; "Companhia Ferry. Regata!!!," *Diário do Povo*, November 29, 1868; Henrique de Beaurepaire Rohan, "Passeio Maritimo a Paquetá em Benefício da Sociedade Emancipadora Nitherohyense," *Diário do Rio de Janeiro*, April 22, 1871.

84. C. Gracchus, "As Carambolas do Governo e o Sr. Rainey," *Jornal do Commercio*, January 23, 1869. Enhancing the humoristic effect of the passage, the reporter transcribed Rainey's rant in grammatically incorrect Portuguese and used the word "goddam" in English.

85. *A Vida Fluminense*, November 28, 1868.

86. Noronha Santos, *Meios de Transporte no Rio de Janeiro: História e Legislação* (Rio de Janeiro: Typographia do Jornal do Commercio, 1934), 56–57.

87. "Dr. Thomas Rainey, Bridge Father, Dead," *New York Times*, March 30, 1910.

88. Charles J. Dunlop, *Apontamentos para a História dos Bondes no Rio de Janeiro: A Companhia Ferro-Carril do Jardim Botanico* (Rio de Janeiro: Editora Gráfica Laemmert, 1953), 11–14.

89. "Chronica," *Opinião Liberal*, October 10, 1868.

90. "Pontos e Virgulas," *Semana Illustrada*, October 18, 1868.

91. Christopher Columbus Andrews, *Brazil, Its Conditions and Prospects* (New York: D. Appleton, 1887), 30.

92. Hastings Charles Dent, *A Year in Brazil, with Notes on the Abolition of Slavery, the Finances of the Empire, Religion, Meteorology, Natural History, Etc.* (London: K. Paul, Trench, 1886), 235.

93. Confucio, "Maximas, Sentenças e Pensamentos Políticos do Celeste Imperial," *Semana Illustrada*, October 17, 1869.

94. Dunlop, *Apontamentos para a História dos Bondes no Rio de Janeiro*, 67.

95. "Estrada de Ferro do Jardim Botanico," *Jornal do Commercio*, October 18, 1868.

96. O Moleque da Semana, "Dentro de um Bond," *Semana Illustrada*, January 15, 1871.

97. Examining how new means of transportation challenged old habits in nineteenth-century Rio de Janeiro, Teresa Cribelli explains that "complaints about rude employees were in part an expression of frustration with this impersonal structure of the trolley or railway company, where higher-ups were removed from direct public interaction and conductors represented the human face of the trolley." *Industrial Forests and Mechanical Marvels*, 191–192.

98. "Os Bonds do Gonçalves Dias ao Jardim," *Semana Illustrada*, April 16, 1871.

99. According to Sandra Lauderdale Graham, the streetcars redesigned the urban geography of nineteenth-century Rio de Janeiro: "Following the tram lines the exclusive residential parts of the city spread up past the convent into the steep hillsides of Santa Thereza, and out beyond the established suburbs of Botafogo and Laranjeiras to the more recent Jardim Botanico, as well as to cool and tranquil Tijuca on the edge of the rain forest from which the area took its name. At the same time, the city center grew in upon itself as the slums, tellingly nicknamed cortiços or beehives, multiplied in the ever more congested older sections that became home to arriving immigrants, free blacks, and to the slaves who hired out their own labor." *House and Street: The*

Domestic World of Servants and Masters in Nineteenth-Century Rio de Janeiro (Austin: University of Texas Press, 1988), 26.

100. "Questão de Bonds," *Revista Illustrada*, November 24, 1877.

101. William S. Auchincloss, *Ninety Days in the Tropics or Letters from Brazil* (Wilmington, DE, 1874), 73.

102. Herbert Huntington Smith, *Brazil: The Amazons and the Coast* (New York: C. Scribner's Sons, 1879), 459–460.

103. Henry Washington Hilliard, *Politics and Pen Pictures at Home and Abroad* (New York: G.P. Putnam's Sons, 1892), 375.

104. For the details of this riot, see Sandra Lauderdale Graham, "The Vintem Riot and Political Culture: Rio de Janeiro, 1880," *Hispanic American Historical Review* 60, no. 3 (August 1980): 431–449.

105. Lamoureux, *Rio News Handbook of Rio de Janeiro*, 147.

106. In a chapter titled "South America—Impotent Anglophobia," David M. Pletcher argues that, between the 1860s and the 1890s, "expansionists in the United States chafed at the impotence of their businessmen." He goes on to claim that, try as they might, Americans failed to challenge the predominant influence of British capital in Brazil. Among other things, Pletcher explains, Americans "were criticized for faulty merchandising—for consigning coffins or mowing machines to a country where undertaking was a government-supervised monopoly and hay virtually unknown, for sending bolts of cloth in unpopular designs or widths and too heavy for hot climate, for glutting a moderate market with overshipment, and for refusing even sixty-day credit." *Diplomacy of Trade and Investment*, 180–195. From the perspective of cultural history, Frank Ninkovich emphasizes Americans' insecurity in the global arena: "Being universally acknowledged as culturally inferior, Americans could not point to a single area of preeminence by way of compensation. Wherever the spotlight was aimed—at social reform, higher education, civic administration, or the quality of political leadership—Europe appeared to be clearly in the lead. Even the nation's strong suit, its leadership in 'material development and mechanical contrivance,' offered surprisingly little opportunity for vainglory because the fruits of industrialization had not fallen into American laps alone." *Global Dawn*, 79.

107. "Interesting from Brazil. Correspondence of the *Philadelphia Bulletin*. Rio de Janeiro, May 26, 1858," *New York Times*, July 12, 1858.

108. John D. Billings, *Hardtack and Coffee: The Unwritten Story of Army Life* (Boston: George M. Smith, 1888), 129–130.

109. Mark Pendergrast, *Uncommon Grounds: The History of Coffee and How It Transformed Our World* (New York: Basic Books, 2010), 46.

110. "Cotton Seed Coffee," *Charleston Courier*, January 28, 1862.

111. Arthur James Lyon Fremantle, *Three Months in the Southern States: April–June, 1863* (Mobile: S. H. Goetzel, 1864), 41.

112. For a biographical account, see Carlos Pontes, *Tavares Bastos (Aureliano Candido), 1839–1875* (São Paulo: Companhia Editora Nacional, 1975).

113. Aureliano Candido Tavares Bastos, *Cartas do Solitário: Estudos sobre Reforma Administrativa, Ensino Religioso, Africanos Livres, Tráfico de Escravos, Liberdade de Cabotagem, Abertura do Amazonas, Communicação com os Estados Unidos, etc.* (Rio de Janeiro, 1863).

114. On the origins of the Brazilian liberal tradition, see Miriam Dolhnikoff, *O Pacto Impe-rial: Origens do Federalismo no Brasil* (São Paulo: Globo, 2005). On Tavares Bastos's interpreta-tion of this tradition, see Gabriela Nunes Ferreira, *Centralização e Descentralização no Império: O Debate entre Tavares Bastos e Visconde de Uruguai* (São Paulo: Editora 34, 2000).

115. Tavares Bastos, *Cartas do Solitário*, 413. On the intertwining of nationalism and capitalism during the nineteenth century, see Jürgen Osterhammel, *The Transformation of the World: A Global History of the Nineteenth Century* (Princeton: Princeton University Press, 2014), 403–419.

116. By the middle decades of the nineteenth century, emerging nationalism was forcing liberals to refashion their cosmopolitanism. As Eric J. Hobsbawm puts it, "Whatever the long-term prospects, it was accepted by contemporary liberal observers that, in the short and me-dium term, development proceeded by the formation of different and rival nations. The most that could be hoped was that these would embody the same type of institutions, economy and beliefs. The unity of the world implied division." *The Age of Capital, 1848–1875* (New York: Scrib-ner, 1975), 66.

117. Tavares Bastos, *Cartas do Solitário*, 344–345. On Tavares Bastos's ideas about the United States, see Bruno Gonçalves Rosi, "The Americanism of Aureliano Candido Tavares Bastos," *Almanack* 19 (August 2018): 244–277.

118. Aureliano Candido Tavares Bastos to George N. Davis, Valença, March 15, 1863, in Ta-vares Bastos, *Cartas do Solitário*, 425–427. Representative John B. Alley of Massachusetts read a translation of this letter before the US Congress on April 15, 1864. *The Congressional Globe: Containing the Debates and Proceedings of the First Session of the Thirty-Eighth Congress* (Wash-ington: Congressional Globe, 1864), 1655.

119. Tavares Bastos, *Cartas do Solitário*, 220.

120. Aureliano Candido Tavares Bastos to George N. Davis, Valença, March 15, 1863.

121. Aureliano Candido Tavares Bastos to Antonio Francisco de Paula Souza, n.p., Decem-ber 28, 1865, Arquivo Paula Souza, PS865.12.28/2, BMA.

122. Cristiano Benedito Ottoni to Aureliano Candido Tavares Bastos, Rio de Janeiro, April 19, 186_, Coleção Tavares Bastos, I3.32.5, FBN; Cristiano Benedito Ottoni to Aureliano Candido Tavares Bastos, Rio de Janeiro, December 19, 186_, Coleção Tavares Bastos, I3.32.9, FBN.

123. Andrew Ellison Jr. to Aureliano Candido Tavares Bastos, Macacos, March 16, 1863, Coleção Tavares Bastos, I3.31.5, FBN; Andrew Ellison Jr. to Aureliano Candido Tavares Bastos, Macacos, April 6, 1863, Coleção Tavares Bastos, I3.31.7, FBN; Andrew Ellison Jr. to Aureliano Candido Tavares Bastos, Macacos, March 29, 1864, Coleção Tavares Bastos, I3.31.8, FBN.

124. Tavares Bastos, *Cartas do Solitário*, 379.

125. Tavares Bastos, *Cartas do Solitário*, 379–385.

126. Barbara Weinstein emphasizes "the strong association between slavery and backward-ness in the Brazilian intellectual milieu from the early nineteenth century on. While the concept of underdevelopment would not appear for another century, Brazilian politicians and essayists in the first half of the nineteenth century already characterized their homeland as backward in terms of technology, culture, wealth, and power compared to those societies where mechaniza-tion and industrialization were advancing productivity, efficiency, and national prestige. This close and persistent association between progress and free labor, reinforced by Brazil's own apparent backwardness and repeated subjection to Britain's will, made it extremely difficult for

defenders of slavery to find a position from which to construct positive arguments for building a nation on the basis of slave labor." "The Decline of the Progressive Planter and the Rise of the Subaltern Agent: Shifting Narratives of Slave Emancipation in Brazil," in *Reclaiming the Political in Latin American History*, ed. Gilbert M. Joseph (Durham, NC: Duke University Press, 2001), 91.

127. "Projectos sobre a Navegação a Vapor para os Estados-Unidos e a Abertura do Amazonas: Observações na Sessão de 8 de julho de 1862, da Camara dos Deputados," in Tavares Bastos, *Cartas do Solitário*, 414.

128. James Watson Webb to Aureliano Candido Tavares Bastos, Petrópolis, January 3, 1863, Coleção Tavares Bastos, I3.32.40, FBN.

129. James Watson Webb to Aureliano Candido Tavares Bastos, Petrópolis, January 3, 1863.

130. Aureliano Candido Tavares Bastos to George N. Davis, Valença, March 15, 1863.

131. Aureliano Candido Tavares Bastos to George N. Davis, Valença, March 15, 1863.

132. Aureliano Candido Tavares Bastos to George N. Davis, Valença, March 15, 1863.

133. James Cooley Fletcher, *International Relations with Brazil: Proceedings on the Reception of H. E. Senhor D'Azambuja, Envoy Extraordinary and Minister Plenipotentiary from Brazil, by the Chamber of Commerce of the State of New York November 2nd, 1865, with Remarks by James C. Fletcher on the Mail Communication between the United States and Brazil* (New York: John W. Amerman, 1865).

134. Aureliano Candido Tavares Bastos, report presented at the Chamber of Deputies, April 22, 1864, in *Annaes do Parlamento Brazileiro, Câmara dos Srs. Deputados, Primeiro Anno da Duodécima Legislatura, Sessão de 1864, Volume III* (Rio de Janeiro: Typographia Imperial e Constitucional de J. Villeneuve, 1864), 246.

135. "Steam Communication with Brazil: Interesting Address by Rev. J.C. Fletcher, before the Boston Board of Trade," *New York Times*, August 14, 1863. The proceedings of this meeting were translated to Portuguese and published in Brazilian newspapers: "Exterior—Nova-York, 14 de Agosto—Comunicação a Vapor com o Brasil," *Correio Mercantil*, September 30, 1863.

136. George N. Davis to Aureliano Candido Tavares Bastos, Rio de Janeiro, February 1, 1864, Coleção Tavares Bastos, I3.31.63, FBN.

137. John B. Alley, speech at the House of Representatives, April 15, 1864, in *Congressional Globe*, 1653–1655.

138. John V. L. Pruyn, speech at the House of Representatives, April 15, 1864, in *Congressional Globe*, 1655–1656.

139. Alley, speech at the House of Representatives, April 15, 1864, 1655.

140. In regard to the immediate post–Civil War period, Jay Sexton notes that "the nation that had been the world's leading defender of slavery now joined Britain in the ranks of antislavery. This diminished the national political power of the former Southern slaveholding elite, as well as further isolating the remaining slave systems in the Western Hemisphere, the Spanish colonies of Cuba and Puerto Rico, and the independent and monarchical Brazil." *Monroe Doctrine*, 159. The steamship line initiative, however, tells a very different story about changing American attitudes toward Brazil—the largest slave society in the Western world after the Confederacy was defeated. First, the American government did not join forces with the British Empire but openly challenged it by proposing an alternative form of antislavery to Brazil. Second, the steamship line—along with American investment in transportation and increased coffee imports—brought slaveholding Brazil closer to the United States. As mentioned

elsewhere in this chapter, the fact that Brazil still preserved slavery made American Republicans all the more interested in engaging with it.

141. James Cooley Fletcher to Aureliano Candido Tavares Bastos, Newburyport, April 22, 1864, Coleção Tavares Bastos, I3.31.76, FBN.

142. "An Act Authorizing the Establishment of Ocean Mail Steamship Service between the United States and Brazil," in *Statutes at Large, Treaties and Proclamations of the United States of America: from December 1867, to March 1869, Volume 13* (Boston: Little, Brown, 1863), 93. On the economic policies of the Republican Party during the American Civil War, see Heather Cox Richardson, *The Greatest Nation of the Earth: Republican Economic Policies during the Civil War* (Cambridge, MA: Harvard University Press, 1997); Mark Wilson, *The Business of Civil War: Military Mobilization and the State, 1861–1865* (Baltimore: Johns Hopkins University Press, 2006).

143. James Cooley Fletcher to Aureliano Candido Tavares Bastos, Rio de Janeiro, August 8, 1864, Coleção Tavares Bastos, I3.31.77, FBN.

144. Aureliano Candido Tavares Bastos to James Cooley Fletcher, n.p., September 23, 1864, Coleção Tavares Bastos, I3.32.61n1, FBN.

145. Fletcher, *International Relations with Brazil*.

146. Martinho Álvares da Silva Campos, speech at the Chamber of Deputies, August 29, 1864, in *Annaes do Parlamento Brazileiro, Câmara dos Srs. Deputados, Primeiro Anno da Duodécima Legislatura, Sessão de 1864, Volume IV* (Rio de Janeiro: J. Villeneuve, 1864), 256.

147. Antonio Francisco de Paula Souza, speech at the Chamber of Deputies, August 31, 1864, in *Annaes do Parlamento Brazileiro, Volume IV*, 275.

148. Paula Souza, speech at the Chamber of Deputies, August 31, 1864.

149. Fletcher, *International Relations with Brazil*.

150. J. Navarro to Aureliano Candido Tavares Bastos, New York, July 7, 1865, Coleção Tavares Bastos, I3.32.4, FBN.

151. "Communication from the Exchange of Rio de Janeiro," in Fletcher, *International Relations with Brazil*, 11–12.

152. Aureliano Candido Tavares Bastos, "Subvenções às Empresas de Navegação," speech at the Chamber of Deputies, May 17, 1865, in *Discursos Parlamentares* (Brasília: Senado Federal, 1977), 319.

153. On the central role that the SAIN played in monarchical Brazil, see Cribelli, *Industrial Forests and Mechanical Marvels*.

154. "Sessão do Conselho Administrativo em 16 de Junho de 1865," *O Auxiliador da Industria Nacional*, 1865.

155. João Lustosa da Cunha Paranaguá, speech at the Senate, June 16, 1865, in *Annaes do Senado do Império do Brasil, Terceira Sessão em 1865 da 12ª Legislatura de 1º a 30 de Junho, Volume II* (Rio de Janeiro: Typographia do Correio Mercantil, 1865), 98.

156. Overlooking such transnational connections, some historians of Brazilian politics portray the Liberals as a weak faction subjugated by proslavery hegemons. See Ilmar Rohloff de Mattos, *O Tempo Saquarema: A Formação do Estado Imperial* (São Paulo: Hucitec, 1987); Jeffrey Needell, *The Party of Order: The Conservatives, the State, and Slavery in the Brazilian Monarchy, 1831–1871* (Stanford, CA: Stanford University Press, 2006); Ricardo Salles, *E o Vale Era o Escravo: Vassouras, Século XIX: Senhores e Escravos no Coração do Império* (Rio de Janeiro: Civilização Brasileira, 2008); Tâmis Parron, *Política da Escravidão no Império do Brasil, 1826–1865* (Rio de Janeiro: Civilização Brasileira, 2011). This is an unjustified contention. By the 1860s, antislavery

Liberals such as Tavares Bastos and Paula Souza had become highly influential in Brazilian politics by allying themselves with international forces revolutionizing the global economy.

157. Francis O. Braynard, "The First American Steam Passenger Line to South America," *American Neptune* 4 (1944): 137–163.

158. "New York as a Commercial Centre," *Harper's Weekly*, July 27, 1867.

Chapter 3

1. John Greenleaf Whittier, "Freedom in Brazil," *Atlantic Monthly*, July 1867.

2. Gregory Downs, *After Appomattox: Military Occupation and the Ends of War* (Cambridge, MA: Harvard University Press, 2015).

3. Eric Foner, *Reconstruction: America's Unfinished Revolution, 1863–1877* (New York: Harper & Row, 1988), 176–280; Mark Summers, *The Ordeal of Reunion: A New History of Reconstruction* (Chapel Hill: University of North Carolina Press, 2014), 81–152; Laura Edwards, *A Legal History of the Civil War and Reconstruction: A Nation of Rights* (New York: Cambridge University Press, 2015), 90–173.

4. Wilma Peres Costa, *A Espada de Dâmocles: O Exército, a Guerra do Paraguai e a Crise do Império* (São Paulo: Hucitec, 1996), 221–306; Francisco Doratioto, *Maldita Guerra: Nova História da Guerra do Paraguai* (São Paulo: Companhia das Letras, 2002), 255–276, 383–402; Thomas Whigham, *The Road to Armageddon: Paraguay versus the Triple Alliance, 1866–70* (Calgary: University of Calgary Press, 2017).

5. Sérgio Buarque de Holanda, *História Geral da Civilização Brasileira. Tomo II: O Brasil Monárquico. Volume 7: Do Império à República* (Rio de Janeiro: Bertrand Brasil, 2005 [1972]), 13–156; Angela Alonso, *Idéias em Movimento: A Geração 1870 na Crise do Brasil-Império* (São Paulo: Paz e Terra, 2002), 97–262; Celso Thomas Castilho, *Slave Emancipation and Transformations in Brazilian Political Citizenship* (Pittsburgh: University of Pittsburgh Press, 2016), 22–52.

6. Brent E. Kinser, *The American Civil War in the Shaping of British Democracy* (Farnham: Ashgate, 2011); Andre M. Fleche, *The Revolution of 1861: The American Civil War in the Age of Nationalist Conflict* (Chapel Hill: University of North Carolina Press, 2014); Don H. Doyle, *The Cause of All Nations: An International History of the American Civil War* (New York: Basic Books, 2015); W. Caleb McDaniel, *The Problem of Democracy in the Age of Slavery: Garrisonian Abolitionists and Transatlantic Reform* (Baton Rouge: Louisiana State University Press, 2015).

7. On Martius's exploration, see Karen Macknow Lisboa, *A Nova Atlântida de Spix e Martius: Natureza e Civilização na "Viagem pelo Brasil" (1817–1820)* (São Paulo: Hucitec, 1997).

8. Louis Menand, *The Metaphysical Club* (New York: Farrar, Straus and Giroux, 2001), 97–148.

9. On Louis Agassiz's social networks, Louis Menand writes that "it is an indication of how commanding a presence Agassiz was in Boston in the years before the [American Civil] war that the Saturday Club—the literary dinning and conversation society which he was a founding member and whose participants included [Ralph Waldo] Emerson, [Nathaniel] Hawthorne, [Henry Wadsworth] Longfellow, [John Greenleaf] Whittier, [James Russell] Lowell, [Charles] Sumner, and [Oliver Wendell] Holmes, all at the peak of their fame—was popularly referred to as 'Agassiz Club.'" *Metaphysical Club*, 99. During the 1860s, Fletcher, who lived in Newburyport, became part of Agassiz's circle.

10. "Curiosities for Professor Agassiz," *Boston Daily Advertiser*, February 12, 1863.

11. *Diário do Imperador D. Pedro II, Volume 9*, July 12, 1862 (Petrópolis: Museu Imperial, 1999), CD-ROM.

12. Louis Agassiz to Dom Pedro II, n.p., n.d., Louis Agassiz Correspondence and Other Papers, Am 1419, HOL-HU.

13. Louis Agassiz to Dom Pedro II, n.p., n.d.

14. Dom Pedro II to Louis Agassiz, Rio de Janeiro, November 3, 1863, Louis Agassiz Correspondence and Other Papers, Am 1419, HOL-HU.

15. "Rev. Mr. Fletcher's Lectures on Brazil," *New York Times*, February 28, 1863.

16. "Legislative Visit," *Boston Daily Advertiser*, March 16, 1865.

17. James Cooley Fletcher to Dom Pedro II, Boston, March 8, 1865, Arquivo da Casa Imperial do Brasil, Documento 6635, AMIP.

18. For more details on the expedition, see Menand, *Metaphysical Club*, 117–148; Maria Helena P. T. Machado, "A Ciência Norte-Americana Visita a Amazônia: Entre o Criacionismo Cristão e o Poligenismo 'Degeneracionista,'" *Revista USP* 75 (2007): 68–75.

19. *Relatório Apresentado à Assembléa Geral Legislativa na Primeira Sessão da Décima Segunda Legislatura pelo Ministro da Agricultura, Comércio e Obras Públicas* (Rio de Janeiro: Typographia Perseverança, 1864), 33.

20. Vitor Marcos Gregório, "O Progresso a Vapor: Navegação e Desenvolvimento na Amazônia do Século XIX," *Nova Economia* 19 (January–April 2009): 199–207.

21. "South America," *New York Herald*, June 13, 1865.

22. "O Sr. Dr. L. Agassiz," *Jornal do Commercio*, June 6, 1865; "O Professor Agassiz," *Diário do Rio de Janeiro*, June 11, 1865; "Conversações do Sr. Agassiz. Noite de Quinta-Feira 15 de Junho," *Jornal do Commercio*, June 16, 1865; "Conversações do Sr. Agassiz. Noite de Sabbado 17 de Junho," *Jornal do Commercio*, June 18, 1865.

23. *Semana Illustrada*, June 18, 1865.

24. "Banquete ao Sr. Agassiz," *Jornal do Commercio*, July 8, 1865.

25. "Professor Agassiz," *Boston Daily Advertiser*, June 4, 1866.

26. *Relatório Apresentado à Assembléa Geral Legislativa na Quarta Sessão da Décima Segunda Legislatura pelo Ministro e Secretário dos Negócios da Agricultura, Commercio e Obras Públicas* (Rio de Janeiro: Typographia Perseverança, 1866), 28.

27. Louis Agassiz to Antonio Francisco de Paula Souza, Rio de Janeiro, July 1, 1865, Arquivo Paula Souza, PS865.07.01, BMA.

28. On Coutinho's professional trajectory, see Marina Jardim e Silva, Antonio Carlos Sequeira Fernandes, and Vera Maria Medina da Fonseca, "Silva Coutinho: Uma Trajetória Profissional e sua Contribuição às Coleções Geológicas do Museu Nacional," *História, Ciências, Saúde-Manguinhos* 20, no. 2 (April–June 2013): 457–479.

29. Louis Agassiz to Antonio Francisco de Paula Souza, Pará, February 25, 1866, Arquivo Paula Souza, PS866.02.25, BMA.

30. João Martins da Silva Coutinho to Antonio Francisco de Paula Souza, on board of the *Icamiaba*, September 22, 1865, Arquivo Paula Souza, PS865.09.22, BMA; João Martins da Silva Coutinho to Antonio Francisco de Paula Souza, n.p., June 22, 1865, Arquivo Paula Souza, PS865.06.22, BMA; João Martins da Silva Coutinho to Antonio Francisco de Paula Souza, Pará, February 25, 1866, Arquivo Paula Souza, PS866.02.25, BMA.

31. João Martins da Silva Coutinho to Antonio Francisco de Paula Souza, Belém, February 11, 1866, Arquivo Paula Souza, PS866.02.11/2, BMA.

32. Louis Agassiz and Elizabeth Agassiz, *A Journey in Brazil* (Boston: Ticknor and Fields, 1868), 252–253.

33. Elizabeth Agassiz, "An Amazonian Picnic," *Atlantic Monthly*, March 1866.

34. Aureliano Candido Tavares Bastos, *Cartas do Solitário: Estudos sobre Reforma Administrativa, Ensino Religioso, Africanos Livres, Tráfico de Escravos, Liberdade de Cabotagem, Abertura do Amazonas, Communicação com os Estados Unidos, etc.* (Rio de Janeiro, 1863), 315, 380–381.

35. Aureliano Candido Tavares Bastos, *O Valle do Amazonas: A Livre Navegação do Amazonas, Estatística, Producções, Commercio, Questões Fiscaes do Valle do Amazonas* (Rio de Janeiro: Companhia Editora Nacional, 1937 [1867]), 101.

36. "Brazil," *New York Herald*, June 24, 1866.

37. John Greenleaf Whittier to Dom Pedro II, Amesbury, March 18, 1865, Arquivo da Casa Imperial do Brasil, Documento 6658, AMIP.

38. Harvard had been a center of antislavery sentiment before and during the American Civil War. According to Phillip Shaw Paludan, "Harvard sent 56 percent of its graduates in 1861 to serve in the Union army." Paludan explains that there was much of self-interest in this willingness to serve: "The heroism of Harvard aristocrats validated the moral qualities of America's upper class." *A People's Contest: The Union and Civil War, 1861–1865* (New York: Harper & Row, 1988), 132–133.

39. Elizabeth Cary Cabot Agassiz to Quincy A. Shaw, Rio de Janeiro, June 5, 1865, in Lucy Allen Paton, *Elizabeth Cary Agassiz: A Biography* (Boston: Houghton Mifflin, 1919), 80.

40. Agassiz and Agassiz, *Journey in Brazil*, 65, 121.

41. Agassiz and Agassiz, *Journey in Brazil*, 112–115.

42. Andre M. Fleche, for example, writes that "Union supporters increasingly believed that the defeat of the Slave Power held universal importance. The institution of slavery threatened republican government by creating a powerful class of wealthy landholders whose political values proved antagonistic to democracy and equality for white men." *Revolution of 1861*, 131.

43. "Professor Agassiz's Expedition," *Daily Age*, November 25, 1865.

44. Gregório, "Progresso a Vapor," 207–209.

45. Aureliano Candido Tavares Bastos to Quintino Antonio Ferreira de Souza Bocaiuva, Rio de Janeiro, December 23, 1866, Coleção Quintino Bocaiuva, CP 855.08.21, Pasta V, FGV.

46. "Opening of the River Amazon," *New York Herald*, January 18, 1867.

47. Andrew Johnson, "Third Annual Message," December 3, 1867, in *A Compilation of the Messages and Papers of the Presidents, 1789–1897, Volume VI* (Washington: Government Printing Office, 1900), 578.

48. Historians who assume that proslavery Conservatives held hegemonic power in monarchical Brazil argue that a sense of shame and isolation took over the Brazilian elite after the Union defeated the Confederacy. Jeffrey Needell writes that Dom Pedro II became preoccupied "with the Empire's reputation among 'civilized' states after the 'Emancipation Proclamation' of 1863." *The Party of Order: The Conservatives, the State, and Slavery in the Brazilian Monarchy, 1831–1871* (Stanford, CA: Stanford University Press, 2006), 233. Ricardo Salles posits that after Lincoln signed the Emancipation Proclamation "it became evident to the attentive observer,

like the emperor and most statesmen of the Empire were, that slavery's days were numbered in Brazil as well as in the United States." "As Águas do Niágara. 1871: Crise da Escravidão e o Ocaso Saquarema," in *O Brasil Imperial. Volume III—1870–1889*, ed. Keila Grinberg and Ricardo Salles (Rio de Janeiro: Civilização Brasileira, 2009), 63. Rafael de Bivar Marquese notes that "the development of the North American conflict risked isolating the country once again, leading the Brazilian government to consider alternative solutions to the problem of slavery." "The U.S. Civil War and the Crisis of Slavery in Brazil," in *American Civil Wars: The United States, Latin America, Europe, and the Crisis of the 1860s*, ed. Don H. Doyle (Chapel Hill: University of North Carolina Press, 2017), 226. The evidence shows otherwise. During and immediately after the conflict, Brazil was becoming closer than ever before to the United States. It was a sense not of isolation but of opportunity—more trade, investment, and economic development—that inspired reform in Brazil. Liberals like Tavares Bastos led the way.

49. Stephanie McCurry, *Confederate Reckoning: Power and Politics in the Civil War South* (Cambridge, MA: Harvard University Press, 2010), 318.

50. Angela Alonso, *Flores, Votos e Balas: O Movimento Abolicionista Brasileiro, 1868–1888* (São Paulo: Companhia das Letras, 2015), 58.

51. "Exterior. Correspondencia do Jornal do Commercio. Londres, 23 de Dezembro de 1862," *Jornal do Commercio*, February 28, 1863.

52. "Revista da Europa. Conclusão da Carta do Correspondente. Paris, 24 de Dezembro," *Diário do Rio de Janeiro*, January 21, 1863.

53. *Diário do Rio de Janeiro*, February 25, 1863.

54. "Correspondencia do Jornal Commercio. Washington, 20 de Fevereiro de 1863," *Jornal do Commercio*, March 7, 1863.

55. "Retrospecto Politico do Anno de 1862 II. Parte Exterior. Estados-Unidos da America do Norte," *Jornal do Commercio*, January 3, 1863.

56. *Times*, October 7, 1862, in *Abraham Lincoln, a Press Portrait: His Life and Times from the Original Newspapers of the Union, the Confederacy, and Europe*, ed. Herbert Mitgang (Chicago: Quadrangle Books, 1971), 319–320.

57. Doyle, *Cause of All Nations*, 240–256.

58. Karl Marx, "Comments on North American Events," *Die Presse*, October 12, 1862, in *Collected Works, Volume 19. Marx and Engels: 1861–1864* (New York: International, 1984), 250. In England, like in Brazil, organized groups on the left and the right engaged in the debate on the meaning of the Emancipation Proclamation. Analyzing pro-Union and pro-Confederate rallies in places like Lancashire, R. J. M. Blackett notes that "there was little that was spontaneous about any of this: resting on a firm foundation of national and local societies, the agitation was organized, well financed, and aimed to reach the broadest audience." *Divided Hearts: Britain and the American Civil War* (Baton Rouge: Louisiana State University Press, 2001), 193.

59. "Be not be" is in English in the original. "Retrospecto Politico do Anno de 1864. Parte Exterior. America Septentrional," *Jornal do Commercio*, January 2, 1865.

60. "O Anno de 1864 III. Estados-Unidos da America do Norte," *Diário do Rio de Janeiro*, January 4, 1865.

61. Agassiz and Agassiz, *Journey in Brazil*, 79.

62. "Exterior. Correspondencia do Jornal do Commercio. Londres, 8 de Maio de 1865," *Jornal do Commercio*, June 12, 1865.

63. "Noticias dos Estados Unidos," *Diário do Rio de Janeiro*, May 25, 1865.

64. José Manoel da Conceição, *As Exequias de Abrahão Lincoln, Presidente dos Estados Unidos da America, com um Esboço Biographico do Mesmo Offerecido ao Povo Brasileiro* (Rio de Janeiro: Eduardo & Henrique Laemmert, 1865).

65. Felix Ferreira, *A Morte de Lincoln: Canto Elegiaco* (Rio de Janeiro: Typ. Popular de Azeredo Leite, 1865); A. G. Simonton, *A Discourse on the Occasion of the Death of President Lincoln* (Rio de Janeiro: G. Leuzinger, 1865).

66. *Jornal do Commercio*, June 4, 1865.

67. "Grande Oriente do Brasil," *Jornal do Commercio*, June 28, 1865.

68. On the causes of the conflict, see Thomas Whigham, *The Paraguayan War, Volume 1: Causes and Early Conduct* (Lincoln: University of Nebraska Press, 2002).

69. José Antonio Pimenta Bueno, "Ata de 5 de Novembro de 1866," in *Atas do Terceiro Conselho de Estado, 1865–1867* (Brasília: Centro Gráfico do Senado Federal, 1978).

70. José Tomás Nabuco de Araújo, "Ata de 5 de Novembro de 1866," in *Atas do Terceiro Conselho de Estado, 1865–1867*; American Freedman's Inquiry Commission, *Preliminary Report Touching the Condition and Management of Emancipated Refugees* (New York: J.F. Trow, 1863), 12.

71. Francisco de Sales Torres Homem, "Ata de 5 de Novembro de 1866," in *Atas do Terceiro Conselho de Estado, 1865–1867*.

72. The war became highly unpopular in Brazil as the death toll increased and the government adopted brutal means of conscription. Peter M. Beattie points out that "as the war dragged on, criticisms of the emperor coalesced around impressment." Meanwhile, in Paraguay, "many soldiers died from preventable diseases and treatable injuries. Those who survived endured harsh discipline, grueling marches, and a frequent lack of food, potable water, clothing, munitions, and shelter." *The Tribute of Blood: Army, Honor, Race, and Nation in Brazil, 1864–1945* (Durham, NC: Duke University Press, 2001), 47, 54.

73. For a comparison between recruitment in the American Civil War and the Paraguayan War, see Vitor Izecksohn, *Slavery and War in the Americas: Race, Citizenship, and State Building in the United States and Brazil, 1861–1870* (Charlottesville: University of Virginia Press, 2014), 128–162.

74. As Gregory P. Downs points out, "While the Civil War created expectations for the end of global slavery and the triumph of democracy, it did not in fact lead directly to either outcome. At the end of the 1870s, slavery limped along in reduced form in Cuba and Brazil, monarchies flourished, and U.S. politicians flailed against political and financial limitations on U.S. power." *The Second American Revolution: The Civil War-Era Struggle over Cuba and the Rebirth of the American Republic* (Chapel Hill: University of North Carolina Press, 2019), 97.

75. On the Native American question in the Civil War and Reconstruction eras, see Alvin Josephy Jr., *The Civil War in the American West* (New York: Knopf, 1991); C. Joseph Genetin-Palawa, *Crooked Paths to Allotment: The Fight over Indian Policy after the Civil War* (Chapel Hill: University of North Carolina Press, 2012); Mary Jane Warde, *When the Wolf Came: The Civil War and the Indian Territory* (Fayetteville: University of Arkansas Press, 2013).

76. "From Buenos Ayres," *New York Times*, March 30, 1865.

77. "South America," *New York Herald*, June 13, 1865.

78. "South America," *New York Herald*, June 13, 1865.

79. "South America," *New York Herald*, November 12, 1867.

80. "South America," *New York Times*, December 24, 1867.

81. "The Military Situation of South America," *Boston Daily Advertiser*, August 22, 1865.

82. *Boston Daily Advertiser*, June 1, 1868.

83. "South America," *New York Herald*, February 23, 1869.

84. "The Paraguayan War—Brazil and Her Allies," *New York Herald*, December 17, 1869.

85. "Going to War," *New York Times*, June 5, 1867.

86. Lawrence F. Hill, *Diplomatic Relations between the United States and Brazil* (Durham, NC: Duke University Press, 1932), 201–213.

87. *Report of the Committee on Foreign Affairs, on the Memorial of Porter C. Bliss and George F. Masterman, in Relation to Their Imprisonment in Paraguay* (Washington: Government Printing Office, 1870), 226.

88. "The War in Paraguay—Lecture by General M. T. McMahon," *New York Times*, February 15, 1870.

89. James Cooley Fletcher to Dom Pedro II, Newburyport, July 20, 1866, Arquivo da Casa Imperial do Brasil, Documento 6818, AMIP.

90. Louis Agassiz to Dom Pedro II, Cambridge, October 29, 1865, Arquivo da Casa Imperial do Brasil, Documento 6836, AMIP.

91. John Greenleaf Whittier to James Cooley Fletcher, Amesbury, July 27, 1868, Arquivo da Casa Imperial do Brasil, Documento 7047, AMIP.

92. James Cooley Fletcher to Dom Pedro II, New York, May 23, 1868, Arquivo da Casa Imperial do Brasil, Documento 6984, AMIP.

93. "The War in South America," *Harper's Weekly*, September 16, 1865.

94. "Brazil," *Harper's Weekly*, October 21, 1865.

95. James Cooley Fletcher, "Preface to the Sixth Edition," in Daniel Parish Kidder and James Cooley Fletcher, *Brazil and the Brazilians: Portrayed in Historical and Descriptive Sketches* (Boston: Little, Brown, 1868), ix.

96. James Cooley Fletcher to Dom Pedro II, Newburyport, July 20, 1866.

97. "Brazil," *New York Times*, December 23, 1866.

98. Louis Agassiz to Dom Pedro II, New York, January 18, 1867, Arquivo da Casa Imperial do Brasil, Documento 6945, AMIP.

99. "Brazil," *Harper's Weekly*, October 21, 1865.

100. "Chevalier D'Azambuja, the New Minister from Brazil," *Harper's Weekly*, December 2, 1865.

101. "Abyssinia and Paraguay," *Harper's Weekly*, May 9, 1868.

102. "View of Humaita," *Harper's Weekly*, May 9, 1868.

103. Agassiz and Agassiz, *Journey in Brazil*, 215.

104. H. Hargrave, "Paraguay and the Lopez Family," *Lippincott's Monthly Magazine*, June 1870.

105. Thomas L. Whigham and Barbara Potthast, "The Paraguayan Rosetta Stone: New Insights into the Demographics of the Paraguayan War, 1864–1870," *Latin American Research Review* 34, no. 1 (1999): 174–186.

106. José Inácio Silveira da Mota, speech at the Brazilian Senate, May 17, 1861, in *Annaes do Senado do Império do Brasil, Primeiro Ano da 11ª Legislatura de 27 de Abril a 31 de Maio, Volume I* (Rio de Janeiro: Typographia do Correio Mercantil, 1861), 45.

107. *A Abolição no Parlamento: 65 Anos de Luta (1823–1888), Volume 1* (Brasília: Senado Federal, 2012), 28.

108. Francisco Gê Acayaba de Montezuma and Felix Dupanloup, *Carta do Exmo. e Revmo. Bispo De Orleans ao Clero de sua Diocese sobre a Escravidão Traduzida e Offerecida ao Clero Brasileiro pelo Visconde de Jequitinhonha* (Rio de Janeiro: Typographia Universal de Laemmert, 1865), 29–30.

109. Francisco Gê Acayaba de Montezuma, speech at the Senate, June 5, 1865, in *Annaes do Senado do Império do Brasil, Terceira Sessão em 1865 da 12ª Legislatura de 1º a 30 de Junho, Volume II* (Rio de Janeiro: Typographia do Correio Mercantil, 1865), 19, 24.

110. Kidder and Fletcher, *Brazil and the Brazilians*, 139.

111. Tavares Bastos, *Cartas do Solitário*, 382.

112. "Books on Emancipation for Brazil," *Liberator*, March 17, 1865.

113. "Emancipation in Brazil," *American Missionary*, May 1865.

114. A. Chameroozow to Aureliano Candido Tavares Bastos, London, May 8, 1865, Coleção Tavares Bastos, I3.31.47a, FBN.

115. "Africains et Esclaves: Exposição de Tavares Bastos sobre o Problema da Escravidão no Brasil Enviada a L. A. Chameroozow," 1865, Coleção Tavares Bastos, I3.31.48, FBN.

116. Joaquim Nabuco, *Um Estadista do Império. Nabuco de Araújo: Sua Vida, Suas Opiniões, Sua época, Volume II* (Rio de Janeiro: H. Garnier, 1897), 388–395.

117. Aureliano Candido Tavares Bastos, speech at the Chamber of Deputies, June 27, 1866, in *Annaes do Parlamento Brazileiro, Câmara dos Srs. Deputados, Quarto Anno da Duodécima Legislatura, Sessão de 1866, Volume II* (Rio de Janeiro: Typographia Imperial e Constitucional de J. Villeneuve, 1866), 238–239.

118. On the causes of this political change in the late 1860s, see Holanda, *História Geral da Civilização Brasileira*, 13–19.

119. Angela Alonso argues that the return of the Conservative Party to power generated a crisis that fractured the Brazilian political elite: "The crisis had an unexpected effect. The intra-elite clash opened opportunities for the expression of varied kinds of criticisms to the imperial institutions. . . . Tavares Bastos's faction, self-styled Liberal Radicals, created newspapers, clubs, public conferences and manifestos, all of which demanded the gradual termination of slavery along with political and economic modernization." *Flores, Votos e Balas*, 39.

120. Antonio Frederico de Castro Alves, "O Século," in *Antologia Brasileira: Castro Alves*, ed. Afrânio Peixoto and Constâncio Alves (Lisbon: Livraria Aillaud e Bertrand, 1921), 48.

121. Antonio Frederico de Castro Alves, "Versos do Solitário," in Peixoto and Alves, *Antologia Brasileira: Castro Alves*, 85.

122. According to Andrew J. Kirkendall, antislavery provided Brazilian students with a powerful political tool: "By embracing a liberalism that rejected slavery and the status quo, students renewed their claim to lead Brazilian society. While only a minority actually became abolitionists, abolitionism became a key component of the student ideal from 1860 on. From that point on, the student ideal required a young man to reject a central institution of his society. . . . The model served, in part, to question the role of patronage in the formation of identity and to demonstrate the students' independence. If sons and clients of slave owners could join in the call to abolish the institution responsible for their families' economic well-being—challenging that which made it possible for them to study at law school—then

patronage and family were not all. A student was not just his father's son or his patron's client. He was, as liberalism would have it, an independent individual actor." *Class Mates: Male Student Culture and the Making of a Political Class in Nineteenth-Century Brazil* (Lincoln: University of Nebraska Press, 2002), 121.

123. Luiz Gama apud Lígia Fonseca Ferreira, "Luiz Gama: Um Abolicionista Leitor de Renan," *Estudos Avançados USP* 21, no. 60 (August 2007): 284.

124. Rui Barbosa, "Quinta Conferencia Radical," *Radical Paulistano*, September 25, 1869.

125. *A Republica*, December 8, 1870.

126. "Abrahão Lincoln," *A Republica*, February 11, 1871.

127. Antonio da Silva Neto, *Estudo sobre a Emancipação dos Escravos no Brasil* (Rio de Janeiro: Typographia Perseverança, 1866), 31–32.

128. Antonio da Silva Neto, *A Coroa e a Emancipação do Elemento Servil* (Rio de Janeiro: Typographia Universal de Laemmert, 1869), v–vi.

129. Celso Thomas Castilho highlights the broad appeal of Brazilian abolitionism: "If organized locally with regional, national, and transnational connections, abolitionism formed as an explicitly 'national' movement. Framing it as such, abolitionists were legitimizing broad political participation and arguing that everyone, not just the slaveowners, had a stake in this debate." *Slave Emancipation*, 38.

130. "Elemento servil" (servile element) was a common euphemism for "slavery" in monarchical Brazil. José Tomás Nabuco de Araújo, speech at the Brazilian Senate, July 12, 1870, in *Annaes do Senado do Império do Brasil, Segunda Sessão em 1870 da Décima Quarta Legislatura de 1 a 31 de Julho, Volume II* (Rio de Janeiro: Typographia do Diário do Rio de Janeiro, 1870), 74.

131. *Manifesto e Programma do Centro Liberal* (Salvador: Typographia do Diario, 1869), 75.

132. José Martiniano de Alencar, *Ao Imperador: Novas Cartas Políticas de Erasmo* (Rio de Janeiro: Typographia de Pinheiro, 1867–1868), 24.

133. Alencar, *Ao Imperador*, 40.

134. Alonso, *Flores, Votos e Balas*, 53–56.

135. Few Brazilians ever defended slavery as a positive good. And the property-rights defense of slavery made for a weak kind of proslavery ideology in Brazil. As Barbara Weinstein puts it, "While much has been written about the slaveholders' use of liberal notions of property to defend their ownership of slaves, this is an even weaker argument given the recent abolition of slave property in the resolutely liberal British Empire, and the widespread acknowledgement that property rights were not absolute. The private property argument was a strong basis on which to claim indemnification, but a shaky basis for defending slavery as a permanent, or even long-term, institution." "The Decline of the Progressive Planter and the Rise of the Subaltern Agent: Shifting Narratives of Slave Emancipation in Brazil," in *Reclaiming the Political in Latin American History*, ed. Gilbert M. Joseph (Durham, NC: Duke University Press, 2001), 88.

136. José Maria da Silva Paranhos, speech at the Chamber of Deputies, July 14, 1871, in *Annaes do Parlamento Brazileiro, Câmara dos Srs. Deputados, Terceiro Anno da Décima Quarta Legislatura, Sessão de 1871, Volume III* (Rio de Janeiro: Typographia Imperial e Constitucional de J. Villeneuve, 1871), 146. Very likely, the way the Paraguayans referred to Brazil's black soldiers compounded Rio Branco's shame. According to Francisco Doratioto, "The use of slaves in the Brazilian Army became a topic for Paraguayan newspapers and for Solano López. The newspaper

Cabichuí often referred to the imperial forces as *the monkeys*, associating the black soldiers with the supposed cowardice of the Brazilians." *Maldita Guerra*, 272.

137. Robert Edgar Conrad, *The Destruction of Brazilian Slavery, 1850–1888* (Berkeley: University of California Press, 1972), 90–91.

138. Luiz d'Alvarenga Peixoto, *Apontamentos para a Historia. O Visconde do Rio Branco* (Rio de Janeiro: Typographia do Imperial Instituto Artistico, 1871), 99.

139. *A Emancipação: Breves Considerações por um Lavrador Bahiano* (Salvador: Typographia Constitucional, 1871), 29.

140. José Maria da Silva Paranhos, speech at the Chamber of Deputies, May 29, 1871, in *Annaes do Parlamento Brazileiro, Câmara dos Srs. Deputados, Terceiro Anno da Décima Quarta Legislatura, Sessão de 1871, Volume I* (Rio de Janeiro: Typographia Imperial e Constitucional de J. Villeneuve, 1871), 108.

141. Francisco de Paula Negreiros de Saião Lobato, speech at the Chamber of Deputies, May 31, 1871, in *Annaes do Parlamento Brazileiro 1871, Volume I*, 145.

142. *Analise e Commentario Critico da Proposta do Governo Imperial as Camaras Legislativas sobre o Elemento Servil* (Rio de Janeiro: Typographia Nacional, 1871), 63.

143. Paranhos, speech at the Chamber of Deputies, May 29, 1871, 108.

144. According to Steven Hahn, Brazilian planters successfully navigated the process of modernization in the nineteenth century: "In the course of emancipation and nation-building, the landed classes throughout Brazil retained their property, control over labor, and local prerogatives." "Class and State in Postemancipation Societies: Southern Planters in Comparative Perspective," *American Historical Review* 95, no. 1 (February 1990): 98, 88.

145. Scholars have debated the idea of conservative modernization for over a century. The foundational work of this tradition is Vladimir I. Lenin, *The Development of Capitalism in Russia: The Process of the Formation of a Home Market for Large-Scale Industry* (Moscow: Progress Publishers, 1964 [1899]). In the American academic context, the most influential work to examine conservative modernization is Barrington Moore Jr., *Social Origins of Dictatorship and Democracy: Lord and Peasant in the Making of the Modern World* (Boston: Beacon, 1966). In Brazil, the concept appears in Florestan Fernandes, *A Revolução Burguesa no Brasil: Ensaio de Interpretação Sociológica* (Rio de Janeiro: Zahar Editores, 1974).

146. Domingos de Andrade Figueira, speech at the Chamber of Deputies, May 30, 1871, in *Annaes do Parlamento Brazileiro, Câmara dos Srs. Deputados, Terceiro Anno da Décima Quarta Legislatura, Sessão de 1871, Volume V, Appendice* (Rio de Janeiro: J. Villeneuve, 1871), 32.

147. Paulino José Soares de Souza, *Discurso Proferido na Sessão de 23 de Agosto de 1871 sobre a Proposta do Governo Relativa ao Elemento Servil pelo Conselheiro Paulino José Soares de Sousa, Deputado pelo 3º Districto da Provincia do Rio de Janeiro* (Rio de Janeiro: Typographia Imperial e Constitucional de J. Villeneuve, 1871), 43.

148. José Martiniano de Alencar, speech at the Chamber of Deputies, July 13, 1871, in *Annaes do Parlamento Brazileiro 1871, Volume III*, 134.

149. *Elemento Servil: Parecer da Commissão Especial Apresentado à Camara dos Srs. Deputados na Sessão de 30 de Junho de 1871 sobre a Proposta do Governo, de 12 de Maio do Mesmo Anno* (Rio de Janeiro: Typographia Nacional, 1871), 16.

150. Joaquim Pinto de Campos, *Discurso Pronunciado pelo Senhor Deputado Monsenhor Pinto de Campos, Relator da Commissão do Projecto sobre a Reforma do Elemento Servil* (Rio de Janeiro:

Typographia de Julio Villeneuve, 1871). Comparing the two regions, James McPherson shows that "the North was more urban than the South and was urbanizing at a faster rate. In 1820, 10 percent of the free-state residents lived in urban areas (defined by the census as towns or cities with a population of 2,500 or more) compared with 5 percent in the slave states. By 1860 the figures were 26 percent and 10 percent, respectively. More striking was the growing contrast between farm and nonfarm occupations in the two sections. In 1800, 82 percent of the Southern labor force worked in agriculture compared with 68 percent in the free states. By 1860 the Northern share had dropped to 40 percent, while the Southern proportion had actually increased slightly, to 84 percent. Southern agriculture remained traditionally labor-intensive while Northern farming became increasingly capital-intensive and mechanized. By 1860 the free states had nearly twice the value of farm machinery per acre and per farmworker as the slave states. And the pace of industrialization in the North far outstripped that in the South. In 1810 the slave states had an estimated 31 percent of the capital invested in manufacturing in the United States; by 1860 this had declined to 16 percent." *Drawn with the Sword: Reflections on the American Civil War* (Oxford: Oxford University Press, 1996), 12–13.

151. Examining Anglo-American relations, W. Caleb McDaniel writes that "transatlantic liberals . . . saw the Civil War not as a demonstration of democracy's failure but as a proof of its viability and a summons to perfect free institutions for the sake of the world." *Problem of Democracy in the Age of Slavery*, 267. Don H. Doyle argues that the Union upheld the "ideals of human equality and liberty against those of aristocracy and slavery." As the conflict unfolded, the Union "embraced the expectation abroad that the Civil War was indeed Liberty's war, a war to destroy slavery, but also presented it, in Lincoln's words, as 'a people's contest' in defense of democratic principles." *Cause of All Nations*, 9, 185.

152. Peixoto, *Apontamentos para a Historia*, 125.

Chapter 4

1. Joel E. Matthews, *Brazil: Reflections on the Character of the Soil, Climate, Inhabitants, and Government* (Selma: William, Chambliss, 1867), 14. On the tensions rising from the transplantation of Northern ideas of development to the American South in the wake of the Civil War, see Lawrence Powell, *New Masters: Northern Planters during the Civil War and Reconstruction* (New Haven, CT: Yale University Press, 1980).

2. Walter Licht, *Industrializing America: The Nineteenth Century* (Baltimore: Johns Hopkins University Press, 1995), 79–101; William G. Roy, *Socializing Capital: The Rise of the Large Industrial Corporation in America* (Princeton: Princeton University Press, 1997); Sven Beckert, *The Monied Metropolis: New York City and the Consolidation of the Bourgeoisie, 1850–1900* (New York: Cambridge University Press, 2001), 145–154.

3. James L. Roark, *Masters without Slaves: Southern Planters in the Civil War and Reconstruction* (New York: Norton, 1977), 111–155; Carole Emberton, *Beyond Redemption: Race, Violence, and the American South after the Civil War* (Chicago: University of Chicago Press, 2013); Gregory P. Downs, *After Appomattox: Military Occupation and the Ends of War* (Cambridge, MA: Harvard University Press, 2015), 11–38, 137–160.

4. Warren Dean, *With Broadax and Firebrand: The Destruction of the Brazilian Atlantic Forest* (Berkeley: University of California Press, 1995), 93–270; Francisco Vidal Luna and Herbert S.

Klein, *Slavery and the Economy of São Paulo, 1750–1850* (Stanford, CA: Stanford University Press, 2003), 53–78.

5. *Fazendeiro* was the common word for planter in nineteenth-century Brazil. The term *fazenda* usually meant plantation.

6. Emília Viotti da Costa, *Da Senzala à Colônia* (São Paulo: Editora Unesp, 1998 [1966]), 169–249; Warren Dean, *Rio Claro: A Brazilian Plantation System, 1820–1920* (Stanford, CA: Stanford University Press, 1976), 1–87.

7. The term "ex-Confederate" describes the ambiguous national identity of the people who left the defeated South because they refused to rejoin the American Union and reincorporate an American national identity.

8. David M. Pletcher, *The Diplomacy of Trade and Investment: American Economic Expansion in the Hemisphere, 1865–1900* (Columbia: University of Missouri Press, 1998); Fareed Zakaria, *From Wealth to Power: The Unusual Origins of America's World Role* (Princeton: Princeton University Press, 1998); Thomas F. O'Brien, *Making the Americas: The United States and Latin America from the Age of Revolutions to the Era of Globalization* (Albuquerque: University of New Mexico Press, 2007); George C. Herring, *From Colony to Superpower: U.S. Foreign Relations since 1776* (New York: Oxford University Press, 2008); Richard H. Immerman, *Empire for Liberty: A History of American Imperialism from Benjamin Franklin to Paul Wolfowitz* (Princeton: Princeton University Press, 2010); Jay Sexton, *The Monroe Doctrine: Empire and Nation in Nineteenth-Century America* (New York: Hill & Wang, 2011); A. G. Hopkins, *American Empire: A Global History* (Princeton: Princeton University Press, 2018).

9. Isaac Watts, *The Cotton Supply Association: Its Origin and Progress* (Manchester: Tubbs & Brook, 1871), 85–86. On British dependence on cotton from the American South and the search for new suppliers, see Sven Beckert, *Empire of Cotton: A Global History* (New York: Knopf, 2014), 98–174.

10. Watts, *Cotton Supply Association*, 86.

11. John James Aubertin to Antonio Francisco de Paula Souza, São Paulo, September 4, 1865, Arquivo Paula Souza, PS865.09.04, BMA; João da Silva Carrão to Antonio Francisco de Paula Souza, São Paulo, June 4, 1866, Arquivo Paula Souza, PS866.06.04, BMA; John James Aubertin to Antonio Francisco de Paula Souza, São Paulo, February 4, 1866, Arquivo Paula Souza, PS866.02.04, BMA; John James Aubertin to Antonio Francisco de Paula Souza, São Paulo, July 24, 1866, Arquivo Paula Souza, PS866.07.24, BMA.

12. *Relatório Apresentado à Assembléa Legislativa da Provincia de São Paulo na 1ª Sessão da 14ª Legislatura pelo Presidente Doutor João Jacyntho de Mendonça* (São Paulo: Typ. Imparcial, 1862), 43.

13. On the role of Brazilian authorities and institutions in fostering cotton cultivation in São Paulo, see Alice Canabrava, *O Desenvolvimento da Cultura do Algodão na Província de São Paulo, 1861–1875* (São Paulo, 1951), 20–68.

14. "Correspondencia do Correio, Sorocaba, Novembro de 1865," *Correio Paulistano*, November 21, 1865.

15. Whitelaw Reid, *After the War: A Southern Tour, May 1, 1865 to May 1, 1866* (London: Samson Low, Son, & Marston, 1866), 374.

16. John James Aubertin, *Eleven Days Journey in the Province of Sao Paulo, with the Americans Drs. Gaston and Shaw, and Major Mereweather* (London: Bates, Hendy, 1866).

17. Cristina de Campos, *Ferrovias e Saneamento em São Paulo: O Engenheiro Antonio de Paula Souza e a Construção da Rede de Infra-Estrutura Territorial Urbana Paulista, 1870–1893* (São Paulo: Fapesp/Pontes, 2010), 40–41.

18. James McFadden Gaston, *Hunting a Home in Brazil. The Agricultural Resources and Other Characteristics of the Country. Also, the Manners and Customs of the Inhabitants* (Philadelphia: King & Baird, 1867), 42.

19. Ballard S. Dunn, *Brazil, the Home for Southerners: Or, a Practical Account of What the Author, and Others, Who Visited That Country, for the Same Objects, Saw and Did while in That Empire* (New York: George B. Richardson / New Orleans: Bloomfield & Steel, 1866), 25–26.

20. João da Silva Carrão to Antonio Francisco de Paula Souza, São Paulo, October 14, 1865, Arquivo Paula Souza, PS865.10.14/1, BMA; João da Silva Carrão to Antonio Francisco de Paula Souza, São Paulo, October 1865, Arquivo Paula Souza, PS865.10/1, BMA; Antonio Francisco de Paula Souza to João da Silva Carrão, Rio de Janeiro, March 14, 1866, Arquivo Paula Souza, PS866.03.14, BMA; Antonio Francisco de Paula Souza to João da Silva Carrão, Rio de Janeiro, May 11, 1866, Minutas Ministérios da Agricultura, 1866, Secretaria da Agricultura, Livro 29, Caixa 7, Ordem 7855, AESP.

21. Manoel Francisco Oliveira, Francisco Correa de Arruda, and José Aranha da Amaral, "Address of Welcome," Araraquara, October 29, 1865, in Gaston, *Hunting a Home in Brazil*, 152–153.

22. José Ribeiro de Camargo to Antonio Francisco de Paula Souza, Jaú, April 4, 1866, Arquivo Paula Souza, PS866.04.04, BMA.

23. Ricardo Gumbleton Daunt to Antonio Francisco de Paula Souza, Campinas, October 24, 1865, Arquivo Paula Souza, PS865.10.24/2, BMA.

24. Gaston, *Hunting a Home in Brazil*, 85–86.

25. Gaston, *Hunting a Home in Brazil*, 105–108.

26. Robert Meriwether and H. A. Shaw, "Shall Southerners Emigrate to Brazil?," *De Bow's Review*, July 1866.

27. Gaston, *Hunting a Home in Brazil*, 106–107. On cotton production in Ibicaba, see Canabrava, *Desenvolvimento da Cultura do Algodão*, 76.

28. Dunn, *Brazil, the Home for Southerners*, 149.

29. On cotton planters' expansionism in North America, see Adam Rothman, *Slave Country: American Expansion and the Origins of the Deep South* (Cambridge, MA: Harvard University Press, 2007).

30. Laura Jarnagin posits that the ex-Confederates' choice for Brazil was not related to slavery, pointing to business and family networks. *A Confluence of Transatlantic Networks: Elites, Capitalism, and Confederate Migration to Brazil* (Tuscaloosa: University of Alabama Press, 2008), 181–228. Yet the evidence pointing to the centrality of slavery for this choice is just too strong to be ignored. For white Southerners' attachment to slavery until the final moments of the Civil War, see Stephanie McCurry, *Confederate Reckoning: Power and Politics in the Civil War South* (Cambridge, MA: Harvard University Press, 2010). For the proslavery views of the ex-Confederates who moved to Brazil, see Célio Antônio Alcântara Silva, "Capitalismo e Escravidão: A Imigração Confederada para o Brasil" (PhD diss., Universidade Estadual de Campinas, 2011); Célio Antônio Alcântara Silva, "Confederates and Yankees under the Southern Cross," *Bulletin of Latin American Research* 34, no. 3 (July 2015): 370–384.

31. Gaston, *Hunting a Home in Brazil*, 160, 235.

32. Dunn, *Brazil, the Home for Southerners*, 40.

33. Meriwether and Shaw, "Shall Southerners Emigrate to Brazil?" On the domestic slave trade in Brazil, see Robert W. Slenes, "The Brazilian Internal Slave Trade: Regional Economies, Slave Experience, and the Politics of a Peculiar Market," in *The Chattel Principle: Internal Slave Trades in the Americas*, ed. Walter Johnson (New Haven, CT: Yale University Press, 2005), 325–370.

34. Dunn, *Brazil, the Home for Southerners*, 39.

35. Patriarchal independence was the foundational ideology of the antebellum South, affecting major planters and yeoman farmers alike. As Stephanie McCurry explains in her study of South Carolina, "Independence had powerful meanings for lowcountry yeomen. Not the least was that manifest in the household itself: in the virtually unlimited authority conferred over the property and dependents that lay within the enclosure. . . . In a society in which the authority of masters over domestic dependents was a matter of paramount political significance, state authorities were seriously disinclined to interfere, limit, or even regulate the power of household heads over their subordinates, familial or otherwise. Within the household, the master's word was virtual law." *Masters of Small Worlds: Yeoman Households, Gender Relations, and the Political Culture of the Antebellum South Carolina Low Country* (New York: Oxford University Press, 1995), 85–86.

36. A Southern Gentleman, "The Great Immigration Question," *Anglo-Brazilian Times*, July 8, 1868.

37. "Araraquara. A Lavoura e a Emigração," *Diário de São Paulo*, October 13, 1865.

38. Pinto Junior, "Communicado," *Diário de São Paulo*, October 17, 1865.

39. "O Sr. General Wood," *Diário de São Paulo*, October 15, 1865.

40. *Correio Paulistano*, October 12, 1865.

41. Antonio Francisco de Paula Souza to Antonio Francisco de Paula Souza, Rio de Janeiro, October 9, 1865, Arquivo Paula Souza, PS865.10.09/3, BMA.

42. *Relatório Apresentado à Assembléa Geral Legislativa na Quarta Sessão da Décima Segunda Legislatura pelo Ministro e Secretario de Estado dos Negócios da Agricultura, Comércio e Obras Públicas Dr. Antonio Francisco de Paula Souza* (Rio de Janeiro: Typographia Perseverança, 1866), 43.

43. "The Future of Cotton in Brazil," *Anglo-Brazilian Times*, January 8, 1866; "Immigrant Labor," *Anglo-Brazilian Times*, June 23, 1868.

44. Carlos Ilidro da Silva apud Canabrava, *Desenvolvimento da Cultura do Algodão*, 106.

45. "Future of Cotton in Brazil."

46. "Sociedade Internacional de Immigração," Coleção Quintino Bocaiuva, CP855.08.21, Pasta V, FGV.

47. "Farmers" is in English in the original. Aureliano Candido Tavares Bastos, "Memoria sobre a Immigração pelo Director A. C. Tavares Bastos," in *Sociedade Internacional de Immigração. Relatório Annual da Directoria, Numero 1* (Rio de Janeiro: Typographia Imperial e Constitucional de J. Villeneuve, 1867), 6.

48. Antonio Francisco de Paula Souza to Diretores da Sociedade Internacional de Imigração, Rio de Janeiro, August 7, 1866, Arquivo Paula Souza, PS866.08.07/1, BMA.

49. Aureliano Candido Tavares Bastos to Antonio Francisco de Paula Souza, Rio de Janeiro, March 3, 1866, Arquivo Paula Souza, PS866.03.03, BMA.

50. "Cópia. Contracto que Celebram de um Lado o Governo Imperial do Brasil, do outro B. Caymari, como Representante da Companhia United States & Brazil Mail Steamships para o Transporte de Emigrantes," Coleção Quintino Bocaiuva, CP855.08.21, Pasta V, FGV.

51. Antonio Francisco de Paula Souza to Quintino Antonio Ferreira de Souza Bocaiuva, August 24, 1866, Coleção Quintino Bocaiuva, CP855.08.21, Pasta V, FGV.

52. "Emigração Norte-Americana para o Brasil," *Correio Paulistano*, March 6, 1867.

53. Manoel Pinto de Souza Dantas to Quintino Antonio Ferreira de Souza Bocaiuva, December 24, 1866, Coleção Quintino Bocaiuva, CP855.08.21, Pasta V, FGV.

54. *Relatório Apresentado à Assembléa Geral Legislativa, na Primeira Sessão da Décima Terceira Legislatura pelo Ministro e Secretário dos Negócios da Agricultura, Commercio e Obras Publicas Manoel Pinto de Souza Dantas* (Rio de Janeiro: Typographia Perseverança, 1867), 67.

55. Manoel Pinto de Souza Dantas to Antonio Francisco de Paula Souza, Rio de Janeiro, November 3, 1865, Arquivo Paula Souza, PS865.11.03, BMA.

56. Charles Grandison Gunter to William A. Gunter, Rio de Janeiro, December 21, 1865, Charles G. Gunter Family Papers, SPR635, ADAH.

57. Charles Grandison Gunter to William A. Gunter, Rio de Janeiro, August 23, 1866, Charles G. Gunter Family Papers, SPR635, ADAH.

58. Julia L. Keyes, "Our Life in Brazil (1874)," *Alabama Historical Quarterly* 28, nos. 3–4 (Fall and Winter 1966): 240–247.

59. Lansford Warren Hastings, *Emigrant's Guide to Brazil* (Mobile, 1867), 213.

60. Herbert Huntington Smith, *Brazil, the Amazons and the Coast* (New York: Charles Scribner's Sons, 1879), 136–141.

61. Petition of Guilherme Bowen, American Colony, N. 3, November 10, 1867, Requerimentos Diversos, Anos 1852–1904, Secretaria da Agricultura, Caixa 1, Ordem 7217, AESP.

62. Guilherme Bowen, "To His Excellency the President of the Province of São Paulo," N. 1, November 9, 1867, Requerimentos Diversos, Anos 1852–1904, Secretaria da Agricultura, Caixa 1, Ordem 7217, AESP.

63. George Scarborough Barnsley to Godfrey Barnsley, Rio de Janeiro, June 22, 1868, Godfrey Barnsley Papers, Box 5, DMR-DU.

64. Scholars have described proslavery expansionism as an influential historical force in the nineteenth century. See Edward B. Rugemer, *The Problem of Emancipation: The Caribbean Roots of the American Civil War* (Baton Rouge: Louisiana State University Press, 2008); Matthew Pratt Guterl, *American Mediterranean: Southern Slaveholders in the Age of Emancipation* (Cambridge, MA: Harvard University Press, 2008); Walter Johnson, *River of Dark Dreams: Slavery and Empire in the Cotton Kingdom* (Cambridge, MA: Belknap, 2013); Rafael de Bivar Marquese and Tâmis Parron, "Proslavery International: The Politics of the Second Slavery," in *The Politics of the Second Slavery*, ed. Dale W. Tomich (Albany: SUNY Press, 2016), 25–56; Matthew Karp, *This Vast Southern Empire: Slaveholders at the Helm of American Foreign Policy* (Cambridge, MA: Harvard University Press, 2016). Its repeated failures suggest otherwise.

65. Harris Gunter to William A. Gunter, Rio de Janeiro, December 23, 1866, Charles G. Gunter Family Papers, SPR635, ADAH.

66. George Scarborough Barnsley to Godfrey Barnsley, Rio de Janeiro, June 22, 1868.

67. Keyes, "Our Life in Brazil," 298.

68. E. P. Thompson remains the main authority on the changing labor conditions in nineteenth-century factories: "Time, Work-Discipline, and Industrial Capitalism," *Past & Present* 38 (1967): 56–97. For a similar approach to the American context, see Herbert G. Gutman, "Work, Culture, and Society in Industrializing America, 1815–1919," *American Historical Review*

78, no. 3 (June 1973): 531–588. On the coffee commodity chain, see Steven Topik and Mario Samper, "The Latin American Coffee Commodity Chain: Brazil and Costa Rica," in *From Silver to Cocaine: Latin American Commodity Chains and World*, ed. Steven Topik, Carlos Marichal, and Zephyr Frank (Durham, NC: Duke University Press, 2006), 118–146.

69. Mark Pendergrast, *Uncommon Grounds: The History of Coffee and How It Transformed Our World* (New York: Basic Books, 2010), 46; Jon Grinspan, "How Coffee Fueled the Civil War," *Opinionator, New York Times*, July 9, 2014, https://opinionator.blogs.nytimes.com/2014/07/09/how-coffee-fueled-the-civil-war.

70. Dean, *Rio Claro*, 30–34.

71. Costa, *Da Senzala à Colônia*, 169–199; Dean, *Rio Claro*, 50–123.

72. Barbara Weinstein, "The Decline of the Progressive Planter and the Rise of the Subaltern Agent: Shifting Narratives of Slave Emancipation in Brazil," in *Reclaiming the Political in Latin American History*, ed. Gilbert M. Joseph (Durham, NC: Duke University Press, 2001), 93.

73. Paula Beiguelman, *A Formação do Povo no Complexo Cafeeiro: Aspectos Políticos* (São Paulo: Edusp, 2005 [1968]), 89–94.

74. José Sebastião Witter, "Ibicaba Revisitada," in *História Econômica da Independência e do Império*, ed. Tamás Szmrecsányi and José Roberto do Amaral Lapa (São Paulo: Imprensa Oficial, 2002), 131–146.

75. Gaston, *Hunting a Home in Brazil*, 90, 103.

76. Dean, *Rio Claro*, 37–38.

77. Costa, *Da Senzala à Colônia*, 226–228.

78. *Diário do Imperador D. Pedro II, Volume 9*, July 14, 1862 (Petrópolis: Museu Imperial, 1999), CD-ROM.

79. Stephen Vail Journals, January 1848–February 1865, HM9 Vail, MMTL.

80. William Van Vleck Lidgerwood to Stephen Vail, Steamship *Constitution*, New York to Rio de Janeiro, 200 Miles N.E. of Cape Frio, July 1862, Stephen Vail Family Correspondence, Unit 1, Folder 20, Shelf 4, Box 1, HSAR.

81. "Ordem do Dia," *O Auxiliador da Industria Nacional*, 1862. On the Brazilian law of patents and its importance for agricultural machinery in the late nineteenth century, see Luiz Cláudio Moisés Ribeiro, "Ofício Criador: Invento e Patente de Máquina de Beneficiar Café no Brasil (1870–1910)" (master's thesis, Universidade de São Paulo, 1995).

82. William Van Vleck Lidgerwood to Stephen Vail, Rio de Janeiro, February 21, 1863, Stephen Vail Family Correspondence, Unit 1, Folder 20, Shelf 4, Box 1, HSAR.

83. Teresa Cribelli, *Industrial Forests and Mechanical Marvels: Modernization in Nineteenth-Century Brazil* (New York: Cambridge University Press, 2016), 26.

84. "Industria Agricola. Uma Visita ao Estabelecimento de Maquinas Americanas, do Sr. G. Van V. Lidgerwood, na Rua da Misericórdia, N. 52," *O Auxiliador da Industria Nacional*, 1863.

85. "The Brazil Paraguay War," *New York Herald*, September 19, 1865.

86. William Van Vleck Lidgerwood to Stephen Vail, Rio de Janeiro, September 12, 1863, Stephen Vail Family Correspondence, Unit 1, Folder 20, Shelf 4, Box 1, HSAR.

87. William Van Vleck Lidgerwood to Stephen Vail, Rio de Janeiro, February 21, 1863.

88. Flávio Azevedo Marques de Saes, *As Ferrovias de São Paulo, 1870–1940* (São Paulo: Hucitec, 1981), 37–67.

89. William R. Summerhill notes that "railroad expansion in São Paulo pushed out the extensive margins of agriculture, attracted large-scale immigration from abroad, and stimulated investments in the form of improvement to land. Such increases in the stock of the economy's resources generated dynamic gains that escape the social savings estimates. These gains appeared in the increase in output that was due to the newly acquired factors of production." By the 1850s, Brazil claimed 52 percent of the world's production of coffee; by the 1900s, its share had risen to 77 percent. *Order against Progress: Government, Foreign Investment, and Railroads in Brazil, 1854–1913* (Stanford, CA: Stanford University Press, 2003), 140. Similarly, Steven Topik writes that "the railroad meant that the quality of coffee was better, and more important, cheaper, since more fertile lands were now accessible in the interior. This also meant that once slavery was abolished in 1888, Brazil could become the only country to attract millions of European immigrants to work in semitropical agriculture." "The Integration of the World Coffee Market," in *The Global Coffee Economy in Africa, Asia and Latin America: 1500–1989*, ed. William Gervase Clarence-Smith and Steven Topik (Cambridge: Cambridge University Press, 2003), 33.

90. "St. Paul's Railroad, Brazil," *Harper's Weekly*, December 5, 1868.

91. "Correspondência do Diário. Limeira, 13 de Janeiro de 1868," *Diário de São Paulo*, January 29, 1868.

92. "Ao Público," *Diário de São Paulo*, March 24, 1868.

93. *Relatório Apresentado a Assembléa Legislativa Provincial de S. Paulo pelo Presidente da Provincia, o Exm. Sr. Dr. Antonio da Costa Pinto Silva, no Dia 5 de Fevereiro de 1871* (São Paulo: Typ. Americana, 1871), 42.

94. Manoel Ferraz de Campos Sales, "Campinas em 1872," in *Almanak de Campinas para 1873 Organizado e Publicado por José Maria Lisboa, Anno III* (Campinas: Typographia da Gazeta de Campinas, 1872), 78.

95. Campos Sales, "Campinas em 1872," 78.

96. "Fabrica a Vapor de Machinas de Beneficiar Café Bierrembach & Irmão," in *Almanak de Campinas para 1871 Organizado e Publicado por José Maria Lisboa* (Campinas: Typographia da Gazeta de Campinas, 1870), 54–55. For the industrialization of nineteenth-century Campinas, see Ulysses C. Semeghini, *Do Café à Indústria: Uma Cidade e seu Tempo* (Campinas: Editora Unicamp, 1991). On the social and cultural impacts of industrialization on Campinas, see José Roberto do Amaral Lapa, *A Cidade: Os Cantos e os Antros: Campinas, 1850–1900* (São Paulo: Edusp, 1996).

97. "Aviso," *Diário de São Paulo*, May 5, 1868.

98. Lidgerwood v. Engelberg, Ação: Libelo Civel, Ano: 1868, Tribunal de Justiça de São Paulo, Comarca de Campinas, Ofício: 2, Caixa: 347, Processo: 6684, Folha: 127, CMAH-UEC.

99. Lidgerwood v. Bierrembach & Irmão, Ação: Libelo Civel, Ano: 1870, Tribunal de Justiça de São Paulo, Comarca de Campinas, Ofício: 1, Caixa: 199, Processo: 04162, CMAH-UEC; Lidgerwood v. Stirp, Ação: Corpo Delito, Ano: 1870, Tribunal de Justiça de São Paulo, Comarca de Campinas, Ofício: 1, Caixa: 199, Processo: 04175, CMAH-UEC; Lidgerwood v. Mac-Hardy, Ação: Ordinária, Ano: 1877, Tribunal de Justiça de São Paulo, Comarca de Campinas, Ofício: 2, Caixa: 401, Processo: 8003, CMAH-UEC.

100. Ema Elisabete Rodrigues Camillo, "Modernização Agrícola e Máquinas de Beneficiamento: Um Estudo da Lidgerwood Mfg. Co. Ltd., Década de 1850 a de 1890" (master's thesis, Universidade Estadual de Campinas, 2003).

101. Olivier Zunz argues that the exchange between industrialists and farmers was a key factor in the agricultural improvement of the American Midwest during the 1870s: "Technical innovation, for instance, involved a constant dialogue between implement manufacturers and their rural customers." *Making America Corporate: 1870–1920* (Chicago: University of Chicago Press, 1995), 154. A similar pattern developed in the Oeste Paulista at the time.

102. "Despolpador," *Gazeta de Campinas*, November 11, 1879.

103. "Secção Particular. Ao Público," *Gazeta de Campinas*, February 28, 1877.

104. "Ao Público," *Gazeta de Campinas*, February 18, 1877.

105. Manoel Francisco de Oliveira Junior to Lidgerwood Mfg. Co. Ltd, Amparo, May 21, 1879, "Secção Particular," *Gazeta de Campinas*, June 29, 1879.

106. Um Lavrador, "Machinas de Beneficiar Café," *Gazeta de Campinas*, August 17, 1876.

107. Club da Lavoura de Campinas, "A Exposição de Paris," *A Província de São Paulo*, December 4, 1877.

108. Nicolau Joaquim Moreira, *Breves Considerações sobre a Historia e Cultura do Cafeeiro e Consumo de seu Producto* (Rio de Janeiro: Typographia do Imperial Instituto Artistico, 1873), 64.

109. G. A. Cruwell and A. Scott Blacklaw, *Brazil as a Coffee-Growing Country: Its Capabilities, the Mode of Cultivation, and Prospects of Extension* (Colombo: A.M. & J. Ferguson, 1878), 17.

110. "Despolpador," *Gazeta de Campinas*, September 12, 1880. Teresa Cribelli finds a similar reasoning among SAIN intellectuals, who maintained that "*máquinas aperfeiçoadas* (perfected machines) promised a peaceful transition from slavery to free labor without overturning the social order." *Industrial Forests and Mechanical Marvels*, 72.

111. Thomas O'Brien provides an accurate analysis when he points out that, in the post–Civil War era, "American ventures in transportation and communication proved that U.S. technology could rival or surpass British investments as a spur to the economic growth sought by Latin American elites. Furthermore, U.S. businesspeople had demonstrated a willingness to enter directly into the production process and upgrade output with improved technology and management techniques, something British interests had rarely done. U.S. investors clearly saw themselves as important agents of economic growth and more generally as a civilizing force in Latin America." *Making the Americas*, 59. However, like other historians of foreign relations, O'Brien does not explain how Latin American elites shaped and benefited from American enterprise. As the case of the Oeste Paulista demonstrates, local planters used American enterprise to concentrate capital in their own hands.

112. "Sessão do Conselho Administrativo em 1º de Agosto de 1868," *O Auxiliador da Industria Nacional*, 1868.

113. "Maquina de Tecer," *O Ypiranga*, January 22, 1869. On the development of textile production in the Oeste Paulista, see Anicleide Zequini, *O Quintal da Fábrica: A Industrialização Pioneira do Interior Paulista, Salto-SP, Séculos XIX e XX* (São Paulo: Annablume, 2004).

114. "Estabelecimento Industrial," *Gazeta de Campinas*, March 29, 1874.

115. Antonio Francisco de Paula Souza to the President of São Paulo, letters of January 3, January 5, January 10, June 25, and July 6, 1866, 3ª Directoria das Terras Publicas e Colonização,

Rio de Janeiro, Ministério dos Negócios da Agricultura, Commercio e Obras Públicas, Secretaria da Agricultura, Livro 29, Caixa 7, Ordem 7855, AESP.

116. Manoel Pinto de Souza Dantas to the President of São Paulo, Directoria das Terras Publicas e Colonização, Rio de Janeiro, Ministério dos Negócios da Agricultura, Commercio e Obras Públicas, March 26, 1867, Secretaria da Agricultura, Livro 30, Caixa 7, Ordem 7855, AESP.

117. Police Chief of Jundiaí to the President of São Paulo, Estrada de Ferro de São Paulo, Telegrama Recebido, March 30, 1867, Secretaria da Agricultura, Livro 30, Caixa 7, Ordem 7855, AESP.

118. Among those who managed to acquire their own farms, the purchase of uncultivated small properties was most common. Out of 232 land titles belonging to ex-Confederates that Alessandra Ferreira Zorzetto found in Santa Bárbara for the years between 1866 and 1900, 75 percent registered lands of less than one hundred twenty acres. "Propostas Imigrantistas em Meados da Década de 1860: A Organização de Associações de Apoio à Imigração de Pequenos Proprietários Norte-Americanos—Análise de uma Colônia" (master's thesis, Universidade Estadual de Campinas, 2000), 90–100.

119. "Atenção," *Correio Paulistano*, August 8, 1871.

120. "A Pedido. Santa Barbara, Janeiro 1870," *Correio Paulistano*, January 28, 1870.

121. "De como a Liberade Nobilita o Trabalho," *Correio Paulistano*, November 27, 1869.

122. "De como a Liberade Nobilita o Trabalho."

123. Guilherme Whitaker, speech at the Legislative Assembly of São Paulo, June 21, 1869, in *Annaes da Assembléa Legislativa Provincial de São Paulo 1869* (São Paulo: Typographia Americana, 1869), 218.

124. Campos Sales, "Campinas em 1872," 77.

125. Whitaker, speech at the Legislative Assembly of São Paulo, June 21, 1869, 219.

126. George Matthews to Imo, Santa Bárbara, October 4, 1868, William H. Norris Family Papers, LPR191, ADAH.

127. George Matthews to Imo, Santa Bárbara, October 4, 1868.

128. George Matthews to Imo, Santa Bárbara, August 3, 1870, William H. Norris Family Papers, LPR191, ADAH.

129. Jane and George Matthews to Imo, Santa Bárbara, January 5, 1871, William H. Norris Family Papers, LPR191, ADAH.

130. George Matthews to Imo, Santa Bárbara, August 3, 1870.

131. Jane and George Matthews to Imo, Santa Bárbara, April 8, 1872, William H. Norris Family Papers, LPR191, ADAH. On domesticity in the antebellum South, Thavolia Glymph writes that "not only, mistresses believed, could they not live without 'Negro help,' neither could they practice 'true economy,' if doing so meant living without extravagance. Women of the South's ruling class defined themselves in part by their consumption of luxury goods, from household furnishings to clothing." *Out of the House of Bondage: The Transformation of the Plantation Household* (New York: Cambridge University Press, 2008), 77.

132. Jane Matthews to Imo, Santa Bárbara, March 7, 1874, William H. Norris Family Papers, LPR191, ADAH.

133. George Matthews to Imo, Santa Bárbara, August 10, 1872, William H. Norris Family Papers, LPR191, ADAH.

134. Steven Hahn further explains that "falling prices for agricultural produce on the international market, discriminatory freight rates, the erection of high protective tariffs, the demonetization of silver, and land policies that favored engrossment combined to squeeze farmers throughout the United States as a national economy was consolidated under the auspices of industrial and financial capital." *The Roots of Southern Populism: Yeoman Farmers and the Transformation of the Georgia Upcountry, 1850–1890* (New York: Oxford University Press, 1983), 168.

135. Orville Whitaker to Frank O. Adams, Santa Bárbara, November 11, 1874, Israel L. Adams and Family Papers, Mss. 3637, LSUL.

136. Orville Whitaker to Frank O. Adams, Santa Bárbara, November 11, 1874.

137. Cruwell and Blacklaw, *Brazil as a Coffee-Growing Country*, 128.

138. Orville Whitaker to Frank O. Adams, Santa Bárbara, September 14, 1875, Israel L. Adams and Family Papers, Mss. 3637, LSUL.

139. William Hutchinson Norris to Francis Johnson Norris, Sítio New Alabama, Province of São Paulo, August 1, 1869, William H. Norris Family Papers, LPR191, ADAH.

140. William Hutchinson Norris to Francis Johnson Norris, Sítio New Alabama, Province of São Paulo, August 1, 1869.

141. Jane Matthews to Imo, Santa Bárbara, August 7, 1872, William H. Norris Family Papers, LPR191, ADAH.

142. Thavolia Glymph notes that "to function and to meet the standards of domesticity, the plantation household required the labor of enslaved women—to beautify, clean, order, and thus civilize it. At the same time, it required negative representations of enslaved women and their labor—filthy, disordered—to deny them consideration as anything more than tools of the civilizing mission." *Out of the House of Bondage*, 65.

143. William Hutchinson Norris to J. W. Shomo, M.D., Sítio New Alabama, Province of São Paulo, April 9, 1873, William H. Norris Family Papers, LPR191, ADAH.

144. William Hutchinson Norris to J. W. Shomo, M.D., Sítio New Alabama, Province of Sao Paulo, April 9, 1873.

145. Zorzetto, "Propostas Imigrantistas em Meados da Década de 1860," 105–113.

146. Cruwell and Blacklaw, *Brazil as a Coffee-Growing Country*, 12.

147. George Scarborough Barnsley to Godfrey Barnsley, Rio de Janeiro, May 23, 1867, Godfrey Barnsley Papers, Box 5, DMR-DU.

148. George Scarborough Barnsley to Godfrey Barnsley, Tatuí, June 8, 1870, Godfrey Barnsley Papers, Box 6, DMR-DU.

149. George Scarborough Barnsley to Godfrey Barnsley, Tatuí, September 7, 1870, Godfrey Barnsley Papers, Box 6, DMR-DU.

150. George Scarborough Barnsley, "Notes on Brazil during the Years of 1867 to 1880," George Scarborough Barnsley Papers, Subseries 3.1, Folder 23, Volume 4, SHC-CH.

151. Robert Cicero Norris to Francis Johnson Norris, Santa Bárbara, September 6, 1885, William H. Norris Family Papers, LPR191, ADAH.

152. William Hutchinson Norris to Francis Johnson Norris, Sítio New Alabama, Province of São Paulo, January 13–14, 1887, William H. Norris Family Papers, LPR191, ADAH.

153. Barnsley, "Notes on Brazil during the Years of 1867 to 1880."

154. James McFadden Gaston Jr., "A Pathfinder of Yesterday: James McFadden Gaston, Patriot, Explorer, Scientist," James McFadden Gaston Papers, Series 2, Folder 19, SHC-CH.

155. Historians of foreign relations have surveyed how the United States exported expertise abroad. George C. Herring, for example, writes that, in addition to tourists and missionaries, "the Gilded Age also saw the first organized and officially sponsored efforts to export Yankee know-how." The author adds that "after the Civil War, U.S. business became more involved internationally. . . . For the first time, the nation had surplus capital to export. American entrepreneurs exploited mines and built railroads in other countries, especially in such friendly environs for foreign investors as Porfirio Diaz's Mexico. With the backing of J. P. Morgan & Co., James Scrymers linked the United States to much of South America by cable. United States companies dominated Russian markets in such diverse areas as farm machinery and life insurance. No firm exceeded John D. Rockefeller's Standard Oil in the breadth of its overseas operations. From the outset, Rockefeller set out aggressively to capture 'the utmost market in all lands.'" *From Colony to Superpower*, 273, 276. Not all Americans engaging with foreigners were like Rockefeller, however. Local elites often had the power and the resources to make some Americans—like the ex-Confederates of the Oeste Paulista—work for them.

156. On PCUSA missions in nineteenth-century Brazil, see David Gueiros Vieira, *O Protestantismo, a Maçonaria e a Questão Religiosa no Brasil* (Brasília: Editora Universidade de Brasília, 1980), 135–161.

157. James Cooley Fletcher to Dom Pedro II, Boston, January 22, 1869, Arquivo da Casa Imperial do Brasil, Documento 7050, AMIP.

158. Alexander Latimer Blackford, "Algumas Considerações sobre os Obstáculos ao Progresso do Evangelho no Brazil, Apresentadas ao Prebyterio do Rio de Janeiro em sua Sessão de 16 de Julho de 1867," Relatórios dos Campos de Trabalho Enviados por estes Missionários e Pastores ao Presbitério do Rio de Janeiro em 1861 a 1872, MPRF.

159. "Escola Americana," *Correio Paulistano*, December 5, 1872; "Estatutos Provisórios da Escola Americana," *Correio Paulistano*, June 29, 1873; "Metodo Rapido para Aprender a Ler," *Correio Paulistano*, October 21, 1874.

160. "Escola Americana," *Correio Paulistano*, August 20, 1872.

161. "Escola Americana. Rua de S. José n. 1 S. Paulo," *Correio Paulistano*, February 21, 1873.

162. "Relatório de J. B. Howell. São Paulo 1875," Relatórios dos Campos de Trabalho Enviados por estes Missionários e Pastores ao Presbitério do Rio de Janeiro em 1861 a 1872, MPRF.

163. "Missions in Brazil," in *The Forty-First Annual Report of the Board of Foreign Missions of the Presbyterian Church in the United States of America* (New York: Mission House, 1878), 24. According to Thomas O'Brien, in Latin American countries in the late nineteenth century, "even those not interested in the Protestant faith might well send their children to a missionary school for the opportunity to expose them to the benefits of an American-style education. Others saw in their conversion not merely a personal spiritual decision but the moral validation of new values that they wished to adopt, including concepts of individualism, competition, and personal freedom." *Making the Americas*, 62. This was certainly the case in São Paulo.

164. "Festa Escolar," *Correio Paulistano*, June 7, 1873.

165. "Escola Americana," *Diário de São Paulo*, April 3, 1877.

166. "Festa de Caridade," *Correio Paulistano*, January 27, 1878.

167. Júlio Andrade Ferreira, *História da Igreja Presbiteriana do Brasil* (São Paulo: Casa Editora Presbiteriana, 1959), 196.

168. "Relatório do Reverendo Geo. W. Chamberlain, Pastor da Igreja de San Paulo, Apresentado ao Presbítero do Rio de Janeiro na Sessão de 1870," Relatórios dos Campos de Trabalho Enviados por estes Missionários e Pastores ao Presbitério do Rio de Janeiro em 1861 a 1872, MPRF.

169. On how the problem of slavery created religious schisms in the antebellum United States, see Mark A. Noll, *The Civil War as a Theological Crisis* (Chapel Hill: University of North Carolina Press, 2006).

170. "Relatório de G. W. Chamberlain, Pastor da Igreja de São Paulo, Lido perante o Presbitério do Rio de Janeiro na Sessão aos 19 de Agosto 1872," Relatórios dos Campos de Trabalho Enviados por estes Missionários e Pastores ao Presbitério do Rio de Janeiro em 1861 a 1872, MPRF.

171. "O Collegio dos Srs. Morton e Lane," *Gazeta de Campinas*, December 14, 1872.

172. "Collegio Internacional," *Imprensa Evangélica*, September 19, 1874.

173. William S. Auchincloss, *Ninety Days in the Tropics or Letters from Brazil* (Wilmington, DE, 1874), 36.

174. "Discurso Proferido no Collegio Internacional por Ocasião da Distribuição de Prêmios," *Gazeta de Campinas*, January 7, 1875.

175. "Collegio Internacional," *Gazeta de Campinas*, January 5, 1874.

176. Francisco Rangel Pestana, "Uma Festa no Collegio Internacional," *Gazeta de Campinas*, July 1, 1876.

177. "Revista Literária do Collegio Internacional," *Gazeta de Campinas*, March 22, 1876.

178. George Nash Morton, "Educação Nacional," *A Província de São Paulo*, November 20, 1879.

179. "O Estabelecimento de Instrução projetado pelo Sr. Morton," *A Província de São Paulo*, November 22, 1879.

180. For an analysis of Positivism in nineteenth-century Brazil, see Angela Alonso, *Idéias em Movimento: A Geração 1870 na Crise do Brasil-Império* (São Paulo: Paz e Terra, 2002), 165–262.

181. George Nash Morton, "Positivismo," *A Província de São Paulo*, February 13, 1880.

182. Luiz Pereira Barreto, "O Sr. G. N. Morton e o Positivismo," *A Província de São Paulo*, February 17, 1880.

183. George Nash Morton, "Positivismo," *A Província de São Paulo*, February 22, 1880.

184. Ferreira, *História da Igreja Presbiteriana do Brasil*, 123.

185. José Custódio Alves de Lima, *Recordações de Homens e Cousas do Meu Tempo* (Rio de Janeiro: Livraria Editora Leite Ribeiro, 1926), 57.

186. "Relatório Annual de J. F. Dagama Apresentado ao Presbytero do Rio de Janeiro em Sessão em São Paulo 9 de Agosto de 1873," Relatórios dos Campos de Trabalho Enviados por estes Missionários e Pastores ao Presbitério do Rio de Janeiro em 1861 a 1872, MPRF.

187. "Missions in Brazil," in *The Forty-Second Annual Report of the Board of Foreign Missions of the Presbyterian Church in the United States of America* (New York: Mission House, 1879), 22.

188. "Missions in Brazil," in *The Forty-Eighth Annual Report of the Board of Foreign Missions of the Presbyterian Church in the United States of America* (New York: Mission House, 1885), 39.

189. William Buck Bagby, "Brazilian Mission. Report of Brother Bagby," *Foreign Mission Journal*, May 1881.

190. Bagby, "Brazilian Mission."

191. William Buck Bagby, "Letter from Brother Bagby. Santa Barbara, Sao Paulo, Brazil, Sept. 2nd, 1881," *Foreign Mission Journal*, November 1881.

192. William Buck Bagby, "Good News from Brazil. Campinas, Sao Paulo, Brazil, June 30, 1881," *Foreign Mission Journal*, September 1881.

193. James M. Dawsey, "The Methodists: The Southern Migrants and the Methodist Mission," in *The Confederados: Old South Immigrants in Brazil*, ed. Cyrus B. Dawsey and James M. Dawsey (Tuscaloosa: University of Alabama Press, 1998), 126–129.

194. Martha Watts, "Letter from Brazil, N. 4, October, 1881," in *Evangelizar e Civilizar: Cartas de Martha Watts, 1881–1908* (versão bilíngue), ed. Zuleica Mesquita (Piracicaba: Unimep, 2001), 172.

195. Martha Watts, "Brazil Mission, Probably May, 1883," in Mesquita, *Evangelizar e Civilizar*, 198.

196. "Collegio Piracicabano," *Gazeta de Piracicaba*, February 11, 1883.

197. In a list containing information on 329 students registered at the Colégio Piracicabano between 1881 and 1890, there were 43 Americans, 22 Germans, 10 Italians, 10 British, 5 Portuguese, 3 Swiss, 2 French, and 1 Spanish. "Lista de Alunos do Colégio Piracicabano," Acervo do Colégio Piracicabano, CCMW.

198. "A Educação da Mulher. Composição da aluna do Collegio Piracicabano, D. Anna de Barros, Lida por Occasião da Festa Collegial na Noute de 8 do Corrente," *Gazeta de Piracicaba*, February 11, 1883. On maternal duties in the nineteenth-century United States, see Nora Doyle, *Maternal Bodies: Redefining Motherhood in Early America* (Chapel Hill: University of North Carolina Press, 2018). On motherhood in nineteenth-century Brazil, see Okezi T. Otovo, *Progressive Mothers, Better Babies: Race, Public Health, and the State in Brazil, 1850–1945* (Austin: University of Texas Press, 2016).

199. Martha Watts, "From Piracicaba, N. 1, July 1889," in Mesquita, *Evangelizar e Civilizar*, 229.

200. Scholars of foreign relations acknowledge the importance of American missionaries. According to George C. Herring, "Persuaded that God had blessed them with modern technology to facilitate their evangelizing of the world and fervently committed to 'bring light to heathen lands,' they brought to their task a self-righteous arrogance that would make them an easy target for critics in later centuries. In some areas, they were the advance guard for American commercial penetration. While spreading their gospel, they were often guilty of the worst kind of cultural imperialism." *From Colony to Superpower*, 274. Thomas O'Brien argues that the missionaries' "primary and secondary schools offered exposure to Protestantism as well as training in academic disciplines, especially mathematics, science, and English, which were often lacking in Latin American institutions. Missionaries also provided a steady dose of American values as they urged on their pupils the importance of promptness, cleanliness, and the competitive spirit." *Making the Americas*, 62. By only emphasizing this sense of cultural superiority—which most American missionaries certainly carried with them abroad—historians have overlooked the fact that local elites engaged them to promote class interests.

201. Pondering questions of racial identity and national interests, some historians argue that Americans became increasingly more aligned with European imperialists in the post–Civil War period. According to Jay Sexton, "When Republicans looked across the Atlantic in the 1860s, they saw much that they liked. They identified racially with Europeans, particularly their fellow 'Anglo-Saxons' of England. . . . In terms of economics, the importance of the markets and capital of the Old World far exceeded the largely undeveloped economic connections between the United States and Latin America. . . . In short, despite the diplomatic complications arising from the civil wars of the period, the United States found itself more closely connected to the Old World, particularly its former colonial master." *Monroe Doctrine*, 149–150. A. G. Hopkins writes

that after the Civil War "the United States joined states on the continent of Europe in undergoing the transition to modern globalization and becoming an imperial power. The transformation ... was the greatest and by far the most successful of all the 'self-strengthening' movements that made their mark in the late nineteenth century." *American Empire*, 285. Accounts like these leave out the class dimensions of American influence in Latin America and the ways in which Latin American elites absorbed American capital and expertise.

Chapter 5

1. William S. Auchincloss, *Ninety Days in the Tropics or Letters from Brazil* (Wilmington, DE, 1874), 76–77.

2. Alan Trachtenberg, *The Incorporation of America: Culture and Society in the Gilded Age* (New York: Hill & Wang, 1982), 11–100; David Montgomery, *The Fall of the House of Labor: The Workplace, the State, and American Labor Activism, 1865–1925* (Cambridge: Cambridge University Press, 1987), 9–170; Olivier Zunz, *Making America Corporate: 1870–1920* (Chicago: University of Chicago Press, 1995), 11–101; Richard White, *Railroaded: The Transcontinentals and the Making of Modern America* (New York: Norton, 2011).

3. Eric Foner, *Reconstruction: America's Unfinished Revolution, 1863–1877* (New York: Harper & Row, 1988), 460–563; Sven Beckert, *The Monied Metropolis: New York City and the Consolidation of the Bourgeoisie, 1850–1900* (New York: Cambridge University Press, 2001), 207–236; Nicolas Barreyre, *Gold and Freedom: The Political Economy of Reconstruction* (Charlottesville: University of Virginia Press, 2016).

4. Sérgio Buarque de Holanda, *História Geral da Civilização Brasileira. Tomo II: O Brasil Monárquico. Volume 7: Do Império à República* (Rio de Janeiro: Bertrand Brasil, 2005 [1972]), 159–205.

5. Angela Alonso, *Idéias em Movimento: A Geração 1870 na Crise do Brasil-Império* (São Paulo: Paz e Terra, 2002), 51–163; Teresa Cribelli, *Industrial Forests and Mechanical Marvels: Modernization in Nineteenth-Century Brazil* (New York: Cambridge University Press, 2016), 37–177.

6. Seymour Drescher, *Abolition: A History of Slavery and Antislavery* (Cambridge: Cambridge University Press, 2009); Maria Helena P. T. Machado, *O Plano e o Pânico: Os Movimentos Sociais na Década da Abolição* (São Paulo: Edusp, 2010); Robin Blackburn, *The American Crucible: Slavery, Emancipation and Human Rights* (London: Verso, 2011); John T. Cumbler, *From Abolition to Rights for All: The Making of a Reform Community in the Nineteenth Century* (Philadelphia: University of Pennsylvania Press, 2013); David Brion Davis, *The Problem of Slavery in the Age of Emancipation* (New York: Vintage, 2014); Angela Alonso, *Flores, Votos e Balas: O Movimento Abolicionista Brasileiro, 1868–1888* (São Paulo: Companhia das Letras, 2015); Celso Thomas Castilho, *Slave Emancipation and Transformations in Brazilian Political Citizenship* (Pittsburgh: University of Pittsburgh Press, 2016); Manisha Sinha, *The Slave's Cause: A History of Abolition* (New Haven, CT: Yale University Press, 2017).

7. Luiz Gama to José Carlos Rodrigues, São Paulo, November 26, 1870, in *Anais da Biblioteca Nacional 9: Correspondência Passiva de José Carlos Rodrigues* (Rio de Janeiro: Divisão de Publicações e Divulgação, 1971), 271. For biographical accounts, see Hugh C. Tucker, *Dr. José Carlos Rodrigues, 1844–1923: A Brief Sketch of His Life* (New York: American Bible Society, 1925); Charles A. Gauld, "José Carlos Rodrigues, o Patriarca da Imprensa Carioca," *Revista de História*

7, no. 16 (1953): 427–438; George C. A. Boehrer, "Jose Carlos Rodrigues and *O Novo Mundo*, 1870–1879," *Journal of Inter-American Studies* 9, no. 1 (January 1967): 127–144.

8. On the political culture of law students in nineteenth-century São Paulo, see Andrew J. Kirkendall, *Class Mates: Male Student Culture and the Making of a Political Class in Nineteenth-Century Brazil* (Lincoln: University of Nebraska Press, 2002).

9. J. Carlos, *O Futuro*, May 17, 1862.

10. J. Carlos, "Os Patriotas," *O Futuro*, September 7, 1862.

11. James Cooley Fletcher, "Preface to the Ninth Edition," in Daniel Parish Kidder and James Cooley Fletcher, *Brazil and the Brazilians: Portrayed in Historical and Descriptive Sketches* (Boston: Little, Brown, 1879), vii.

12. *O Novo Mundo*, October 24, 1870.

13. "O Valor das Machinas," *O Novo Mundo*, May 23, 1875.

14. The postwar political economy, Rodrigues knew well, had its roots in the urban North. Noam Maggor highlights the importance of elite Bostonians' investment in the American West in the Gilded Age: "Groping for success (but hardly immune to failure), the Bostonians fundamentally rethought their place in a national economy. They traveled staggering distances and went to great strenuous lengths to forge these new vehicles of accumulation. Driven by the disintegration of the cotton economy and the prospects of their decline as a hegemonic class, they acted with a marked sense of urgency. They leveraged their entrepreneurial instinct and values, stretched their organizational skills to the utmost limit, drew on the latest scientific and technical expertise, and where necessary took aggressive and even violent measures in mobilizing labor. Their access to the large financial resources back east gave them the confidence and ability to lead and play a pivotal role in shaping the American political economy of the following decades." *Brahmin Capitalism: Frontiers of Wealth and Populism in America's First Gilded Age* (Cambridge, MA: Harvard University Press, 2017), 40.

15. "Mr. Cyrus W. Field," *O Novo Mundo*, January 23, 1871.

16. "Cultura em Grande Escala," *O Novo Mundo*, November 1878.

17. "As Gravuras," *O Novo Mundo*, February 1879.

18. "Alguns Retratos," *O Novo Mundo*, February 1877.

19. "As Classes Operarias nos Estados Unidos," *O Novo Mundo*, December 23, 1870.

20. "Importancia do Trabalho Individual," *O Novo Mundo*, February 23, 1872.

21. "Self-made man" is in English in the original. "Iniciativa Individual," *O Novo Mundo*, March 1877.

22. "O Aspecto Politico," *O Novo Mundo*, April 23, 1872.

23. When examining the Anglo-American context, Marc-William Pallen notes that "Cobdenite cosmopolitans, many of whom were leading radical abolitionists, viewed the 'unshackling' of the fetters of trade as but the next step in the universal emancipation of mankind and as a tool for 'civilizing' less advanced societies." *The "Conspiracy" of Free Trade: The Anglo-American Struggle over Empire and Economic Globalization, 1846–1896* (New York: Cambridge University Press, 2016), xxix. See also Foner, *Reconstruction*, 488–511; Andrew L. Slap, *Doom of Reconstruction: The Liberal Republicans in the Civil War Era* (New York: Fordham University Press, 2006).

24. "Grant e Greeley," *O Novo Mundo*, August 23, 1872.

25. Beckert, *Monied Metropolis*, 159.

26. "Estados Unidos: Como um Grande Povo se Governa," *O Novo Mundo*, November 23, 1874.

27. "Negócios Americanos," *O Novo Mundo*, June 23, 1875.

28. "O Anno de 1870," *O Novo Mundo*, December 23, 1870.

29. "O Trabalho dos Emancipados," *O Novo Mundo*, October 23, 1872. On the restructuring of the plantation economy in the postwar South, see Gavin Wright, *Old South, New South: Revolutions in the Southern Economy since the Civil War* (Baton Rouge: Louisiana State University Press, 1986), 51–123. For a parallel analysis of capitalist development in the South and the West, see Emma Teitelman, "The Properties of Capitalism: Industrial Enclosures in the South and the West after the American Civil War," *Journal of American History* 106, no. 4 (March 2020): 879–900.

30. On black workers' mobility in the postwar South, see Steven Hahn, *A Nation under Our Feet: Black Political Struggles in the Rural South from Slavery to the Great Migration* (Cambridge, MA: Belknap, 2003), 163–316.

31. "O Trabalho dos Libertos," *O Novo Mundo*, February 1879.

32. "Condição Economica do Sul dos Estados Unidos," *O Novo Mundo*, October 24, 1871.

33. "Trabalho dos Libertos."

34. "Fabricas de Tecer," *O Novo Mundo*, April 23, 1872.

35. On the rise of manufacturing in the postwar American South, see Wright, *Old South, New South*, 124–197.

36. "Prosperidade Industrial de 1870," *O Novo Mundo*, January 23, 1871.

37. "Trabalho dos Emancipados."

38. "Trabalho dos Libertos."

39. On the Brazilian perception of how slavery bred backwardness, see Barbara Weinstein, "The Decline of the Progressive Planter and the Rise of the Subaltern Agent: Shifting Narratives of Slave Emancipation in Brazil," in *Reclaiming the Political in Latin American History*, ed. Gilbert M. Joseph (Durham, NC: Duke University Press, 2001), 91–93.

40. "Beneficios da Emancipação," *O Novo Mundo*, November 1879.

41. "Progresso Agrícola em Pernambuco," *O Novo Mundo*, February 1877.

42. "História da Escravidão nos Estados Unidos," *O Novo Mundo*, August 24, 1871.

43. According to Robert Edgar Conrad, "A decade after the passage of the Rio Branco Law its failure to produce impressive immediate results was widely recognized. Even proslavery spokesmen admitted that the law had not been implemented energetically, that its provisions no longer corresponded with national aspirations, and that its results were insignificant when compared with the effects of private initiative and the high costs of administration." *The Destruction of Brazilian Slavery, 1850–1888* (Berkeley: University of California Press, 1972), 116–117.

44. "O Futuro dos Ingênuos," *O Novo Mundo*, April 23, 1875; "A Pena de Açoites," *O Novo Mundo*, April 23, 1875.

45. "Disposição das Terras Públicas," *O Novo Mundo*, November 24, 1871.

46. "O Nosso Café," *O Novo Mundo*, April 1877.

47. "Notes," *Nation*, November 3, 1870.

48. "Nova Ferry," *O Novo Mundo*, May 23, 1875.

49. "C. B. Greenough," *O Novo Mundo*, February 1877.

50. "Colégio Internacional de Campinas," *O Novo Mundo*, May 1878.

51. "Revista Industrial," *O Novo Mundo*, November 1877.

52. "O Novo Mundo, A Monthly Illustrated Family Journal of Literature, Politics and the Arts, Edited by J. C. Rodrigues, LL. B.," *O Novo Mundo*, November 1877.

53. "A Última Crise Americana," *Revista Industrial*, September 1877. For a historical account of the strike, see David O. Stowell, *Streets, Railroads, and the Great Strike of 1877* (Chicago: University of Chicago Press, 1999).

54. "A Questão entre o Trabalho e o Capital," *Revista Industrial*, December 1877.

55. Sven Beckert explains that "free-labor ideology prepared industrialists to blame workers for their social standing and to see workers' collective action as a threat to their core beliefs. As proletarianization widened, workers organized, and the social distance between manufacturers and their employees increased; commitment to a shared social contract centered on social mobility became more difficult to maintain. With notions of a mutuality of interest between workers and their employers diminishing, industrialists eventually would recast their relationship to the people in their employ." *Monied Metropolis*, 177. During the Great Railroad Strike, the New York elite concluded that only the use of military force against the labor movement would guarantee social order and the safety of private property. Rodrigues agreed.

56. "Aos Leitores," *Revista Industrial*, July 1877.

57. "Monopolio Territorial," *Revista Industrial*, February 1878.

58. "Irrigação," *Revista Industrial*, July 1879. On destructive agricultural practices in nineteenth-century Brazil, see Warren Dean, *With Broadax and Firebrand: The Destruction of the Brazilian Atlantic Forest* (Berkeley: University of California Press, 1995), 93–270.

59. "O Dr. Nicolau J. Moreira," *O Novo Mundo*, June 24, 1872; "O Sr. Cristiano Ottoni," *O Novo Mundo*, October 23, 1873.

60. Aureliano Candido Tavares Bastos to José Carlos Rodrigues, February 3, 1872, in *Anais da Biblioteca Nacional 9*, 162–163.

61. "O Brasil visto dos Estados Unidos," *Correio Paulistano*, January 30, 1874.

62. "Revista Industrial Illustrada," *Correio Paulistano*, August 12, 1877.

63. Manoel Ferraz de Campos Sales, "Questão do Dia," *Gazeta de Campinas*, November 5, 1871.

64. "O Instituto do Novo Mundo em Itu," *A Província de São Paulo*, January 4, 1875.

65. "O Instituto do 'Novo Mundo' em Itu," *Correio Paulistano*, December 30, 1874.

66. "Self-help" is in English in the original. "Navegação Fluvial," *O Novo Mundo*, June 24, 1876.

67. "Caminhos de Ferro de S. Paulo," *O Novo Mundo*, May 23, 1875.

68. "Barão de Piracicaba," *O Novo Mundo*, January 1877.

69. João Guilherme de Aguiar Whitaker, "O Progresso de S. Paulo," *O Novo Mundo*, February 22, 1875.

70. José Carlos Rodrigues, *The Panama Canal: Its History, Its Political Aspects, and Financial Difficulties* (New York: C. Scribner's Sons, 1885). On the American takeover of the canal, see Julie Greene, *The Canal Builders: Making America's Empire at the Panama Canal* (New York: Penguin, 2009), 37–122.

71. Manisha Sinha, for example, identifies antislavery with the early struggle against capitalist exploitation and other modern forms of oppression: "Contrary to conventional wisdom, they [abolitionists] developed an incipient critique of capitalism that linked the emancipation of the slaves with that of all laboring people. . . . As the movement matured, it remained ideologically consistent, sympathizing with labor and communitarian movements, the radical side of the

revolutions in Europe, and the emergence of anti-imperialism in Ireland and India. Far from reinforcing the sanctity of bourgeois society, the nation-state, and empire, abolition bolstered radical internationalism." *Slave's Cause*, 339.

72. On Paula Souza's professional and political trajectory, see Cristina de Campos, *Ferrovias e Saneamento em São Paulo: O Engenheiro Antonio de Paula Souza e a Construção da Rede de Infra-Estrutura Territorial Urbana Paulista, 1870–1893* (São Paulo: Fapesp/Pontes, 2010).

73. Antonio Francisco de Paula Souza to Antonio Francisco de Paula Souza, May 5, 1861, Arquivo Paula Souza, PS 861.05.05, BMA.

74. Antonio Francisco de Paula Souza to Antonio Francisco de Paula Souza, São Paulo, October 18, 1863, Arquivo Paula Souza, PS 863.10.18, BMA.

75. Antonio Francisco de Paula Souza to Antonio Francisco de Paula Souza, January 4, 1866, Arquivo Paula Souza, PS 866.01.04, BMA.

76. Antonio Francisco de Paula Souza, "Notícias Diversas em Forma de um Diário," August 15, 1869, Arquivo Paula Souza, PS 1868, BMA.

77. Antonio Francisco de Paula Souza, *A República Federativa no Brazil* (São Paulo: Typ. Ypiranga, 1869), 3.

78. Paula Souza, "Notícias Diversas em Forma de um Diário," August 15, 1869.

79. Antonio Francisco de Paula Souza, "Victorias do Trabalho Livre," *O Ypiranga*, November 30, 1869.

80. Paula Souza, "Victorias do Trabalho Livre."

81. Paula Souza, "Victorias do Trabalho Livre."

82. Before the Civil War, wage labor had become the prevalent form of organizing production in Northern cities and farms. In his study of western Massachusetts, Christopher Clark notes that "data on farm laborers from the 1850 and 1860 censuses suggests not only that their numbers were growing but that their condition was becoming more permanent. This was especially evident in Hatfield, which had the largest concentration of farm workers in its population. Laboring was becoming less a young man's occupation. . . . Both in 1850 and in 1860 just over half the laborers were immigrants. But while at the beginning of the 1850s over three-quarters of these immigrant workers were French-Canadians, many of them young summer migrants, by 1860 seven out of ten were Irish or German immigrants who were more permanently settled and less likely to move seasonally. The fastest-growing segment of the work force, however, was local. The number of Massachusetts-born laborers increased by three-quarters, from forty-eight to eighty five men, 45 percent of the whole group in 1860. On farms, just as in industry, the number of American-born wage workers grew along with the immigrants." *The Roots of Rural Capitalism: Western Massachusetts, 1780–1860* (Ithaca, NY: Cornell University Press, 1992), 308.

83. Paula Souza, "Victorias do Trabalho Livre."

84. Paula Souza, "Notícias Diversas em Forma de um Diário," August 25, 1869.

85. Paula Souza, "Notícias Diversas em Forma de um Diário," November 3, 1869.

86. Paula Souza, "Notícias Diversas em Forma de um Diário," November 3, 1869.

87. Paula Souza, "Notícias Diversas em Forma de um Diário," November 3, 1869.

88. Paula Souza, "Notícias Diversas em Forma de um Diário," November 3, 1869.

89. Paula Souza, "Notícias Diversas em Forma de um Diário," January 1, 1870.

90. Richard White argues that the railroad boom of the late nineteenth century generated "dumb growth": "The railroads seemed incapable to achieve a balance between too much and

too little. They enabled farmers and miners to produce far more cattle, wheat, and silver than the world needed. They opened up some of the most productive farmlands in the world and some of the most unproductive." *Railroaded*, 461. From Paula Souza's perspective, however, the more stuff to carry, the better for integrating the national economy, regardless of how much small producers and workers suffered.

91. Antonio Francisco de Paula Souza, "John Deere," in *Almanach Litterario de S. Paulo para o Anno de 1878* (São Paulo: Typographia da Provincia de São Paulo, 1877), 65–66. Examining agricultural production in nineteenth-century Illinois, William Cronon explains that "the grasses formed a mat so dense that in upland areas rainwater rarely sank more than six inches into the ground, preventing all but the hardiest of competing plants from taking root. Wooden plows with cast-iron edges quickly came to grief here. What farmers needed was a steel plow that could cut the tangled roots and still hold its edge—exactly the sort of plow that John Deere and other prairie manufacturers began to produce in their shops during the 1840s." *Nature's Metropolis: Chicago and the Great West* (New York: Norton, 1991), 99.

92. Paula Souza, "John Deere," 66–67.

93. Paula Souza, "John Deere," 68–70.

94. Antonio Francisco de Paula Souza, "Anotações de Viagem aos Estados Unidos," 1869, Arquivo Paula Souza, PS 1869, BMA.

95. Paula Souza, "Anotações de Viagem aos Estados Unidos."

96. Cronon, *Nature's Metropolis*, 212.

97. Antonio Francisco de Paula Souza, "Esboço Rápido de Algumas de Nossas Industrias Comparadas às dos Estados Unidos," in *Almanach Litterario Paulista para 1876* (São Paulo: Typ. da Província de São Paulo, 1875), 55.

98. Paula Souza, "Esboço Rápido de Algumas de Nossas Industrias Comparadas às dos Estados Unidos," 51, 56.

99. On the life, ideas, and career of André Pinto Rebouças, see Maria Alice Rezende de Carvalho, *O Quinto Século: André Rebouças e a Construção do Brasil* (Rio de Janeiro: Revan, 1998); Alexandro Dantas Trindade, *André Rebouças: Um Engenheiro do Império* (São Paulo: Hucitec, 2011).

100. André Pinto Rebouças, May 23, 1873, in *Diário e Notas Autobiográficas: Textos Escolhidos e Anotações por Ana Flora e José Veríssimo* (Rio de Janeiro: J. Olympio, 1938), 245.

101. Rebouças, June 9, 1873, in *Diário e Notas Autobiográficas*, 245.

102. Rebouças, June 9, 1873, in *Diário e Notas Autobiográficas*, 245–246.

103. Rebouças, June 11, 1873, in *Diário e Notas Autobiográficas*, 247.

104. Rebouças, June 10, 1873, in *Diário e Notas Autobiográficas*, 246.

105. André Pinto Rebouças, "Viagem aos Estados Unidos em junho de 1873," Arquivo Joaquim Nabuco, PI, Pasta 3, Documento 7, FJN.

106. Rebouças, June 11, 1873, in *Diário e Notas Autobiográficas*, 247.

107. Rebouças, "Viagem aos Estados Unidos em junho de 1873."

108. Rebouças, June 12, 1873, in *Diário e Notas Autobiográficas*, 247–248.

109. Rebouças, "Viagem aos Estados Unidos em junho de 1873."

110. Rebouças, June 12, 1873, in *Diário e Notas Autobiográficas*, 247–248.

111. Rebouças, June 13, 1873, in *Diário e Notas Autobiográficas*, 248–249.

112. Rebouças, "Viagem aos Estados Unidos em junho de 1873."

113. Rebouças, "Viagem aos Estados Unidos em junho de 1873."

114. Rebouças, June 13, 1873, in *Diário e Notas Autobiográficas*, 248.

115. Rebouças, "Viagem aos Estados Unidos em junho de 1873."

116. Rebouças, June 15–June 16, 1873, in *Diário e Notas Autobiográficas*, 250.

117. Rebouças, "Viagem aos Estados Unidos em junho de 1873."

118. Rebouças, "Viagem aos Estados Unidos em junho de 1873."

119. Rebouças, June 18, 1873, in *Diário e Notas Autobiográficas*, 253.

120. Rebouças, June 16, 1873, in *Diário e Notas Autobiográficas*, 251.

121. On the emergence of the petroleum industry in Pennsylvania, see Brian Black, *Petrolia: The Landscape of America's First Oil Boom* (Baltimore: Johns Hopkins University Press, 2000).

122. Rebouças, June 19, 1873, in *Diário e Notas Autobiográficas*, 254.

123. Rebouças, "Viagem aos Estados Unidos em junho de 1873."

124. Rebouças, June 21, 1873, in *Diário e Notas Autobiográficas*, 255.

125. "Self-help" is in English in the original.

126. André Pinto Rebouças, *Garantia de Juros: Estudos para a sua Applicação às Emprezas de Utilidade Pública do Brazil* (Rio de Janeiro: Typographia Nacional, 1874), 18, 146–148.

127. Rebouças, *Garantia de Juros*, 245.

128. Seymour Drescher makes a compelling argument when he concludes that "the global achievements of antislavery a century ago left two indelible legacies. In the course of a century and a half (1770s–1920s), it destroyed or sharply restricted an institution, which had devastated and abbreviated the lives of tens of millions of human beings in two hemispheres. By the mid-twentieth century, it succeeded in reasserting slavery's position at the top of the list of practices condemned in the Universal Declaration of Human Rights. For more than sixty years, reviving slavery has remained beyond the bounds of any contemporary movement's dream or any states' ambition." *Abolition*, 461–462. Historians seeking to explain why slavery did not reemerge in the modern world, however, need to analyze the labor system that replaced it. The entrenchment of a more efficient system of exploitation—wage labor—was a decisive factor in the virtual extinction of slave labor in the western hemisphere.

129. *Thayer Expedition: Scientific Results of a Journey in Brazil by Louis Agassiz and His Travelling Companions; Geology and Physical Geography of Brazil by Ch. Fred. Hartt* (Boston: Fields, Osgood, 1870).

130. For an intellectual biography of Charles Frederick Hartt, see Marcus Vinicius de Freitas, *Charles Frederick Hartt: Um Naturalista no Império de Pedro II* (Belo Horizonte: Editora UFMG, 2002).

131. "Geologia do Brazil," *O Novo Mundo*, October 24, 1870.

132. Charles Frederick Hartt to José Carlos Rodrigues, on board of the steamer *Pará*, Tapajós River, September 17, 1871, in *Anais da Biblioteca Nacional 9*, 138.

133. On technical education in nineteenth-century Brazil, see José Murilo de Carvalho, *A Escola de Minas de Ouro Preto: O Peso da Glória* (Rio de Janeiro: Finep, 1978).

134. According to Nathan Sorber, "Through the advancement, dissemination, and application of useful knowledge, the land-grant colleges contributed new ideas, technologies, and technical specialists that supported emerging industries (including scientific agriculture) premised on mechanization and scientific principles." *Land-Grant Colleges and Popular Revolt: The Origins of the Morrill Act and the Reform of Higher Education* (Ithaca, NY: Cornell University

Press, 2018), 5. Paul Nienkamp makes a similar point: "During the second half of the nineteenth century, educators across America embraced and fostered a national character and identity intricately tied to Morrill Land-Grant Colleges Act. College administrators and professors recognized a dire need for technically skilled individuals who could adapt quickly to changes in equipment and processes and implement advances in scientific knowledge in American homes, fields, and factories. They wanted highly trained students to become leaders, managers, and field experts." "Engineering National Character: Early Land-Grant College Science and the Quest for an American Identity," in *Science as Service: Establishing and Reformulating Land-Grant Universities, 1865–1930*, ed. Alan I. Marcus (Tuscaloosa: University of Alabama Press, 2015), 115–116.

135. "A Universidade de Cornell," *O Novo Mundo*, June 24, 1871.

136. *The Cornell University: What It Is and What It Is Not* (Ithaca, NY: University Press, 1872), 23.

137. *A Exposição de Obras Publicas em 1875* (Rio de Janeiro: Publição Official, 1876), 460. On the surveys of the American West, see Richard A. Bartlett, *Great Surveys of the American West* (Norman: University of Oklahoma Press, 1980).

138. "Universidade de Cornell."

139. Charles Frederick Hartt to José Carlos Rodrigues, Ithaca, June 18, 1870, in *Anais da Biblioteca Nacional 9*, 138.

140. T. A. Castro, "Impressões de Viagem do Rio de Janeiro a Ithaca," *Aurora Brasileira*, May 20, 1874.

141. Andrew J. Kirkendall argues that, when compared with the more prestigious law degree, engineering "received little acclaim in imperial Brazil's agrarian society. Few plantation owners would have welcomed a son's choice of engineering as a profession." *Class Mates*, 5. This was certainly not the case of the fazendeiros of the Oeste Paulista in the 1870s.

142. Whitaker, "Progresso de S. Paulo."

143. On the intellectual tenets of the *Aurora Brasileira*, see Marcus Vinicius de Freitas, *Contradições da Modernidade: O Jornal Aurora Brasileira (1873–1875)* (Campinas: Editora Unicamp, 2011).

144. "O Novo Mundo," *Aurora Brasileira*, January 20, 1874.

145. "Propagadora da Instrução," *Aurora Brasileira*, April 20, 1874.

146. F. A. Vieira Bueno, "Necessidade de uma Academia de Agricultura no Brazil I," *Aurora Brasileira*, January 20, 1875.

147. Willard Fiske to the Rev. Edmund Burke Wilson, Library of Cornell University, Ithaca, February 15, 1871, American Slavery Collection, no. 194249, AAS.

148. F. A. Vieira Bueno, "Necessidade de uma Academia de Agricultura no Brazil II," *Aurora Brasileira*, February 20, 1875.

149. "Aurora Brasileira," *Aurora Brasileira*, October 22, 1873.

150. T. A. Castro, "Impressões de Viagem do Rio de Janeiro a Ithaca," *Aurora Brasileira*, June 20, 1874.

151. In the Old Testament (Daniel 5:25), the words "mene, mene, tekel, upharsin" appear on the wall during Belshazzar's feast, and Daniel interprets them as God dooming the kingdom of Belshazzar. "Educação no Exterior," *O Novo Mundo*, January 23, 1874.

152. "A Universidade de Lehigh, em Bethlehem, Estado da Pennsylvania," *Aurora Brasileira*, November 20, 1873.

153. "O Lafayette College," *O Novo Mundo*, October 23, 1874; J. P. D. Carneiro, "O Lafayette College," *Aurora Brasileira*, November 20, 1874.

154. "Aurora Brazileira," *Aurora Brazileira*, March 1877.

155. "Aurora Brazileira," *Aurora Brazileira*, December 1875.

156. "Verdadeira Economia," *Aurora Brazileira*, October 1877.

157. "Advertise in the Aurora Brazileira," *Aurora Brazileira*, May 1877–January 1878.

158. "Bombas para Uso Domestico," *Aurora Brazileira*, December 1875.

159. "Aurora Brazileira," *Aurora Brazileira*, December 1875.

160. "O Segador de Bradley," *Aurora Brazileira*, January 1876.

161. "Museus de Machinas em Movimento," *Aurora Brazileira*, June 1877.

162. "Nossa Resposta," *Aurora Brazileira*, May 1876.

163. "Machina a Vapor para Lavradores," *Aurora Brazileira*, August 1877.

164. "Influencia da Machina sobre o Trabalho," *Aurora Brazileira*, December 1875.

165. "Porque É que S. Paulo Progride," *Aurora Brazileira*, May 1877.

166. "Locomotivas e Machinas a Vapor Para o Brazil," *Aurora Brazileira*, December 1877.

167. "Em Geral," *Aurora Brazileira*, April 1876.

168. Focusing on a declining sector of the Brazilian elite, the coffee planters of the Paraíba Valley, historians have argued that Brazil had a "second," industrial form of slavery. See, for example, Mariana Muaze and Ricardo Salles, eds., *O Vale do Paraíba e o Império do Brasil nos Quadros da Segunda Escravidão* (Rio de Janeiro: Faperj, 2015); Rafael de Bivar Marquese and Ricardo Salles, eds., *Escravidão e Capitalismo Histórico no Século XIX: Cuba, Brasil, Estados Unidos* (Rio de Janeiro: Civilização Brasileira, 2016); Rafael de Bivar Marquese and Ricardo Salles, "Slavery in Nineteenth-Century Brazil: History and Historiography," in *Slavery and Historical Capitalism during the Nineteenth Century*, ed. Dale Tomich (Lanham, MD: Lexington Books, 2017), 123–169. Brazilians who had access to the newest technology of the time—the sons of the most powerful slaveholders in the country—would not go down the uncertain path of maintaining and expanding slavery. In the end, the vision formed in the Oeste Paulista and expanded in American universities prevailed, while the Paraíba Valley sank into backwardness.

169. James O'Kelly, "Dom Pedro II," *New York Herald*, April 17, 1876.

170. "Dom Pedro II, of Brazil," *Phrenological Journal and Science of Health*, July 1876. On the history of phrenology in the Anglo-American context, see James Poskett, *Materials of the Mind: Phrenology, Race, and the Global History of Science, 1815–1920* (Chicago: University of Chicago Press, 2019). Phrenology was also popular among Brazilian scientists during the second half of the nineteenth century. See Lilia Moritz Schwarcz, *The Spectacle of the Races: Scientists, Institutions, and the Race Question in Brazil, 1870–1930* (New York: Hill & Wang, 1999).

171. "Our Imperial Guest," *New York Herald*, April 16, 1876.

172. "Our Yankee Emperor," *New York Herald*, April 21, 1876.

173. "Our Imperial Guest," *New York Evangelist*, April 20, 1876.

174. S. R., "Freedom in Brazil," *Friends' Intelligencer*, May 13, 1876.

175. On the Northern retreat from Reconstruction, see Foner, *Reconstruction*, 524–534.

176. According to Robert W. Rydell, "Rather than merely offering an escape from the economic and political uncertainties of the Reconstruction years, the [Centennial Exhibition] was a calculated response to these conditions. Its organizers sought to challenge doubts and restore confidence in the vitality of America's system of government as well as in the social and

economic structure of the country." *All the World's a Fair: Visions of Empire at American International Expositions, 1876–1916* (Chicago: University of Chicago Press, 1999), 11. The presence of Dom Pedro II was part of this effort.

177. *Frank Leslie's Illustrated Historical Register of the Centennial Exposition* (New York: Frank Leslie Publisher, 1876), 112.

178. *Catalogue of the Brazilian Section, Philadelphia International Exhibition, 1876* (Philadelphia: Hallowell, 1876).

179. "The Century—Its Fruits and Its Festivals," *Lippincott's Monthly Magazine*, January 1876.

180. "A Comissão Brazileira," *O Novo Mundo*, May 27, 1876. On Rodrigues's coverage of the Centennial Exhibition, see Krista Brune, "Retranslating the Brazilian Imperial Project: *O Novo Mundo*'s Depictions of the 1876 Centennial Exhibition," *Journal of Lusophone Studies* 3, no. 2 (Fall 2018): 1–23.

181. Nicolau Joaquim Moreira, *Brazilian Coffee* (New York: O Novo Mundo Printing Office, 1876).

182. *Catalogue of the Brazilian Section*, 78–82.

183. Palácio do Governo da Província de São Paulo, November 16, 1874, Secretaria da Agricultura, Caixa 5652, Livro E00942, AESP.

184. Palácio do Governo da Província de São Paulo, October 28, 1874 and January 7, 1875, Secretaria da Agricultura, Caixa 5652, Livro E00942, AESP.

185. Felippe Lopes Netto to Alfred T. Goshorn, April 2, 1876, United States Centennial Commission, RG 230, Box A-1525, DRPHI.

186. Moreira, *Brazilian Coffee*.

187. "Lista dos Premiados Brazileiros na Exposição da Philadelphia," *O Novo Mundo*, September 1876; "O Café do Brazil," *O Novo Mundo*, September 1876.

188. *Diário do Imperador D. Pedro II, Volume 17*, April 29, 1876 (Petrópolis: Museu Imperial, 1999), CD-ROM.

189. James O'Kelly, "Dom Pedro's Tour," *New York Herald*, May 11, 1876.

190. Francisco de Assis Vieira Bueno, "Carta de um Engenheiro Brazileiro," *Aurora Brazileira*, March 1877.

191. According to Steven Hahn, "The driving forces of western development were the railroads. . . . They drove the expansion of mining and lumbering, not least because they became prodigious consumers of wood (for tracks, rolling stock, and fuel) and then coal (replacing wood to fire the engines). They would be of immense benefit to the emerging iron and steel industries as well." *A Nation without Borders: The United States and Its World in an Age of Civil Wars, 1830–1910* (New York: Viking, 2016), 242.

192. James O'Kelly, "Pedro Segundo," *New York Herald*, April 20, 1876.

193. P. D. G. Paes Leme, "Um Brazileiro no Oeste Americano," *O Novo Mundo*, January 1877. On how Chicago's slaughterhouses became a touristic attraction, see Dominic A. Pacyga, *Slaughterhouse: Chicago's Union Stock Yard and the World It Made* (Chicago: University of Chicago Press, 2015).

194. Francisco de Assis Vieira Bueno, "Carta de um Engenheiro Brazileiro (Continuação)," *Aurora Brazileira*, April 1877.

195. James O'Kelly, "Dom Pedro," *New York Herald*, April 21, 1876.

196. James O'Kelly, "An Emperor Abroad," *New York Herald*, April 22, 1876.

197. *Diário do Imperador D. Pedro II, Volume 17,* April 29–May 6, 1876.

198. James O'Kelly, "Dom Pedro," *New York Herald,* May 8, 1876.

199. Vieira Bueno, "Carta de um Engenheiro Brazileiro."

200. "Dous Commisarios Brazileiros em Syracusa," *Aurora Brazileira,* May 1877.

201. Vieira Bueno, "Carta de um Engenheiro Brazileiro (Continuação)."

202. Paes Leme, "Brazileiro no Oeste Americano."

203. Paes Leme, "Brazileiro no Oeste Americano."

204. Vieira Bueno, "Carta de um Engenheiro Brazileiro (Continuação)."

205. Donald J. Pisani explains that "the decline of the mining industry, the adoption of no-fence laws, and the expansion of rail transportation into the San Joaquin Valley and southern California contributed to a dramatic increase in irrigation during the 1870s. Irrigated land nearly tripled during the decade, even as the state suffered through its first protracted economic depression. The transition from a frontier economy characterized by individual entrepreneurs and loose confederations of investors, to an economic system dominated by large corporations, accelerated during the 'terrible seventies.' . . . Proponents of corporate water development pointed to the irrigation colonies adjoining Fresno as proof of how private enterprise had encouraged diversified, small farms; but critics maintained that farmers could never be independent and self-sufficient when they depended on greedy capitalists for their water." *From the Family Farm to Agribusiness: The Irrigation Crusade in California and the West, 1850–1931* (Berkeley: University of California Press, 1984), 103.

206. Paes Leme, "Brazileiro no Oeste Americano."

207. P. D. G. Paes Leme, "Agricultura Americana em 1876," *O Auxiliador da Industria Nacional, Volume XLVI,* 1878.

208. P. D. G. Paes Leme, "Machinas Agricolas na Exposição da Philadelphia," *O Novo Mundo,* September 1876.

209. Nicolau Joaquim Moreira, *Relatório sobre a Immigração nos Estados-Unidos da America Apresentado ao Ex. Sr. Ministro da Agricultura, Commercio e Obras Publicas* (Rio de Janeiro: Typographia Nacional, 1877), 23–24.

210. According to Richard Slotkin, "The Myth of the Frontier is the American version of the larger myth-ideological system generated by the social conflicts that attended the 'modernization' of the Western nations, the emergence of capitalist economies and nation-states. The major cultural tasks of this ideology were to rationalize and justify the departures from tradition that necessarily accompanied these developments. Progress itself was to be asserted as a positive good against the aristocratic and peasant traditions that emphasized stasis and permanence in productive techniques and social relations." *The Fatal Environment: The Myth of the Frontier in the Age of Industrialization: 1800–1890* (Norman: University of Oklahoma Press, 1998), 33. Because nineteenth-century Brazil, like the United States, had vast interior territories occupied by subsistence agriculture and unproductive latifundia, the American version of the development myth was easily adaptable to the Brazilian modernizers' projects.

211. Paes Leme, "Agricultura Americana em 1876."

212. Moreira, *Relatório sobre a Immigração nos Estados-Unidos da America,* 71.

213. James D. McCabe, *The Illustrated History of the Centennial Exhibition* (Philadelphia: National, 1876), 431; "Carro de Estado Brazileiro," *Aurora Brazileira,* May 1876; *Diário do Imperador D. Pedro II, Volume 17,* June 27, 1876.

214. "Agricultural Department of the Exhibition," *New York Observer and Chronicle*, November 23, 1876.

215. Paes Leme, "Machinas Agricolas na Exposição da Philadelphia."

216. *Diário do Imperador D. Pedro II, Volume 17*, May 31, 1876.

217. *Diário do Imperador D. Pedro II, Volume 17*, May 24, 1876.

218. *Diário do Imperador D. Pedro II, Volume 17*, May 20, 1876.

219. James O'Kelly, "The Brazilian Emperor," *New York Herald*, May 26, 1876.

220. *Diário do Imperador D. Pedro II, Volume 17*, May 26, 1876.

221. Paes Leme, "Agricultura Americana em 1876."

222. *Diário do Imperador D. Pedro II, Volume 17*, May 27, 1876.

223. Vieira Bueno, "Carta de um Engenheiro Brazileiro (Continuação)."

224. David Brion Davis presents a nuanced analysis when he writes that "the issue of legacies is complex. Despite the dismal failure of American Reconstruction, the succeeding century of Jim Crow discrimination, and the legacy of racism even in the Caribbean and South America, Anglo-American emancipation had a profound influence on the freeing of slaves in the French, Dutch, and Danish colonies, and especially in Cuba and Brazil. We should also note that in the twentieth century the legacy of new emancipation extended, thanks in part to the League of Nations and the United Nations, to the outlawing of chattel slavery throughout the world." *Problem of Slavery in the Age of Emancipation*, 335–336. Like other historians, however, Davis does not examine how the labor system that replaced slavery in the United States contributed to its demise in the western hemisphere.

225. *Diário do Imperador D. Pedro II, Volume 17*, June 10–June 15, 1876.

226. *New York Herald*, July 13, 1876.

Chapter 6

1. "Emancipation in Brazil," *Boston Daily Advertiser*, May 17, 1888.

2. David Montgomery, *The Fall of the House of Labor: The Workplace, the State, and American Labor Activism, 1865–1925* (Cambridge: Cambridge University Press, 1987), 9–213; Nancy L. Cohen, *The Reconstruction of American Liberalism, 1865–1914* (Chapel Hill: University of North Carolina Press, 2002), 86–109; Sven Beckert, *The Monied Metropolis: New York City and the Consolidation of the Bourgeoisie, 1850–1900* (New York: Cambridge University Press, 2001), 205–322.

3. Steven Hahn, *The Roots of Southern Populism: Yeoman Farmers and the Transformation of the Georgia Upcountry, 1850–1890* (New York: Oxford University Press, 1983), 137–268; Jeffrey Ostler, *Prairie Populism: The Fate of Agrarian Radicalism in Kansas, Nebraska, and Iowa, 1880–1892* (Lawrence: University Press of Kansas, 1993), 12–90.

4. Leon Fink, *Workingmen's Democracy: The Knights of Labor and American Politics* (Urbana: University of Illinois Press, 1985); Roy Rosenzweig, *Eight Hours for What We Will: Workers and Leisure in an Industrial City, 1870–1920* (Cambridge: Cambridge University Press, 1983), 9–168; James R. Green, *Death in the Haymarket: The Story of Chicago, the First Labor Movement, and the Bombing That Divided Gilded Age America* (New York: Pantheon, 2006).

5. Robert Edgar Conrad, *The Destruction of Brazilian Slavery, 1850–1888* (Berkeley: University of California Press, 1972), 121–182; Celso Thomas Castilho, *Slave Emancipation and Transformations in Brazilian Political Citizenship* (Pittsburgh: University of Pittsburgh Press, 2016), 105–191.

6. Angela Alonso, *Flores, Votos e Balas: O Movimento Abolicionista Brasileiro, 1868–1888* (São Paulo: Companhia das Letras, 2015), 186–329.

7. Emília Viotti da Costa, *Da Senzala à Colônia* (São Paulo: Editora Unesp, 1998 [1966]), 489–517; Paula Beiguelman, *A Formação do Povo no Complexo Cafeeiro: Aspectos Políticos* (São Paulo: Edusp, 2005 [1968]), 95–134.

8. Eric Williams, *Capitalism and Slavery* (Chapel Hill: University of North Carolina Press, 1944); Manuel Moreno Fraginals, *El Ingenio: Complejo Económico Social Cubano del Azúcar* (Havana: Comisión Nacional Cubana de la Unesco, 1964); Costa, *Da Senzala à Colônia*; Eric Foner, *Free Soil, Free Labor, Free Men: The Ideology of the Republican Party before the Civil War* (New York: Oxford University Press, 1970); Florestan Fernandes, *A Revolução Burguesa no Brasil: Ensaio de Interpretação Sociológica* (Rio de Janeiro: Zahar Editores, 1974); David Brion Davis, *The Problem of Slavery in the Age of Revolution: 1770–1823* (Ithaca, NY: Cornell University Press, 1975); Warren Dean, *Rio Claro: A Brazilian Plantation System, 1820–1920* (Stanford, CA: Stanford University Press, 1976); Eric Foner, *Nothing but Freedom: Emancipation and Its Legacy* (Baton Rouge: Louisiana State University Press, 1982); Hahn, *Roots of Southern Populism*; Steven Hahn, "Class and State in Postemancipation Societies: Southern Planters in Comparative Perspective," *American Historical Review* 95, no. 1 (February 1990): 75–98; Thomas C. Holt, *The Problem of Freedom: Race, Labor, and Politics in Jamaica and Britain, 1832–1938* (Baltimore: Johns Hopkins University Press, 1992); Julie Saville, *The Work of Reconstruction: From Slave to Wage Laborer in South Carolina, 1860–1870* (New York: Cambridge University Press, 1994); Rebecca J. Scott, *Degrees of Freedom: Louisiana and Cuba after Slavery* (Cambridge, MA: Harvard University Press, 2005); Sven Beckert, *Empire of Cotton: A Global History* (New York: Knopf, 2014).

9. For Hilliard's biography, see David I. Durham, *A Southern Moderate in Radical Times: Henry Washington Hilliard, 1808–1892* (Baton Rouge: Louisiana State University Press, 2008).

10. The novel came out in 1865 with the title *De Vane: Story of Plebeians and Patricians*. According to David I. Durham, it was "a defense of Methodism presented through the story of a Virginia patrician who associates with Methodist plebeians in the Alabama backcountry and eventually is converted." *Southern Moderate in Radical Times*, 148.

11. Eric Foner further notes that "many scalawags possessed considerable political experience; their ranks included prewar Congressmen, judges, and local officials. Most such man were former Whigs who viewed the Republican party as the 'legitimate successor' to Whiggery." *Reconstruction: America's Unfinished Revolution, 1863–1877* (New York: Harper & Row, 1988), 297–298.

12. Henry Washington Hilliard, *Politics and Pen Pictures at Home and Abroad* (New York: G.P. Putnam's Sons, 1892), 358.

13. Durham, *Southern Moderate in Radical Times*, 179.

14. Henry Washington Hilliard to William Evarts, Rio de Janeiro, December 31, 1877, in *Papers Relating to the Foreign Relations of the United States Transmitted to Congress, with the Annual Message of the President, December 2, 1878* (Washington: Government Printing Office, 1878), 63.

15. Henry Washington Hilliard to William Evarts, Rio de Janeiro, January 16, 1878, in *Papers Relating to the Foreign Relations of the United States, 1878*, 64.

16. Henry Washington Hilliard to William Evarts, Rio de Janeiro, November 4, 1878, in *Papers Relating to the Foreign Relations of the United States Transmitted to Congress, with the Annual Message of the President, December 1, 1879* (Washington: Government Printing Office, 1879), 130.

17. Hilliard, *Politics and Pen Pictures*, 381.

18. While some scholars see in this act the opening of the abolitionist movement in Brazil, Celso Thomas Castilho argues that Nabuco "entered electoral politics with a recognizable abolitionist mobilization in place in [his hometown of] Recife. It was a mobilization that he had helped energize almost a decade prior. . . . Certainly the beginning of his legislative career adds a very significant dimension to Brazilian abolitionism, but it did not instigate the movement." *Slave Emancipation*, 80.

19. Joaquim Nabuco to Henry Washington Hilliard, Rio de Janeiro, October 19, 1880, in *Cartas do Presidente Joaquim Nabuco e do Ministro Americano H. W. Hilliard sobre a Emancipação nos Estados-Unidos* (Rio de Janeiro: G. Leuzinger & Filho, 1880). For the English translation, see Hilliard, *Politics and Pen Pictures*, 412–414.

20. Alonso, *Flores, Votos e Balas*, 91–101.

21. Joaquim Nabuco to Henry Washington Hilliard, Rio de Janeiro, October 19, 1880.

22. Nicolau Joaquim Moreira, "Discurso Manifesto," in *Associação Central Emancipadora, Boletim N. 1* (Rio de Janeiro: Typ. Primeiro de Janeiro, 1880).

23. Moreira, "Discurso Manifesto."

24. Henry Washington Hilliard to Joaquim Nabuco, Rio de Janeiro, October 25, 1880, in *Cartas do Presidente Joaquim Nabuco e do Ministro Americano H. W. Hilliard.* For the English translation, see Hilliard, *Politics and Pen Pictures*, 414–426.

25. Sven Beckert adds that "by 1877 they had regained their prewar market share in Great Britain. By 1880 they exported more cotton than they had in 1860. And by 1891 sharecroppers, family farmers, and plantation owners in the United States grew twice as much cotton as in 1861 and supplied 81 percent of the British, 66 percent of the French, and 61 percent of the German market." *Empire of Cotton*, 291–292.

26. Henry Washington Hilliard to Joaquim Nabuco, Rio de Janeiro, October 25, 1880.

27. "A. J. Lamoureux Dead; Funeral This Afternoon," *Cornell Daily Sun*, February 27, 1928.

28. "Brazilian Agriculture," *Rio News*, July 5, 1879.

29. André Pinto Rebouças, *Agricultura Nacional: Estudos Economicos. Propaganda Abolicionista e Democrática, Setembro de 1874 a Setembro de 1883* (Rio de Janeiro: A. J. Lamoureux, 1883).

30. *Rio News*, November 15, 1880.

31. "Carpetbaggers" is in English in the original.

32. Pedro Dias Gordilho Paes Leme, "A S. Ex. o Muito Honrado Sr. Henry Washington Hilliard, Enviado Extraordinário e Ministro Plenipotenciário da União Americana, junto ao Governo do Brasil," *Jornal do Commercio*, November 5, 1880.

33. *Banquete Offerecido ao Exm. Sr. Ministro Americano Henry Washington Hilliard a 20 de Novembro de 1880* (Rio de Janeiro: Typ. Primeiro de Janeiro, 1880).

34. "Sessão Extraordinaria em 22 de Novembro de 1880," in *Annaes do Parlamento Brazileiro, Camara dos Deputados, Terceiro Anno da Decima-Setima Legislatura, Sessão de 1880, Tomo V, Prorrogação* (Rio de Janeiro: Typ. Nacional, 1880), 308–318.

35. *Rio News*, December 5, 1880.

36. "The Emancipation Question," *Rio News*, December 15, 1880.

37. P. D. G. Paes Leme, "Um Brazileiro no Oeste Americano," *O Novo Mundo*, January 1877.

38. Nicolau Joaquim Moreira, "Discurso," in *Associação Central Emancipadora, Boletim N. 4* (Rio de Janeiro: Typ. Primeiro de Janeiro, 1880).

39. "Emancipation in Brazil," *New York Times*, December 20, 1880.

40. *North American*, December 25, 1880.

41. *Georgia Weekly Telegraph*, February 25, 1881.

42. *Rio News*, March 24, 1881.

43. *Rio News*, March 24, 1881.

44. Examining the postemancipation South, Edward L. Ayers points out that "people of both races hoped that emancipation had given the South a fresh start, a chance to catch up with the rest of the nation while avoiding the mistakes of the North." *The Promise of the New South: Life after Reconstruction* (New York: Oxford University Press, 2007), viii.

45. Herbert Huntington Smith, *Brazil: The Amazons and the Coast* (New York: C. Scribner's Sons, 1879).

46. Smith, *Brazil*, 517, 526, 520–522.

47. Smith, *Brazil*, 470, 529, 535–536, 539.

48. Smith, *Brazil*, 466–467.

49. "Coffee: Quality, Modes of Preparation, &c. Number 3," *Spice Mill*, October 1880.

50. W. H. Ukers, *All about Coffee* (New York: Tea and Coffee Trade Journal Company, 1922), 634–637.

51. "Coffee: Quality, Modes of Preparation, &c. Number 5," *Spice Mill*, December 1880.

52. Steven Topik, "The Integration of the World Coffee Market," in *The Global Coffee Economy in Africa, Asia and Latin America: 1500–1989*, ed. William Gervase Clarence-Smith and Steven Topik (Cambridge: Cambridge University Press, 2003), 37.

53. Michael F. Jimenez highlights additional connections between industrialization and the coffee business in the United States: "The restructuring of industrial capitalism in this period spurred coffee consumption. A new phase of manufacturing with novel energy and production technologies led to an increasing homogenization of the working class as factory hands were deskilled and leveled. The resulting cultural unity and coherence of a large portion of the United States population served as the core of a national market enlarged and consolidated by two additional factors: first, a rise in discretionary incomes as a result of dramatic increases in agricultural productivity in the trans-Mississippi granary from the 1870s which reduced foodstuff prices, and, second, the greater, more efficient carrying capacity of the national and world-wide transportation system which substantially diminished transfer costs within the United States and globally, thereby affecting the demand for products such as coffee from abroad." "'From Plantation to Cup': Coffee and Capitalism in the United States, 1830–1930," in *Coffee, Society, and Power in Latin America*, ed. William Roseberry, Lowell Gudmundson, and Mario Samper (Baltimore: Johns Hopkins University Press, 1995), 40–41.

54. Francis Beatty Thurber, *Coffee: From Plantation to Cup. A Brief History of Coffee Production and Consumption* (New York: American Grocer Pub. Association, 1881), 22.

55. Ukers, *All about Coffee*, 521–526.

56. Ukers, *All about Coffee*, 521–526.

57. John Roach, *The American Carrying Trade: An Address to Our Public Men and People Who Desire the Revival of Our Ocean Carrying Trade, and the Steady Development of the Resources and Industries of the United States; and Who Recognize the Need of Opening Up New Markets to Keep Pace with the Nation's Growth* (New York: H. B. Grose, 1881), 70.

58. Leonard Alexander Swann, *John Roach Maritime Entrepreneur: The Years as Naval Contractor, 1862–1886* (Annapolis, MD: US Naval Institute, 1966), 103–113.

59. "Nova Linha de Paquetes," *O Novo Mundo*, September 1877.

60. Henry Washington Hilliard to William Evarts, Rio de Janeiro, November 6, 1877, in *Papers Relating to the Foreign Relations of the United States, 1878*, 61.

61. Henry Washington Hilliard to William Evarts, Rio de Janeiro, June 7, 1878, in *Papers Relating to the Foreign Relations of the United States, 1878*, 67–70.

62. Swann, *John Roach Maritime Entrepreneur*, 99–102.

63. Smith, *Brazil*, 503–505.

64. Swann, *John Roach Maritime Entrepreneur*, 114–124.

65. "A New Line to Brazil," *New York Daily Tribune*, June 1, 1882.

66. Robert Hewitt, *Coffee: Its History, Cultivation, and Uses* (New York: D. Appleton, 1872), 10.

67. "Coffee on Wheels," *Harper's Weekly*, November 20, 1880. On the history of the temperance movement in the United States, see John J. Rumbarger, *Profits, Power, and Prohibition: Alcohol Reform and the Industrializing of America, 1800–1930* (Albany: SUNY Press, 1989); Carol Mattingly, *Well-Tempered Women: Nineteenth-Century Temperance Rhetoric* (Carbondale: Southern Illinois University Press, 1998).

68. "Use of Alcohol and Coffee in Brazil," *Spice Mill*, November 1883.

69. According to John J. Rumbarger, not all temperance advocates shared this conservative approach. Many contended that alcoholism was caused by poor working and living conditions, not vice versa. Yet as industrialization advanced and corporate capitalists embraced the cause of temperance, it became another tool for labor exploitation. For elite temperance advocates, "intemperance was dysfunctional in at least two respects. First, there was its obvious connection with industrial inefficiency. Second, and perhaps more important, was its connection to social instability. . . . Temperance advocates believed that American workers' own profligacy—manifested by drinking—dissipated their high wages, and thus left them with no reserves to set against downturns in the business cycle. In turn 'necessary' reductions in wages triggered in such workers discontent, which in turn let to strikes for higher wages. As this line of argument went, abstemious temperance, as an instance of frugality, would prepare workers for recessions, thereby eliminating the need to strike." *Profits, Power, and Prohibition*, 66–67.

70. "Capital and Labor," *Spice Mill*, July 1882.

71. Thurber, *Coffee*, 172.

72. Hewitt, *Coffee*, 44.

73. Hewitt, *Coffee*, 84.

74. Jackson Lears notes that, due to the pressures of the Gilded Age, many Americans came to fantasize about self-transformation, which often "took an inner alchemical change, a regeneration." "The language of rebirth," Lears adds, "had begun to refocus from soul to body." Pauperism was often linked to disease, femininity, and lack of energy; wealth to health, masculinity, and power. *Rebirth of a Nation: The Making of Modern America, 1877–1920* (New York: Harper Perennial, 2010), 36–37. Coffee consumption was part of this search for bodily regeneration.

75. William H. Daniels, *The Temperance Reform and Its Great Reformers: An Illustrated History* (New York: Nelson & Phillips, 1878), 556.

76. Rebouças, *Agricultura Nacional*, 38, 43, 25.

77. Rebouças, *Agricultura Nacional*, 76.

78. Hewitt, *Coffee*, 60.

79. Thurber, *Coffee*, 121–122.

80. Smith, *Brazil*, 469, 540.

81. "A Progressive Empire," *Spice Mill*, October 1885.

82. "Santos Coffee," *Spice Mill*, May 1884.

83. M. Mulhal, "The Highlands of São Paulo," *Littell's Living Age*, February 19, 1887. On how coffee fostered the growth of São Paulo City, see Warren Dean, *The Industrialization of São Paulo, 1880–1945* (Austin: University of Texas Press, 1969).

84. Dean, *Rio Claro*, 44.

85. According to Anne G. Hanley, "From 1880 on, banks, brokers, and two separate stock and bond exchanges arose to create complementary institutions that first helped improve the conditions under which the economy operated (liquidity) and then helped raise finance capital for the sorts of large-scale domestic enterprises that built São Paulo's industrial base (investment). Stimulated by economic expansion on the one hand and regulatory legislation on the other, these increasingly formal institutions channeled the seemingly limitless wealth generated by the robust coffee economy into local business and development projects. These businesses and projects would lay the groundwork for explosive regional development." *Native Capital: Financial Institutions and Economic Development in São Paulo, Brazil, 1850–1920* (Stanford, CA: Stanford University Press, 2005), 20.

86. *Almanach da Provincia de São Paulo Administrativo, Commercial e Industrial para 1888* (São Paulo: Jorge Seckler, 1888), 199–286. On quotidian life in the city by the late nineteenth century, see Fraya Frehse, *O Tempo das Ruas na São Paulo de Fins do Império* (São Paulo: Edusp, 2005).

87. Christopher Columbus Andrews, *Brazil, Its Conditions and Prospects* (New York: D. Appleton, 1887), 137.

88. Andrews, *Brazil*, 146–147.

89. Andrews, *Brazil*, 147–148.

90. On port improvements in nineteenth-century Brazil, see Cezar T. Honorato, "O Estado Imperial e a Modernização Portuária," in *História Econômica da Independência e do Império*, ed. Tamás Szmrecsányi and José Roberto do Amaral Lapa (São Paulo: Hucitec/Edusp, 2002), 161–176.

91. William Milnor Roberts, "Port of Santos Report, 1879," William Milnor Roberts Papers, Box 6, Folder 26, MGB-MSU.

92. Roberts, "Port of Santos Report."

93. *Rio News*, March 15, 1881.

94. Roberts, "Port of Santos Report."

95. Flávio Azevedo Marques de Saes, *As Ferrovias de São Paulo, 1870–1940* (São Paulo: Hucitec, 1981); William R. Summerhill, *Order against Progress: Government, Foreign Investment, and Railroads in Brazil, 1854–1913* (Stanford, CA: Stanford University Press, 2003).

96. Andrews, *Brazil*, 150–151.

97. On the rapid urban growth of Campinas, see Ulysses C. Semeghini, *Do Café à Indústria: Uma Cidade e seu Tempo* (Campinas: Editora Unicamp, 1991); José Roberto do Amaral Lapa, *A Cidade: Os Cantos e os Antros: Campinas, 1850–1900* (São Paulo: Edusp, 1996).

98. "Machinas de Secar Café Taunay-Telles," *Correio Paulistano*, October 14, 1881.

99. "Machinas Lidgerwood," *A Província de São Paulo*, July 1, 1887.

100. Rebouças, *Agricultura Nacional*, 27, 133.

101. "Exposição Provincial," *Correio Paulistano*, August 25, 1885.

102. Andrews, *Brazil*, 246–247.

103. Lapa, *Cidade*, 91–93.

104. Petição de John Sherrington, advogado de Lidgerwood Mfg. Co. Ltd., à Câmara Municipal de Campinas, Campinas, June 20, 1885, ACMC.

105. Petição de John Sherrington, advogado de Lidgerwood Mfg. Co. Ltd., à Câmara Municipal de Campinas, Campinas, July 14, 1885, ACMC.

106. *The Lidgerwood Cableway. A Hoisting and Conveying Device Employed in Construction of Canals, Dry Docks, Dams, Locks, Filter Beds, Piers, Log Handling, Fortifications, Open Pit Mining, Quarrying, Discharging Vessels, Etc. Coaling at Sea and Logging by Steam. Cane Hoisting and Lidgerwood Transfer* (1904), Lidgerwood Manufacturing Company, Unit 1, Folder 3, Shelf 3, Box 1, HSAR.

107. Andrews, *Brazil*, 159.

108. Henry Clay Armstrong, "Report of Consul-General Armstrong on the Commerce and Industries of Brazil in 1885," in *Report upon the Commercial Relations of the United States with Foreign Countries for the Years 1884 and 1885* (Washington: Government Printing Office, 1886), 748–749.

109. William Hutchinson Norris to Francis Johnson Norris, Santa Bárbara, March 7, 1886, William H. Norris Family Papers, LPR191, ADAH.

110. Armstrong, "Report of Consul-General Armstrong," 749.

111. *Almanak Administrativo, Mercantil e Industrial do Imperio do Brazil para 1884* (Rio de Janeiro: H. Laemmert, 1884), 185.

112. Armstrong, "Report of Consul-General Armstrong," 750.

113. Andrews, *Brazil*, 250.

114. Robert Cicero Norris to Francis Johnson Norris, Santa Bárbara, September 6, 1885, William H. Norris Family Papers, LPR191, ADAH.

115. Armstrong, "Report of Consul-General Armstrong," 750.

116. "Dossiê Referente à Proibição da Venda de Melancias Enviado pela Secretaria do Interior," 1896, Secretaria da Agricultura, AESP.

117. C. F. Van Delden Laërne, *Brazil and Java: Report on Coffee-Culture in America, Asia and Africa, to H. E. the Minister of the Colonies* (London: W. H. Allen, 1885), 355.

118. Laërne, *Brazil and Java*, 354–364.

119. Laërne, *Brazil and Java*, 359–361.

120. On the conflicts involving sharecroppers in the Oeste Paulista, see Emília Viotti da Costa, *The Brazilian Empire: Myths and Histories*, rev. ed. (Chapel Hill: University of North Carolina Press, 2000), 94–124.

121. Rebouças, *Agricultura Nacional*, 115.

122. Laërne, *Brazil and Java*, 366.

123. Thomas H. Holloway, *Immigrants on the Land: Coffee and Society in São Paulo, 1886–1934* (Chapel Hill: University of North Carolina Press, 1980), 72–74.

124. Andrews, *Brazil*, 157–165, 153.

125. Andrews, *Brazil*, 246.

126. By the 1880s, acquiring slaves did not seem like a good option for coffee producers like Detlef Brune Schmidt. As Robert Slenes puts it, "When the small agriculturalist of the nineteenth century acquired slaves to use in commercial agriculture, he assumed particularly high risks (especially if he contracted debt to do so) because he immobilized resources in a productive 'machine' that could disappear at any moment, given their propensity for morbidity and mortality and the possibility of running away." "Senhores e Subalternos no Oeste Paulista," in *História da Vida Privada no Brasil, Volume 2, Império: A Corte e a Modernidade Nacional*, ed. Luiz Felipe de Alencastro (São Paulo: Companhia das Letras, 1997), 245.

127. Laërne, *Brazil and Java*, 364.

128. Andrews, *Brazil*, 165.

129. Andrews, *Brazil*, 168.

130. Martha Watts, "Letter from Miss Watts—the School at Piracicaba, N. 4, October 1884," in *Evangelizar e Civilizar: Cartas de Martha Watts, 1881–1908*, ed. Zuleica Mesquita (Piracicaba: Unimep, 2001), 213.

131. Andrews, *Brazil*, 168.

132. Andrews, *Brazil*, 107.

133. Cristina de Campos, *Ferrovias e Saneamento em São Paulo: O Engenheiro Antonio Francisco de Paula Souza e a Construção da Rede de Infra-Estrutura Territorial e Urbana Paulista, 1870–1893* (Campinas: Fapesp/Pontes, 2010).

134. *The Ten-Year Book of Cornell University, Volume II, 1868–1888* (Ithaca, NY: Andrus & Church, 1888), 125, 189, 146.

135. *Alumni Record and General Catalogue of Syracuse University, 1872–1910* (Syracuse: Alumni Association of Syracuse University, 1911), 637.

136. *University of Cincinnati: Catalogue of the Academic Department, 1890–1891* (Cincinnati: Office of the University, 1891), 59.

137. *Catalogue of the Governors, Trustees, and Officers, and of the Alumni and Other Graduates of Columbia College* (New York: McGowan & Slipper, 1882), 200.

138. *Rensselaer Polytechnic Institute, Troy N.Y., Annual Register, April 1897* (Troy, NY: Wm. H. Young, 1897), 72.

139. Laërne, *Brazil and Java*, 362.

140. *Cornell Daily Sun*, December 8, 1880.

141. *Ten-Year Book of Cornell University*, 56, 159.

142. G. A. Cruwell and A. Scott Blacklaw, *Brazil as a Coffee-Growing Country: Its Capabilities, the Mode of Cultivation, and Prospects of Extension* (Colombo: A.M. & J. Ferguson, 1878), 102.

143. *Record of the Men of Lafayette: Brief Biographical Sketches of the Alumni of Lafayette College from Its Organization to the Present Time* (Easton, PA: Skinner and Finch, 1879), 102.

144. *University of Cincinnati: Catalogue*, 60.

145. *Alumni Record and General Catalogue of Syracuse University*, 643, 653, 649.

146. Overlooking the case of the Oeste Paulista, scholars argue that slaveholders throughout the Americas could—and did—use industrial technology and management techniques to perpetuate and expand slave labor by the second half of the nineteenth century. Dale Tomich has first formulated the idea of a "second slavery," which at times relied on industrial technology. See *Through the Prism of Slavery: Labor, Capital, and World Economy* (Lanham, MD: Rowman

& Littlefield, 2004). Historians of Brazil and the United States have adapted Tomich's concept to their case studies. See, for example, Walter Johnson, *River of Dark Dreams: Slavery and Empire in the Cotton Kingdom* (Cambridge, MA: Belknap, 2013); Rafael de Bivar Marquese, "Capitalismo, Escravidão e a Economia Cafeeira do Brasil no Longo Século XIX," *Saeculum* 29 (2013): 289–321; Joshua D. Rothman, *Flush Times and Fever Dreams: A Story of Capitalism and Slavery in the Age of Jackson* (Athens: University of Georgia Press, 2014); Mariana Muaze and Ricardo Salles, eds., *O Vale do Paraíba e o Império do Brasil nos Quadros da Segunda Escravidão* (Rio de Janeiro: Faperj, 2015); Rafael de Bivar Marquese and Ricardo Salles, eds., *Escravidão e Capitalismo Histórico no Século XIX: Cuba, Brasil, Estados Unidos* (Rio de Janeiro: Civilização Brasileira, 2016); Edward E. Baptist, *The Half Has Never Been Told: Slavery and the Making of American Capitalism* (New York: Basic Books, 2016); Caitlin Rosenthal, *Accounting for Slavery: Masters and Management* (Cambridge, MA: Harvard University Press, 2018). This scholarship does not take into consideration that attempts to combine chattel slavery and industrial technology were never long-lived. In reality, these experiments were eventually crushed by the very forces they sought to control.

147. André Pinto Rebouças, "A Provincia de S. Paulo depois da Abolição," *Gazeta da Tarde*, May 31, 1883.

148. Conrad, *Destruction of Brazilian Slavery*, 210–216.

149. *Rio News*, August 24, 1884.

150. Conrad, *Destruction of Brazilian Slavery*, 222–224.

151. *Rio News*, August 24, 1885.

152. On the repressive measures against abolitionists during the 1880s, see Alonso, *Flores, Votos e Balas*, 287–293.

153. On the abolitionist movement in São Paulo, see Maria Helena P. T. Machado, *O Plano e o Pânico: Os Movimentos Sociais na Década da Abolição* (São Paulo: Edusp, 2010).

154. Conrad, *Destruction of Brazilian Slavery*, 250–251.

155. *Rio News*, July 15, 1887.

156. On the changing attitudes of the São Paulo republicans in relation to slavery, see Antonio Carlos Galdino, "Campinas, uma Cidade Republicana: Política e Eleições no Oeste Paulista (1870–1889)" (PhD diss., Universidade Estadual de Campinas, 2006), 23–93.

157. *Rio News*, September 24, 1887.

158. *Rio News*, December 24, 1887.

159. *Rio News*, October 24, 1887.

160. *Rio News*, December 24, 1887.

161. A biographer of the Prado family, Darrell E. Levi observes that Martinho Prado Junior, "a republican, represented the new, labor-starved, and relatively poor Ninth Assembly District [the Mogiana Region] in São Paulo's legislature, while his older brother Antonio, an imperial minister, represented the interests of São Paulo city in the Provincial Assembly and spoke for the already-prosperous, developed coffee regions. It was thus not surprising that differences occurred." *The Prados of São Paulo, Brazil: An Elite Family and Social Change, 1840–1930* (Athens: University of Georgia Press, 1987), 76.

162. *Rio News*, July 15, 1886.

163. Beiguelman, *Formação do Povo no Complexo Cafeeiro*, 95–134.

164. Mark I. Choate highlights the push factors influencing Italian migration: "Crushed under one of Europe's highest tax burdens, threatened by malaria, isolated by a lack of roads,

with their vineyards devastated by phylloxera disease, many families found a better future abroad." *Emigrant Nation: The Making of Italy Abroad* (Cambridge, MA: Harvard University Press, 2008), 24.

165. On Italians' early preference for the United States and Argentina, see Samuel L. Baily, *Immigrants in the Lands of Promise: Italians in Buenos Aires and New York City, 1870–1914* (Ithaca, NY: Cornell University Press, 1999).

166. Martinho Prado Junior apud Beiguelman, *Formação do Povo no Complexo Cafeeiro*, 112.

167. *Rio News*, July 15, 1886.

168. Walter J. Hammond, "S. Paulo Immigration Question," *Rio News*, August 5, 1886.

169. *Rio News*, April 15, 1888.

170. Cristiano da Luz, speech at the Chamber of Deputies, August 27, 1888, in *Annaes do Parlamento Brazileiro, Camara dos Srs. Deputados, Terceira Sessão da Vigésima Legislatura, de 3 de Agosto a 1 de Setembro de 1888, Volume IV* (Rio de Janeiro: Imprensa Nacional, 1888), 321.

171. *Rio News*, January 24, 1888.

172. *Rio News*, August 24, 1888.

173. *Relatório Apresentado à Assembléa Legislativa Provincial de São Paulo pelo Presidente da Província Barão do Parnahyba no Dia 17 de Janeiro de 1887* (São Paulo: Jorge Seckler, 1887), 120.

174. Holloway, *Immigrants on the Land*, 70–110. On the wage system that emerged in the Oeste Paulista, Barbara Weinstein writes that "the relatively weak pro-slavery sentiment laid the groundwork for rapid transition to free labor in São Paulo, rather than a resort to some form of quasi-slavery or apartheid-like labor system. At the same time, it reinforced racist notions that associated free, efficient labor with European immigrants rather than with African, Afro-Brazilian, or Chinese workers." "The Decline of the Progressive Planter and the Rise of the Subaltern Agent: Shifting Narratives of Slave Emancipation in Brazil," in *Reclaiming the Political in Latin American History*, ed. Gilbert M. Joseph (Durham, NC: Duke University Press, 2001), 94.

175. *Rio News*, November 5, 1887.

176. *Rio News*, March 15, 1888.

177. *Rio News*, May 15, 1888.

178. Fernandes, *Revolução Burguesa no Brasil*, 103.

179. *Rio News*, February 24, 1888.

180. *Rio News*, July 15, 1888.

181. James McFadden Gaston Jr., "A Pathfinder of Yesterday: James McFadden Gaston, Patriot, Explorer, Scientist," James McFadden Gaston Papers, Series 2, Folder 19, SHC-CH.

182. William Hutchinson Norris to Francis Johnson Norris, Sítio New Alabama, Province of São Paulo, January 13–14, 1887, William H. Norris Family Papers, LPR191, ADAH.

183. Jane Matthews to Imo, Santos, Florida, October 21, 1885, William H. Norris Family Papers, LPR191, ADAH.

184. William H. Norris to Francis, Sítio New Alabama, Province of São Paulo, May 25, 1888, William H. Norris Family Papers, LPR191, ADAH.

185. *Rio News*, January 28, 1889.

186. André Pinto Rebouças, Alfredo d'Escragnolle Taunay, Carlos A. Raynsford, Wenceslau de Souza Guimarães, Henrique David de Sanson, and Luiz A. de Magalhães, "Difficuldades na Immigração," *A Immigração*, February 1889.

187. *Rio News*, August 26, 1889.

188. André Pinto Rebouças, "Imposto Territorial," *Revista de Engenharia*, September 14, 1889.

189. Steven Hahn, *A Nation without Borders: The United States and Its World in an Age of Civil Wars, 1830–1910* (New York: Viking, 2016), 93–94.

190. André Pinto Rebouças, "Pequena Propriedade VII," *Cidade do Rio*, July 7, 1888.

191. *Rio News*, April 15, 1889.

192. "Coffee Cultivation," *Spice Mill*, January 1888.

193. "Brazilian Emancipation," *St. Paul Daily Globe*, May 19, 1888.

194. "Brazilian Statesmen," *Daily Inter Ocean*, June 30, 1888.

195. "Brazil," *Macon Telegraph*, January 7, 1889.

196. "A False Prophet," *Daily Inter Ocean*, July 21, 1889.

197. Herbert S. Klein and Francisco Vidal Luna quantify the growth of coffee production in São Paulo: "Especially after the abolition of slavery, the state of São Paulo finally assumed a hegemonic role in the world production of coffee as it replaced Rio de Janeiro as the leading producer in Brazil. This was accomplished through the gradual penetration of western São Paulo, with its high-quality virgin soils. Between 1854 and 1900, Paulista coffee production grew by a factor of ten, yielding 9 million sacks of coffee by 1900, which was two-thirds of national production and 62 percent of the coffee consumed in the world in that year. The frontier regions also allowed the average size of coffee fazendas to increase significantly." *An Economic and Demographic History of São Paulo, 1850–1950* (Stanford, CA: Stanford University Press, 2018), 12. See also Topik, "Integration of the World Coffee Market," 24–36.

198. "The Platform," *Daily Inter Ocean*, July 2, 1888.

Epilogue

1. Joaquim Nabuco, "The Share of America in Civilization," *American Historical Review* 15, no. 1 (October 1909); W. T. Stead, *The Americanization of the World: or, The Trend of the Twentieth Century* (New York: Horace Markley, 1902).

2. Nabuco, "Share of America in Civilization," 57.

3. Nabuco, "Share of America in Civilization," 57.

4. Nabuco, "Share of America in Civilization," 58.

5. Nabuco, "Share of America in Civilization," 62.

6. George Scarborough Barnsley, "Original of Reply to a Circular Asking for Information of the ex-Confederates Emigrants, April 1915," George Scarborough Barnsley Papers, Subseries 3.1, Folder 25, Volume 6, SHC-CH.

7. Barnsley, "Original of Reply."

8. Barnsley, "Original of Reply."

INDEX

Page numbers in italics refer to figures and tables.

A NOTE ON THE TYPE

This book has been composed in Arno, an Old-style serif typeface in the classic Venetian tradition, designed by Robert Slimbach at Adobe.

GPSR Authorized Representative: Easy Access System Europe - Mustamäe tee
50, 10621 Tallinn, Estonia, gpsr.requests@easproject.com